Abstracts of

Cumberland County

Pennsylvania

WILLS

1785-1825

F. Edward Wright

WILLOW BEND BOOKS
2007

WILLOW BEND BOOKS
AN IMPRINT OF HERITAGE BOOKS, INC.

Books, CDs, and more—Worldwide

For our listing of thousands of titles see our website
at
www.HeritageBooks.com

Published 2007 by
HERITAGE BOOKS, INC.
Publishing Division
65 East Main Street
Westminster, Maryland 21157-5026

International Standard Book Number: 978-1-58549-454-2

INTRODUCTION

These wills were abstracted under the auspices of the Genealogical
Society of Pennsylvania in the early 1900s. Copies of these abstracts
were made available to various libraries in Pennsylvania and microfilm
copies made by the Genealogical Society of Utah (LDS). Recently
bound photostat copies of the abstracts were offered for sale by the
Genealogical Society of Pennsylvania.

We extend our appreciation to the Genealogical Society of Pennsylvania
and encourage membership in the Society (1305 Locust Street,
Philadelphia, PA 19107-5699), whose collections are mainly housed at
the Library of the Historical Society of Pennsylvania (1300 Locust
Street, Philadelphia, PA 19107). We encourage use of its holdings and
facilities which are available at a modest fee.

F. Edward Wright
Westminster, Maryland
1998

GREGG, ANDREW, yeoman, Middleton. 19 Jan 1771. 14 Jan 1785.
Wife Jean.
Eldest son John.
Sons James, Matthew and Andrew.
Eldest dau. Leah.
Daus. Elizabeth, Margaret, Jennet and Mary.
Youngest dau. Margery.
Exs.: Wife Jean Gregg and John Montgomery of Carlisle.
Wit.: John McKee, William Alexander.
Codicil 15 June 1782.
Wit.: John Davis, William McNelly.   E. 1-3.

HUDSON, JOSEPH, East Pennsborough. 8 Aug 1784. 24 Aug 1784.
Letters 1785.
Son William.
Son Joseph, a minor.
Son-in-law Thomas Davison.
Son-in-law William Harvy.
Son-in-law John McCormick.
Exs.: David Bell and Matthew London.
Wit.: Andrew Erwin, Walter Buchanan, James Irvine.   E. 4.

McTEER, JAMES, Sr., yeoman, Allen. 2 Aug 1784. 16 March 1785.
Sons James, Samuel and Robert.
Daus. Elizabeth Boyd, and Eale Carothers.
Sons William and John McTeer.
Dau. Sarah Pauly.
Granddau. Elizabeth McTeer, dau. of son James McTeer.
Exs.: Sons James McTeer and Samuel McTeer.
Wit.: Hugh Laird, John Warden.   E. 5.

ARMSTRONG, WILLIAM, Derry. 4 Oct 1784. 16 March 1785.
Wife Rebecca.
Nephew James McCord.
Land adj. *Willson's Tract.*
Indentured girl Nancy McLearn.
Land adj. David Steel on the River Juniata.
Exs.: Thomas Martin, William Smith and Captain William Armstrong.
Wit.: James Lyon, Edw. Purcell, Plunket Armstrong, Robert Martin son
of Thomas Martin.   E. 6-10.

ARMSTRONG, ROBERT, yeoman, Fermanagh. 24 June 1783. 21 Jan 1785.
Bro. George's eldest dau. Ann.
Said George's second dau. Sarah.
Sister Eliza.'s dau. Sarah.
Bro. Alexr. youngest son Robert, a minor.
Sd. Alexr.'s eldest dau. Mary, and his eldest son James.
Sarah Pawley, wife of John Pawley.
Bro. Alexr.'s son George, sd. Alexr.'s dau. Sarah.
Land in Greewood Twp. adj. late Richard Hays.
Exs.: James Armstrong, bro. Alex's son, and Epinetas Hart.
Wit.: Mary Hart, Willm. Sketch (Stretch?).   E. 11.

DUNNON (DUNNIN), SAMUEL, West Pennsborough. ----. 25 Feb 1785.
Sister Liddy Dunn.
Land in County New Castle.
Uncle Ezekiel Dunnon.
Thomas Buchanan.
Exs.: Uncle Ezekiel Dunnon and Mr. Wm. McFarlin.
Wit.: James Jackson, Wm. Clark, Mary Murray.   E. 12-13.

HICK, JOHN CONRAD, Carlisle. 5 Feb 1785. 7 March 1785.
Wife Elizabeth.
Eldest son Christian Hick. Plantation in Dover Twp., York Co.
Son Frederick.
Eldest dau. Anna Maria Greaver.
Dau. Catherine Ottenberger, wife of Jacob Ottenberger.
Dau. Philipina Hoffman.
Fourth dau. Susanah Fisher.
Exs.: Wife Elizabeth Hick and Jacob Greaver.
Wit.: Casper Crapts, John George Huber, Jacob Kartt.   E. 14-18.

STEWART, ROBERT, yeoman, West Pennsborough. 6 Oct 1784. 28 March 1785.
Wife Elizabeth.
Granddau. Rachel Starr.
Land sold to John Brown in sd. Twp.
Grandchildren Elizabeth Starr, Mary Starr, Moses Starr.
Land near Shippensburgh called *Stewart's Tract* sold to William Blyth.
Exs.: Stephen Duncan and John Starr.

Wit.: Hugh Laird, Moses Starr.   E. 18-19.

BEARD, JAMES. 30 March 1785. 4 April 1785.
Mother Rebecca Sterret.
William Smith son of Robert Smith of Carlisle.
Bros. Robert Beard and John Beard.
Samuel Robinson and John Boggs.
Exs.: Friend Robert Smith and bro. John Beard.
Wit.: William McSherry, William Smith.   E. 20.

CULBERTSON, WILLIAM, East Pennsborough. 9 Aug 1784. 20 April
1785.
Wife Marget.
Two sons Samuel and William Culbertson.
Land in Allen Twp. where Thomas Williamson lives.
Dau. Francis Johnston.
Exs.: Wife and son Samuel Culbertson
Wit.: Robert Denny, William Denny, John Urie.   E. 21.

PORTER, HUGH. 22 March 1785. 21 April 1785.
Wife Mary.
Sons William, Hugh, Robert and Joseph Porter.
Land in Westmoreland County.
Exs.: Sons William Portr and Hugh Porter.
Wit.: Jas. Blair, William Kerr, Hugh McCutchen, William Blain. E. 22-23.

BAUM, JONAS, Derry. 1 Oct 1784. 21 April 1785.
Wife Eve.
Nine children, names not given, three youngest minors.
Letters to Eve Baum and John Baum.
Exs.: None appointed.
Wit.: James Burns, Frederick Baum, Robert Buchanan.   E. 24.

OGDEN, JOSEPH. 21 Feb 1775. 22 April 1785.
Wife Ann.
Children Mary, Elizabeth and Joseph, minors.
Exs.: Wife Ann, Henry Gass and Garawant Ogden.
Wit.: John Neel, Jas. McCabe, Owen McCabe, James Lamb.   E. 25-26.

TORRANCE, HUGH, farmer, Newton. 12 June 1784. 13 Aug 1784.
Three children James, Hugh and Sarah.

Son-in-law Alexander McClintock.
Step dau. Jean Blair.
Overseers Daniel McDaniels and Samuel McCormick.
Exs.: Alexander McClintock and Hugh and Alexr. Laughlin.
Wit.: John Allison, Thomas Allison.   E. 28.

DENNY, JOHN, Cumberland County. 27 Sept 1782. 5 Nov 1782.
Letters 15 Feb 1786.
Wife Margery.
Daus. Sarah, Ann and Elizabeth Denny.
Son Walter Denny.
Three married daus., viz., Jean Burns, Margret Denny and Margery
Ferguson.
Bound children Edward Byan and Agness Penewell.
William Paton's land.
Exs.: Wife Margery Denny and son-in-law James Ferguson.
Wit.: Wm. McFarlane, Thos. Buchanan.   E. 29.

GEMMILL, JOHN, Clock and watch maker, Derry. 18 June 1770. 1 July
1785.
Wife Elizabeth.
Sons John and William, minors.
Daus. Elizabeth Gemmill and Mary Ann Gemmill, minors.
Property in Carlisle.
Land in Berree Twp., called *Clover Lick*.
Land in sd. Twp. in partnership with William Call, goldsmith.
Overseer: George Stevenson.
Exs.: Wife Elizabeth Gemmill, Matthew Wakefield and James Lyon.
Wit.: William Armstrong, John Brown, James Lyon.
Codicil 2 Sept 1784.
Wit.: Shobert McHarg, James Lyon.   E. 30-32.

MARTIN, SAMUEL, Allen. 2 March 1781. 2 July 1785.
Wife (no name).
Sons Samuel and Andrew.
Dau. Margaret Crocket and her son John.
Dau. Jean Bringham.
Son Thomas Martin.
Exs.: Wife and son Samuel Martin.
Wit.: Alexr. Trindle, John Trindle.   E. 33.

McKINNEY, JOSEPH, husbandman, Hopewell. 2 Feb 1785. 12 Aug 1785.
Eldest son Thomas, land to John McKee's line.
Son David.
Dau.-in-law Elizabeth, widow of son Samuel, dec'd.
Son Joseph.
Son-in-law John Macon.
Dau. Mary.
Son-in-law William McCord and dau. Agness, his wife, dec'd.
Grandchildren Joseph, Samuel, Grizel, and Andrew McCord, minors.
Son William, decd, his widow Elizabeth and his four daus., viz., Elinor, Jean, Mary and Agness McKinney.
Grandchildren Jean and Grizell McKinney.
Exs.: Sons Thomas McKinney and David McKinney.
Wit.: Andrew Thompson, Joseph Miller, John McKee.   E. 34-36.

PORTER, DAVID, Shippensburgh. 29 June 1785. 24 Aug 1785.
Wife Mary.
Eldest son Robert, two youngest sons, viz., Washington and David Porter.
Oldest dau. Agness Porter.
Youngest dau. Sarah Porter.
When youngest son David comes to age of twenty-one years.
Exs.: Alexander Pebles of Shippensburg and Saml. Porter.
Wit.: Peter Dickey, Alexander Donnald, Wm. Rippey.   E. 37.

MOUTZ, STOPHEL, miller, Greenwood. 5 March 1785. 1 Aug 1785.
Oldest dau. Barbara Albright, wife of George Albright.
Youngest dau. Elizabeth Whealand.
Grandson Stophel Whealand.
Andrew Struube and Michael Herman.
Exs.: Jacob Buck and Michael Herman.
Wit.: Jacob Fritle(?), Willm. Cook, Philip Mathews.   E. 37-38.

MARSHALL, JOSEPH, yeoman, Rye. 2 July 1785. 26 Aug 1785.
Sons Michael, Joseph, John and David.
Daus. Catherine and Elinor.
Dau. Mary.
Dau. Jean.
William Griffith, bound boy.
Exs.: Sons John Marshall and Michael Marshall.

Wit.: David McClure, Richard Douglass Smith, Hugh Gormly, Jr.

E. 40-41.

ANDERSON, MARY, widow, Carlisle. 7 Aug 1785. 9 Sept 1785.
Eldest son Allen Anderson.
Granddau. Mary Phillips, minor.
Grandson William Phillips, minor.
Son John.
Exs.: Son John Anderson.
Wit.: William Wallace, John Steel.   E. 42.

PATTEN, THOMAS, farmer, Tyrone. 9 July 1785. 7 Oct 1785.
Wife (no name).
Two youngest sons Robert and David Patten, minors.
Two oldest sons Thomas and William, minors.
Exs.: James Adams and William Foster of Tyrone.
Wit.: James Dixon, Patrick McCanna, Samuel Thompson.
Codicil 2 Aug 1785.
To step dau. Janet Bell, her father's Bible.   E. 43-45.

McNELEY, GEORGE, Carlisle. 3 Sept 1785. 19 Oct 1795.
Bro. James McNeley.
Father James McNeley in Ireland.
Wit.: John Hunter, John Richmond, Abrm. Lochridge.
Exs.: None named.
Adm: James McNelly.   E. 46.

CULBERTSON, JOHN, yeoman, Armagh. 25 Jan 1785. 18 May 1785.
Wife Agness.
Eldest son Samuel Culbertson.
Son-in-law John Campble.
Daus. Jean McFarlin, Frances Orr and Agness Thompson.
Sons John and William Hanna Culbertson.
Dau. Elizabeth Culbertson.
Exs.: Wife Agness Culbertson and son John Culbertson.
Wit.: Edmd. Richardson, James Johnston, William Brown.   E. 46-47.

HOLDEN, THOMAS, Fermanagh. 11 Oct 1784. 20 Oct 1785.
Two daus., viz., Sarah and Agness.
Ex.: James Smith.
Wit.: William McCay, Hugh McCormick.   E. 48.

RYANS, CORNELIUS, Rye. 14 April 1785. 15 Nov 1785.
Wife Agness.
Son Robert.
Son John Ryans and his son William.
Daus. Elizabeth, Agness, Elen, Rebeka and Margret.
Son William, if he is alive.
Exs.: Wife Agness Ryans.
Wit.: Laurence Mealy, Hugh Gormly.   E. 49.

McCULLOGH, JAMES, farmer, West Pennsborough. 5 Aug 1785. 21
Nov 1785.
Wife Elizabeth.
Dau. Elizabeth.
Son-in-law James Boyle.
Son-in-law John Chambers.
Son-in-law William Lemmond.
Son James McCullogh.
Son Robert to be schooled and clothed.
Grandchildren Samuel Lemmond and Samuel Boyle, minors.
Dau. Sarah Chambers.
Son Archibald.
Grandchild Rosana Adair, minor.
Exs.: Wife Elizabeth and son-in-law William Lemmond.
Wit.: John Sproat, William Sproat, Joshua Marlin.   E. 50-51.

TRINDLE, WILLIAM, Allen. 8 April 1784. 7 Nov 1785.
Wife Agness.
Children William, John, Agness, James and the child not yet born.
Joshua Miars land.
Exs.: Wife Agness, bro. Alexr. Trindle and John Lamb.
Wit.: Hugh McCay, John Lamb.   E. 52.

HORRELL, CLEMENT, yeoman, Milford. 7 Aug 1784. 22 Oct 1785.
Wife Sarah.
Son Chirstopher, a minor.
Son James.
Line to land of William Bell, Esq.
Land to Thomas Beal's line.
Son Robert Horrell, minor.
Son John.
Daus. Margret, wife of Hugh Hardy and Mary, wife of John Brown.

Exs.: Son John Horrall and William Bell, Esq.
Wit.: John Stuart, James Stuart.   E. 53-54.

ALEXANDER, THOMAS, farmer, Hopewell. 28 Sept 1778. 26 Nov 1785.
Wife Mary.
Son William.
To David.
Land joining Nicholas Evert.
Daus. Elizabeth, Amey and Margaret Alexander.
Son Joseph Alexander.
Land where James Burns lives, adj. Edd. Shippen, Esq.
Exs.: Wife Mary Alexander and son William Alexander.
Wit.: Joseph Ferguson, Samuel Perry, James Cisney.   E. 55-56.

LOVE, JAMES, West Pennsborough. 17 April 1783. 6 Dec 1785.
Wife Elee (Elce?) Love.
Son-in-law Josiah McGuire.
Son David.
Sons John, James and Thomas.
Son Josiah, minor.
Exs.: Sons John Love, James Love and cousin John White.
Wit.: Thomas Bullen, Wm. Clark, Jr., Wm. Clark, Wm. McNelly, David Mitchel.   E. 57.

BAUR, MARTIN, free holder, Middleton. 19 Aug 1777. 14 Jan 1786.
Wife Elizabeth Catherine.
Only son Martin.
Daus. Mary, Catherine and Elizabeth.
Exs.: Son Martin Baur.
Wit.: Jacob Snibul, Jronny [sic] Kayt, Henry Eby.   E. 58-59.

BOWER, CATHERINE, wife of Martin Bower, dec'd, Middleton. 19 April 1785. 14 Jan 1786.
Oldest dau. Catherine.
Dau. Elizabeth.
Three sons of George Wytsil, blacksmith, viz., Jacob, George and John Wytsil, grandsons.
Son Martin Bower.
Exs.: George Wytsil and Martin Bower.
Wit.: T. S. Wetzel, George Crean.   E. 59.

BROWN, ELIZABETH, Middle Twp. 26 Feb 1777. 14 March 1786.
David Russel of East Twp., son of James Russel and Jean Russel of Chester Co.
Joseph Semple of Middleton.
James Russel of East Twp., Chester Co.
Joseph Russel of County aforesd.
Mary Russel dau. of sd. James Russel.
Exs.: Joseph McClun of East Pennsboro and Jos. Semple.
Wit.: Joseph Adair, Robert Young, Joseph Semple.   E. 60.

CARHART, WILLIAM, Carlisle. 3 Jan 1786. 10 April 1786.
Wife Rosanna.
Son Seth.
Plantation in Shearman's Valley, adj. lands of widow Smiley, John Smiley, Esaiah Reese and Craff's.
Lott in Carlisle bounded by Archibald Kenneday and by a certain Leany.
Dau. Rebecca wife of Peter Alenberger.
Exs.: Son Seth Carhart.
Wit.: John Anderson, Hugh Boden, John Jordan.   E. 61.

SMITH, WILLIAM, farmer, Middleton. 14 April 1786. 15 May 1786.
Wife Jean.
Son Robert Smith in Carlisle.
Son Brice Smith.
Land in Shearman's Valley bought from James Steelman, where Thomas Shortlass lives.
Sons Hugh, James and William.
Father's estate in Ireland.
Dau. Mary.
Elizabeth Christy, Jean Christy and Mary Christy.
William Smith, Robert's oldest son.
Exs.: Wife Jean and sons Hugh Smith and James Smith.
Wit.: Robert Patterson, William Boyd.   E. 62-63.

WOLFE, LEONARD, Allen. 1 July 1786. 29 July 1786.
Wife Margaret.
Christiana Wolfe, Mary Wolfe, Henry Wolfe, Elizabeth Wolfe, Catharine Wolfe and eldest son Jacob Wolfe.
Daus. to be considered of age when married, sons to have same privilege.
Exs.: Jacob Wise and David Kishler.
Wit.: Jacob Halsher, Wm. Scott, Andreas Wolf.   E. 64.

GALBREATH, JAMES, Esq., East Pennsborough. 27 May 1782. 3 Aug 1786.
Wife Elizabeth.
Son Bartram.
Tract of land in Donegal, Lancaster Co.
Son Robert and his daus. Elizabeth, Agness and Mary.
Son Thomas.
Place called the Tan yard.
Son Andrew.
Dau. Dorcas wife of John Buchanan.
Dau. Elizabeth wife of Charlenes (Charlena?) Torrance.
Exs.: Wife Elizabeth and son Bartram Galbraith.
Wit.: Robt. Magaw, William Geddis, James McCormick.
Codicil 8 Dec 1784.
Wit.: Wm. Irvine, Robt. Magaw.   E. 65-67.

TATE (TEAT), JOHN, Shippensburgh. 29 May 1786. 4 Aug 1786.
Wife Isabella.
Plantation in Southampton Twp.
Sister Elizabeth Eskin.
Nephew John Humphreys.
Bro. Alexander Eskin.
Bro. Samuel Tate, near Plymouth in England.
Exs.: Friends Alexander Peebles and Robt. Donavan.
Wit.: John Frazer, Josiah Griffen, Samuel Huey.   E. 68.

KIMMELL, PHILIP, East Pennsborough. 10 Jan 1786. 19 Aug 1786.
Wife Ann Mary.
Son Samuel, when twenty-one years of age.
Daus. Elizabeth and Susanna.
Land of Robert Patterson and Tobias Hendrick's, dec'd.
Surveyor William Lyon, Esq.
Exs.: Adam Croyster and George Cover.
Wit.: John Kissler, Adam Weaver.   E. 71-73.

WOOLF, JEREMIAH, Middleton. 20 June 1786. 6 Sept 1786.
Wife Elizabeth.
Sons John and Jacob.
Daus. Mary, Reagina, Catherina and Elizabeth, some of them minors.
Exs.: Jacob Miller and Adam Brand.
Wit.: Samuel Irwin, John Walter.   E. 74-75.

JOHNSTON, ROBERT, Carlisle. 15 Aug 1786. 15 Sept 1786.
Wife Elizabeth.
John Brown.
Exs.: Wife Elizabeth Johnston.
Wit.: Nathaniel Steel, James Little. E. 76.

KIDD, BENJAMIN, Carlisle. ----. 5 Aug 1786.
Wife Mary.
Sons John and James.
Land in Woodcock Valley, Bedford Co.
Dau. Sarah.
First wife "since she eloped from me."
Exs.: Son John Kidd and George Elder of Woodcock Valley.
Wit.: Saml. Postlethwaite, John Jordan, Saml. Laird. E. 78-79.

SMITH, WILLIAM. 13 Aug 1786. 1 Sept 1786.
Nephew William Brown.
Lott of ground left by Bro. Robert Smith in Town of New London,
Connecticite (Connecticut).
Francis Irwin and Elizabeth his wife.
Andrew Irwin son of sd. Francis and Elizabeth.
Messrs. Tedford of Philadelphia. James Carson and Francis Carson, both
of Philadelphia.
William Bell, Esq., of Milford.
John Shaw, near Cocolamus.
Demands against the United States or the State of Pennsylvania as a
soldier.
Exs.: Francis Irwin.
Wit.: John Creeg, Margaret Irwin, Geo. Robinson. E. 80-81.

BRICE, SAMUEL, West Pennsborough. 27 May 1783. 3 Oct 1786.
Wife Elizabeth.
Five daus., viz., Sarah wife of John Murdock and her children,
Ann wife of Paul Reed and her children, Elizabeth wife of Robert Walker
and her children, Margaret wife of Petter Smith, Isabel wife of Samuel
Walker.
Exs.: Petter Smith, Andrew Carter and John Scouller.
Wit.: Hugh Boden, Thomas Dickson, James Dawson, Jr. E. 82.

QUIGLEY, HENRY, Sr., yeoman, Allen. 8 April 1781. 10 Oct 1786.
Wife Martha.

Sons Henry and Christopher.
Grandson Henry.
Exs.: Sons Henry Quigley and Christopher Quigley.
Wit.: Robert McQuillen, Hugh Laird, William Morrow.   E. 83.

McCUNE, SAMUEL, yeoman, Hopewell. 13 March 1786. 12 Oct 1786.
Wife Elenor.
Son John.
Daus. Elizabeth, Rosanna, Peggy, Kezia and Nelly.
Land in Southampton, Franklin Co. in tenure of Joseph Arbucle.
Exs.: Alexander Laughlin, James McCune and son John McCune.
Wit.: Jas. Arbuckle, Robt. Barr, Rob. Scott.   E. 84-85.

CRISWELL, JAMES, Wayne. 20 Oct 1785. 25 Oct 1786.
Two sons John and Michael.
Daus. Jane, Elizabeth and Susannah.
Exs.: Son John Criswell and bro.-in-law John Beatty.
Wit.: William Junkin, James Johnston, Geo. Bratton.   E. 86-87.

BRATTON, JAMES, Wayne. 3 July 1786. 25 Oct 1786.
Wife Issable.
Dau. Jean when eighteen years of age.
Youngest dau. Elizabeth.
Rest of children, viz., Phebe, William, George and Robert, all minors.
Exs.: Wife Issable Bratton and William Junkin.
Wit.: Wm. Bratton, Geo. Bratton, Hugh Robison.   E. 88.

CLOUSER, SIMON, Middleton. 7 Sept 1786. 4 Nov 1786.
Wife Margaret.
Oldest son John.
Minor children, names not given.
Land joining Robt. Morrison and Wm. Drennon.
Exs.: Wife Margaret Clouser, Jacob Wolf and George Wetzel.
Wit.: George Crean, William Drennon.   E. 90-91.

McCLEAN, ALLAN, Tyrone. 1 Aug 1786. 26 Nov 1786.
Wife Agness.
Two sons Allan and John.
Dau. Jean.
Son-in-law William Reed.
Dau. Elizabeth.

Exs.: Son Allan McClean and John Sharp, Sr.
Wit.: William McClure, John Sharp, Sr., George Hamilton.   E. 92.

McCONNELL, ESTHER. 13 May 1786. 24 Nov 1786.
Children, viz., Ann McConnell, Elizabeth McConnell, Robert McConnell
and Mary Dickey.
Sons-in-law William Dickey and Peter Sturgeon.
Exs.: John Johnston.
Wit.: Samuel Lamond, Thomas Johnston.   E. 95.

BLACK, WILLIAM, farmer, Allen. 14 Nov 1785. 12 April 1786.
Wife Susannah.
Son John.
Sons George and William, minors.
Daus. Ann, Ruth, Rachel, Mary and Lydia.
Exs.: Son John Black and James Kightley.
Wit.: George Eppley, Jacob Knop.   E. 94-95.

GORDON, JAMES, farmer, West Pennsborough. 16 Nov 1784. 16 Dec
1786.
Wife Agness.
Daughter's son and dau. James Ewin and Jane Ewin.
To my John Gordon's three sons, viz., James, Samuel and John Gordon.
Robert Gutery (Guthrie?).
Richard Dun.
Nancy Gordon, widow.
Exs.: Bros.-in-law William Douglass and James Douglass.
Wit.: Patrick McCanna, Mary Douglass, Jennet Douglass.   E. 96.

GARRET, ROBERT, Rye. 27 Oct 1782. 20 Feb 1787.
Wife Jean.
Son Alexander and other children, minors.
Exs.: Wife and Samuel Shaw.
Wit.: John Gill.   E. 97.

WITZEL, GEORGE, Middleton. 10 Nov 1786. 20 Feb 1787.
Wife Mary.
Oldest son Jacob.
Second son George.
Sons John and Martin Witzel, minors.
Exs.: Martin Bower and Andrew Sigler.

Wit.: William Fleming, George Creane.   E. 98.

WILLSON, WILLIAM, Tyrone. 27 Aug 1776. 20 Feb 1787.
Wife Esther.
Son-in-law James Thorn.
Grandsons William Crawford, son to dau. Margaret and William Thorn,
son of dau. Mary.
Exs.: Wife Esther Willson and George Robison, Esq.
Wit.: Robert Miller, Jean Miller, Mary Thorn.
Letters to William Green and Mary his wife, late Mary Thorn, the widow
Esther Willson, being dec'd.   E. 99-100.

GARVIN, JAMES, Tyrone. 22 Dec 1785. 21 March 1787.
Wife Mary.
Five youngest children, viz., Margaret, John, Elizabeth, David and
Easter.
Son Thomas.
Dau. Mary.
Exs.: Wife Mary Garvin and John Davidson.
Wit.: Robert Welch, Jane Welch.   E. 101.

GUNSALUS, JAMES, Wayne. 7 March 1787. 2 April 1787.
Wife (no name).
Sons Manuel, Richard, Daniel, James and Benjamin.
Dau. Sarah, minor under fourteen years.
Exs.: Wife and son Daniel Gunsalus.
Wit.: George Mitchell, Samuel Wallace, Archibald Moore.   E. 102.

THOMPSON, ROBERT, Fermanagh. 24 Feb 1787. 5 April 1787.
Wife (no name).
Son William, a minor.
Other children, minors.
Exs.: Wife and David Boal.
Wit.: Gerard Ferrill, Saml. Willy, Thos. Palley.   E. 103.

McMURRAY, WILLIAM, Carlisle. 6 March 1787. 9 April 1787.
Wife Elizabeth.
Son Samuel, minor.
Land in Northumberland Co.
Land in the State of New York.
Annis Kearns, my father's sister.

Exs.: Wife and John Buchanan of Cumberland Co., William McClay, William Gray and William Wilson of Northumberland Co. and Thomas Wilcox of Chester Co.
Wit.: John Anderson, John Steel. E. 104-105.

McFARLANE, MARGARET. 4 Feb 1780. 17 May 1787.
Son William.
Granddau. Margaret, dau. of son John.
Granddau. Ann Buchanan.
Son Robert.
Daus. Ann and Jennet.
For schooling of son John's children.
Exs.: Sons Robert and William.
Wit.: James McFarlane, Jno. Byers. E. 106.

FRAZER, ARON, husbandman, Allen. 12 4th mo. 1780. 31 May 1787.
Wife Jane.
Children, minors, Ruth, Alexander, Aron, John.
Exs.: Wife Jane and Peter Cleversole.
Wit.: John Garetson, John Cowdrey, James Kightley. E. 107.

BRADY, HUGH, farmer, Hopewell. 16 May 1782. 26 May 1787.
Wife
Son James.
Sons John, Samuel and Joseph, minors.
Four daus. Mary, Hannah, Rebeccah and Jean, minors.
Exs.: Son James and bro. Ebenezer.
Wit.: John Thompson, William Baron, James Young. E. 108.

STAIR, JOHN, East Pennsborough. Nuncupative Will. 16 May 1787. 31 May 1787.
Wife Mary Magdalane.
Sons and one dau., names not given.
Wit.: Peter Smith, Mary Magdalene Stair, Rudy Pickle.
Said John Stair died 17 May 1787. E. 109.

McCARTNEY, JOHN, Fermanagh. 9 Nov 1786. 2 June 1787.
Wife Sibilla.
Three daus. Rebecca, Sarah and Margret.
Exs.: Wife Sibilla and James Adair.
Wit.: Robert Nelson, William McCartney, James Thompson. E. 110.

BRADY, JOSEPH, farmer, Hopewell. 7 Sept 1776. 22 June 1787.
Wife Mary.
Eldest dau. Marget.
Other daus. Mary, Jean, Hannah and Elizabeth, at their marriage or at
age of twenty-two years.
Sons Hugh and Joseph, when last is of age.
Exs.: Wife Mary and James McCane, of sd. Twp.
Wit.: Hugh Laughlin, John Mitchel.   E. 111-112.

GALBRAITH, ROBERT, Hopewell. 30 March 1787. 3 July 1787.
Wife Hannah.
Oldest son Samuel.
Second son James.
Dau. Sarah.
Four youngest children John, William, Elizabeth and Nancy Galbraith.
Son William to be bound to Samuel Hannah till he is eighteen years of
age.
John Elliott.
Exs.: Hannah Galbraith and Nathaniel Wilson.
Wit.: David Sterrett, Samuel Hanna.   E. 113.

ADAIR, WILLIAM, Carlisle. 20 Jan 1787. 4 July 1787.
Wife Elizabeth.
Bro. Joseph's son John Adair.
Exs.: John Buchanan and Thos. Dixon, both of Carlisle.
Wit.: Thomas Dickson, John Barber, John Pollock.   E. 114.

DONALY, PHILIP, Greenwood. 12 Jan 1779. 21 Sept 1787.
Wife Easter.
Sons James and Hugh Donaly.
Three daus. Elianor, Rosana and Margaret Donaly, minors.
Exs.: Wife Easter Donaly and James Custaloe.
Wit.: F. Watts, John Smith.   E. 114-115.

McKINNEY, THOMAS, husbandman, Hopewell. 2 June 1787. 23 Oct
1787.
Wife (no name).
Dau. Lidia.
Dau. Nancy.
Daus. Jean and Grizel, minors.
Son Joseph.

Son David.
Sons Andrew, Samuel and Thomas, minors.
Exs.: Two sons, Joseph and David McKinney.
Wit.: Alexr. Laughlin, Joseph Miller.   E. 116.

BASKINS, JAMES, Rye. 30 Jan 1788. 11 Feb 1788.
Wife Elizabeth.
Daus. Elizabeth McCay, Catherine Stephen, Sarah Dougherty and Jane
Jones.
Sons Mitchell Baskins and Francis Baskins.
Exs.: Frederick Watts, David Watts and son Mitchell Baskins.
Wit.: Cornelius Atkinson, Jr., Patrick Martin, David Watts.   E. 117.

McCORMICK, JANE, Tyrone. 18 Jan 1788. 13 Feb 1788.
Son John McCormick.
Dau. Margaret Quigley.
Granddau. Elizabeth Quigley, dau. of Margaret Quigley.
Remainder of grandchildren, viz., Samuel McClure, Thomas McClure,
John McClure, James McClure, William McClure, Wilson McClure, David
McClure, Jane McClure, John Quigley, William Quigley, Samuel Quigley,
Elizabeth Quigley, Easter Quigley, Jane Quigley, Sarah Quigley,
Elizabeth Sharon, Sarah Sharon, Mary Sharon, Issabella Sharon,
William Sharon, Jane Sharon, William Adams, Ann Adams, Thomas
McCormick and Hudson McCormick.
To grandson John McClure, his grandfather John McCormick's Bible.
Exs.: David McClure, Esq., and James McCormick, Sr.
Wit.: Patrick McCanna, James Adams, William Foster.   E. 118-119.

O'NEIL, JOHN. 9 Jan 1788. 5 Feb 1788.
"To be buried in Carlisle."
To the Big Spring Congregation, to the use of the Meeting house now
building.
To friend and neighbor Margaret Espy.
Lands in any other state.
Exs.: William Douglass and William Lindsay.
Wit.: John Dunn, William Espy.
Letters to Thomas Espy and Wm. McFarland.   E. 120.

BYERS, JOHN, West Pennsborough. 7 Feb 1788. 18 Feb 1788.
Only son James.
Daus. Mary and Jane.

Dau. Elizabeth, her late husband.
George Lewis' land.
John Alexander.
Exs.: Son James and son-in-law John Alexander.
Wit.: Robert Davidson, John Montgomery, Sam. Laird, Chas. McClure.

E. 120-121.

WILSON, JAMES, Toboine. 13 Feb 1787. 22 April 1788.
Wife Mary.
Dau. Sarah, another dau. not named.
Son William Wilson.
Exs.: George McMullen and James Baxter.
Wit.: John Gray.   E. 122.

WILSON, JAMES ARMSTRONG. Nuncupative will. 11 March 1788. 25
March 1788.
Wife (no name).
Son James, a minor.
Daus. names not given.
Wit.: Joseph Thornburgh and Robt. Miller, Jr.
Letters to Margaret Wilson, Joseph Thornburgh and Robt. Miller, Jr.

E. 123-124.

PORTERFIELD, JOHN, farmer, Newton. 20 Jan 1788. 5 April 1788.
Daus. Jean and Sarah.
Sons Samuel and William.
Dau. Agness.
Dau. Hannah.
Son James.
Bro.-in-law Samuel Cunningham.
Exs.: William Stevenson and David Sterrett.
Wit.: Alexr. Laughlin, John Patton, Isaac Shannon.   E. 125.

BREDEN, WILLIAM, now of Hamilton, Franklin Co. 25 April 1786. 7
April 1788.
Son Robert Breden.
Daus. Agness and Sarah.
Dau.-in-law Margaret, wife to Elder Bredin.
Grandson William son to Elder Breden, when fourteen years old.
Exs.: Abraham Dar and Josiah Cander of Dafen Co.
Wit.: William Withrow, Joseph Swan, William McClure.   E. 126.

McCLINTOCK, JOHN, Newton. 24 July 1787. 7 May 1788.
Son Alexander.
Three daus., viz., Mary, Ann and Elizabeth.
Son Daniel McClintock.
Exs.: Son Alexander McClintock.
Wit.: Alexr. Laughlin, Thos. Buchanan.   E. 127.

MURRAY, THOMAS, Tyrone. 8 May 1780. 2 June 1788.
Wife Sophia.
Dau. Margaret.
Sons William, Michael and Thomas Murray.
Dau. Elizabeth.
Exs.: Sophia Murray and Michael Murray.
Wit.: Thomas Gray, Thomas Kensloe.   E. 128.

BAIRD, SAMUEL, Armagh. 8 April 1788. 13 Aug 1788.
Wife Martha.
Children, viz., John, James, Martha and Agness.
Plantation in Westmoreland Co.
Sons William and Samuel.
Heirs of dau. Mary.
Son Hugh Baird.
Grandson Samuel (son of Hugh Baird), a minor.
Exs.: Wife Martha, son John Baird and John Wilson.
Wit.: John Wilson, John Cooper, James Cowan.   E. 129-130.

SHOP, ULERY, East Pennsborough. 11 Jan 1786. 12 Feb 1788.
Wife Mary.
Sons Henry, John and Christian.
Daus. Magdalen and Elizabeth.
Sons Abraham and Jacob.
Child of dau. Barbara, dec'd.
Exs.: George Cover and John Snevly.
Wit.: John Mappan, Adm. Wever.   E. 131-133.

MICHAL, MARINAS, East Pennsborough. 21 Jan 1788. 27 Aug 1788.
Wife Eve.
Daus. Mary Quin and Magdalen Michel.
Son-in-law Torrance Quin.
Exs.: Jacob Wormley.
Wit.: Richard Whitehill, Agness Murdock.   E. 134.

WATTS, ALEXANDER, Teboyn. 21 Dec 1786. 4 Sept 1788.
Wife Isabel.
Son Archibald.
Grandson Alexander Hunter, a minor.
Jane Watts, Archibald Watts's wife.
Son James.
Daus. Elizabeth and Jean.
Exs.: John Watts and Alexander Watts of Teboyn.
Wit.: Andrew Watts, Thomas Carshadon.   E. 134-135.

HULINGS, MARCUS, farmer, Greenwood. 6 Feb 1788. 22 Sept 1788.
Oldest son Marcus.
Dau. Mary Stewart.
Son Samuel.
Son James.
Lands in Dauphin Co.
Mill near Shearman's Creek in Rye Twp., Cumberland County.
Son Thomas Hulings.
Exs.: David Watts and son Thomas Hulings.
Wit.: James Alreight, David Mathews, David Watts.   E. 136.

STEWART, ALEXANDER, yeoman, Wayne. 16 April 1787. 22 Oct 1788.
Wife Catherine.
Sons James and Alexander Stewart.
Land joining Mitchell's.
Land next to Archd. Stewarts.
Dau. Jean Stewart.
Exs.: Sons James Stewart and Alexander Stewart.
Wit.: James Gunsalus, Nathl. Stanly, Marg. Forggy.   E. 136-137.

LEEPER, ALLAN, Westpensbro. 14 July 1788. 29 Oct 1788.
Wife Elizabeth.
Son Allen.
Five grandchildren, viz., Allen son of James Leeper, David Ewing son of
James Ewing, Allen son of Charles Leeper, John Ewing son of Thomas
Ewing and James Leeper son of Allen.
Exs.: Sons James Leeper and Charles Leeper.
Wit.: Samuel Wilson, Daniel Boyle, John Lesler (Leslie).   E. 138.

BROWNFIELD, JOHN, yeoman, Hopewell. 15 Sept 1788. 18 Nov 1788.
Wife Elizabeth.

Son James.
Daus. Jean and Elizabeth.
Dau. Maryann, a minor.
Exs.: Wife Elizabeth and Alexander Laughlin, Esq.
Wit.: James Hathorn, George Clark, John Clark.   E. 139.

COOK, JOHN, West Pennsborough. 3 Dec 1788. 10 Jan 1789.
To Barbary Wilson's son John.
Armstrong Carothers and Elizabeth his wife.
Martin Carothers and his mother Isabella.
Shusannah McQueen.
Jean Linsey.
Robert Cook's son John.
Land in Tuscarora.
Exs.: James Carothers and William Lindsey, also guardians of John, son
of Barbary Wilson.
Wit.: Geog. Cook, Rennel Blair, John Carothers.   E. 139-140.

BOOR, MICHAEL, East Pennsborough. 7 April 1786. 7 Jan 1788.
Wife Margaret.
Son Nichalaus Boor.
Dau. Mary.
Willary Bucholder.
Dau. Margaret Longstorf.
Son Michael.
Land at Northumberland, near the big Island.
Susannah, wife of Michael Boor.
Nicholaus Boor's son, Michael.
Dau. Margaret Longstorf's dau. Mary.
Exs.: Son Michail Boor.
Wit.: John Walker, Philip Longstorf.   E. 141.

CARTER, ANDREW. 24 Sept 1788. 7 Jan 1789.
Wife Margaret.
Children Sally, Elizabeth and Esther, minors.
Exs.: Wife Margaret and George Logue.
Wit.: Alexander Murdock, Hugh Breden, Peter Smith.   E. 142.

WILLIAMSON, SAMUEL, East Pennsboro. 7 Dec 1786. 23 Jan 1789.
Wife (no name).
Children, two sons, minors, names not given.

Exs.: Bro. Thomas Williamson and bro.-in-law Matw. Miller.
Wit.: Samuel Irvine, George Williamson. E. 143.

MAXWELL, ALBERT, Rye. 20 Dec 1788. 24 Jan 1789.
Three children, viz., William, Andrew and Margaret Maxwell.
Five other children, viz., James, Alexander, Robert, Ann Maxwell alias
Taylor, and Mary Maxwell alias Woodburn.
Where James Hackett lives.
Exs.: Son Alexander Maxwell and Frederick Watts, Jr.
Wit.: Robert Walker, Frederick Watts, Jr. E. 144.

HAYS, ADAM, yeoman, West Pennsborough. 7 Sept 1785. 9 March
1789.
Son Adam Hays, Jr.
Son John.
Dau. Lacey, wife of Joseph Connelly.
Sons George, Henry and Nathan Hays.
Dau. Charity Hays.
Son Joseph.
Grandchildren, viz., Adam Hays, son of son Adam; Adam Connelly, son of
dau. Lacey; Adam, son of son George; Adam, son of son Henry; and John,
son of son John.
Exs.: Sons George, Joseph and Henry Hays.
Wit.: William Wallace, Thos. Foster, Robert Magaw. E. 145-146.

PATTERSON, ESTHER, East Pennsborough. 18 Oct 1788. 4 April
1789.
Children John, William, James and Isabella Patterson.
Exs.: Son John Patterson, Robt. Whitehill and John A. Hanna, Esq.
Wit.: Moses Gilmor, Jas. Duncan, John Harris.
Codicil 11 Jan 1789.
Wit.: Japheth Morton, Edward Morton, Jr., Moses Gilmor. E. 146-147.

HANNA, SAMUEL, farmer, Hopewell. 16 May 1785. 9 April 1789.
Wife (no name).
Two youngest sons Ebenezer and Samuel, minors.
Four daus. Margaret, Elizabeth and Mary and dau. last born, not yet
named.
Eldest son Joseph.
Exs.: Wife and friend William Trimble.
Wit.: Joseph Brady, Adam McCormick. E. 147-148.

HODGE, JOHN, yeoman, West Pennsborough. 13 Nov 1789. 20 Dec 1789.
Wife Agness.
Son William.
Grandson John, son of William.
Exs.: Samuel Finley and Samuel Mathers.
Wit.: John Rippeth (Ripley), John Barns.   E. 148.

STUART, SAMUEL, Hopewell. 15 April 1789. 30 April 1789.
Wife (no name).
Son-in-law John McKnight of Hopewell.
Son-in-law John McKee.
Grandson-in-law John McCarrell, married to grandau. Mary McKnight.
Dau. Margaret McKee, wife of John McKee.
Mr. Daniel Duncan, merchant of Shippensburgh, Alexander Laughlin, Esq., of Hopewell Twp. and Robert Donovan, late of Shippenburgh, now of Franklin Co.
Exs.: Son-in-law John McKnight.
Wit.: David Hill, clk., David McKiney, Samuel Whery.   E. 148-150.

McDANIEL, DAVID, Newton. 30 Jan 1787. 28 April 1789.
Wife Jean.
Oldest son Daniel.
Dau. Katrine McDaniel.
Dau. Mary, wife of Alexander McNickle.
Son Joseph.
Granddau. Jean McNickle, a minor.
Exs.: Son Daniel McDaniel.
Wit.: John Scouller, Sam McCormick, Alexander McClintock.   E. 151.

KNOPF, JACOB, Allen. 14 April 1785. 11 May 1789.
Wife Anely.
Sons Michael and Jacob.
Son John, a minor.
Dau. Anely, wife of Roger Lannon.
Dau. Elizabeth.
Sons Benjamin and Christian, minors.
Dau. Mary and son David, minors.
Exs.: Wife Annely, son Jacob and Conrad Reinenger.
Wit.: Christian Jacobs, Alexander Wilson, Jno. Postlethwaite.
                                                  E. 152-153.

CARSON, JOHN, yeoman, Tyrone. 5 Aug 1788. 12 May 1789.
Wife Margaret.
Son James.
Son-in-law Archibald London.
Son William Carson.
Dau. Jean Carson, Jennet Carson, Martha and Margret Carson.
Exs.: Son-in-law Archd. London and Isaac Thompson of Rye.
Wit.: David McClure, James Adams, John Peden.   E. 154-155.

WILSON, CHRISTOPHER. 7 Dec 1784. 1 Aug 1785.
Wife Sarah.
Dau. Sarah and her present husband.
Eldest son Jacob.
Sons John and Henry.
Dau. Susanna.
Dau. Elizabeth and her husband.
Wit.: Henry Richards, Stephen Sinslow, Henry Slachart.
Exs.: None named.   E. 156.

STONES, PETER, Sr., Tyrone. 8 Jan 1789. 8 Aug 1789.
Wife Margaret.
Sons Peter, Andrew and John.
Dau. Elizabeth Douty.
Eldest son James Stones.
Dau. Ann Stones.
Dau. Margaret, a minor.
Dau. Mary Talbot, widow.
Exs.: Sons Peter Stones and Andrew Stones.
Wit.: George Ferguson, John Davidson.   E. 157.

McMURRAY, THOMAS, Carlisle. 9 July 1789. 1 Sept 1789.
Bro. William McMurray's two sons, viz., Thomas and William, of the
Kingdom of Ireland.
Bro. Samuel McMurray, his children, if he has any living.
Two sisters Jean and Sarah.
Bro. William.
Sister Ann Kerns and her three daus., viz., Jean, Ann, and Sarah.
Bro.-in-law John Kerns and his five children, viz., sd. three daus. Jean,
Ann and Sarah, and two sons James and William.
Dau.-in-law Elizabeth McMurray.
Jean Boden wife of Hugh Boden.

Exs.: William Blair, Sr., John Jordan, Ephraim Steel and Abraham Longbridge.
Wit.: John Morrison, John Anderson, Michael Marshall.   E. 158-159.

KENNAGHAN, RICHARD. Nuncupative Will. 15 March 1788. 2 Sept 1789.
To Mrs. Wilson.
Wit.: Catherine Duey, John Moore, Susannah Hall.
Admin.: John Agnes, Esq.   E. 160.

YORTY, HENRY, Allen. 2 Sept 1789. 22 Sept 1789.
Wife Agness.
Son John.
Dau. Mary Poorman.
Dau. Mattelen.
Sons George, Peter, Samuel, David, and Christy, "if any die in their minority."
Exs.: George Coover and John Snevley.
Wit.: Christopher Quigley, Henry W. Faber.   E. 161.

GEDDIS, WILLIAM, East Pennsborough. 7 March 1786. 1 Oct 1789.
Wife Cathrine.
Six children, viz., James, Margaret, John, Paul, Robert and Thomas. Thomas McCallen.
Exs.: Son Thomas, son James Geddis and Abraham Adams.
Wit.: John McConnell, John Story, James Gilfillen.   E. 162.

FISHER, THOMAS, Tyrone. 21 June 1788. 27 Oct 1789.
Wife Margaret.
Sons Samuel, John and Thomas, minors.
Five daus. Mary, Jean, Elizabeth, Margaret and Sarah Fisher, minors.
Land sold to Jacob Stumbaugh.
"If wife and children, remove to Kentucky."
Bro. James Fisher and bro.-in-law Isaac Gibson, guardians of three sons.
Exs.: Bro. Samuel Fisher and bro.-in-law Robert Scot.
Wit.: David McClure, William Foster, Thomas Matier.   E. 163-164.

PATTERSON, WILLIAM, Letort Spring. 16 Nov 1789. 7 Dec 1789.
Wife Mary.
Dau. Elizabeth Chester.
Granddau. Ruth Patterson.

26

Grandson Richard Chester, minor.
Granddau. Mary Chester, minor.
Son William.
Exs.: Son William Patterson and Charles McClure.
Wit.: Andrew Holmes, Matthew Laird.   E. 165.

CEAGLE, FREDERICK, yeoman, Greenwood. 1 March 1789. 25 Jan
1790.
Wife Margaret.
Son Jacob.
Daus. Elizabeth and Mary.
Exs.: Jacob Pfoutz and son Jacob Ceagle.
Wit.: Peter Besan, John Lewes.   E. 166.

McCUE, ANTHONY, yeoman, Allen. 8 Feb 1790. 18 March 1790.
Wife Jane.
Sons John, Abraham and Thomas.
Son-in-law Thomas Cannon and Mary Cannon, his wife.
Son-in-law Samuel Johnston and Agness, his wife.
Grandson James Johnston, minor.
Grandson Anthony Johnston, minor.
Granddau. Mary Rodgers.
Exs.: Henry Quigley and Abraham McCue.
Wit.: C. Quigley, Isaack Norton.   E. 167-168.

HENRY, WILLIAM, East Pennsbro. 13 June 1783. 2 April 1790.
Wife Sarah.
Sons James, John and Hugh, minors.
Other children Robert, Joseph, William, Jean and Sarah.
Exs.: John Quigley, Samuel Fisher and William Henry.
Wit.: John Buchanan, William Geddis, Nat Nelson.   E. 169-170.

MAGAW, ROBERT, Carlisle. 22 Nov 1789. 9 April 1790.
Wife Marietta.
Dau. Elizabeth, minor.
House in tenure of James Hamilton.
Son Vanbrunt, minor.
Lands in Mifflin Co., in tenure of Robert Howe.
Plantation near Carlisle, in tenure of Abraham Swanger.
Exs.: Wife Marietta, father-in-law Rutgart Vanbrunt, bro.-in-law George
Covenhaven and friends, Saml. Laird and James Hamilton.

Wit.: Thos. Foster, Lewis Foulk.   E. 171-172.

AGNEW, JOHN, Carlisle. 2 April 1790. 12 April 1790.
To Sarah Wilson, "for long and faithful service," land in Rye Twp.
Land In Wayne Twp.
Nephew John Henry.
Nephew John Agnew, son of bro. James, of the Kingdom of Ireland.
Ephm. Blaine.
Exs.: Saml. Postlethwaite, John Miller and Samuel Laird of Carlisle.
Wit.: Robert Miller, Jr., John Gesham, John Armor.   E. 173.

REED, JAMES R., Esq. ----. 12 April 1790.
Wife Frances.
Bro. John Reed.
Nephew James Reed, one of sons of sd. John Reed.
Nephew Joseph Reed, son of sd. John.
Father James Reed.
Land on Juniata River, in Huntingdon Co., formerly estate of Jacob
Hare.
Nephew, the son of Thomas Reed.
Plantation in Hamilton Bann Twp. (York Co.).
Nephew James Stephens.
Land in District of Kentucky conveyed by William Alexander.
Niece Mary Reed, dau. of bro. Samuel Reed.
Land in Northumberland Co., warrant in name of Thomas Duncan.
Bro. Samuel Reed.
Nephew James, son of bro. William Reed.
Land in Northumberland Co., warrant in name of William Chambers.
Nephew James Reed, son of bro. Benjamin Reed.
Land in William Powers district, No. 63.
Nephew John McKassen.
Lot of ground in Pittsburg, the north side of Allegahaney River, title
from Gen. Wm. Irvine.
William Irvine, son of Genl. Wm. Irvine.
A military bounty right assigned to Col. Henry Lee.
Calender Duncan, son of Thomas Duncan.
Son Robert Callender (step-son?).
Friend Thomas Shippen, son of Dr. William Shippen, my eagle, in hopes
the Society of Council will admit as member, a man who abroad has done
so much honor to his country."
Thomas Duncan.

Mary Thompson, wife of George Thompson.
To Catherine Callender.
Exs.: Wife Frances Reed, Bro. William and Gen. Wm. Irvine.
Wit.: George Gibson, Wm. Crawford.   E. 174-176.

HAWTHORN, ROBERT, Hopewell. 30 April 1790. 5 May 1790.
Wife Sarah.
Step son Robert McCune.
Land at George Clark's line.
Adam Hawthorne.
Son John McCollum.
Son Moses Glen.
Exs.: Robert McCune.
Wit.: William Hisnut, John Rainy, William Rainy.   E. 177.

McCANA, PATRICK, schoolmaster, Tyrone. 4 April 1790. 14 May 1790.
To Samuel Fisher.
David McClure, Esq., and his dau. Jean.
Exs.: Samuel Fisher.
Wit.: James Adams, Samuel Thompson.   E. 178.

GRIMES, JOHN ADAM, Shippensburgh. 14 Feb 1790. 21 May 1790.
Son-in-law John Sailor.
Samuel Sailor, son of John Sailor, aforesd., a minor.
Exs.: John Ditrick.
Wit.: Conrad Beamer, Frederick Shepfley, Abraham Beitleman, John
Beck (Beek), Christian Etinger.   E. 179.

KELLY, ROBERT, Tyrone. 28 Dec 1778. 29 May 1790.
Daus. Mary, Jean, Nancy and Sarah.
Four sons Henry, Samuel, Archibald and William, minors.
Exs.: Samuel McCullough and Hugh Wallace.
Wit.: Robert Allen, Mary Allen, Hugh Wallace.   E. 180.

McTEER, JOHN, Allen. 10 Sept 1789. 9 June 1790.
Wife Mary.
Son James.
Seven youngest children, viz., Samuel Huston, John, Andrew, Alice,
Isabel, Mary and Ann; three of the children minors.
Exs.: Wife Mary and sons Samuel Huston and John.
Wit.: William McMeen, Robert McMeen, Hugh Wallace.   E. 181-183.

MARTIN, ALEXANDER, Hopewell. 2 April 1789. 18 June 1790.
Bro. Robert.
John and Robert Watson in Franklin Co.
Andrew McCalla in the city of Philadelphia.
Exs.: Bro. Robert Martin.
Wit.: Samuel Hanna, William Montgomery. E. 184.

ERWIN, JOHN, Tyboine. 1 Oct 1786. 13 Aug 1790.
Son Francis and his children.
Dau. Mary, wife of Thomas Hawitt, and her children.
Dau. Jean, wife of William Murray, and her children.
James Erwin, son of Richard Erwin, dec'd, and Margaret Erwin, dau. of
sd. Richard Erwin, dec'd.
Exs.: Alexr. Murray, Esq., and son Francis Erwin.
Wit.: Mary Armstrong, Abel Armstrong, James Johnston. E. 185.

NEWTON, EDWARD, West Pennsborough. 16 Aug 1790. 28 Aug 1790.
Robert McIntire.
William McIntire, son of sd. Robert McIntire.
William McIntire, bro. of sd. Robert.
George Newton, son of Robert Newton, dec'd, of New Jersey.
Ann Keasby, dau. of Saml. Keasby.
Henry McIntire.
Ann McIntire, wife of sd. Robert.
Exs.: Robert McIntire and John Kelly.
Wit.: James Irwin, David Blean, James Brown. E. 186.

KINKADE, GEORGE, Tyboine. 20 Aug 1790. 18 Sept 1790.
Wife Jean.
Two sons Andrew and John and their sons.
Son Matthew McClaren.
Dau. Mary.
Exs.: Nephews Archibald and Andrew Kinkade.
Wit.: Alexander Murray, John Nelson, Robert Adams. E.187-188.

NEILL, WILLIAM, Baltimore, Md. 13 Aug 1782. Proved in Baltimore
Co., Md., 18 April 1785. in Cumberland Co., Penna., Sept 1790.
Wife Isabella.
Present dwelling house in Calvert Street.
Son Alexander, a minor.
Other children, names not given, minors.

Samuel Holmes.
Exs.: Wife Isabella, bro. Thomas Neill, Hercules Courtnay and Joseph Donaldson.
Wit.: Thorougd. Smith, John Boyd, Danl. Bowly.   E. 189-190.

MILLER, MATTHEW, farmer, Middleton. 11 Sept 1784. 1 Oct 1790.
Eldest dau. Mary, wife of Samuel Irwin.
Matthew Irwin, son of dau. Mary.
Second dau. Sarah, wife of Samuel Williamson.
Matthew Williamson, son of dau. Sarah.
Eldest son John Miller.
Ann and Elizabeth, when eighteen years of age.
Third dau. Jenny, wife of James Gallespie.
Matthew Miller Gallespie, son of dau. Jenny.
Fourth dau. Elizabeth.
Fifth dau. Ruth.
Sixth dau. Catherine.
Youngest son Matthew.
Exs.: Two sons John Miller and Matthew Miller.
Wit.: Martha Skinner, Robert Skinner, James Adams.   E. 191-193.

SMITH, PETER. 15 July 1790. 11 Sept 1790.
Wife Margaret.
Children, viz., Elizabeth Dunbar, Ann Gregg, Margaret Carter, Sarah Dunlop, Esther Smith, Issabella Smith.
Exs.: Wife Margaret Smith.
Wit.: Hugh Boden, Adam Logue, Geo. Logue.   E. 194.

BLACK, JOHN, Sr., Tyrone. 9 April 1790. 28 Sept 1790.
Wife Abigal.
Son James Black.
Plantation in Rye Twp.
Sons John, George, William, Samuel.
Dau. Jean and her husband Jonathan Robinson.
Dau. Rachel and her husband Thomas Stevenson.
Dau. Rebekah and her husband, Samuel Shaw.
Son Jonathan.
Granddau. Abigal McCrakon.
Granddau. Rebekah McCrakon.
Grandson John McCrakon.
To my eight grandsons named John.

Exs.: Sons George Black and Jonathan Black.
Wit.: William Elliott, James Elliott, Robert Elliott.   E. 195.

McNAIR, JOHN. 19 May 1790. 28 Sept 1790.
Bro. David McNair's sons, viz., Robert, John, David, Dunnen (Duncan?),
Ezekiel and Alexander and his dau. Mary.
Four step sons John, Samuel, William and Matthew Davidson.
Bro. Alexr. McNair.
Exs.: Alexander Murray, Esq., and John Davidson.
Wit.: James McCrea, John Morrison.   E. 196.

DENISON, ANDREW, Newton. Jan 1788. 8 Oct 1790.
Wife Sarah.
Dau. Martha French.
Son Andrew Denison.
Agness, wife of John Shanon.
Dau. Sarah, wife of Thomas Little.
Dau. Maryann, wife of James McEwen.
Children of dau. Elizabeth Miller, dec'd.
Son-in-law John Scott.
Dau. Margaret, wife of Robt. Little.
Exs.: John Scouller and Andrew Thompson.
Wit.: John Mitchell, William Richey, John Sheilds.   E. 197.

QUIGLEY, JAMES, farmer, Hopewell. 4 March 1782. 20 Oct 1790.
Wife Janet.
Dau. Mary Brady.
Son John's heirs, if any.
Son Robert.
Exs.: Son Robert Quigley.
Wit.: Alexr. Laughlin, Robert McComb, James McCune.   E. 198.

GREGG, MATTHEW, Middleton. 6 Sept 1783. 22 Oct 1790.
Bro. Andrew Gregg.
Sister Mary Hays' four children, viz., Sarah Hays, Denniston Hays, Jean
Hays and Charity Hays.
Sister Margery Buchanan.
Nancy McAnulty.
Bro. James Gregg's son, Smith Gregg.
Exs.: James Gregg and Andrew Gregg.
Wit.: John Gregg, John McNelly.   E. 199.

LAWRENCE, CALEB, Greenwood. 9 Oct 1789. 27 Oct 1790.
Wife Elenor.
James Neal, son of John Neal.
Ann Neal, dau. of John Neal.
Wife's sister, Rachel Gummery.
Wife's bro. Ezakel James.
Elizabeth Lawrence, dau. of Edward Lawrence, dec'd.
Wife's bro. Isaac James.
Exs.: Wife Elenor and Isaac James.
Wit.: Samuel Osborne, Benjamin Hunt.   E. 200.

BEATY, JOHN, Cordwinder, Rye. 9 July 1784. 22 Oct 1790.
Wife Margaret.
Oldest son William.
Sons Andrew, James and John.
Other children, viz., Robert, Elizabeth, Alexander, Samuel and Joseph.
Grandson James.
Exs.: Sons Andrew and John Beaty.
Wit.: Hugh Miller, Hugh Miller, Jr.   E. 201-202.

WOODS, JOHN, West Pensborough. 5 June 1790. 26 Nov 1790.
Son George Woods.
William Woods.
Son Hugh.
Son-in-law Isaack Skiles.
Son James.
Plantation in Leacock Twp., Lancaster Co.
Dau. Esbel.
Sons Richard and Robert, and John Woods.
Granddau. Jean Skiles.
Exs.: Sons Richard Woods and Robert Woods.
Wit.: William Wallace, William Gladen, Wm. Clark.   E. 203.

HARKNESS, WILLIAM, Allen. 13 Feb 1789. 26 Nov 1790.
Sons William and David.
Daus. Jain and Margaret.
Exs.: Son William Harkness and Samuel Irwin, Esq.
Wit.: Ephraim Brown, Saml. Irwin, James Graham.   E. 204.

CROCKET, JAMES, Allen. 16 July 1790. 31 Dec 1790.
Wife Margaret.

Dau. Elizabeth, wife of Thomas McCormick.
Dau. Agness, wife of James Magoveney.
Dau. Mary Brodrick.
Dau. Margaret, wife of Robt. Thompson.
Dau. Jean and Rebecka Crocket.
Son John.
Exs.: Wife Margaret Crocket and son John Crocket.
Wit.: George Dickie, James Crocket, Wm. Scott.   E. 205.

COLLIER, JOSEPH, Carlisle. 4 Aug 1790. 10 Jan 1791.
Mother Hannah Collier.
Land in Westmoreland Co., 1st and 7th Districts of Donation Lands.
Land warrant in hands of Major Willm. Alexander, Surveyor General,
granted for publick services.
Exs.: Mother Hannah Collier and William Thompson.
Wit.: John Trow, James Horwick.   E. 206.

ELLIOTT, EDWARD, Tyrone. 6 Jan 1786. 15 Feb 1791.
Wife Margaret.
Sons William and James.
Dau. Elizabeth.
Son John.
Son and dau. Moses Leathern and Margaret, his wife.
Granddau. Elizabeth Elliott, dau of son Edward, dec'd, a minor.
Grandchildren.
Exs.: Sons William and James.
Wit.: Andrew Kincaid, Archibald Kincaid.   E. 207-208.

BOW, MICHAEL, Carlisle. 10 Jan 1791. 4 March 1791.
Wife Catherine.
Daus. Catherine, wife of John Gaw, and Nancy Bow.
Son Andrew Bow, in Kingdom of Ireland.
Exs.: Wife Catherine and son-in-law John Gaw.
Wit.: Samuel Boyd, John Rodgers, John Jordan.   E. 209.

CAMPBLE, FRANCIS, Esq., Shippensburg. 8 Aug 1790. 9 March 1791.
Wife Elizabeth.
Estate in Hopewell Twp., called *The Forest*.
Son John.
Land in Bedford, or perhaps now in Huntingdon Co., adj. land of John
Burd and Ramsey.

Son James.
Land in Letterkenny, Franklin Co. in name of John Mitchell.
Son Francis.
Land in tenure of Michael Traxler.
Son Ebenezer.
Son Parker, a minor.
Son George.
Land in tenure of John Neff.
Son-in-law Robert Tate.
Dau. Elizabeth.
Parker, Elizabeth and George, minors.
Exs.: Wife Elizabeth and sons Francis, Ebenezer and Parker.
Wit.: John Simpson, Jean Woods, Mattw. Henderson.   E. 209-211.

CLARK, THOMAS, Toboine. 31 Jan 1791. 10 March 1791.
Wife Mary.
Children minors, names not given.
Exs.: Wife Mary and Thomas Adams, son to Robt. Adams.
Wit.: Robert Richey, Richard Murray.   E. 211.

DINSMOOR, MARGARET, widow of John Dinsmoor, Middleton. 8 Aug 1790. 25 March 1791.
Son Samuel.
Three daus. Jean, Mary and Sarah.
Elizabeth Farra, "that now lives with me."
Sons Henry and John.
Dau. Margaret Wilhollem.
Dau. Elizabeth Vanmeater.
Exs.: None given.
Wit.: George Crean, James Harper.
Letters to son Samuel Dinsmoor.   E. 212.

SHARP, ROBERT, Hopewell. 18 Feb 1790. 23 March 1791.
Wife Catherine.
Children William, Mary, Elizabeth, Robert, James and Jean. The three sons and dau. Jean, minors.
Exs.: Wife Catherine Sharp and Josias Brown.
Wit.: William Highlands, Elizabeth Highlands.   E. 213-214.

STUART, MARY, widow of Samuel Stuart, Hopewell. 16 Jan 1790. 23 March 1791.

Dau. Elizabeth McNeight.
Son-in-law John McNeight.
Exs.: John McNeight (McKnight).
Wit.: Josias Brown, Robert Coffey, John Coffey.   E. 215.

McCOLLUM, NEAL, Tyrone. 6 Feb 1790. 2 April 1791.
Wife Christian.
Exs.: Son Thomas McCollum.
Wit.: James McCord, James Diven.   E. 216.

STERRETT, DAVID, Newton. 22 Aug 1790. 19 April 1791.
Wife Rachel.
Son William, minor.
Sons Robert and Brice Innes.
Land in Paxtown.
Sons David, and John, a minor.
Dau. Elizabeth, a minor.
Legacy to son Brice Innes Sterrett from his grandfather Brice Innes.
Exs.: Wife Rachel and sons Robert and Brice Innes Sterrett.
Wit.: James Starrett, Jr., Willm. Montgomery.   E. 216-220.

GARDNER, WILLIAM, Toboine. 12 Dec 1790. 20 April 1791.
Sons William and John.
Daus. Elizabeth, wife of John Ewing, and Rebecca, wife of John Gardner.
Exs.: John Walker and John Nelson.
Wit.: Alexander Murray, Stephan Cessna, John Gardner.   E. 220.

SALSBURY, WILLIAM. -- April 1791. 11 April 1791.
Wife (no name).
Peter, Philip, Daniel, Henry, Christian and Salome Salsbury.
Other children, minors.
William's age is seventeen in August 1791.
Exs.: Charles Crislip and Peter Crislip.
Wit.: George Buck, Charles Crislip.   E. 221.

EARL, RICHARD. 22 April 1784. 5 May 1791.
Wife Jannot.
Daus. of Malcolm Wright.
Joseph Clark and his mother.
William Linton and his children.
Wit.: John Buchanan, Malcom [sic] Wright, An [sic] McMullan.

No Exs. Letter to widow Jannet *[sic]* Erle. E. 222.

CHAMBERS, JOHN. 8 Dec 1756. 28 Dec 1756. Filed 8 Aug 1791.
Wife Mary.
Sons Randle Chambers and William Chambers.
Son John, a minor.
Dau. Elizabeth Smith.
Daus. Jean and Mary Chambers.
A child not yet born.
Exs.: Arthur Foster and James Henderson, farmer.
Wit.: Andrew Dalton, Thomas Adams, Robert Renick. E. 222.

KEROWER, JOHN, Allen. 2 May 1789. 9 June 1791.
Wife Ann.
Dau. Margaret.
Grandchildren Jacob and David Kishler, children of the late Barbara Kishler.
Dau. Catherine.
Son Jacob Kerower.
Land bounded by those of Joseph Strock, Hartman Morret, Phollex Wise, Daniel McNeal and Frederick Elephritz.
Exs.: David Kishler and Andrew Albert.
Wit.: Wm. Scott, Hartman Morret, Joseph Strock.
Codicil 2 Aug 1789.
Grandson David Kishler being now dec'd. E. 223-225.

SWARTZ, JOHN, East Pennsborough. 25 May 1791. 11 July 1791.
Wife Elizabeth.
Son John.
Other children, viz., sons George, Leonard, Caspar and Christian, and daus. Katrin, Susana and Annamare.
Dau. Cradlets.
Exs.: John Sheffer and son Casper Swartz.
Wit.: Abraham Adams, Jonathan Hoge, John Seffer. E. 226.

McCORMICK, ADAM, Hopewell. 30 Dec 1790. 19 July 1791.
Wife Elizabeth.
Sons James and Robert.
Dau. Jean.
Son Adam.
Dau. Elizabeth.

Son George.
Dau. Isabella.
Some of the children, minors.
Exs.: Wife Elizabeth, son James and John McKee.
Wit.: William Montgomery, John Wills.   E. 227-228.

BUTLER, THOMAS, gunsmith, West Pennsborough. 20 Sept 1787. 23
July 1791.
Wife Elienor.
Son Richard Butler and his spouse.
Son William and his spouse.
Dau. Elinor Butler.
Sons Edward and Pierce Butler.
Son Captain Thomas Butler.
Exs.: Wife Elioner Butler and sons Thomas and Edwd. Butler.
Wit.: Pat. Wallace, Jas. Armstrong, Mark Kerr.   E. 229.

RYAIN, AGNESS, Rye. 6 June 1791. 29 July 1791.
Son Robert Ryain.
Daus. Agness Jones, Elinor Boyd and Rebeka Pue.
Grandson William Ryain, son of John and Elizabeth Ryain.
Exs.: Son Robert Ryain.
Wit.: William Wallace, Thomas Scott, George Leonard.   E. 230.

ELLIOTT, JAMES, farmer, Eastpensbro. 16 Aug 1791. 2 Sept 1791.
Wife Mary.
Grandson James Dodds.
Granddau. Elizabeth Dodds.
Grandson James Atchley.
Granddaus. Nancy Dodds and Catherine Atchley.
Grandson Jessy Atchley.
Exs.: Andrew Irvine and Joseph Junkin.
Wit.: Robert Patterson, John Douglass.   E. 231.

MITCHELL, ISABELL. 19 June 1789. 12 Sept 1791.
Son Ezekiel Mitchell.
Dau. Susanah.
Son Robert.
Daus. Jean and Ruth.
Exs.: Dau. Ruth Mitchell.
Wit.: Josias Brown, Hannah Brown.   E. 232.

SMITH, JAMES, Westpensbro. 15 Sept 1776. 7 Oct 1791.
Wife Margaret.
Children, viz., Mary, Nathaniel, James, William, Margaret, and an unborn child.
Exs.: Wife Margaret Smith and Charles McClure.
Wit.: John Watson, Sarah McMurray, John Byers.
Codicil 13 Sept 1791.
Youngest dau. Sidney. Oldest dau. Polly, now Mrs. Butler. Appoints Exs.: son James Smith and Charles McClure.
Wit.: Robt. Davidson, Lemuel Gustine, Saml. Weakley.   E. 232-233.

McBETH, ANDREW, Middleton. 28 Jan 1791. 7 Oct 1791.
Wife Ann.
Dau. Margaret, a minor.
Son Alexander.
Daus. Mary and Jean.
Exs.: Wife and William Blair, Jr. of Carlisle.
Wit.: David Elliott, Robert Elliott, Jean Elliott.   E. 234.

GIVEN, JOSEPH, merchant, Carlisle. 23 Oct 1791. 2 Nov 1791.
Bro. Samuel.
Bros. John, Robert, Benjamin and James.
Exs.: John Morrison, bro. James Given and Lemuel Gustine.
Wit.: Robert Given, John Webber, Robt. Miller.   E. 235.

REED, WILLIAM, Southampton. 6 March 1791. 8 Nov 1791.
Wife Margaret.
Sons John and Thomas.
Dau. Jean Reed.
Exs.: Wife Margaret Reed.
Wit.: Josias Brown, William Highlands.   E. 236.

CROCKET, ANDREW, Allen. 15 Oct 1791. 14 Nov 1791.
Wife Elizabeth.
Three youngest children James, Sarah and Andrew, minors.
Plantation whereon James Williamson dwells.
Other children Elizabeth McGowan and Alice Keepers.
Grandson Andrew Keepers.
Exs.: Wife Elizabeth, George Logue and Thomas Clark.
Wit.: James Williamson, John Williamson, George Dickie.   E. 236-239.

IRWIN, GEORGE, Teboin. 5 Nov 1791. 22 Nov. 1791.
Sister's son William Young.
William Irwin.
Land on Shevers Creek.
Francis Irwin's children.
Thomas Hewet's children.
William Fisher's children.
William Morrow's children.
Allen Nesbit's children.
Alexander Morrow and Nancy his wife.
Elizabeth Irwin.
Francis Irwin.
George Irwin, son of cousin John Irwin.
Said Irwin's son Alexander Irwin.
Margaret Nelson.
Exs.: Alexander Morrow, Francis Irwin and John Nelson.
Wit.: George McKeehan, George Flaghart, John Fleicher.   E. 238-239.

LINDSEY, SAMUEL, West Pennsborough. 25 Oct 1791. 7 Dec 1791.
Wife Agness.
Son John.
Dau. Margaret Hammon.
Sons James and William.
Daus. Jenny and Nancy.
Son Samuel.
Son Robert.
Exs.: Wife Agness and sons William and Robert Lindsey.
Wit.: Joseph Hays, Nancy Hays.   E. 239-240.

MURRAY, ALEXANDER, Toboyne. 17 Sept 1791. 21 Dec 1791.
Wife Margaret.
Oldest son John Murray and his son Alexander, a minor.
Oldest dau. Mary Armstrong.
Son Halbert.
Mother-in-law Ann Adams.
Son James.
Dau. Jane Adams.
Sons William, Alexander, Thomas, Richard and dau. Ann.
Some of the children, minors.
Exs.: Wife Margaret, son John Murray and 2nd son Halbert Murray.
Wit.: Alexander Murray, John Morrison.   E. 241.

BLAINE, WILLIAM. ----. 2 Feb 1792.
Wife (no name).
Eldest dau. Mary.
Sons Alexander, William, Ephraim and James Armstrong.
Boys all to be put to trades.
Exs.: Samuel Lyon and John Armstrong.
Wit.: Thomas Purdy, Robert Hunter.   E. 242.

KILGORE, ELIZABETH, Newton. 14 Aug 1782. 14 Feb 1792.
Sons Hugh and Benjamin Kilgore.
Dau. Mary Borland.
Sons Joseph, Oliver, Patrick, David, Jonathan, John and William.
Sons Jesse and Robert, minors.
Exs.: Son William Kilgore and Alexander Laughlin.
Wit.: Saml. Cunningham, Alexr. Laughlin, James Scrogs.   E. 243-244.

McENAIR, ALEXANDER, gentleman, Teboin. 23 Sept 1791. 17 Feb
1792.
Wife Mary.
Nephew Alexander McEnair, Junior.
Mary Thorn.
Hannah Thorn.
Margaret Garvin.
Nephews Robert McEnair, Dening McEnair, David McEnair.
Exs.: Wife Mary McEnair and John Clark.
Wit.: Joseph Henderson, Sarah Clark.   E. 245-246.

JACOBS, JOSEPH, farmer, West Pennsborough. 2 Jan 1783. 3 April
1792.
Wife Elinor.
Dau. Mary, wife of Robert Quigley.
Dau. --- wife of Daniel Duncan.
Sons Thomas and John Jacobs.
Lot of ground in Charlestown, Cecil Co., Maryland.
Dau. Elinor, wife of John Reed.
Son Jerman.
Land bought of Andrew Gibson, next to John Scouller's mill.
Exs.: Wife Elinor Jacobs and son Jerman Jacobs.
Wit.: John Scouller, David Ralston, James Ralston.
Caveat entered 3 March 1787 against probate of will.   E. 247-248.

THOMPSON, ANDREW, Hopewell. 14 May 1792. 24 May 1792.
Wife Martha.
Dau. Mary, wife of John Wilson.
Daus., viz., Jean, Elizabeth, Sarah, Prudence, Hannah and Rosanna.
Grandson Andrew Wilson, a minor, and his bro. and sister.
Exs.: Wife Martha, David Wills and John Snody.
Wit.: Willm. Montgomery, Robert Bell.   E. 249-250.

WOODS, THOMAS, West Pennsborough. 4 May 1792. 26 May 1792.
Wife Janet.
Four children Mary Woods, Elizabeth Woods, William and Samuel
Woods, all minors.
Father-in-law Samuel Woods, Sr.
David Woods.
Exs.: William Woods and Nathan Woods.
Wit.: James Weakley, Robert Weakley.   E. 251-252.

BUTLER, RICHARD, Carlisle. At Fort McIntosh 29 Sept 1785. 31 May
1792.
Wife Mary.
Son William and dau. Mary Butler, minors.
Bro. William Butler.
Honored father.
House and lot in Carlisle.
Land on Plumb Creek, Westmoreland Co., taken out in name of John
Beard, adj. land of Col. George Croghan.
Land in name of George McCully on the Alleghany River.
Land in name of Robert George on Plumb Creek.
Lots in Pittsburgh adj. lots of William Butler.
Lots in town of Appleby on the Alleghany River.
Donation Lands for services as Colonel in Army of the United States.
James O'Hara.
Exs.: Wife Mary, bro. William Butler and Thomas Smith, Esq., Attorney
at Law in Carlisle.
Wit.: John McDowell, James O'Hara.   E. 253-256.

RODOCKER, CHRISTOPHER, farmer, West Pennsborough. 26 May
1792. 1 June 1792.
Wife Ann Dority.
Son Fredrick.
Daus. Morriah and Barbarow.

Son Jacob Rodocker.

Exs.: Ann Dority Rodocker, John Smith and Armstrong Carothers.

Wit.: Martin Carothers, Armstrong Carothers.   E. 256-257.

PARKER, MARGARET, widow of John Parker, West Pennsboro. 12 May 1791. 5 June 1792.

Grandson Parker Campbell, son to Francis Campbell, dec'd.

Great grandson Alexander Lyon.

Son Alexander Parker, dec'd.

Daus. Mary Flemming, Elizabeth Campbell, Margaret Calhoon and Agness Denny.

Granddau. Margaret Parker, dau. of son Alexander Parker, dec'd.

Granddau. Mary and her youngest sister, daus. of sd. son Alexander Parker.

Revd. Mr. Davidson.

Dr. Lemuel Gustine.

Granddau. Elizabeth Denny.

Exs.: Grandson James Flemming.

Wit.: George Crean, Willm. Lyon.   E. 257.

JUNKIN, JOHN. 4 July 1792. 21 July 1792.

Oldest bro. Joseph and his male children, when of age.

Exs.: Bro. Joseph Junkin.

Wit.: James Clayton, John Mackey, John Black.   E. 258.

LAUGHLIN, JAMES, farmer, Newton. 25 Jan 1792. 23 July 1792.

Dau. Elizabeth.

Other children James, Mary, John, William, Robert and Hugh.

Exs.: Sons Robert Laughlin and Hugh Laughlin.

Wit.: Atcheson Laughlin, Wm. Thompson.   E. 259.

RAMSEY, JAMES, Dickenson, formerly West Pennsboro. 30 May 1792. 28 July 1792.

Wife Janet.

Son Nathan.

Daus. Mary Ramsey, Nancy Ramsey, Elizabeth Ramsey and Margaret Ramsey.

Daus. Janet Donaldson and Rebecca Armstong, her son James Ramsey Armstrong, a minor.

Dau. Martha Means.

James Woods son of William Woods, Jr., a minor.

William Donaldson, bound by Abraham Brooks, when of age.
Exs.: Son Nathan Ramsey and Samuel Woods.
Wit.: David King, Wm. Woods, Adam Hauck.   E. 260-261.

LONGSTROFF, HENRY, farmer, Eastpennsbro. 11 Dec 1789. 8 Aug
1792.
Eldest son Martin.
Children of son Philip Longstrof, dec'd.
Son Adam.
Dau.-in-law Ann Longstrof, son Philip's wife.
Guardian of son Philip's children.
Exs.: Son Martin Longstroff and Michael Hawk.
Wit.: John Walker, Archd. London.   E. 262-263.

CAROTHERS, GERARD, Carlisle. 6 June 1792. 21 Aug 1792.
Wife Nancy.
Bro. John Carothers.
Sister Margaret Carothers.
Exs.: Wife Nancy Carothers and Samuel Greer.
Wit.: Saml. Greer, Mary Hazlett, John Jordan.   E. 264.

PATERSON, ROBERT, Eastpennsborough. 6 Sept 1792. 9 Oct 1792.
Wife (no name).
Sons William, Samuel, Robert, Timothy, John and Millard.
Dau. Hannah Paterson.
Jane, wife of Henry Furry.
Martha Patrson.
Exs.: Wife and son-in-law Henry Furry.
Wit.: William Diven, Jonathan Hoge.   E. 265-266.

RHEINIER, JOHN. 26 May 1790. 12 Sept 1792.
Wife Elizabeth.
Son John Rheinier.
Dau. Elizabeth Lackey.
Dau. Esther Jones.
Dau. Hanna.
Dau. Margret.
Exs.: Dau. Hannah and Edward West.
Wit.: Enock Lewes, Emy Lewes.
Letters to Hannah and her husband Geo. Painter.   E. 264-265.

McCLURE, ROBERT, Sr., yeoman, Westpennsbro. 20 Sept 1792. 16 Oct 1792.
Oldest son William.
Dau.-in-law Sarah, wife of son Alexander, dec'd, and her unborn child.
Son Robert.
Bro. William McClure of Lack Twp., Mifflin Co.
Daus. Jane, Margaret and Elizabeth.
Exs.: Son William McClure and son-in-law James Laird.
Wit.: John McKighan, James Woodburn.   E. 267.

McKEAN, JAMES, Carlisle. 13 Aug 1792. 21 Sept 1792.
Bro.-in-law Hugh Patton of Carlisle.
Exs.: Hugh Patton and bro.'s son Hugh McKean.
Wit.: Saml. Laird, Wm. Wallace, James Brown.   E. 267-268.

PURDY, WILLIAM, Teboyn. 13 Aug 1784. 1 Nov 1792.
Wife Elizabeth.
Father Thomas Purdy.
Bros. John, Thomas and Robert Purdy.
Nephew William Purdy, son of bro. Thomas, a minor.
Exs.: Wife Elizabeth Purdy and bro. John Purdy of Newtown.
Wit.: Alexr. Murray, Elizabeth Purdy.   E. 269.

STEWART, ARCHIBALD. 3 Sept 1792. 7 Nov 1792.
Wife Isabella.
Sons John, James, William and Archibald.
Plantation in Morison's Cove.
Dau. Mary and Jeney.
Sons Thomas and Samuel, some of children, minors.
Exs.: Wife Isabella, Robert Scot and Hugh Wallace.
Wit.: Elizabeth Sunbay, John Dunbar, Robert Dunbar.   E. 270.

ALLEN, DAVID, Carlisle. 30 July 1792. 16 Dec 1792.
Wife Sarah.
Mother.
Bro. Joseph Allen.
Plantation in Londonderry Twp., Dauphin Co.
John, son of bro. James Allen.
William, son of bro. James Allen.
Plantation in Northumberland Co., near Montoor's Hill.
Bros. James Allen and John Allen.

Nephew Robert Allen, eldest son of bro. James.
David Allen, son of bro. James.
Exs.: Wife Sarah Allen and bro. Joseph Allen.
Wit.: Lemuel Gustine, James Ross, John Jordan.   E. 271-272.

DUNLOP, JAMES, West Pennsborough. ----. 16 Nov 1792.
Wife Mary.
Son William.
Dau. Isbel and her children.
Son John and his son James.
Dau. Mary and her children.
Dau. Easter.
Daus. Nancy and Sarah.
Exs.: Son William Dunlop and Zunnel (Tunnel?) Blair.
Wit.: David Crookshanks, John Sproat, Agness McDoud.   E. 273.

COLWELL, ROBERT, merchant, Shippensburgh. 10 Sept 1792. 21 Nov
1792.
Wife Ann.
Bro. Samuel Colwell.
Father James Colwell.
Mother Agness Colwell.
Bros. John, James, Joseph and Abdiel Colwell.
Matthew Miller.
Sisters Martha, Nancy, Mary and Betsy Colwell.
Some of bros. and sisters, minors.
Exs.: Wife Anne Colwell and bros. John and Samuel Colwell.
Wit.: Patrick Cochran, John Redett, John Scott.   E. 274-275.

ECHLEBERGER, HENRY. Nuncupative will. Proved 7 Dec 1792.
Two children, names not given.
Wit.: Jacob Witzel and Elizabeth Bower.
Admin.: father-in-law Martin Herman and Martin Bower.   E. 276.

COOTS, RICHARD, West Pennsbro. 2 May 1789. 15 Feb 1793.
David Murray and Mary Murray.
Plantation in Tuscorora.
Heirs of Andrew McFarlane, dec'd.
Ann Dunning, wife of Ezekiel Dunning.
Exs.: William French.
Wit.: Ez. Dunning, Thos. Buchanan.   E. 277.

McCUNE, JOHN, farmer, Newton. 24 Dec 1792. 6 March 1793.
Wife Mary.
Land bought from John McKewen.
Sons Andrew and David McCune.
Dau. Susanna Barr.
Dau. Margaret Wier.
Grandson John McCune, son of Samuel McCune, dec'd.
Dau. Mary McCune.
Sons John, Robert and William McCune, minors.
Exs.: James Sharp, Alexander Laughlin and John McCune.
Wit.: Alexander Laughlin, John Woods, George Wier.   E. 278-280.

NICHOLSON, RICHARD, farmer, Newton. 26 April 1791. 6 March
1793.
Wife Mary.
Daus. Margery, Sarah, Ann and Margaret.
Sons James and William.
William Stevenson.
Mary Stevenson, dau. of Wm. Stevenson.
Grandson Isaac Shannon.
Two grandsons John and Richard McElwain.
Granddaus. Mary and Ruth McElwain.
James Stevenson, son of John Stevenson, dec'd.
Grandson Benjamin Gamble.
Exs.: Son James Nicholson and stepson William Stevenson.
Wit.: Hugh Laughlin, Alexr. Laughlin.   E. 281.

CHAMBERS, JAMES, Tyrone. 23 July 1792. 13 March 1793.
Wife Margaret.
Ground adj. Samuel Rosses.
James Chambers' children.
Eldest dau. Margaret.
Daus. Mary and Jean.
David Chambers.
Cathrine Chambers, Nancy Chambers, and Esabel Chambers, when they
come to age of sixteen.
Exs.: Wife Margaret Chambers and James Hearse.
Wit.: Robert McCally, Peter Stones.   E. 282-283.

RUPLEY, JACOB, yeoman, East Pennsborough. 6 July 1789. 16 March
1793.

Wife Mary.

Grandchildren, viz., the seven children of son George, dec'd.

Sons Jacob, Conrad, Michael, Frederick, John and Abraham Rupley.

Daus. Dorothea, wife of Daniel Frank, Magdalene, wife of Dewrett Erford, Margaret, wife of Adam Fonderan, Barbara, wife of John Swineford, Mary Rupley, Elizabeth, Ann, Catherine, Susanna and Sophia Rupley.

Exs.: Wife Mary and son-in-law Adam Fonderan.

Wit.: Jacob Wormley, George Wiernolz.   E. 284-287.

HIATHERS (HOLTTER), GEORGE, cooper, Westpensbro. 25 Feb 1793. 30 March 1793.

Oldest son John. Other children, names not given.

Exs.: Bro.-in-law David Snyder.

Wit.: Jacob Brown, David Kyser.   E. 288.

McFARLANE, PATRICK, Newton. 3 March 1793. 4 April 1793.

Wife Rosanah.

Daus. Margaret, Elizabeth and Mary.

Son Robert, a minor.

Son William.

Son James.

Exs.: Sons William McFarlane and bro. William McFarlane.

Wit.: Robt. Laughlin, William Thompson, Alexr. Laughlin.   E. 289.

GLEN, GABRAEL, farmer, Big Spring, Westpennsbro. 15 Nov 1791. 26 April 1793.

Wife Jane.

Daus. Jane, Rachel and Rebecca, minors.

Land in tenure of Dr. Isaiah Blair.

Sons William, David and Alexander, minors.

Land at late William Laughlin's line.

To Robert Walker's line.

Exs.: Wife Jane and Benjamin McKeehan.

Guardians of children: James McKeehan and Dr. Isaiah Blair.

Wit.: Isaiah Blair, Gennet N. Blair, Mary McGaughey, David McKeehan.
                    E. 290-293.

DAVIES, JOHN, yeoman, Tyrone. 10 Oct 1791. 3 May 1793.

Wife Jeane.

Dau. Saran Dean.

Dau. Elizabeth.
Son William.
Exs.: Hannah Collier and James Sharon.
Wit.: James Sharon, Andrew Keyser.   E. 294.

HALL, ISABELLA, Newton. 1 Feb 1790. 14 May 1793.
Dau. Mary, wife of Robert McQueen, her dau. Rosy McQueen.
Granddau. Isabella McQueen.
To each of dau. Mary's children.
Granddau. Ruth Cook, minor.
Dau. Sarah Bogle.
Hugh Hall.
Exs.: Son-in-law James Bogle and bro.-in-law Saml. McCormick.
Wit.: George Little, John Scouller, Francis Donahd. *[sic]*.   E. 295.

BOYCE, WILLIAM, yeoman, East Pennsborough. 22 April 1791. 16
April 1793.
Sons John and Robert.
Dau. Ann.
Robert Boyce's son william.
Robert's dau. Mary.
Joseph Clerk's dau. Mary.
Samuel Fleming to school him.
Dau. Sarah Montgomery.
Exs.: Son John Boyce and David Bower.
Wit.: Lewes Lewes, Robert Chamber, Solomon Kees.   E. 296-297.

MURRAY, ALEXANDER, Tyboin. 11 April 1793. 31 May 1793.
Wife Agness.
Daus., viz., Margaret Nesbit, Mary Fisher, Isabella Murray and Jean
McCree.
Grandsons Alexander Fisher and Alexander Nesbit, minors.
Lands up the river.
James and Margaret Irwin, heirs of Richard Irwin, dec'd.
Land in Chillisquaka Creek.
Exs.: Wife, William Fisher and Allen Nesbit.
Wit.: James McCree, Elonar McCree.   E. 298.

WOODS, WILLIAM, Dickinson. 11 Feb 1791. 25 July 1793.
Children Nathan, James, Richard, Mary and Janet, all minors.
Land on Alleghany River, Westmoreland Co.

Guardians of children: Nathan Ramsey and Nathan woods.
Exs.: Bro. Richard Woods and uncle Samuel Woods, Sr.
Wit.: Saml. Woods, David Woods, Adam Hauck.   E. 299-300.

McCLINTOCK, ROBERT, joiner, Toboin. 11 Feb 1791. 25 July 1793.
Wife Martha.
Children John, James, Betsy and Samuel.
Father William McClintock.
Exs.: James Powers, Moses Thompson and Joseph McClintock.
Wit.: James Robison, William McCoord.   E. 301.

RODGERS, JOHN, Middleton. 26 March 1784. 7 April 1792.
To mother-in-law Jane Hashey.
Exs.: Matthew Gregg and Samuel Laird, Esq.
Wit.: Job Johnson, John Cochran.   E. 302.

HART, MATTHEW, Tyrone. 5 July 1793. 3 Aug 1793.
Eldest son John Hart.
Dau. Rosana Bowen.
Charles McCarty.
Dau. Jean Gillespie.
Dau. Mary (Mc)Carty [sic] and her children, Mary and Charles Carty [sic].
Exs.: William Dreaner and Daniel MCarty (McCarty).
Wit.: Peter Stones, Andrew Stones.   E. 303.

CALDWELL, JOHN, Newton. March 1793. 20 Aug 1793.
Wife Ann.
Sons John and Samuel.
Son Joseph.
Land adj. Leonard Thrush, Andrew Ganets and Thomas Niel's houses.
Land adj. William McCracan's.
Daus. Elizabeth and Ann.
Patrick McKenny.
Exs.: Wife, son Joseph Caldwell, William McCracan and Samuel Findley.
Wit.: John Russell, Solomon Clyd.   E. 304.

DEVLIN, ROGER, Carlisle. 19 Aug 1793. 15 Sept 1793.
Wife Sarah.
Children John Devlin, Thomas Atcheson, Alice King and John Love.
Exs.: Wife Sarah Devlin and George Logue, Esq.

Wit.: Thomas Dickson, Adam Logue, George Weiest.   E. 305.

HENRY (McHENRY), JOHN, Carlisle. 21 Aug 1793. 10 Sept 1793.
Daus. Polly Henry and Martha Henry, minors.
House in possession of --- White.
Sister Nancy Moore, widow of John Moore, dec'd, of Bellessequgh(?), Co. Antrim, Ireland.
Sister Elizabeth Cowan, widow of Isaac Cowan of Learn, Co. of Antrim, Ireland.
Sister Martha.
Nephews John Moore and William Cowan of Path Valley, Franklin Co.
Bro. James Henry of Ireland.
Exs.: William Alexander and Robert Miller, Jr., of Carlisle.
Wit.: James Davis, George Pattison, Thomas Creigh.   E. 306.

WALKER, RACHEL, Newtonship. 1 March 1791. 30 Sept 1793.
Youngest children, when fourteen years of age.
Exs.: Son-in-law Samuel Crewell.
Wit.: William Walker, Alexander Work, Robert Walker.   E. 307.

SMILEY, GEORGE, Rye. 5 Aug 1793. 31 Oct 1793.
Wife Margaret.
Son Frederick Smiley.
Land on the big run adj. Samuel Smiley.
Sons David and George.
Plantation knows as Watson's Place.
Land adj. Thomas Such, John Stuart and others.
Other children Elizabeth, Jane, Margaret, Mary and Sarah.
Exs.: Wife Margaret and bro. Samuel Smiley.
Wit.: Frederick Watts, Hugh Wallace, Thos. Smiley.   E. 308.

MILLER, PHILIP, Carlisle. 17 Sept 1793. 4 Nov 1793.
Father and mother, Jeremiah and Elizabeth Miller.
Children of bros. and sisters.
Exs.: Bro. Michael Miller and William Levi.
Wit.: Saml. Postlethwait, John McCurdy.   E. 309.

CARNAHAN, ADAM, farmer, Newton. 10 Sept 1793. 3 Dec 1793.
Wife (no name).
Son James.
Sons Adam and Andrew, minors.

Exs.: Robert Carnahan, son James Carnahan and bro.-in-law William McFarlane.
Wit.: Wm. McFarlane, Alexr. Laughlin, William Wilson.   E. 310.

ROSS, JOHN, yeoman, Tyrone. 2 March 1793. 19 Dec 1793.
Mother Elizabeth Ross.
Sisters Jane Ross, Nancy Ross and Margaret Ross.
Exs.: David Robb.
Wit.: John Ross, Robert McMedrim.   E. 311.

BAIRD, JOHN, West Pennsborough. 4 Nov 1793. 18 Jan 1794.
James Carothers, Sr., sole legatee.
Ex.: John Carothers.
Wit.: Nicholas Laing, James Walsh.   E. 312.

CAROTHERS, WILLIAM. 5 Nov 1786. 25 Jan 1794.
Bros. James, Martin, Andrew and Armstrong.
Mother.
Sisters Margaret, Jean and Isabel.
Exs.: William Clark, James Carothers, Jr., and John Carothers.
Wit.: Armstrong Carothers, John Keane, James Carothers.   E. 313.

CLOUSER, JOHN, Rye. 4 Oct 1790. 11 Feb 1794.
Wife Margaret.
Children Michael, Elizabeth, Margaret, George and Peter Clouser, all minors.
Exs.: Wife Margaret Clouser and friend Solenberger.
Wit.: David McClure, Matthew McBride.
Codicil 19 June 1793.
Dau. Elizabeth, dec'd.
Dau. Sydney, born since 1790.   E. 314-315.

BEATTY, SAML., Ensign, 2 Regt. U.P.L., Letter purporting to be the last will, "Miami River, fifty miles from its mouth." 24 Sept 1791. Letters 11 Feb 1794.
Commission with Mr. Wilky (Wilkins), merchant, in Pittsburgh, now in Fort Washington.
Mr. Brotherton.
Major Butler.
Mother.
Joseph.

Wit.: Alexander Power and James Beatty.
Admin.: Alexander Power and James Beatty.
The dec'd was killed at Saint Mary's in the defeat of Genl. St. Clair, by
the Indians, 4 Nov 1791. E. 316.

MARSHALL, MICHAEL, Carlisle. 29 Jan 1794. 14 Feb 1794.
Wife Letitia.
Eldest son Michael.
Sons John and Samuel.
Eldest dau. Isabella English.
Second dau. Grizzle Powers.
Youngest dau. Martha Cox.
Exs.: William Levis of Carlisle and nephew Michael Marshall.
Wit.: David Irvine, Edwd. Little. E. 316-317.

ALLEN, SARAH, widow, Carlisle. 21 Feb 1794. 4 March 1794.
Nephew David Craig, minor.
Lot adj. Dr. Lemuel Gustine.
Nephew Allen Watson.
Lot adj. Alexander Makehan's (Mahon).
William, bro. of sd. David Craig.
Bro. John Craig.
Sister Mary Sloan's children, viz., George, Isabel, Sarah and Rosana, the
estate of their grandfather John Craig in possession of Wm. Wilson, of
Hanover Twp., Dauphin Co.
Sister Watson.
Bro. John Craig's children by his present wife.
William, the eldest son.
Bro. John, wife and dau.
Exs.: James Ross and William Alexander, Esq.
Wit.: Lemuel Gustine, James Ross, John Jordan. E. 317-318.

CARUTHERS (CARITHERS), RODGERS, Dickinson. ----. 28 March
1794.
Wife Sarah.
Two sons John and Andrew.
Exs.: Joshua Martin and James Turner of Newton.
Wit.: Percival Kean, John Neal. E. 319.

HAYS, WILLIAM, Rye. 12 April 1793. 19 March 1794.
Wife Elizabeth.

Daus. Margaret Kirkpatrick, Esther Matthews and Elizabeth Steel.
Son Moses Hays.
Exs.: Robert Wallace and Isaac Jones.
Wit.: Samuel Hogg, Sarah Hogg, Susannah Mathews.   E. 320.

McWHINNEY, ROBERT. ----. 25 March 1794.
"The will was destroyed, when the home and office of Wm. Lyon,
Register, were consumed by fire, about eighteen years ago. The contents
sworn to by Jonathan Hope, Esq., who wrote it."
To wife Margaret McWhinney.
House and lot in Carlisle.
Land in East Pennsborough, where the testator lived.
His sister Bedcom's children.
Wit.: Isabella Buchanan, names of the others not remembered.
                                                               E. 321-322.

DUNCAN, WILLIAM, yeoman, Southampton. 16 Oct 1793. 19 April
1794.
Wife Mary.
Sons David and John Duncan.
Grandson William Duncan, son of sd. John.
Land in Hopewell, West Pennsborough and Newton Twps.
Son William.
Son Stephen, where he now lives in Shippensburgh.
Sons Daniel, Joseph and James.
Grandson William, son of son James Duncan.
Grandson William, son of son Joseph Duncan.
Dau. Margaret Blyth.
Grandson William Blyth.
Dau. Jane Culbertson.
Grandson William Culbertson.
Dau. Anne Culbertson.
Grandson William Culbertson, son of sd. dau. Anne.
Exs.: Wife Mary Duncan and sons John and David Duncan.
Wit.: Matthew Henderson, James Rainey.   E. 323-325.

WALTENBERGER, GEORGE, yeoman, Westpensbro. 4 March 1794. 9
April 1794.
Children, when of age, names not given.
Exs.: Peter Diller and Henry Shank.
Wit.: Jacob Kyser, Jacob Bleaser.   E. 326.

Copy of will and probate of MATTHEWS, JAMES, Woolwich Twp.,
Gloucester Co., New Jersey. 7 Oct 1788. 8 Aug 1792.
Estate in Pennsylvania and New Jersey.
Grandson Samuel Parsons, son of dau. Catherine Dugan, alias Parsons.
Grandson James Campbell, son of dau. Elizabeth Campbell.
Both grandsons under age.
Dau. Jane Mathews.
Son Richard Mathews.
Dau. Phoebe Morison.
Grandchildren, viz., William Dugan and George Dugan, sons of dau.
Catherine, aforesd., and Elizabeth Dugan and Margaret Dugan, daus. of
sd. Phoebe Morrison, alias Dugan.
Exs.: Sons-in-law John Campbell and Daniel Morrison.
Wit.: Vanderver Homan, Thos. Denny, Gideon Denny.
"A true copy, taken from the original."   E. 327.

PATTON, JOHN, Middleton. 31 May 1790. 19 May 1794.
Son William Patton.
Plantation in Tuskerora Valley where sd. son now lives.
Son Robert Patton.
Grandchildren, viz., John and Mary Thompson.
Exs.: Sons William Patton and Robert Patton.
Wit.: George Robinson, Sr., George Robinson, Thos. Robinson.
                                                      E. 328-329.

BLAINE, JAMES, Toboin. 11 Aug 1792. 19 May 1794.
Wife Elizabeth.
Son James Shadden Blaine.
Dau. Margaret Blain.
Son Alexander.
Daus. Eleanor Lions, Agness McMurray, Mary Davidson and Isabella
Mitchell.
Son James Carshaden Blaine and other children, not of age.
Exs.: Son Ephraim Blain and wife Elizabeth Blaine.
Wit.: James Carshadan, John Morrison, Jas. Morrison.   E. 330.

COLHOON, ANDREW, carpenter, Carlisle. 20 March 1794. 23 June
1794.
Wife Esther.
Four daus. Sarah, Rebecca, Elizabeth and Lydia Colhoon.
Land in Middleton Twp. adj. land of Robert Miller and Saml. Laird, Esq.

When youngest dau. is eighteen years of age.
Exs.: Wife Esther Colhoon and Robert Miller, Jr.
Wit.: George Pattison, Wm. Armor.   E. 331.

HENDRICKS, PETER, Southampton. 29 July 1793. 5 Sept 1794.
Wife Elizabeth.
Son James.
Other seven children, viz., Margaret, Elizabeth, Susanna, Mary, Sarah,
Peter and John.
Some of children, minors.
Exs.: Son James Hendricks and Christy Miller.
Wit.: Allen Leeper, Frainey Miller.   E. 332.

SAMPLE, JOHN, East Pennsbro. 3 Sept 1792. 14 Oct 1794.
Wife Kesiah.
Son James Sample.
Children of dau. Sarah Little by John Little.
Daus. Jane Shannon, Margaret Gilmore, Mary Ewalt and Elizabeth
Sample.
Sons John, Chambers and Samuel Sample, minors.
Exs.: William Chambers and Joseph Sample.
Wit.: Jonathan Hoge, James Anderson, Henry Brenizer.   E. 333.

PARKER, JAMES, East Pennsborough. 8 June 1792. 14 Oct 1794.
Wife Rebeca.
Son-in-law Dr. Gustine.
Son Andrew.
Grandson James Gustine.
Exs.: Son Andrew Parker.
Wit.: Jonathan Hoge, Matthew London.   E. 334.

ORR, JOHN, East Pennsborough. 13 Dec 1793. 12 Dec 1794.
Wife Martha.
Son William, a minor.
Son John.
Farm, late property of William Orr, dec'd.
Daus., viz., Mary, Rachel and Jean.
Exs.: Son John Orr and Robert Whitehill.
Wit.: John Young, Andrew Moore.
Codicil 19 Aug 1794.
Wit.: Andrew Moon, Isaac Kuntz.   E. 335.

RUPLEY, MARY, East Pennsborough. 26 Nov 1794. 12 Dec 1794.
Children Frederick, Mary, John, Elizabeth, Nancy, Katrine, Abraham,
Susana and Sophia.
Exs.: Son John Rupley and Robert Whitehill.
Wit.: Elizabeth Wormly, Robert Whitehill.   E. 336.

DUNCAN, STEPHEN, Carlisle. 10 Aug 1793. 9 Jan 1795.
Wife Ann.
Dau. Mary.
Children of son John, dec'd, viz., Matilda, Stephen, Samuel, Mary Ann
and Amelia.
Sons Robert and James.
Son Stephen, a minor.
Dau. Lucy, wife of Jonathan Walker.
Dau. Ann, wife of Samuel Mahon.
Oldest living son, Thomas Duncan.
Exs.: Wife Ann and sons Thomas, Robert and James.
Wit.: Saml. Postlethwait, John Lyon, James Dill, Jr.   E. 337-340.

ESPY, GEORGE, Westpennsbro. 15 Dec 1794. 3 March 1795.
Wife Rachel.
Dau. Jane, a minor.
Sisters Jane and Christy.
Sons George Espy and John Espy, minors.
Exs.: Thomas Kennedy and George Brown.
Wit.: James Graham, Samuel McDowell.   E. 340-341.

BEATTY, JAMES, Greenwood. 11 Jan 1795. 7 March 1795.
Bros. William and John.
Mother.
Sister Elizabeth Marshall.
Exs.: Bros. Robert and Joseph.
Wit.: David Miller, James Craven, James Sterrett.   E. 342.

MICKEY, ROBERT, Newton. 16 Jan 1792. 8 April 1795.
Son Robert.
Daus. Elizabeth, Mary, Agness, Janet, Eleanor and Hannah.
Heirs of dau. Margaret, dec'd.
Heirs of dau. Frances, dec'd.
Sons James, David and John, minor.
Exs.: Sons James Mickey and David Mickey.

Wit.: David Ralston, Alexr. Laughlin, William Boyd.   E. 342-343.

McCALL, ANN, Shippensburgh. Dec 1794. 18 April 1795.
Son Ezra.
Dau. Mary, wife of David Tate.
Son James Campbell.
Exs.: Son Ezra McCall and Col. William McFarlane.
Wit.: Jas. Crawford, John Scott, Isaac Cook.   E. 344.

DICKEY, JOHN, East Pennsborough. 16 Nov 1784. 30 April 1795.
Sons James, Samuel and John.
Dau. Margaret.
Exs.: John Clendenin and dau. Margaret Dickey.
Wit.: Samuel Clendenin, Elizabeth Clendenin.   E. 345.

TOWNSLEY, WILLIAM, Teboyne. 8 April 1795. 2 June 1795.
Wife (no name).
Daus. Janet Kincaid, Agness Innes, Martha Kincaid, Elizabeth
McCraken, Eleanor McCree, Margart McMillen and Joanna Townsley.
Sons Thomas, John and George Townsley.
Exs.: George McMillen and William Martin.
Wit.: Abraham Thomas, Martin Motzer, William Colwell.   E. 345-346.

HEACK, JOHN, Allen. 13 June 1795. 25 July 1795.
Wife (no name).
Son Jacob.
Daus. Mary Elizabeth and Catherine.
Sons John and William.
Exs.: Frederick Long, Jr., and Jonas Rupe, Jr.
Wit.: Frederick Switzer, Jr., Philip Kock.   E. 347.

McALLISTER, TOBIAS, yeoman, Rye. 15 June 1795. 25 July 1795.
Wife Hester.
Sister Mary McAlliser.
James Donnelly, eldest son of wife Hester.
Son Daniel McAllister, a minor.
Exs.: Samuel Deane and James Diven, both of Tyrone.
Wit.: James Cunningham, John Dea, John Connelly.   E. 348.

GEDDIS, WILLIAM, West Pennsboro. 10 June 1794. 22 Aug 1795.
Dau. Peggy and son-in-law Andrew Carothers.

Only son James.
Indentured girl Cathrine Dixon.
Exs.: Son James Geddis.
Wit.: William Lindsay, James Laird, Robert Lindsey.   E. 349-350.

KOACH (KOCK), PETER, Juniata. 22 Jan 1795. 2 Sept 1795.
Wife Margaret.
Children John, Peter, Christiana and Sally, all minors.
Exs.: Caspar Lopher of Juniata and Daniel Brown of Reading Twp.,
York Co.
Wit.: Roger Brown, Adam Conkel, Peter Yego.
Letters issued to Joseph Bradley.   E. 351.

SMITH, PETER, yeoman, Middleton. 4 Aug 1795. 5 Sept 1795.
Wife Catheren.
Sons Peter and David Smith.
Land joining land of Caspar Diller and Eppesam Blaine.
Daus. Barbara Smith and Ester Smith.
Grandchild Catheren.
Exs.: William Bore and Henry Witmore.
Wit.: Jacob Wynkoop, Jacob Witmer.   E. 352-353.

McCALLESTER (McCALLISTER), JOHN, Rye. 18 Feb 1792. 4 April
1792. Letter 5 Oct 1795.
Kinsman John Cain and his wife.
Donation land in Alleghany Co.
Land in Muskingum.
James Cain, son of John Cain.
Exs.: John Cain and his wife.
Wit.: George Dickson, Joseph Hare.
Letters to Catherine McCallister.   E. 354.

GILLESPIE, JAMES, West Pennsborow. 8 Aug 1795. 4 Nov 1795.
Wife Jain.
Children, names not given, some minors.
Exs.: Wife Jain and friends Robert Gillespie and Saml. Irwin.
Wit.: Nathl. Gillespie, Elizabeth Miller, Samuel Irwin.   E. 355-357.

HATHORN, JAMES, Newton. 10 Sept 1795. 18 Nov 1795.
Wife Martha.
Son-in-law Abraham Boyd.

Grandchildren Hugh Boyd, James Boyd, Robert Boyd, Martha Boyd and Alexander Boyd.
Son-in-law William Adams.
Grandchildren James Adams, Matthew Adams, William Adams and Richard Adams, all minors.
Son Alexander Hathorn.
Son James Hathorn.
Exs.: Robert Quigley and Robert McCune.
Wit.: Robert McCormick, Robert Quigley, Robert McCune. E. 358.

SIMONDS, WILLIAM, Dickinson. 9 Oct 1795. 26 Nov 1795.
Wife Margaret.
Sons Edward, Richard and John.
Daus. Susanna, Jean and Margaret.
Exs.: Wife Margaret and sons Richard and John Simonds.
Wife Margaret Simonds, guardian of dau. Margaret.
Wit.: Jno. Alexander, Robert Semple, James Graham. E. 359.

ESPY, JEAN, Frankford. 12 Sept 1795. 28 Nov 1795.
Sister Ann Mitchell.
Sister Elizabeth Callwell.
Sister Christian.
Sister Ann's dau. Christian Mitchell.
Mother.
Exs.: Sister Christian Espy.
Wit.: Samuel McDowel, John Brown. E. 360.

STEEL (STAHL), ANTHONY, Greenwood. 4 Oct 1795. 8 Dec 1795.
Wife Mary.
Daus. (all married), viz., Ann, Elizabeth and Eve.
Sons Paul, Anthony and Morris.
Exs.: Wife Mary, son Paul Steel and Jacob Buck.
Wit.: John Elliott, Philip Leidig. E. 361-363.

MILLER, ROBERT, tanner, Carlisle. 18 Jan 1791. 28 Dec 1795.
Wife Elizabeth.
Son Robert.
Plantation on the Conodoguinet Creek, adj. lands of heirs of Hugh McCormick, dec'd.
Land in the dry lands or *Propactory Manor*, near Boiling Springs.
House in tenure of William Armor in Carlisle.

Dau. Margaret.
Granddaus., viz., Elizabeth, Jean and Rebecca Wilson, daus. of dau. Margaret Wilson.
Dau. Rebecca, wife of Joseph Thornburgh.
Children of dau. Rebecca, viz., Deborah, Elizabeth, Margaret and Sarah Thornburgh.
Grandchildren, children of son John, dec'd, viz., William, John and Elizabeth Miller, minors.
Heirs of son-in-law James Armstrong Wilson.
Exs.: Son Robert Miller and son-in-law Joseph Thornburgh.
Wit.: Willm. Lyon, George Pattison, John Armor.
Codicil 6 Oct 1794.
Dau. Rebecca, dec'd, her four daus. minors, under eighteen years of age.

F. 1-3.

MILLER, WILLIAM, Tyrone. 28 Jan 1795. 7 Jan 1796.
Wife Sarah.
Wife's son Joseph, a minor.
Dau. Polly, a minor.
William Hays.
William Enslow.
Thomas Copland.
Abraham Enslow.
William Miller and Thomas Miller.
Brother's and sister's children, including William and Abraham Enslow.
Exs.: William McClure and Joseph Mitten.
Wit.: Geo. Robinson, Robert McCally, Margaret McCally.
Codicil 26 Dec 1795.
Wit.: Joseph Mytown, James Tully.

F. 4-5.

BIELMAN (BEILMAN), JOHN, Allen. 18 Jan 1791. 9 Jan 1796.
The children of dau. Christiana Moler.
Exs.: John Brindle and Jacob Wise.
Wit.: Wm. Scott, Jacob Gensiul.

F. 6.

WOODS, ALEXANDER, mason, Carlisle. 25 Dec 1795. 13 Jan 1796.
Wife Jane. Children, names not given.
Sister Ann Woods.
Dec'd father.
Property in the Kingdom of Ireland, viz., the lease of Ardue.
Exs.: Henry Burchsten and James Wood.

Wit.: John Smyth, Thos. Jones. F. 7.

LEIBY, GEORGE, Tyrone. 26 Dec 1795. 21 Jan 1796.
Wife Eve.
Children, minors, names not given.
Exs.: Christopher Bower and George Crowback.
Wit.: Jacob Bergetreser, George Arnolt, John Nelson. F. 8.

HARRIS, JOHN, now in Middleton. 10 Jan 1796. 24 Jan 1796.
Sister Mary Rhea's children.
Bro. Robert dec'd.
Sister Sarah Irwin.
Bro-in-law James Irwin.
Exs.: John Irwin and bro.-in-law James Irwin.
Wit.: David Sample, William Irwin. F. 9.

MORRISON, ANTHONY, Toboyne. 1 June 1795. 20 Nov 1795.
The children of daus. Margaret Black, dec'd, and Eleanor Magee, dec'd,
when of legal age.
Exs.: Daniel McClintock, Wm. McCoard and Geo. Black.
Wit.: John Linn, Robert Hunter. F. 10.

GILMORE, JOHN. 23 Dec 1795. 27 Jan 1796.
Wife Jean.
Sons John and Joseph.
Son-in-law James Vincent.
Sons Hugh, William, Thomas, Robert and James.
Dau. Charity.
Exs.: Wife Jean and James Diven.
Wit.: Edward West, Samuel Killey. F. 11.

PORTER, MARY, widow of Moses Porter, Rye. 2 Nov 1795. 30 Jan
1796.
Jean Watts, alias Morrow.
Thomas Wilson.
Exs.: Jean Morrow.
Wit.: John Elliott, Frederick Watts. F. 12.

SHANNON, ROBERT, Newton. 21 Nov 1795. 19 Feb 1796.
Wife Jean.
Son Robert and his son Robert.

62

Bound boy Samuel Baker.
Son Samuel and his son Robert.
Son Joseph and his son Robert.
Son John.
Son-in-law Samuel Finton.
Son-in law Hugh McElhenny and his son Robert.
Son-in-law John Patton.
Son-in-law Elisha Carson, his step sons William, Robert and Joseph, and
his step dau Mary; his son Ezekiel and his dau Margaret.
Son-in-law Andrew McElwain and his son Robert and dau Jeny
McElwain.
Son-in-law William Porterfield.
Exs.: Sons John Shannon and Joseph Shannon.
Wit.: James Nicholson, James Stevenson.   F. 13-14.

GALBRAITH, SAMUEL, Rye. 8 June 1789. 26 Feb 1796.
Dau. Mary Elliott.
Son James.
Sons Samuel and William.
Island in the River Juniata.
Exs.: Son William Galbraith.
Wit.: Fredk. Watts, John Thompson.   F. 15.

WILSON (WILLSON), MATTHEW, farmer, Middleton. 28 Dec 1795. 18
March 1796.
Jean Wilson, son Archibald's widow.
Two children of Archibald Wilson, dec'd, viz., Mary Wilson and James
Wilson.
Joseph Wilson.
Son-in-law Thomas Cincaid.
Sons James and Joseph Wilson.
Jean Fisher.
Mary Wilson.
Exs.: Robert Smith and Hugh Smith.
Wit.: James Dickey, Henry Hock.   F. 16.

COFFEY, THOMAS, Hopewell. 29 June 1787. 22 March 1796.
Wife Mary.
Sons William, Thomas, Robert, James and George.
Daus. Jean and Martha Coffey.
Son John.

Exs.: Wife Mary Coffey and James Leeper.
Wit.: Josias Brown, James Leeper, John McKnight.   F. 17.

REED, WILLIAM, Middleton. 30 Oct 1795. 26 March 1796.
Dau. Sarah Doran.
William Reed and John Reed, minors, sons of John Reed.
Anne Neil, my housekeeper.
Exs.: Hugh Boden and George Logue, Esq., both of Carlisle.
Wit.: John Sanderson, Martin Bower, Geo. Logue.   F. 18-19.

WHITEHILL, JEAN, East Pennsborough. 25 Sept 1793. 7 April 1796.
To husband Robert Whitehill.
Jean Luckey, eldest dau of sister Mary Luckey.
Exs.: Husband Robert Whitehill.
Wit.: Agness McClintock, James Whitehill.   F. 20.

McCLEAN, CORNELIUS, Hopewell. 23 Nov 1789. 6 April 1796.
Wife Jean.
Dau. Jean McLean.
Son Andrew.
Son Daniel.
Dau. Mary Gordon.
Son Allen McLean.
Exs.: Wife Jean McLean and son John McLean.
Wit.: Jas. Dunlap, David Mahon, George McCleary.   F. 20-21.

SCROGGS, ALEXANDER, Newton. 1 Feb 1794. 15 April 1796.
Wife Rachel.
Land adj. Alexander Sharp's.
Son Aron Scroggs, twenty-one years of age on the 18th day of Oct 1799.
Sons Allen, John and Moses Scroggs.
Daus. Rachel Scroggs and Sarah Scroggs.
Son Elijah Scroggs.
Daus. Mary and Elizabeth Scroggs.
Dau. Miriam, wife of William Work.
First wife's children, viz., James, Alexander and Ebenezer Scroggs, and
Jennet, wife of Joseph McElwain, and Ann, wife of Hugh McElroy.
Wife Rachel Scroggs, Allen Scroggs and John Scouller.
Wit.: Alexr. Thompson, Wm. Thompson, Hugh Thompson.   F. 22.

LEE, RICHARD, waggon maker, Carlisle. 9 April 1796. 3 May 1796.

64

Wife Margaret.
Children of bro. Edward.
Exs.: John Officer and Jeremiah Miller.
Wit.: Richard Hemming, John Orwan. F. 23.

TRESTER, PETER, Toboyne. 24 April 1796. 20 May 1796.
Bro.-in-law Nicholas Shock.
Land bought from Thomas Scaden.
Mother.
Bro.-in-law Michael Snider and his son Frederick, a minor.
Sister Mary.
Exs.: Jacob Knobler, also guardian of Frederick Snider.
Wit.: Michael Brown, William Beyer. F. 24.

SMITH, PHILIP, Millerstown, Greenwood Twp. 9 May 1796. 25 May
1796.
Sister Eve Smith.
Bro. James Smith.
Other bros. and sisters.
Apprentice lad Henry Long.
Exs.: Robert Beatty.
Wit.: Ephraim Williams, John Jordan, Joseph Beatty. F. 25.

SMITH, MICHAEL, Greenwood. 24 Dec 1794. 13 June 1796.
Wife Sarah.
Oldest son Michael.
Son Philip.
Dau. Catran Rollen.
Dau. Fanny Resh.
Dau. Susanna Keepler.
Dau. Eve Smith.
Youngest son James.
Daus. Elizabeth, Matalena, Sarah and Mary, minors.
Exs.: Sarah Smith and Robert McCurdy.
Wit.: Robert McCurdy, William Everly. F. 26-27.

SIMISON, JOHN, Tyrone. 18 March 1796. 2 Aug 1796.
Wife Kathrain.
Sons John and Samuel.
Other sons Andrew and Robert.
Oldest dau. Kathrain Simison.

Dau. Rebecca Simison.
Granddau. Margaret Enslow, minor, and her sister Kathrain Enslow.
Son-in-law Wm. Enslow.
Exs.: John Anderson and William Enslow.
Wit.: Robert Hollyday, William Fitzpatrick.   F. 28-29.

WYLIE, JOHN, Eastpennsborough. 9 Jan 1790. 17 Aug 1796.
Wife Sarah.
William Wylie and Robert Wylie.
Son John.
Daus. Margret, Sarah, Ann and Jean.
Exs.: William Wylie and Robert Wylie.
Wit.: None.   F. 30.

HENDERSON, MATTHEW, Esq., Shippensburgh. 10 Aug 1795. 12
Sept 1796.
Wife Margaret.
Eldest son Daniel.
Land in Potter Twp. occupied by Lot Stratton.
Sons Jonathan, John and Matthew.
Daus. Lydia and Jane, minors.
Four younger children, viz., Robert Cooper, Joseph, Elizabeth and
Isabella, minors.
Exs.: Wife Margaret and sons Daniel and Jonathan.
Wit.: Robert Cooper, Jane Woods, Jno. Simpson.   F. 31-36.

HAMILTON, GEORGE, Teboyne. 6 April 1796. 20 Sept 1796.
Son James.
Son Hugh.
Dau. Martha.
Son George.
Dau. Elizabeth's three children.
Son William.
Exs.: Son William Hamilton.
Wit.: George McMillen, William Martin.   F. 37-38.

WILSON, HUGH, farmer, East Pennsborough. 12 April 1796. 3 Oct
1796.
Wife Isabella.
George Washington Fulton, son of Henry Fulton of Harrisburg, Dauphin
Co., and his sister Jenny Fulton.

Dau. Isabella, intermarried with sd. Henry Fulton.
Hartty Wormley.
Exs.: Wife Isabella Wilson.
Wit.: Samuel Wallace, Jacob Wormley, Alexr. Berryhill.   F. 38-39.

GATZ, MARY, Greenwood. 23 July 1796. 6 Oct 1796.
Dau. Susannah.
Other children, names not given.
Exs.: Son-in-law Adam Rupert.
Wit.: Saml. Utter, William North.   F. 39.

CESSNA, JOHN, Shippensburg. 24 Oct 1793. 13 Oct 1796.
Eldest son John.
Sons Charles, Joseph, Jonathan, dec'd, Evan and William Cessna.
Eldest dau. Mary Neale, dec'd.
Other daus. Elizabeth Jones and Margaret Hall, dec'd.
Youngest son Theophilus Cessna.
Son James.
Land in Southampton Twp. conveyed from William Campble.
Land on Juniata River, above Jack's Narrows.
Island in Juniata River.
Land where Prigmore's Mill now is.
Land from Mr. Blunston in York Co.
Land taken up with Messrs. Fulton and Wallace.
Granddau. Elizabeth, minor, dau. of William Cessna.
Land adj. place formerly Robert Gabey's and Samuel Culbertson's.
Exs.: Son James Cessna.
Wit.: Mattw. Scott, John Hearny, John Scott.   F. 40-42.

GOWDY, SAMUEL, Tyrone. 22 Feb 1791. 24 Oct 1796.
Wife Sarah.
Elizabeth Baskins, widow.
Son Samuel.
Oldest son James.
Estate of James Baskins, dec'd.
Sarah Meharg, when of age.
Exs.: Wife Sarah Gowdy, Edward West and son Samuel.
Wit.: John Davidson, Susannah Davidson.   F. 43.

DILLER, CASPER, Middleton. 11 Sept 1796. 24 Nov 1796.
Wife Margaret.

Son Casper.

Son Martin.

Five sons John, David, Benjamin, George and Solomon, minors.

Dau. Elizabeth, wife of Abraham Pollinger.

Dau. Catherina, wife of George Carle.

Dau. Molly, wife of George Fossler.

Dau. Juliana, wife of Abraham Richter.

Dau. Christina Diller, a minor.

Jacob Craven and Abraham Pollinger, guardians of sons David, Benjamin, George and Solomon and dau. Christiana.

Exs.: John Craven and Philip Baker.

Wit.: James Duncan, Petr Fass, Daniel Harkins.   F. 44-51.

MORRISON, JEANET, widow of William Morrison, Peters. 19 Oct 1775. 12 Dec 1796.

John and William Morrison of the Burrough of Belfast.

Sister Margaret Watt of Dinegore Parish.

Nephew John Morrison of Maharahochel Parish.

Nephew William Richie of Chester Co.

Dau. of Robert Morrison, dec'd (the girl's name not known to me, nor yet the place of her residence).

The Revd. John Culbertson.

Rev. Mr. Dawbing.

To Jean Speedy.

Jno. Clark.

Tabitha Cunningham.

Jno. and William Marshall, Jr., of Peters Twp.

William Anderson.

William Coburn.

Peter January of Westmoreland Co.

Nephews William Marshall, John Marshall and James Marshall, all of Donegore Parish, Ireland.

Nephew Thomas Corman of Donegore Parish.

Jas. Lawson and his wife and dau. Jeanet.

Thomas Lawson and his children.

Bros. John and Robert Morrison.

Exs.: Jas. Lawson, David Humphrey and Oliver Anderson.

Wit.: James McCamis, John Mortimer.

Appeal against probate of will, 19 April 1786.   F. 51-55.

PATTON, WILLIAM, Westpennsborough. 9 Jan 1796. 19 Dec 1796.

68

Wife Jannet.
Dau. Margaret Patten.
Dau. Mary McKeman.
Dau. Rebecca's children.
Grandson Robert Patton.
Son Thomas and his son William Patten.
Son John.
Son-in-law William Adams.
Dau. Margaret's children.
Dau. Mary's children.
Daus. of son John Patton.
Dau. Mary's daus. Bety and Jeannet.
Exs.: John Patton and Robert Lusk.
Wit.: Danl. McGuire, Martha Lusk, Jared Graham.   F. 56.

HOUTZ, PHILIP LAWRENCE, Newton. 6 Dec 1796. 4 Jan 1797.
Wife Ann Katrin.
Dau. Elizabeth Hefflefinger and her children.
Dau. Barbara Smith.
Dau. Eve Ochinbaugh.
All children, viz., Jacob, Barbara, Elizabeth, Henry, Eve Kertren, Ann,
John, Christina, Billy, Philip, Samuel and Polly, some of them minors.
Exs.: George Gilbert and Vendal Weaver.
Wit.: William Montgomery, Philip Pfiester.   F. 57-58.

SMITH, ABRAHAM, Hopewell. 4 March 1796. 5 Jan 1797.
Wife Ann.
Sons Isaac, James and Jacob Smith.
Daus. Ann Smith and Susannah Smith.
Two youngest sons, Samuel and Willson Smith.
Dau. Jenny intermarried with David McKinney.
Two oldest sons John and Abraham Smith.
Exs.: Sons Jacob Smith and James Smith.
Wit.: Joseph McKinney, John McKee, John Woods.   F. 59-61.

McCALL, ROBERT, physician, Shippensburg. 5 June 1796. 10 Jan 1797.
Wife Sarah.
Aged mother Sarah McCall.
Son Robert, a minor.
Three daus. Elizabeth, Sarah and Peggy.
Lot No. 69 purchased from Simon Rice.

Lot adj. William Barr and others.
Exs.: Wife and Captain Alexander Sharp and David McKnight,
merchant.
Wit.: James Lowrey, Alex. Ritchard.   F. 62-63.

RAMSEY, JAMES, Carlisle. 5 April 1796. 27 Feb 1797.
Wife Margaret.
Son David, minor.
Dau. Rebecka Ramsey.
Samuel Greer, late of Carlisle.
Granddau. Violetta Jackson, dau. of Samuel Jackson.
Plantation in Shearman's Valley.
All my children.
Exs.: Wife Margaret, my (son?) James Ramsey and son-in-law Samuel
Jackson.
Wit.: Joseph Young, W. Alexander, John McCoy.
Codicil 18 Jan 1797.
Grandchildren Ezra Jackson Ramsey, James R. Dixon and Violetta
Jackson.   F. 64-65.

BROOKS, WILLIAM, yeoman, Allen. 23 Aug. 1794. 6 April 1797.
Wife Susanna.
Sons James, William, Jr., and Matthew Brooks.
Jean Brooks, a minor, Martha Brooks, Elizabeth Brooks and Susanna
Brooks, a minor, Joseph Brooks and Hays Brooks.
Exs.: Sons Samuel Brooks and James Brooks.
Wit.: William Kelso, James Sayers, John Shields.   F. 66-68.

McCOY, WILLIAM, Rye. 4 June 1796. 6 May 1797.
Wife Rachel.
Sons Thomas and Matthew.
Other children, minors, names not given.
Exs.: Wife Rachel and son John McCoy.
Wit.: John Elliott, Francis Murry.   F. 69.

KENNEDAY, ARCHIBALD, Middleton. 5 June 1788. 11 May 1797.
Wife Kethrine.
Son John.
Heirs of son Thomas, viz., James, John, William and Jean.
Two children of dau. Jean, James and Jean Waugh.
Sons Archibald and David.

70

Dau. Mary Stewart.
Dau. Kathrine.
Son Joseph.
Exs.: William Clark and John Jordan.
Wit.: George Crean, William Drennon. F. 70.

SANDERSON, GEORGE, Middleton. 11 Nov 1775 (1795?). 22 May 1797.
Wife Jane.
Eldest son Robert.
Second son John.
Dau. Catherine, wife of Hugh McCormick.
Dau. Margaret, wife of James Elliott.
Dau. Martha,wife of Robert McCormick.
Dau. Mary, wife of David Elliott.
Exs.: Sons Robert Sanderson and John Sanderson.
Wit.: John Creigh, John Anderson, James Pollock, Alexander Sanderson. F. 71-72.

HOOVER, GEORGE, Carlisle. 27 Dec 1792. 22 May 1797.
Wife Anna Maria.
Bro. Conrad Hoover.
Sister Barbara Hoopack.
Jacob Hoover son of Martin Hoover.
Exs.: Jacob Crever and John Crever.
Wit.: Adam Logue, Alexr. Brown, Geo. Logue. F. 73.

BROWN, ANDREW, Allen. 6 Aug 1796. 31 May 1797.
Wife Martha.
Two sons James and Ephraim.
Two daus. Martha Brown and Mary Brown.
Exs.: Wife Martha Brown and son James Brown.
Wit.: James Graham, William Harkness. F. 74.

BORLAND, THOMAS, Carlisle. 9 Feb 1797. 14 June 1797.
Wife Mary.
Three children in the Kingdom of Ireland, viz., Mary Borland, Samuel and Thomas Borland.
Son Joseph Borland.
Land in Nittany Valley, in partnership with bros.
Exs.: Bro. Samuel Borland and John Pollock of Carlisle.

Wit.: John Pollock, John Jordan.   F. 75.

ARMSTRONG, JOHN, Carlisle. -- Feb 1795. 25 July 1797.
Wife Rebeccah.
Sons James and John.
Rebeccah Turner of Chester Co.
Bro. Andrew of the Kingdom of Ireland.
Plantation in Middleton Twp.
Exs.: Wife Rebeccah and sons James and John Armstrong.
Wit.: George Patterson, David Lindsay, Willm. Lyon.   F. 76-77.

HUNTER, WILLIAM, Sr., Newton. 28 Dec 1796. 29 Aug 1797.
Wife Jean.
Sons Joseph and William.
Daus. Jean and Sarah.
Step dau. Mary Walker.
Step sons James Graham and John Graham.
Dau. Jean's children.
Land in the State of Georgia.
Exs.: Wife and son Joseph Hunter.
Wit.: Leonard Shannon, James Walker.   F. 78.

ERVIN (ERVINE), ANDREW, East Pennsborough. 23 July 1796. 4 Sept
1797.
Wife Agness.
Son Andrew.
Two daus., viz., Ann Quigley and Elizabeth Williamson.
Sons William and John.
Youngest son Armstrong Ervin.
Exs.: Two eldest sons James and William Ervin.
Wit.: John Douglass, John Walker.   F. 79-80.

CLENDENIN, JOHN, Eastpennsboro. 29 Aug 1783. 25 April 1796.
Wife Janet.
Two sons John and Samuel.
Sons-in-law, names not given.
Son James.
Land to John Dickey's.
Exs.: Sons John Clendenin and Samuel Clendenin.
Wit.: Walter Buchanan, David Boyd, Henry Leef.   F. 81-82.

GLENN, MOSES, Southampton. 10 Oct 1797. 28 Nov 1797.
Wife Lettice.
Dau. Elizabeth Glenn.
Sons Matthew and Robert,
Dau. Peggy Glenn.
Sons Thomas and Alexander.
Dau. Lettice Glenn.
John Quigley's land.
Exs.: Robert McCune and Alexander Glenn.
Wit.: Alexander Glenn, Robert Quigley, Thomas Glenn.   F. 85.

NETTLES, ROBERT, Tyrone. 25 Jan 1797. 8 April 1797.
Wife Rebeccah.
Children, names not given.
Exs.: Wife Rebeccah Nettles and Samuel Galbraith.
Wit.: John Walach, Isaac Williams, James Scandrett.   F. 86.

ROBISON, ELLIOTT, Tyrone. 14 Oct 1797. 25 Nov 1797.
To mother.
Nephews Thomas Robison's son George and Robert Robison's son
George.
To bros. and sisters.
Exs.: Bros. Robert and Thomas Robison.
Wit.: Robt. Laughlin, Alexander Kerr.   F. 87.

FIELURE, NICHOLAS, Mifflin. 13 Oct 1797. 25 Oct 1797.
Wife Barbara.
Sons Christopher and Leonard, minors.
Eldest dau. Catherine.
Sons Adam, Andrew and Jacob, a minor.
Dau. Eve, a minor.
Exs.: Son Andrew Fielure and Jacob Mussleman.
Wit.: Thomas McCormick, John Purdy, John Bolton.   F. 88-89.

EARLS, JENNET, Greenwood. 31 July 1797. 1 Nov 1797.
Son John Philips (if to be found).
Jean Mitchell, Jr.
Nancy Mitchell.
Exs.: James Mitchell.
Wit.: Malcolm Wright, Thos. Wilson, Thos. Hulings.   F. 90.

SWARTZ, ELIZABETH, East Pennsbro. 20 Oct 1797. 20 Dec 1797.
Son John Swartz's wife, viz., Elizabeth, my good dau.-in-law.
Sons George, Leonard and Christy Swartz.
Son Caspar Swartz, dec'd.
Dau. Margaret Kuntz and her children.
Other dau., name not given.
Exs.: Sons John Swartz and Christy Swartz.
Wit.: James McGuire, Frederick Kistler, Henry Smith.   F. 91.

REED, JAMES, East Pennsborough. 18 Dec 1796. 16 Dec 1797.
Wife (no name).
Grandson James Reed, a minor.
Son John.
Dau. Rosana.
Grandsons William and John Reed.
Exs.: Jacob Bortneer and Andrew Ferguson.
Wit.: Jacob Bortneer, Andrew Ferguson.   F. 92.

THOMPSON, WILLIAM, Newton. 1 Sept 1784. 31 Oct 1797.
Wife Eleanor.
Daus. Mary, Margaret and Margery.
Son Matthew.
Exs.: Son Matthew Thompson and son-in-law John Moore.
Wit.: Alexr. Laughlin, Alexr. Thompson.   F. 93.

SHEEPSHANKS, RICHARD, Rye. 9 Sept 1797. 2 Nov 1797.
Wife Agness (Ann or Nancy) Sheepshanks, now residing in Warrington
Twp., York Co.
Son William Sheepshanks, now in Leeds, England.
House and lot at corner of Hanover Street, formerly in twp. of
Kensington, but now, I believe, in the city of Philadelphia, owned with
son William's uncles, Captain Samuel Williams and Joseph Spencer.
Elizabeth Lawshe, dau. of John Lawshe.
William Lawshe, Lewis Lawshe and Isaac Lawshe, sons of sd. John
Lawshe.
John Mills.
Lands in Monaghan and Warrington Twps., York Co.
Lines of land of Capt. Thos. Campbell, Gen. Miller, Charles Brewster and
John McClelland.
Land lately in possession of Robert Ryan.
Tract in possession of Richard Wickersham.

Land lately claimed by Isaac Sadler.

Tract lately claimed by George Ross.

Warrants of these lands in name of Nancy Morris.

Witnesses to Deed, Benjamin Carpenter and Elisha Underwood, Esq.

Survey up Beaver Creek made by Capt. Robert Gray (called *Gray's Folly*).

Jane Morris.

Edward O'Hail, Deputy Surveyor in Monaghan.

Land from James Benezet, Esq.

Robert Stevenson, surveyor.

Land in town at St. Ann's Point, conveyed by Bazel Raurison, Esq., a British officer.

Witness to Deed, James Armstrong of Philadelphia.

Personal property &c. in care of Mrs. Jane Graybill in York Town, Alexander Power, Peter Bower in Huntingdon, Joseph Edmondson in Newburg, John Gordon in Hopewell, and Ben Carpenter.

To Elinor Lawshe, wife of John Lawshe.

Exs.: John Lawshe.

Wit.: Michael Marshall, Francis McCown, George Barnet.   F. 94-95.

ARMSTRONG, JAMES, Frankford. 9 Nov 1797. 22 Jan 1798.

Wife Sarah.

John Officer's three children by dau. Agness, when of age.

Dau. Jenny Bratton, wife of Samuel Bratton.

Daus. Susannah wife to James Kenneday, Sarah wife to Robert Patterson, Mary wife of Alexander Johnston and Rebecca, single.

Grandchild Rebecca Bratton.

Exs.: John Brown and Adam Bratton.

Wit.: Horas Bratton, Thomas Kenneday.   F. 96-97.

FISHER, JAMES, East Pennsborough. 18 June 1796. 23 Feb 1798.

Wife Mary. Wife's dau. Sarah Brines.

Son Thomas.

Thomas Fisher, millwright, son to bro. Samuel Fisher.

James Fisher, son to bro. Thomas.

Exs.: Neighbors Abraham Longnecker and Wm. Quigley.

Wit.: William Denning, Peter Wagoner, Joseph Longnecker, Jacob Dill.

       F. 98.

HOGG, SARAH, wife of Samuel Hogg, Rye. ----. 28 Feb 1798.

Husband Samuel Hogg.

Niece Jane Smith, widow, Carlisle.
Exs.: Charles Cooper and William Lewes.
Wit.: William Lewes, Charles Cooper. F. 99.

WISE, JACOB, Middleton. 5 May 1795. 28 April 1798.
Seven children, viz., Martin, Henry, Jacob, John, Sophia Margaret wife
of Mark Brindle, Anna Maria wife of John Wormley, and George Wise.
Grandsons John and Frederick, sons of son Jacob Wise.
Conrad Derr of Dauphin Co.
Plantation in Berwick Twp., York Co.
Exs.: Son Jacob Wise and nephew Jacob Wise, of Allen.
Wit.: Michael Ridner, Wm. Scott, Jean Carothers. F. 100-101.

BAKER, PHILIP, Middleton. 18 April 1798. 28 April 1798.
Wife Catherine. Three children, viz., Michael, Jacob and William, minors.
Aged father.
Exs.: Bro. John Baker and Peter Fishburn.
Wit.: William Levis, Saml. Postlethwait, Saml. McCoskry, John Dunbar.
F. 102.

KARTT, JACOB, Carlisle. ---- 1798. 30 April 1798.
Wife Christiana.
Children, viz., Mary wife of Frederick Rhinehart, Jacob, George,
Elizabeth wife of Andrew Byerly and Margaret.
Exs.: Son Jacob Cart and Jacob Creaver, Esq.
Wit.: Robert Barkely, John Rhine, John Jordan. F. 103-104.

WIER, GEORGE, farmer, Newton. 25 Jan 1798. 30 April 1798.
Wife Margaret Wier, late Martin.
Mother Jane Wier.
Land conveyed by father Samuel Wier, bounded by lands of Jesse
Kilgore and John Eakman, to Mary McCune's line.
Nephew George Clark, son of sister Jane, wife of Robert Clark, and his
bros. and sisters, viz., Jane Clark now wife of Jesse Kilgore, Agness
Clark, Samuel Clark, Mary Clark, Robert, John and David Clark.
Sister Mary Mitchell, now wife of Alexander Mitchell.
Sister Mary's son James Mitchell, and Samuel Mitchell and Mary
Mitchell.
Sister Mary's son George Mitchell, a minor.
Peggy Woodburn and George Woodburn, minors, children of James and
Agness Woodburn, now of Newville.

76

Exs.: Wife Margaret Wier, John McCune of Middle Spring and James Woodburn.
Wit.: Samuel McCune, Hugh McCune, John McCune.   F. 105-106.

GIBSON, ROBERT, Middleton. 26 May 1797. 4 May 1798.
Granddau. Mary Fitzgerald Gibson, minor dau. of son William Gibson, dec'd.
Margaret Gibson, otherwise Thompson, by intermarriage, dau. of son James Gibson, dec'd.
John Gibson, a natural son of son John Gibson, dec'd, a minor.
William Gibson, minor son of nephew George Gibson, dec'd.
Dr. Saml. McCoskry.
Exs.: Ross Mitchell, Robert Miller and Wm. Alexander.
Wit.: Abm. Loughridge, William Brown, Robert Miller.   F. 107.

CULBERSON, WILLIAM, Eastpennsborough. 6 March 1798. 18 May 1798.
Wife Nancy.
Five children John, Sarah, Margaret, Samuel and William, all minors.
Exs.: Thomas Urie and Andrew Parker.
Wit.: Archibald Hamilton, Samuel Culbertson, James Fleming.   F. 108.

WHITE, THOMAS, Rye. 10 June 1782. 22 May 1798.
Wife Mary.
Son John.
Line at Mr. Steretts to Juniata.
Minor sons Thomas and James.
Son William.
Land on Big Run adj. Thos. Shortis.
Daus. Sarah and Nancy.
Dau. Elizabeth in Ireland.
Exs.: Archibald Stuart and Hugh Wallace.
Wit.: Hugh Wallace, Archibald Stuart.   F. 109.

MEHAFFEY, SAMUEL, East Pennsborough. 30 Oct 1795. 17 April 1826.
Letters to Robert Mehaffey in 1826.
Bros. Joseph and Thomas Mehaffey.
Samuel Mehaffey, son of John Mehaffey, of Ireland, County Donegall, Parish of Liffer and town of Drummore.

Two eldest sons, minors, of Moses Mehaffey, son of John Mehaffey, of Ireland, County Donegall.
Exs.: James McCormick and Samuel Wallace.
Wit.: Robert Whitehill, Jr., John Wallace.   F. 110.

SCOTT, MATTHEW, Shippensburgh. 16 May 1798. 15 June 1798.
Wife Elizabeth.
Eldest son John.
Son William.
Daus. Margaret Cook, Mary Kirk and Elizabeth.
Son Joseph.
Son Matthew Thompson.
Exs.: Wife Elizabeth Scott.
Wit.: William Hamil, Robt. Scott, John Scott.   F. 111.

COOVER, ELIZABETH. Nuncupative will. 13 June 1798. 18 June 1798.
Husband Henry Coover.
One child, name not given.
Wit.: Henry Branizer, Michael Philip, John Smith.
Admin.: Henry Coover.   F. 112.

WILLIAMSON, SAMUEL, East Pennsborough. 29 Jan 1789. 29 June 1798.
Wife Susannah.
Sons Thomas and John.
Grandchildren the minor children of son Samuel Williamson, dec'd.
Widow of son Samuel, dec'd.
Son George Williamson.
Land purchased of Mr. Andrew Holmes.
Son Moses Williamson.
Sons-in-law John Brownlee and Samuel Long.
Exs.: Sons Thomas Williamson and John Williamson.
Wit.: Saml. Martin, Wm. Clark.   F. 113-114.

AGNEW, JAMES, Newton. 1 April 1797. 3 Aug 1798.
Brothers and sisters, viz., John, Elizabeth, Matthew, Isaac, Nancy and Samuel N. Agnew.
Friend Samuel Hanna and his children that lives with him.
Exs.: None named.
Wit.: James Lang, Willm. Montgomery.
Admin.: James Agnew.   F. 115.

McKNIGHT, JOHN, Southampton. 5 May 1798. 15 Aug 1798.
Wife Elizabeth.
Sons-in-law John McCarrell and David Williamson.
Three young daus. Elizabeth, Rebecah and Peggy McKnight.
Eldest son William.
Second son Samuel Stuart.
Third son John McKnight.
Exs.: Wife Elizabeth McKnight and son Wm. McKnight.
Wit.: Alexander Pebles, Robert Pebles. F. 116.

MILLER, CHRISTIAN, Southampton. 5 Aug 1798. 15 Aug 1798.
Wife Fronica.
Daus. Betsy and Catherine.
Little children, names not given.
Exs.: Wife Fronica and Frederick Clippenger.
Wit.: Peter Mullershock, Frederick Clippenger. F. 117.

WILSON, WILLIAM, Tyrone. 6 Sept 1798. 20 Oct 1798.
Seven children, viz., James, William, John, Matthew, George, Levy and
Elizabeth.
Son Levy's dau. Elizabeth.
Exs.: Sons James Wilson and Levy Wilson.
Wit.: James Scandrett, John Nelson, Margaret Junkin. F. 118.

WALLACE, SAMUEL, Allen. 4 Nov 1796. 23 Nov 1798.
Eldest son John.
Sons Joseph and Samuel.
Daus. Mary, Martha and Elizabeth.
Dau. Sarah Brooks.
Granddau. Margaret Brooks.
Son William.
Exs.: Sons Joseph Wallace and Samuel Wallace.
Wit.: Jno. Burnet, Richard Millard.
Codicil 14 Nov 1796.
Bequests to children by Elizabeth Patton, dec'd.
Wit.: Robt. Whitehill, Moses Wallace. F. 119.

MAVINS, GEORGE. Nuncupative will. 4 Oct 1798. 24 Nov 1798.
Mary Cox and John Cox, dau. and son of Samuel Cox.
Martha Cochran, dau. of Patrick Cochran.
Wit.: Robert Culbertson, Jacob Kern.

Admin.: Samuel Cox.   F. 120.

THOMPSON, MARGARET, Carlisle. Nuncupative will. 28 Dec 1798. 2
Jan 1799.
Mother Jean Gibson and her child (mother's child).
Wit.: Dr. Lemuel Gustine, Margaret Stewart.   F. 121.

WILSON, WILLIAM, West Pennsbro. 17 Feb 1795. 9 Jan 1799.
Wife Mary.
Sons John, William, James and Samuel.
Three daus. Margaret, Sarah and Mary.
Two grandsons William and Samuel, sons of son James Wilson.
Exs.: Son-in-law Benjamin McKeehan.
Wit.: James Laird, Thomas Espy.   F. 122-123.

GROVE, JACOB, Sr., Teboine. 18 July 1796. 11 Jan 1799.
Sons Abraham, Jacob, Jr. and David Grove.
Daus. Mary Gallespie, Hannah Bumberger and Elizabeth Shank.
Ex.: Son David Grove.
Wit.: Abr. Thomas, Geo. McMillen, Willm. Hamilton.   F. 124.

ALLEN, HUGH, Mufflin. 7 Jan 1799. 21 Jan 1799.
Wife Jenny.
Son John Allen.
Dau. Elizabeth and her husband Robert Barr.
Dau. Jenny Cowan.
All six children, viz., John, Rachel, Mary, Jean, Elizabeth and Jenny.
Exs.: Samuel Bryson and son-in-law Robert Bare.
Wit.: Samuel Bryson, Alexander Laughlin, Esq.
Not signed, Testator died 8 Jan 1799.   F. 125-127.

WOODS, WILLIAM, Dickinson. 17 Nov 1798. 21 Jan 1799.
Son Samuel.
Son Thomas Woods, dec'd, his two sons William and Samuel, and his
widow and her other children.
Son Samuel's three sons, viz., William, James and Samuel.
Nathan Woods, Jr., a minor, son to William Woods.
Indentured boy Philip Warner.
Land on Black Lick Creek, Somerset Co.
Son Richard.
Land bought from Alexander McKeehan.

Daus. Jenny Woods and Mary Woods.
Exs.: Son Samuel Woods and John Woodburn.
Wit.: Patrick Hamilton, William Calder, William Ellison.　　F. 128.

SANDS, JOHN, Allen. 1 July 1798. 28 Nov 1798.
Wife (no name).
Two sons John and George.
Exs.: Said two sons, John Sands and George Sands.
Wit.: Wm. McMeen, Job Moore, John Philips.　　F. 129-130.

CASHT, GEORGE, Middleton. 8 March 1794. 3 Dec 1798.
Wife Mary Ann.
Sons Jacob, Philip, Michael and Leonard.
Exs.: Wife Mary Ann and son Jacob Casht.
Wit.: Jacob Thumma, Nicholas Fordig.　　F. 131.

WORK, JENET, Allen. 15 May 1793. 14 Dec 1798.
Son William.
Son-in-law Thomas Donaldson.
Son John.
Dau.-in-law Martha Work.
Son-in-law James Cunningham and his wife Jane.
Granddau. Sarah Cunningham.
Exs.: Son John Work and son-in-law James Cunningham.
Wit.: C. Quigley, Mary Quigley.　　F. 132.

WUNDERLICK, DANIEL, Middleton. 19 Jan 1799. 16 Feb 1799.
Wife Barbara.
Three oldest sons Daniel, John and David.
Dau. Elizabeth.
Three youngest sons Jacob, Simon and Gotleb Wunderlick.
Exs.: Wife Barbara Wunderlick and son David.
Wit.: Michael Kasht (Casht), John Schlouner (Schlonner).　　F. 133.

WORK, JOHN, Allen. 1 Dec 1798. 4 Feb 1799.
Wife Martha.
Bro. William Work.
Sister Martha Donaldson and her husband Thomas Donaldson.
John Cunningham's dau. Sarah Cunningham.
Sister and bro.-in-law Jane Cunningham and James Cunningham.
John Patterson.

Exs.: Wife Martha Work and John Patterson.
Wit.: James Graham, William Harkness, C. Quigley.   F. 134.

GALBREATH, ELIZABETH, East Pennsborough. 4 Oct 1798. 12 Feb 1799.
Dau. Dorcas Buchanan.
Grandson John Galbreath, son of late son Thomas Galbreath, dec'd.
Dau. Elizabeth Torrance.
Exs.: Moses Gilmore and Robt. Whitehill.
Exs.: Nancy Pollock, Andw. Galbreath, Mary Galbreath.   F. 135-136.

CAROTHERS, ISABELLA. Nuncupative will. Proved 16 Feb 1799.
Bro. James and one of sisters, name not given.
Wit.: John Carothers, Samuel Turner.
Admin.: James Carothers.   F. 137.

McNAIR, MARY, Widow of Alexr. McNair, Toboyne. 13 Nov 1798. 25 Feb 1799.
Sons John and David.
Daus. Margaret, Elizabeth and Esther.
Exs.: Son John Garvin, Allen Nesbit and Robt. Laughlin.
Wit.: Robert Brown, William Anderson.   F. 137.

HENDERSON, SAMUEL, Toboyne. 21 Nov 1798. 5 March 1799.
Wife Mary.
Sons James and Richard.
Dau. Betsy, when married.
Son James' son Samuel.
Son Richard's son Samuel.
Grandsons Samuel Sanderson and Samuel Woodney, minors.
Daus. Ann Patterson, Letice Sanderson, Polly Woodney.
John Patterson.
Bound boy, William Morrison.
Exs.: Wife Mary and son-in-law John Patterson.
Wit.: John Hunter, John Morison.   F. 138-139.

LOPEMAN, THOMAS, West Pennsboro. 22 May 1798. 19 March 1799.
Wife Catherine.
Son William Lopeman.
Land purchased from Peter Good.
Exs.: None named.

Wit.: Henry Rine, Peter Good.
Admin.: Catherine Lopeman.   F. 140.

SMITH, PETER. Nuncupative will. 11 April 1799. 15 April 1799.
Henry Hartman, sole legatee.
Wit.: Ludwick Waltermiers, Jacob Zigler.   F. 141.

BULL, RICHARD, yeoman. 29 Feb 1792. 19 April 1799.
Sons Henry, William, Thomas, John and Richard.
Dau. Joccaminka Richards' son.
Grandson David Maredy (McCready?).
Exs.: Sons Henry Bull and Wm. Bull.
Wit.: Thomas Scott, Roger Brown, William Wallace.   F. 141-142.

McCLINTOCK, JOSEPH, farmer, Toboyne. 13 Oct 1793. 23 May 1799.
Sons Daniel, Alexander, Joseph and Hugh.
Daus. Mary, Sarah, Elizabeth, Agness, Ann and Margaret.
Exs.: William McGuire and Robert Hunter.
Wit.: Hugh McClintock, John Clark.   F. 143.

CRAIG, JOHN, Juniata. 9 April 1798. 6 June 1799.
Sister Jane Craig.
Nephews Isaac and Mitchell Atkinson.
Plantation in Somerset Co.
Exs.: Sister Jane Craig and nephew Isaac Atkinson.
Wit.: John Elliott, Mary Elliott, Barbara Martin.   F. 144.

LUCK, WILLIAM, Dickinson. 12 Feb 1799. 28 Aug 1799.
Nephew William Luck Weakley, a minor.
Land at John Arthur's line.
Land adj. Michael Ege's in South Mountain.
Land adj. Alexr. McBride and Samuel Woods.
Nephew William Luck Campbell, a minor.
Nephew John Luck.
Land in Westmoreland Co.
Bros.-in-law Samuel Weakley and Thomas Campbell.
Land purchased of David King in partnership with Wm. Leeper.
Bro. David Luck.
Sisters Mary, Elizabeth Piper and Isabella.
Nephews William Piper and John Weakley.
Niece Mary Weakley.

Sister Ann Swaney.
Exs.: Bros.-in-law Samuel Weakley and Thomas Campbell.
Wit.: Thomas Weakley, John Arthur, Peter Ege.   F. 145-146.

COLWELL, JAMES, Southampton. 17 Dec 1798. 20 Sept 1799.
Wife Agness.
Sons Samuel, John, James and Abdiel, a minor.
Daus. Martha Brotherton and Nancy.
Son Joseph.
Dau. Polly.
Grandchild James, son of son James.
Exs.: Sons John and Samuel Colwell and John Scott, Esq.
Wit.: Samuel C. McKean, Robert Patterson, Samuel McDowell.
                                                  F. 147-151.

TARR (DARR), NICHOLAS, Shippensburgh. 16 April 1799. 28 Nov
1799.
Wife Catharina.
Son Joseph.
Minor children.
Exs.: Wife and son Joseph Tarr.
Wit.: Fredk. Shepley, Michael Miller, John Mozer.   F. 152.

WALKER, JAMES, Mufflin. 10 Sept 1799. 29 Oct 1799.
Wife Jane.
Children William, John, Jean, Margret and Mary, all minors.
Exs.: John Walker and bro.-in-law Robert Beard.
Wit.: James Nicholson, Andrew Thompson.   F. 153.

SANDERSON, JOHN, farmer, Tyrone. 27 Nov 1799. 17 Dec 1799.
Wife Sarah.
Bro. Robert Sanderson.
Nephew George, son of Robert Sanderson.
Two nephews George Elliott, son of James Elliott and George
McCormick, son of Robert McCormick.
Sister Martha McCormick, wife of Robert McCormick.
Bro.-in-law David Elliott.
Nephews George Elliott and Robert Elliott, sons of David Elliott.
Land at Samuel Fisher's line.
Thomas Ross, a minor, "who lived with me from a child."
Indentured boy, John Power McCabe and his mother.

84

Sister Catherine McCormick, widow of Hugh McCormick.
Sister Margaret Elliott.
Exs.: Major William Linn and Wilson McClure, Esq.
Wit.: Thomas Simonton, William Douglass, Wilson McClure.
Land on the Chenesee River, Northumberland Co. One tract named
Tyrone, the other named *Pleasant Tract*.   F. 154-157.

REED, JOHN, Toboyne. 15 Aug 1799. 20 Dec 1799.
Wife Sarah.
Son Samuel, his son John, and his dau. Sally.
Son John, and his son John, a minor.
Son Robert, and his son John, a minor, under seven years of age.
Son David.
Dau. Rachel Hardy, her son John, a minor, and her dau. Sally.
Exs.: Sons Samuel Reed and David Reed.
Wit.: John Hunter, Jno. Morrison.   F. 158-159.

McCOWN, FINLAW, Juniata. 18 June 1798. 21 Dec 1799.
Son Francis.
Eldest dau. Margaret, wife of William Rogers.
Dau. Elinor, wife of John Beatty.
Youngest dau. Rosana, wife of John Hoge.
Finlaw Beatty, son of dau. Elinor.
Other children of John and Elinor Beatty.
Exs.: David Mitchell and son Finlaw McCown.
Wit.: Roger Brown, George Thomas, Philip Bosserman.   F. 160-161.

COCKLIN, JACOB, Sr., farmer. 24 Sept 1799. 23 Dec 1799.
Dau. Mary Shepler and her husband, Henry Shepler.
Sons Jacob and David Cocklin.
Land adj. James Gregory and John Cocklin.
Dau. Elizabeth Cocklin.
Exs.: Adam Houk, Sr., and Adam Brandt, the one of Allen, the other of
Dickenson Twp.
Wit.: John Brenizer, C. Quigley.   F. 162-163.

HUTTON, SOLOMON, Allen. 17 Dec 1799. 10 Feb 1800.
Wife Rachel.
Children, all minors, names not given.
Land in Newberry Twp., York Co.
Exs.: Bro. Joshua Hutton and James Legget, Sr.

Wit.: Isaac McKinley, John Starr, James Leggett, Jr.   F. 164.

WEAVER, JUCTICE HENRY, farmer, Allan. 1 Sept 1798. 24 Feb 1800.
Wife Ann Margret.
Sons Conrad, Philip and Henry.
Dau. Elizabeth, her two children by her first husband.
Son-in-law Frederick Crumledge.
Daus. Margret, Rebecca and Barbara.
Grandson Christy Deal.
Grandson Frederick Titner.
Dau. Susannah.
Sons John Weaver and Christy Weaver.
Exs.: Sons Henry Weaver and Philip Weaver.
Wit.: Henry Quigley, C. Quigley.   F. 165.

ARMSTRONG, ANDREW, East Pennsborough. 21 July 1797. 26 Feb
1800.
Wife Margret.
Four daus. Nancy Eakins, Isabella Irwin, Rachel Lowry and Jain
Grayson.
Three sons, viz., Andrew, William and John.
Exs.: Sons Andrew Armstrong and William Armstrong.
Wit.: Henry Christy, Jno. Carothers.   F. 166-167.

CAROTHERS, REBECKAH, West Pennsborough. 5 Feb 1800. 7 March
1800.
Son William Orr, a minor, to live with his uncle, my bro. John Carothers.
Sister Jean Carothers.
Estate of father James Carothers.
Exs.: Bros. John and James Carothers.
Wit.: John Carothers, John Forbes, John Black.   F. 168.

YOUNG, ALEXANDER, East Pennsborough. 2 Aug 1798. 10 March
1800.
Wife Martha.
Sons Robert and John.
Dau. Jean.
Exs.: Son Robert Young and Andrew Galbraith, Esq.
Wit.: Edward Morton, Jonas Rupp, Andrew Galbraith.   F. 169.

RIPPTON, JOHN. 24 Jan 1800. 12 March 1800.

Wife Elizabeth.
Youngest son Peter, a minor.
Sons William and John.
Daus. Rebecka, Mary and Elizabeth.
Exs.: Runnell Blair.
Wit.: Andrew Mitchell, Mary Ann McKeehan, John Wilt.   F. 170-171.

McDONNELL, JOHN, Carlisle. 29 Dec 1799. 14 March 1800.
Wife Elizabeth.
Only son Daniel.
Exs.: Son Daniel McDonnell and nephew Daniel McDonnell.
Wit.: Lemuel Gustine, Edward McGauran, John Noble.   F. 172.

FILSON, SAMUEL, Dickinson, 10 April 1799. 8 April 1800.
Wife Mary.
Children, viz., Samuel, Jane, Joseph, John, Benjamin and Steven.
Sons to be put to trades when fit.
Donation lands.
Exs.: Wife Mary, James Maxwell and Benjn. Blackford.
Wit.: Stephen Legget, Elizabeth Haft.   F. 173-174.

CARSON, JOHN, Newton. 11 April 1800. 6 May 1800.
Two sons John and Elija Carson, when twenty two years of age.
Younger children, viz., Hanna, Priscilla, Martha and Eliza.
Dau. Ruth intermarried with James Ralston.
Elishu Carson's eldest son, John Eager, and Elisha's second son Ezekiel.
Exs.: Dr. John Geddis, Alexr. Sharp and Thos. Kenneday.
Wit.: James Brown, John Sheafer.   F. 175-176.

MATHERS, THOMAS, farmer, Mifflin. 2 March 1800. 30 May 1800.
Wife Mary.
Dau. Jane Mathers.
Son William.
Exs.: Son William Mathers and cousin Saml. Mathers.
Wit.: John Mitchell, Alexr. Elliott.   F. 177-179.

DICKIE, GEORGE, Middleton. 7 Nov 1797. 5 June 1800.
Wife Ann.
Children, viz., John, James, Margaret, George and Hugh McKee Dickie, all minors.
Exs.: Wife Ann Dickie and Michael Ege.

Wit.: Matthew Trotter, Saml. Irwin, Michael Ege.   F. 179-180.

VAN CAMP, WILLIAM, Juniata. 22 Nov 1799. 6 June 1800.
Wife Elizabeth.
Sons James, Alexander and Andrew.
Daus. Jane alias Frank, Lydia alias Hawkins, and Deborah Van Camp.
Son William, dec'd.
Exs.: Sons James Van Camp and Andrew Van Camp.
Wit.: John Elliott, Robert Miller.   F. 181-182.

WEAVER, ANN MARGRET, Allen. 4 June 1800. 18 July 1800.
Christian Deal and his wife Susannah.
Sons John and Christy Weaver.
Grandson Frederick Titmore, a minor.
Son Philip Weaver.
Son-in-law Ephraim Strause.
Daus. now alive.
Exs.: Sons John Weaver and Christy Weaver.
Wit.: C. Quigley, Jacob Shelley.   F. 183.

HOFFMAN, GEORGE, Greenwood. 19 July 1800. 5 Aug 1800.
Wife Agatha.
Children, viz., Joseph, Gorge, Lucana, Samuel, Jacob and Nancy.
Exs.: John Bowman and Adam Overly.
Wit.: Henry Bowman, Bery Duncan.   F. 184.

HACKET, GEORGE, blacksmith, Tyrone. 29 June 1800. 23 Aug 1800.
Wife Elizabeth.
Daus. Mary intermarried with Francis Silvers, Isabella Hacket, Elizabeth
and Eleanor.
Sons James, Robert, Henry, George and William.
Plantation bounded by lands of Michael Loy, Wm. Officer, Henry Ricket,
George Loy and Wm. Anderson.
Exs.: Sons James Hacket and Robert Hacket.
Wit.: William Endslow, John McClure, Wilson McClure.   F. 185-189.

GREGORY, JAMES, Jr., Allen. 4 March 1800. 14 March 1800.
Wife Elizabeth.
Sons James and John, minors.
Exs.: Bro. Richard Gregory and bro.-in-law James Given.
Wit.: Robert Holmes, Adam Brandt, George Hogg.   F. 190-191.

BEASLEY, WILLIAM, an invalid of the United States. 6 May 1800. 23 Aug 1800.
Sole Legatee and Ex.: Jane Legget, wife of Patrick Legget of Carlisle.
Wit.: Geo. Logue, Adam Johnston. F. 192.

LINDSEY, AGNESS, Frankford. 9 Jan 1800. 30 Aug 1800.
Four sons, viz., John, William, James and Robert.
Daus. Margaret Hammon, Nancy Graham and Jenny.
Son Samuel.
Exs.: Son William Lindsey and Isaiah Graham.
Wit.: William Connelly, Richard Woods, Joseph Connelly. F. 192-193.

DUCK, PHILIP, Newdown. 26 March 1796. 15 Sept 1800.
Dau. Catharina.
Sons George and Philip.
Daus. Elizabeth, Margratha, Poly and Eve.
Son-in-law George Miller.
Exs.: Jacob Roth.
Wit.: George Peifer, Guerg *[sic]* Miller. F. 194.

ROBESON, JOHN, Rye. 20 Aug 1788. 4 Oct 1800.
Son-in-law William Wattson.
Grandson John Wattson.
Son Alexander Robeson.
Daus. Jane Robeson, Janet Robeson and Sarah Robeson.
Exs.: Dr. Patrick McNaughton and dau. Sarah Robeson.
Wit.: Fredk. Watts, James Brewes. F. 195.

ANDREWS, ABRAHAM, native of Great Britain, now a Methodist preacher in America. 20 March 1800. 7 Nov 1800.
Youngest son George Andrews in England.
Letter to be sent to him at Mr. George Whitfield's, book stewards, at the New Chapel City Road, London.
Exs.: Mr. Jesse Hollingsworth, merchant, Baltimore, Maryland, and Mr. Henry Willis, near Baltimore.
A sure copy sworn to by John Smith and Henry Willis. F. 196.

STAYMAN, JOSEPH, East Pennsboro. 1 Oct 1800. 17 Oct 1800.
Wife Katron.
Son John.
Dau. Elizabeth Stayman.

Sons Jacob, Joseph and Abraham Stayman, minors.
Lots in Harrisburg.
Exs.: Frederick Grame and Christley Coughman.
Wit.: John Clendenin, Andrew Carothers.   F. 197-198.

McTEER, SAMUEL, farmer, Allen. 18 Sept 1800. 9 Oct 1800.
Wife Rosanah.
Sons James, John and Samuel.
Daus. Margret, Jane and Else McTeer.
Son Sherron.
Some of the children minors.
Exs.: Wife, William Bryson and Robert McTeer.
Wit.: C. Quigley, John McDanel.   F. 199-200.

FOULK, STEPHEN, Middleton. 3 Sept 1800. 24 Nov 1800.
Wife Sarah.
Son Willis and daus. Priscilla and Margret Foulk, minors.
House and lot in Baltimore bought from John McGladry.
Sons Stephen and Moses Foulk.

LONDON, MATTHEW, West Pennsborough. 6 April 1799. 15 Jan 1801.
Wife Ann.
Daus. Mary McFarline and Elizabeth Carothers.
Sons John London and James London.
Daus. Cathrine and Ann.
Son Archibald.
Exs.: Wife Ann, James Irwin and Joseph Junkin.
Wit.: Elinor Junkin, Benjn. Junkin, Robert Wylie.   F. 204-206.

STEELE, JOHN, Captain in the 3rd Reg. of Infantry, in the service of the
United State of America. 26 Sept 1800. 15 Jan 1801.
Mother Agness Jordan.
Nephew John Steele, minor son of William Steele of Carlisle.
Exs.: Mother Agness Jordan and Ephraim Steele, merchant of Carlisle.
Wit.: B. Genet, A. Marschalk.
Codicil 6 Nov 1800.
Bros. William and Joseph Steele.
Cousin William Steele.
Wit.: Edward Magauran, Ja. Duncan.   F. 207-208.

BEARD, DAVID, farmer, Tyrone. 24 April 1799. 22 Jan 1801.

Wife Jennet.
Dau. Jean Kelly.
Sons David and John Beard.
James Elliott.
Exs.: Son David Beard and James Divers.
Wit.: John Ross, David Robb. F. 209.

WILLS, DAVID, yeoman, Hopewell. 5 Aug 1800. 5 March 1800.
Sons John, James and David.
Land on Conodoquinct Creek adjoining Richard Rogers' land.
Land adjoining lands of John Laughlin and James Smith.
Exs.: Sons John William and James Wills.
Wit.: Joseph McKinney, John Maclay, Robert Early. F. 210.

LOVE, JOHN, Westpennsboro. 8 March 1800. 28 March 1800.
Wife Margaret.
Son James, a minor.
Exs.: Wife Margaret and George Clark of Frankford.
Wit.: Jos. Peirce, Jas. McFarland. F. 211.

MAGEE, ALEXANDER, Shippensburg. 14 Jan 1801. 10 April 1801.
Two youngest sons Morison and Alexander, minors.
Sons John, Ebenezer and James.
Ground at Mount Pleasant, Virginia.
Land in Northumberland Co.
Exs.: Son James Magee and James Means of Shippensburg.
Wit.: Gibb. McMaster, Thos. McCammon, Robert Porter.
F. 212-213.

JUNKIN, ADAM. Aug 1799. 29 April 1801.
Sister Jane Parkison.
Housekeeper Mary Davidson.
Exs.: Cousin Benjamin Junkin, Eastpensbro., innkeeper.
Wit.: Conrad Carl, Isaiah Carl. F. 214.

MC CLINTOCK, JAMES, yeoman, Rye. 20 March 1801. 28 May 1801.
Wife Barbarah.
Sons John and William.
Daus. Jenny and Nancy.
Son James.
Exs.: Samuel Dean of Tyrone and John Stewart of Rye.

Wit.: William Eccles, David Millagan. F. 214-216.

RUPP, JONAS, yeoman, East Pennsborough. 6 May 1800. 30 May 1801.
Wife Elizabeth.
Sons, viz., Jonas, John, Martin, George and Jacob.
Daus. Mary, Catharina, Elizabeth and Margretta.
Henry Zering, decd., husband of dau. Elizabeth.
Children of sd. Henry and Elizabeth Zering, minors.
Other sons in law, names not given.
Land adjoining Frederick Gromlich, Andrew Sheiley and Henry Sheibley.
Exs.: Son Jonas Rupp and Andrew Sheiley.
Wit.: Baltzer Telter, Frederick Gromlich. F. 217-218.

HOLLIDAY, SAMUEL, Juniata. 15 Dec 1800. 30 May 1801.
Wife Agness.
Son in law George Williams.
Granddau. Agness Power.
Dau. Catharine.
Exs.: Wife Agness and John Miller.
Wit.: Thomas Simonton, John Kerr, John Miller. F. 219.

DOUGLASS, GEORGE, yeoman, Tyrone. 8 July 1798. 2 June 1801.
Wife Martha.
Sons George and Watson Douglass, minors.
Son William.
Daus. Sarah McClure and Margaret Scott.
Minor daus. Martha Douglass and Elizabeth Douglass.
Exs.: Wife, son William and William McClure, Esq. of Tyrone Township.
Wit.: Jno. Darlington, Thomas McClure, John McClure.
F. 220-222.

REES, SOLOMON, blacksmith, Eastpennsborough. 25 April 1801. 3 June
1801.
Children, viz., Erenia Rees, Jonathan, Deborah and Hannah Rees, three
last named minors.
Exs.: Andrew Longnecker and Dewalt Erfort.
Wit.: George Wornelsdorf, Samuel Rees, William Reed. F. 223.

URWIN (IRWIN), JOHN, Carlisle. ---. 3 July 1801.
Wife Susannah.
Eldest son Daniel.

92

Daus. Elizabeth and Jane Urwin.
Youngest dau. Maria, minor.
Exs.: Michael Miller and John Delancey, Esq.
Not witnessed or signed.   F. 224-225.

COCKLIN, JOHN, farmer, Allen. ---. 20 July 1801.
Wife Fanny.
Sons Tedry Cocklin, David and Peter Cocklin.
Son in law Tiebrick Coover and Catherine, his wife.
Dau. Barbara Cocklin.
Exs.: Son Tedry Cocklin and Adam Branet (Brandt), both of Allen
Township.
Wit.: Samuel Kinsley, C. Quigley, Jacop Golklin.   F. 226-229.

BEYENER, JOHN, Shippensburg. 1 July 1801. 5 Aug 1801.
Wife Elizabeth.
Son Jacob and dau. Elizabeth, minors.
Exs.: Jacob Rham of Shippensburg.
Wit.: Frederick Sheply, N. Krehl, John Heck.   F. 230.

CAROTHERS, MARTIN, Westpennsborough. 9 Aug 1801. 15 Aug 1801.
Bro. Andrew Carothors.
Father decd.
Bro. William Carothors, decd.
Sister Jean's dau. Nancy Clark.
Bro. Armstrong.
Sister Isabella Hays.
Robt. Hegney.
Exs.: Bros. Andrew Carothors and Armstrong Carothors.
Wit.: Martha Perry, William McNaughton.   F. 231-232.

BAXTER, JOHN. 5 Feb 1796. 28 Aug 1801.
Dau. Martha Hunter.
Jennet Officer.
Niece, Jenny Baxter.
Sons James and William.
Exs.: Sons James Baxter and William Baxter.
Wit.: Enoch Anderson, Robert Ewing, James Maxwell.   F. 233.

COLWELL, JOSEPH, Southampton. 12 May 1801. 1 Sept 1801.
Bros. John, James, Samuel and Abdiel, a minor.

Sisters Patty now married to John Brotherton and Nancy married to John Brackenridge.
Mother Agness.
Sister Polly.
Exs.: Bro. Samuel Colwell.
Wit.: Robert Patterson, John Scott, Peter Elrod.   F. 234-236.

MC CAY, JOHN. ---. 1 Sept 1801.
Wife Jean.
Children, viz., Agness McCay, Alexander, Mary, James and Elizabeth McCay.
Jean Garelt.
Esquire Beaty.
Exs.: None named.
Wit.: Nancy McKee, Isaac Kirkpatrick, Junr.
Adtrix: Widow Jean McCay.   F. 237.

MC CRAKEN, JAMES, Toboyne. 28 Feb 1801. 9 Oct 1801.
Daus. Jean and Agness.
Sons James and Joshua.
Daus. Peggy and Ann Catherine.
Grandchildren, viz., James McCraken, James Macklin, James Nelson, James McCraken and Sarah Cord.
Exs.: James Carson and dau. Jane McCraken.
Wit.: James Patton, James Carson.   F. 238.

POLLOCK, JAMES, East Pennsborough. 26 Sept 1790. 2 Nov 1801.
Wife Ann.
Bro. Oliver Pollock's children, viz., Jarett Pollock, Mary Pollock and Rosetta Pollock.
Land on west branch of the Susquehanna River, near the Great Island, Northumberland Co.
Property in and near Carlisle.
Galvez Pollock, son of bro. Oliver.
Land in Bedford Co.
Exs.: Charles McClure and Andrew Galbreath.
Wit.: Jonathan Hoge, John Hulings, Francis Silver.   F. 239-240.

LAIRD, HUGH, Allen. 27 Feb 1797. 9 Nov 1801.
Wife Anna.
Sons Arthur and Samuel.

Dau. Jane.
Sons Stewart, William and James.
Exs.: Son James Laird and son in law William McMeen.
Wit.: Wm. Wallace, John Isett, Samuel Laird.　　　　F. 241.

GEOBLE, HENRY, merchant, Carlisle. 20 Oct 1801. 13 Nov 1801.
Step sister Dorothy Heigel (wife to William Heigle of Carlisle) and their dau. Harriet Heigle.
Two bros., viz., John Conrad Geoble of Berdinger, near Frankford, Isenburg, Germany, and John Andrew Geoble, formerly of the same place.
Exs.: James Given, merchant, and Jacob Hendel, silversmith, both of Carlisle.
Wit.: Thomas Foster, John Smith, George Hendel.　　　　F. 242-243.

HERVEY, ANDREW, Frankford. 4 May 1801. 14 Nov 1801.
Wife Margret.
Son William.
Three daus., viz., Jane wife of Andrew Griffen, Rebecca wife of William McClure, and Mary wife of Hugh Lowry.
To members of the session of the Associate Congregation of Big Spring (if any at that time).
Exs.: Son William Harvey and Thomas Kenneday.
Wit.: Thomas Jacob, John Konig, Hugh Holmes.　　　　F. 244-245.

PIPER, WILLIAM, Mount Pleasant, Hopewell. 19 Oct 1801. 20 Nov 1801.
Wife Mary.
Daus. Phebe Laughlin, Mary McCommon, Nancy Laughlin, Elizabeth Piper and Jane Piper.
Exs.: Wife Mary Piper and son in law Thos. McCommon.
Wit.: Robert Quigley, Francis Nesbit.　　　　F. 246.

GROMLICK, ADAM, Allen. 24 Nov 1800. 26 Nov 1801.
Wife Anna Mary.
Sons Adam, Christopher and Peter.
Youngest son John.
Dau. Magdelena.
Other daus., names not given.
Exs.: Sons Adam and Christopher Gromlick.
Wit.: Jacob Slyder, Herman Blaefeer.
Codicil.

Three grandchildren, children of dau. Ann, decd., (formerly wife of Michael Gunkel), viz., Michael, Jacob and Adam Gunkel.

F. 247-249.

MASONER, ELIZABETH, Dickinson. 6 Nov 1801. 30 Nov 1801.
Isaac Titsworth.
Lands adjoining those of Henry Hartman.
Philip Geoop and others.
Exs.: Isaac Titsworth.
Wit.: James Love, Lodowick Waltermiers. F. 250.

ARMSTRONG, ROBERT, Petersburgh. 17 May 1799. 17 Dec 1801.
Wife Ann.
Dau. Rebecca Clark, wife of James Clark, and her two sons, viz., John Armstrong Clark and Armstrong Clark.
Dau. Catherine Baskins, Mary Kemplin.
Exs.: Wife Ann and Col. James Cowden.
Wit.: Alexander Power, Nathan Vanfossen, Robert Chambers, Philip Swisser. F. 251-252.

PURDY, JOHN, Mifflin. 8 Feb 1801. 17 Dec 1801.
Wife Margaret.
Son William.
Eldest son Thomas.
2nd son James.
Eldest dau. Rachel Purdy.
Dau. Martha Brandon.
Son John.
Indentured boy, Christy Saunders.
Exs.: Two sons Thomas Purdy and James Purdy.
Wit.: John Bolton, Sarah McQueen, Jno. Geddis. F. 253-254.

ANDERSON, WILLIAM, Toboyne. 17 Dec 1801. 31 Dec 1801.
Sons William and James.
Plantation in Tyrone Township occupied by George Cropah.
Sons Alexander and Samuel, minors.
Land that James Johnston lives on.
Son George.
Oldest dau. Ruth Anderson.
Daus. Margaret Johnston, Ann Douglass and Mary Anderson.
Exs.: John Nelson and son William Anderson.

Wit.: Matthew Shanks, William Campbell, John Bryner.

F. 255-257.

WEAKLEY, ROBERT, Dickinson. 4 June 1801. 6 Jan 1802.
Wife Elizabeth.
Children, viz., James, William, Jane, Elizabeth, Samuel, Robert, Mary and
Hannah, minors.
Exs.: Wife Elizabeth, bro. James Weakley and bro. in law Nathaniel
Gillespie.
Wit.: Daniel Holmes, David Woods.   F. 258.

MC CORMICK, JAMES, Eastpennsborough. 2 Sept 1793. 15 Jan 1802.
Wife Mary.
Sons Robert and William.
Son James.
Line at Bro. Thomas' land.
Exs.: Sons Robert McCormick and William McCormick.
Wit.: James Armstrong, James Hoge, Jno. Carothers.   F. 259-261.

MC FARLANE, WILLIAM, farmer, Newton. 10 Jan 1802. 5 Feb 1802.
Bro. James McFarlane.
Sisters Margaret Kenedy, Elizabeth McFarlane and Polly Dunbar.
Niece Rosanna Thompson. Nephew William Thompson.
Mother.
Niece Rosanna Boid.
Bro. Robert McFarland.
Land formerly James Lamond's.
Exs.: Bro. Robert McFarlane and Alexr. Thompson.
Wit.: Alexander Thompson, William Thompson, Robert McFarlane.

F. 262-263.

BRITTON, JOHN, yeoman, Southampton. 19 June 1797. 6 Feb 1802.
Dau. Sarah wife of James Russell.
Sons Thomas, James and John Britton.
Exs.: Son John Britton.
Wit.: Andrew Huston, Isabel Scott, John Scott.   F. 264-265.

REIGHTER, GEORGE, Middleton. 6 Feb 1802. 10 Feb 1802.
Wife Catherine.
Sons John and Philip.

Dau. Mary.
Son George.
Exs.: Sons Philip and George Reighter.
Wit.: Jno. McFeeley, Saml. Postlethwait.   F. 266-267.

GLADSTEN, WILLIAM, Senr., Shippensburg. 16 Sept 1801. 16 Feb 1802.
Wife Elizabeth.
Sons David and William Gladsten.
Daus. Polly Johnston wife of William Johnston and her children, and dau.
Jean Gladsten.
Exs.:   Wife Elizabeth Gladsten and David McKnight, merchant, of
Shippensburg.
Wit.: George McCanless, Senr., James McGuiness, James Blair.
                                                            F. 268-269.

FLEMING, WILLIAM, Middleton. Aug 1798. 27 Feb 1802.
Sons James and John.
Daus. Sarah wife of Richard Crain, Susannah wife of Paul Randolph,
Rebecca, and Nancy widow of Charles Gregg.
Grandsons Alexander Gregg, a minor.
Dau. Anna wife of William Lyon.
Daus. Elizabeth wife of William Crain and Mary wife of William Denny.
Exs.: Sons James Fleming and John Fleming.
Wit.: Ichabod Randolph, Martin Bower, Jacob Wetzel.   F. 270-273.

CLIPPINGER, FREDERICK, farmer, Southampton. 11 March 1802. 25
March 1802.
Wife Barbara.
Sons Anthony, George and John.
Daus. Catherine wife of George Kessler, Anna Maria wife of Adam Wolf,
Elizabeth Clippinger and Susanna Clippinger.
Exs.: Eldest son Anthony Clippinger and son in law George Kessler.
Wit.: Jacob Raum, John Clippinger.   F. 274-279.

PARKISON, JOHN, farmer, Tyrone. 1 April 1802. 14 April 1802.
Wife Jean.
Son Richard.
Daus. Catherine, Ann and Elizabeth Parkison.
Exs.: Bro. David Mitchell and son Richard Parkison.
Wit.: James Diven, Christian Hickerdorn.   F. 280-281.

WILLIAMS, JOHN, yeoman, Allen. 12 Feb 1801. 1 May 1802.
Wife Mary.
Son David.
Mill and land in York Co., line at John Wilson's land.
Sons James and Abraham.
Youngest dau. Jenny Williams.
Grandson James Williams, a minor.
Lands bounded by lands of George Myers, Michael Keck and George Webber.
Daus. Catherine, the widow Allen, Margaret wife of Andrew Parker, Mary wife of John McAllister and Elizabeth wife of Richard Doyle.
Exs.: Sons David and Abraham Williams and Adam Brandt.
Wit.: Saml. Irwin, Edward O'Hail.
Land in York Co. conveyed by Dr. George Wilson.   F. 282-285.

BROWN, WILLIAM, Carlisle. 3 April 1802. 6 May 1802.
Wife Mary.
Two youngest children, viz., Lucy Brown and Thompson Brown.
Ground and tan yard on Pompet Street.
Sons Arthur, William and George.
Dau. Isabella wife of Lewis Foulk.
Lands on the Juniata River.
Exs.: Sons William and Thompson Brown and James Duncan.
Wit.: Samuel Gustine, Ephraim Steel, Charles Bovard.
Codicil 4 April 1802.
Land in Juniata in name of son Pitt Brown, decd.   F. 286-293.

HOFFMAN, GEORGE, Senr., Greenwood. 4 April 1801. 8 May 1802.
Wife Elizabeth.
Sons George Hoffman, Junr. and John Hoffman.
Tenement adjoining lands of John Kepner, Frederick Wendt, David Boal and the Cocolamus Creek.
Other children, viz., Philip, Joseph, Daniel, Maria wife of John Shade, Magdalena Mozer, Catherina wife of John Walter.
Property in Millerstown, Juniata.
Exs.: Eldest son Philip Hoffman and Peter Couffman of Greenwood Township.
Wit.: Fredk. Wendt, Fredk. Harter (Houter), John Went.

                                                              F. 294-300.

WRIGHT, GEORGE, hatter, Carlisle. 21 Nov 1801. 10 May 1802.

Wife Jane.
Son William and dau. Maria, minors.
Tract of land called *Brinigh's Property*, 1 mile east of Col. Bonquet's battlefield in Westmoreland Co.
Exs.: Leonard Kellar, Jos. Shrom and Jacob Hendel.
Wit.: Tedrick Uhler, Ha. Boden, Abm. Holmes.   F. 300-301.

WEAVER, VENDEL, Mifflin. 28 Feb 1802. 20 May and 2 June 1802.
Wife Ann Kitrone.
Estate of her former husband Philip L. Houts, decd.
Sons Peter and John.
Where Thomas Butter lives.
Daus. Jean and Eve.
Sons Henry, Christopher, Jacob, Benjamin, a minor, and William, a minor.
Daus. Betsy and Sally, minors.
Guardian of minor children, Ludwick Miller.
Exs.: Sons Peter and John Weaver.
Wit.: Walter Bell, David Sterrett.   F. 302-303.

MARTIN, PAUL, farmer, Mifflin. 15 Feb 1802. 20 May 1802.
Wife Rosana.
Sons Thomas, Charles, Paul and John Martin.
Daus. Rachel Clark, Rosanna McCoy and Jane Dorbrey.
John Bitner.
Exs.: Wife Rosana Martin and Walter Bell.
Wit.: Andw. Lindsay, Robert Lusk.   F. 304-305.

WOODS, SAMUEL, Dickinson. 12 April 1802. 22 May 1802.
Wife Elizabeth.
Dau. Margaret wife of Daniel Hohnes.
Daus. Jane Woods, Elizabeth and Meary.
Sons William, Samuel, Nathan and David.
Bound girl Polly Strunk.
Bound boys John Strunk, Samuel Ross and James Haslett.
Exs.: Sons Nathan Woods and David Woods.
Wit.: Philip Pfeffer, Jas. Weakley, Isaac Weakley.   F. 306-307.

HARPER, SAMUEL, Dickinson. 12 April 1802. 26 May 1802.
Wife Sarah.
Bros. James, William, John and Robert.
Exs.: Wife Sarah Harper and bro. John Harper.

Wit.: William Ramsey, Robert Paterson. F. 308.

KEARSLEY, JANE, widow of Jonathan Kearsley, Shippensburg. Nov 1790.
30 May 1802.
Sons John Kearsley and Samuel Kearsley.
Daus. Elizabeth Cooper, Margaret Henderson, Mary Rogers and Rebecca
McComb.
Son in law Matthew Henderson.
Dau. Jean Woods, widow.
Son Jonathan.
Indentured girl Esther Welsh.
Land in Tuscarora Valley, now Mifflin Co.
Grandchildren Andrew Woods and Jane Woods.
To estate of Daniel Wister of Philadelphia.
Son in law William McComb.
Grandson John Cooper.
Exs.: Son Jonathan Kearsley and Matthew Henderson.
Wit.: John Simpson, Wm. Cowan, Jas. Kelso. F. 309-310.

NOBLE, WILLIAM. 23 Aug 1776. 2 June 1802.
Wife Rosanah.
Sons James, John and William, a minor.
Dau. Hannah.
Daus. Mary and Sarah, minors.
Exs.: Rosanah Noble, James Noble and John Quigley.
Wit.: Hendry Wharton, Michael Dill, George Wood. F. 311-313.

BARNHISLE, MARTIN, Tyrone. 1 June 1799. 22 July 1802.
Wife Jenny.
Dau. Molly, a minor.
Son Jacob, decd.
Sons John, Adam, Henry and Samuel Barnhisle.
Dau. Mattena Lupfer.
Exs.: Wife Jenny Barnhisle and son Samuel.
Wit.: Thomas McClure, John Dunbar, George Stroop. F. 314.

CLENDENEN, JOHN, Eastpennsboro. 18 May 1802. 7 Aug 1802.
Wife Elizabeth.
Sons John, William and Samuel, a minor.
Daus. Mary, Jean, Agness, Elizabeth, Catherine and Isabella, a minor.
Dau. Janet.

Exs.: Sons John Clendenen and William Clendenen.
Wit.: John Dea, Andrew Carothers.   F. 315-317.

FOLK, CHRISTIANA. 8 Aug 1802. 3 Sept 1802.
Sons William, Richard and James Folk.
Daus. Nancy Lucas and Jean Folk.
Exs.: Son William Folk and Abraham Etter.
Wit.: John Thompson, Wm. Jameson.   F. 318.

CHAMBERS, ROBERT, Middleton. 8 May 1802. 23 Sept 1802.
Sons in law John Davidson and John Logan.
Dau. Agness.
Indentured boy Andrew Davidson.
Plantation adjoining Thomas Duncan, Esq. and Saml. Irwine, Esq.
Granddaus. Margaret Davidson, dau. of Mary Davidson, and Margaret
Logan, dau. of Margaret Logan.
House in Carlisle occupied by James Mitchell.
Bros. and sisters, viz., John Chambers, Joseph Chambers, William
Chambers, Agness Chambers and Hannah Chambers.
Land held in partnership with Ephraim Steel.
Nephew John Chambers.
Deceased wife and dau.
Exs.: Dau. Agness Sterrett, sons in law John Logan and John Sterrett,
James McCormick and John Officer.
Wit.: James Armstrong, James Moore, Ja. Duncan.   F. 319-324.

CERFASS, DANIEL. 14 May 1802. 7 Oct 1802.
Wife Mary.
Son Daniel, a minor.
Plantation in Dauphin Co.
Daus. Susannah, Elizabeth, Rebecca, Mary, Ruth and Catherine.
Exs.: Wife Mary Cerfass and David Funk.
Wit.: Natl. Weakley, Saml. Postlethwaite.   F. 325.

ADAMS, ROBERT, Teboine. 7 Aug 1801. 21 Oct 1802.
Wife Hanna.
Sons Thomas and Robert.
Three married daus., viz., Letty, Terra and Polly.
Dau. Betsy.
Land adjoining George Lambert's and James Miller's mill.
Exs.: Sons Thomas and Robert Adams.

Wit.: John Nelson, George Douglass, John Kincaid.   F. 328-329.

MC MURRAY, WILLIAM, Carlisle. 8 Oct 1802. 22 Oct 1802.
Sole Legatee and Ex.: Bro. Thomas McMurray of Carlisle.
Wit.: Thomas Dickson, John Borden.   F. 330.

PARKISON, WILLIAM, yeoman, Middleton. 23 Jan 1794. 27 Oct 1802.
Sons Richard, John, William, David, Joseph and Thomas.
Dau. Elizabeth.
Granddaus. Margaret and Rachel, children of dau. Catreen.
Dau. Margret.
Granddau. Margret, dau. of son Thomas Parkison.
Granddau., dau. of Jeams Parkison.
Granddau. Margaret Doughter.
Exs.: Nathaniel Wilson and Thomas Parkison.
Wit.: David Sample, Robert Anderson.   F. 331.

LUTES, GEORGE, Allen. 25 Sept 1802. 16 Nov 1802.
Daus. Mary, Ann and Margaret and their children when eighteen years of age.
Sons Jonathan and George.
Plantation in Newberry Township, York Co.
Decd. son Isaac's three children when of age.
Sons in law, viz., Frederick Yost, Samuel Wilson and James Moore.
Grandson Joseph, son of son Isaac decd.
Exs.: Son Jonathan Lutes of Newberry Township, York Co.
Wit.: James Legget, Junr., Frederick Schweitzer.   F. 332-333.

GUDLANDER, JACOB. 3 May 1802. 12 Nov 1802.
Wife Justina.
George William Gudlander and his sisters Margaret, Susannah, Elizabeth and Catherine and his bro. John Gudlander.
Exs.: Wife Justina Gudlander and Valentine Gamber.
Wit.: George Shaff, Frederick Leieb.   F. 334.

ELLIOTT, MARY, East Pennsborough. 10 Sept 1799. 31 Nov 1802.
Dau. Mary Dods.
Granddau. Betsy Dods.
to Jean Barnhill.
Exs.: Robert Bell and Samuel Waugh.
Wit.: Elis Woodward, Rachel Bell.   F. 335.

TURNER, JOHN, Dickinson. 2 Nov 1802. 6 Dec 1802.
Oldest son Daniel
Son James.
Dau. now Polly Neal.
Dau. now Eleanor Mathers.
Sons John and Joseph.
Exs.: Sons Daniel Turner and Joseph Turner.
Wit.: William Greaey, Matthew Adams.   F. 336-337.

BLAIR, WILLIAM, Carlisle. 24 Jan 1800. 17 Jan 1803.
Wife.
House and lot in Carlisle adjoining lots of John Delaney and John Cecigh.
Son Mark.
Dau. Jane.
Children of decd. son William.
Dau. Rebecca wife of Charles McClure.
Son Isaiah.
Exs.: Son Isaiah Blair and John Creigh.
Wit.: Saml. McCoskry, Ja. Duncan, Robert Duncan.   F. 338.

GOORLEY, JOHN, Dickinson. 11 July 1798. 1 Feb 1803.
Dau. Isabella.
To son in law Aron Watson and children, the share intended for dau. Mary.
Daus. Jean, Elizabeth and Agness.
Only son John.
Grandsons John Crawford, John Wishard and John Abercrombie and John
Sproat.
Dau. Margret.
Exs.: Samuel Weakley and William Lusk.
Wit.: John Foster, John Weakley, Robt. McCreary.   F. 339-340.

QUIGLEY, JOHN, Southampton. 28 March 1799. 22 March 1803.
Wife Mary.
Sons Robert and Samuel.
Land bought from John Colwell at James Hathorn's line.
Son in law James Beatty.
Grandchildren Isabella Beatty, Nancy Beatty, Robert Beatty, John Beatty,
William Beatty and James Beatty, all minors.
Exs.: Wife Mary Quigley and son Robert Quigley.
Wit.: James Hathorn, Robert McCune.   F. 341-342.

EVERS, PHILIP, Eastpennsborough. 4 Jan 1799. 18 Feb 1803.
Wife Elizabeth.
Son John Evers.
Other children.
Exs.: Mathias Sailor and Martin Longstaff.
Wit.: Nicholas Bobb, Jonathan Hoge.   F. 343.

DICKIE, JAMES, Eastpennsbro. 11 Sept 1802. 25 Feb 1803.
Wife Margret.
Dau. Betsy Anderson.
Sons John, William, James and Benjamin.
Daus. Polly Dickie and Nancy Dickie.
Exs.: Wife Margret and son in law Robt. Anderson.
Wit.: John Dea, Martin Harmon.   F. 344-346.

WILLIAMSON, DAVID, Middleton. 28 Jan 1803. 2 March 1803.
Wife Elizabeth.
Sons John, Samuel, David and Johnston Williamson.
Daus. Eliza Williamson, Mary McCulloch and Margaret Moore.
Exs.: Bro. John Williamson of City of Charleston, S.C., Samuel Laird, Esq.
of Carlisle, James Moreland of Middleton Township, son in law John
McCulloch and son John Williamson.
Wit.: Ja. Duncan, Hugh McFadden.   F. 347-348.

CULVER, JAMES. 1 Feb 1801. 12 March 1803.
Wife Anny.
Children Joseph, Hannah and Sarah, minors.
Step children William and Margaret Peters.
Exs.: Jacob Palen and William Huston.
Wit.: Joseph Turner, Jacob Bysop, John Kean.   F. 349.

SPARK, HENRY LUDOLPH, Tyrone. 15 Feb 1803. 15 March 1803.
A small place bought from Mr. Herman Donath bequeathed forever for a
school for surrounding neighbors.
Exs.: Mr. Anthony Kimmel.
Wit.: Bastian Shober, Frederick Fleck.   F. 350.

KIRKPATRICK, JAMES, Westpennsborough. 28 Feb 1803. 24 March
1803.
Wife Margaret.
Two step daus., viz., Polly McKean and Betsy McKean.

Exs.: Gared Graham of Westpennsborough Township.
Wit.: Henry Davis, Lawrence Lefever. F. 351.

SANDERSON, ALEXANDER, Tyrone. 9 Feb 1803. 30 March 1808.
Wife Mary.
Two sons James and George.
Daus. Catherine Christy, Margaret Little and Sarah Graham.
Son Alexander.
Dau. Mary Sanderson.
Exs.: Sons James Sanderson and George Sanderson.
Wit.: Alexr. Sanderson, Chas. Elliott, Robert Elliott.
F. 352-353.

SANDERSON, GEORGE, Tyrone. 31 March 1803. 12 April 1803.
Wife Elizabeth.
Sons Alexander, William and George.
Daus. Barbara wife of John Mitchell, Margaret wife of Samuel Smiley, Jane wife of Alexander Robinson and Elizabeth wife of John McKnighton (McKnight).
Exs.: Sons William Sanderson and George Sanderson.
Wit.: Robert Elliott, John Irwin. F. 354-356.

WILSON, JOSEPH, Tyrone. 17 March 1802. 31 May 1803.
Wife Isabel.
Son James.
Daus. Martha wife of John Stones, and Mary Wilson.
Grandson Joseph.
Exs.: James McCord and James Wilson.
Wit.: John Creigh, Jacob Lafever. F. 356.

ADAIR, JAMES. 30 March 1803. 1 June 1803.
Wife Polly.
Sons James and William.
Youngest dau. Isable, a minor.
Other daus. Polly Adair, Elsey Adair and Sinny Adair.
Exs.: Wife Polly Adair and Samuel Mathers.
Wit.: David Glean, William Dunlap. F. 357.

BRANDT, PHILIP, farmer, Allen. 11 May 1803. 3 June 1803.
Wife Mary.
Sons Martin and David.

Plantation on Yellow Breeches Creek.
Plantation in Hanover Township, Dauphin Co.
Four daus., viz., Mary wife of George Schenk, Elizabeth, Catherine and Barbara.
Exs.: Son Martin Brandt and his bros. Adam Brandt and Abraham Brandt.
Wit.: Jacob Mohler, David Brandt. F. 358-360.

DOUGLASS, JOHN, storekeeper, Carlisle. 7 Nov 1802. 13 May 1803.
Wife Margaret.
Daus. Hannah wife of Joseph Knox and Isabella Douglass.
Exs.: Dr. Samuel A. McCaskry and James Duncan, Esq.
Wit.: John Holmes, John Creigh. F. 361-362.

HOLMES, JONATHAN, Middleton. 5 Feb 1800. 2 July 1803.
Sons Daniel, John and Robert.
Dau. Jane wife of William Irvine.
Dau. Mary wife of John Carothers.
Sons William,David and Jonathan.
Exs.: Jonathan Holmes and son in law John Carothers.
Wit.: George Pattison, James Craighead, Geo. Logue. G. 1.

WERT, LUDWICK, Toboyne. 2 April 1802. 20 July 1803.
Wife Elizabeth.
Children John, Elizabeth and Catharine.
Guardians of children: Wife, William Brown and Jacob Hickless.
Exs.: Wife Elizabeth and Nicholes Snyder.
Wit.: Peter Brown, John Hubler. G. 2.

FITZGERALD, WILLIAM, Middleton. 10 Aug 1803. 24 Aug 1803.
To friend Roddy Malkolm.
Exs.: Said Roddy Malkolm and John Armstrong.
Wit.: John Armstrong, William Armstrong. G. 3.

CUNKLE, MICHAEL, East Pennsborough. 14 Aug 1797. 23 Sept 1803.
Sons Baltzer and Michael.
Sons in law Peter Barnhart, John Besor and Philip Sender.
Children of dau. Peggy Couffman, minors.
Son in law Christy Wiser.
Exs.: Michael Longsdorf and Andrew Eminger.
Wit.: John Rennick, John Carothers. G. 3.

ADAMS, ABRAHAM, yeoman, East Pennsborough. 26 April 1802. 26 Sept 1803.
Sons Abraham, William, Samuel and Isaac, youngest son.
Line at lands of John Hawk, Samuel Geddis, John Stagman and James McGuire and Henry Ernsberger.
Four daus. Jean, Elizabeth, Nancy and Mary, a minor.
Youngest dau. Maria, a minor.
Grandson Abraham Adams Byson (Bryson).
Exs.: Benjamin Junkin and son Saml. Adams.
Wit.: James McGuire, John Raack, W. Addams.   G. 4-6.

LUPFER, JOHN, yeoman, Rye. 21 March 1791. 7 Oct 1803.
Sons Caspar and Jacob.
Plantation bounded by lands of Thomas Barnet, Edward Clark, Michael Marshall and Joseph Marshall.
Other children, viz., John, Catharine wife of Peter Crafts, Elizabeth wife of John Sherer, Martha wife of Abraham Grove and Mary Lupfer.
Exs.: Caspar Lupfer and Martin Barnhisel.
Wit.: David McClure, John Lawson.   G. 7-8.

MC CORMICK, SAMUEL, Mifflin. 11 Dec 1801. 8 Oct 1803.
Wife Elizabeth.
Sons Joseph and Thomas.
Daus. Mary Elizabeth, Jane and Ann.
The "time of" Elizabeth Bucanan, minor.
Exs.: Son Joseph McCormick and John Davidson.
Wit.: John McFarland, James Harper, John Bowman.   G. 9.

BOWER, HENRY, Dickinson. 13 May 1803. 11 Oct 1803.
Wife Margaret.
Dau. Rebecka.
Son Daniel, minor and his full bros. and sisters, names not given.
Exs.: Philip Pepper.
Wit.: Nathan Woods, Samuel Lockard.   G. 10.

MATEER, JAMES, Senr., Allen. 7 Oct 1803. 19 Dec 1803.
Son James.
Land in Juniata.
Son in law Robert Baily and Elizabeth his wife.
Granddaus. Margaret Bailey, Ann Bailey and Jane Bailey, minors, and grandson Bailey, minor.

108

Son John.
Exs.: Son John Mateer.
Wit.: James Mateer, C. Quigley. G. 10-11.

MILLER, PHILIP, farmer, Juniata. 24 Sept 1803. 19 Oct 1803.
Wife Catharine.
Sons Philip, Jacob and John.
Daus. Kitty, Mary, Peggy and Christiana.
Dau. Ann wife of George Reamer.
Land purchased of Dr. Daniel Fahnestock and Matthew Hale.
Land sold to John McGorry and Jacob Gount.
Exs.: Bro. John Miller and George Monroe of Juniata Township.
Wit.: Hugh Gormley, John Leonard. G. 12.

KISLEY (KNISLEY), SAMUEL, Senr., Allen. 29 Sept 1803. 19 Oct 1803.
Son Samuel Knisley.
Property in York County and elsewhere.
"Maintenance of family," no names given.
Exs.: John Coffman and George Kisley.
Wit.: C. Quigley, Eleanor Roseberry. G. 13.

OFFICER, ALEXANDER, Carlisle. 3 March 1800. 8 Nov 1803.
Sons James and John.
Granddau. Mary dau of son James.
Grandchildren Alexander and Mary, son and dau. of son John.
Exs.: Sons James Officer and John Officer.
Wit.: James Laird, Samuel Linn. G. 14.

KAIRNS, JOHN, Rye. 21 Sept 1802. 17 Nov 1803.
Wife Annis.
Son in law William Galbreath and Sarah his wife.
Sons James and William Kairns.
Dau. Jane.
Dau. Ann (alias Skipton).
Grandson Andrew Galbreath.
Exs.: William Galbreath.
Wit.: John Elliott, John Thompson. G. 15.

WALLACE, MOSES, Allen. 7 Aug 1801. 29 Nov 1803.
Daus. Isabella and Elizabeth Wallace.
Son Richard.

Exs.: Bro. James Wallace and son Richard Wallace.
Wit.: John Whitehill, James Whitehill.   G. 15-16.

BLACKWOOD, WILLIAM, farmer, Westpennsboro. 13 Aug 1803. 30 Nov 1803.
Wife Mary.
Eldest son James.
2nd son John.
Daus. Agness and Mary.
Son William.
Sons George, Robert and Moses.
Some of children, minor.
Exs.: Wife Mary and son William Blackwood.
Wit.: Daniel McDonald, Junr., William Dunlap, John Chambers.
                                                          G. 16.

MC KEEHAN, GEORGE, Westpennsborough. 5 Aug 1803. 3 Dec 1803.
Wife Mary.
Sons Samuel and Robert.
Land joining Richard Woods and William Miller.
Daus. Mary, Jean and Rebecka.
Granddau. Lydia.
Exs.: Benjamin McKeehan and son Samul. McKeehan.
Wit.: George McKeehan, Junr., James McKeehan, Junr.   G. 17.

SCHNEIDER, MICHAEL, Westpensbro. 26 Nov 1803. 19 Dec 1803.
Wife Sera.
Oldest son Samuel.
Son John, minor.
Dau. Eleanora, minor.
An unborn child.
Guardians of children Matthias Klee and John Klee.
Exs.: Wife Sera Schneider and Philip Nely.
Wit.: Daniel Yohe, John Davidson.   G. 17.

BIGGAR, WILLIAM, Allen. 12 Nov 1799. 10 Jan 1804.
Wife Jane, sole heir.
Exs.: Wife Jane and Wm. Bryson.
Wit.: C. Quigley, William McTeer.   G. 18.

BIGGAR (BIGGERT), JANE, Allen. 8 June 1803. 10 Jan 1804.

Sister Esther Bryson.
Jane Trimble, and her grandmother, widow Quigley.
James Bryson's son William Biggert Bryson.
William Bryson and his son Robert.
John Quigley, up the river's, eldest son.
James Quigley, Henry's son.
Christopher Quigley, the younger, C. Quigley's son.
C. Quigley's daus. Jane and Nancy.
Margaret Glass and her son Daniel.
James Graham's two sons.
Widow Quigley's Polly.
Alexander Quigley.
Jane Bryson.
Pricillah Bryson.
Sarah Miller, former Sarah Quigley.
John Quigley, widow Quigley's son.
Exs.: William Bryson and Henry Quigley, Senr.
Wit.: C. Quigley, Widow Quigley.   G. 18.

DREVISH, WILLIAM, merchant, Carlisle. 21 Dec 1803. 20 Jan 1804.
Nephew Wilhelm Vogel, sister's son, whose arrival in this country is looked
for.
Sister Carolina Florentina, formerly wife of --- Vogel.
Sister Gertruda Elizabetta Ludwig, wife of --- Ludwig.
Mother Maria Elizabetta Drevish.
Former partnership with Mr. Wilson Elliott of Chambersburgh.
Exs.: James McCormick and Jacob Hendel, Esq., and Mr. James Given,
merchant.
Wit.: George Hendel, Ja. Duncan, Thos. Bell.   G. 19.

BRIGGS, DAVID, Eastpennsborough. 27 Jan 1801. 8 Feb 1804.
Wife Anna.
Lands formerly belonging to Oliver Pollock, Esq., known by name of Silver's
Spring Estate.
Three sons David, Benjamin and Joseph, a minor.
Dau. Mary Pollock.
Land where Carey's house stands.
House occupied by Jared Pollock.
House in which Henry lives.
Dau. Elinor Hoge.
Grandson David Hoge, a minor.

James Davis' wife's son.
Plantation formerly belonging to Robert Morris, Esq.
Exs.: Wife Anna Briggs and son David Briggs.
Wit.: Andrew Galbreath, Robt. Duncan, James Duncan.
Codicil 2 Feb 1804.
Land adjoining Andrew Sheeley.
Philadelphia. James McGuire, Christopher Coffman. G. 20-21.

HOGE, JOHN, East Pennsborough. 5 Jan 1804. 6 March 1804.
Wife Mary.
Son Michael, minor.
Daus., minors.
Exs.: Wife Mary and Marten Renninger.
Wit.: Abraham Addams, James McQuire, Henry Ansberger. G. 22.

MC GAHAN, ANTHONY. 8 April 1803. 7 March 1804.
Bro. William McGahan.
Sister in law Margaret McGahan.
Exs.: William McGahan.
Wit.: John Walker, Anthony McGahan. G. 23.

DALE, CHRISTIAN, Tyrone. 5 Jan 1804. 8 March 1804.
Wife Martha.
Sons Christian, Paul, Peter and Daniel.
Daus. Martha and Christiana.
Exs.: Son Daniel Dale and John Miller.
Wit.: Thomas Simonton, Daniel Lower, Mathias Best. G. 24.

IRVINE, ROBERT, Tyrone. 20 Aug 1803. 8 March 1804.
Wife Ann.
Three sons James, John and William.
Four daus. Mary Irvine, Nancy Reid, Jane McMullan and Sarah Holliday.
Land where George Wallock and Benjamin Wallock live.
Exs.: Sons James Irwin and William Irwin.
Wit.: William Irwin, James Elliott, Geo. McMullan. G. 24-25.

SANDERSON, ROBERT. 16 Oct 1803. 10 March 1804.
Wife Mary.
Son George.
Deed from Penn.
Another from William Armstrong.

112

Lands bounded by Ross Mitchell, John Baker, William Brown, decd., James Lamberton, Alexander Blaine, decd., and the Glebe.
Where James Simpkins lived adjoining George Sanderson.
To William Hawling.
Land at head of Shearman's Valley in possession of Robert Morrow.
Mill place adjoining John Sanderson's and John Cormans.
Grandchildren Robert McClain, James McClain and Maria McClain, children of dau. Martha McClain.
Dau. Jane Hawling.
Son Alexander Sanderson.
Son William Sanderson and his children.
Exs.: Wife Mary and son George Sanderson.
Wit.: John Wightman, George Elliott.   G. 26.

BLAINE, EPHRAIM, Middleton. 1 Feb 1800. 19 March 1804.
Wife Sarah Elizabeth.
Son Ephraim, a minor.
Grandson Ephraim, son to son James.
Sons James and Robert.
Grandson Ephraim, son to son Robert.
Exs.: Sons James Blaine, Robert Blaine and David Watts.
Wit.: James Armstrong, H. Miller, D. Watts.   G. 27-28.

GANSEE, JOHN. 1 Feb 1804. 20 March 1804.
Wife, sole heir.
Exs.: Wife and Jacob Keggle.
Wit.: John Rafter, David Blocher.   G. 29.

JUMPER, CONRAD, Frankford. 6 Jan 1800. 9 April 1804.
Wife Eve.
Granddaus. Elizabeth and Barbara, daus. of David Herr.
Grandson David, son of sd. David Her.
Unmarried daus. Mary, Nancy and Rosina.
Five living children.
Exs.: Wife Eve, George Logue, Esq., and John Smith, my sons in law.
Wit.: Nicholas Fordig (Fordick), Anthony Houtz.   G. 29.

CLARK, WILLIAM, Middleton. 14 May 1803. 9 April 1804.
Wife Margaret.
Sons Joseph and Robert.
Daus., viz., Margaret Clark, Mary Clark and Ann Clark.

Exs.: Sons Joseph Clark and Robert Clark.
Wit.: Archibald Stewart, Geo. Crean, John Stewart.   G. 30-31.

PATTERSON, OBIDIAH, farmer, Dickinson. 17 Feb 1804. 11 April 1804.
Wife Anne.
Children Polly, Robert, John and Sarah, minors.
Exs.: Wife, bro. John Patterson and bro. in law Thos. Patterson.
Wit.: Andw. Huston, Alexr. McBride.   G. 32.

BELL, SARAH, Eastpennsborough. 24 Sept 1794. 24 April 1804.
Dau. Sarah.
Three sons Robert, James and David.
Exs.: Said sons Robert, James and David Bell.
Wit.: Jno. Carothers, Mary Carothers.   G. 33.

FOSTER, ISABELLA, Tyrone. 19 Feb 1804. 28 April 1804.
Bro. George Foster's two daus., viz., Isabella and Mary Foster, minors.
Bro. William's three daus., viz., Mary, Isabella and Jean Foster.
Exs.: Bro. William Foster.
Wit.: John McClure, Wilson McClure.   G. 33.

MARTIN, THOMAS, Eastpennsborough. 26 April 1804. 3 May 1804.
Bros. David and John Martin.
Sister Jane Leverty.
Exs.: John Orr.
Wit.: John Noble, John Hunter, Dewalt Erford.   G. 34.

CAMP, CHRISTOPHER, Dickinson. 3 May 1804. 17 May 1804.
Wife Catherin.
Son Peter Camp and step son Philip Evert.
Daus. Elizabeth wife of John Clopper and Margaret Camp.
Exs.: Step son Philip Evert and Peter Spangler.
Wit.: John Leas, Philip Fissell.   G. 34-35.

HOLMES, ABRAHAM, Belleford, Centre Co., now in Carlisle. 8 June 1804.
25 June 1804.
Wife Rebecca.
Son James, a minor.
Furs from John Dunlap of Centre Co.
Hatter stock from Rowland Curtin of Bellefont.
House in Carlisle in possession of John Boden and Adam Isett.

Bros. and sisters.
Exs.: Wife Rebecca Holmes, bro. Andrew Holmes and bro. in law George Pattison.
Wit.: Jno. Armor, A. P. Lyon.   G. 35-36.

RAINEY, WILLIAM, Carlisle. 15 June 1804. 3 July 1804.
Wife Mary.
Hugh Woods, son of James Woods.
James Gregg, son of James Gregg, late of Carlisle.
Exs.: Wife Mary, George Logue, Esq. and James Gregg.
Wit.: Jacob Keighley, Daniel Dunlap.   G. 37.

MOORE, HOWARD, Eastpennsborough. 25 Oct 1793. 17 May 1804.
Bro. Robert Moore.
William Moore, son of bro. George Moore.
Land from Robert Whitehill's known by name of John Wormly.
Howard Moore, son of bro. George.
Andrew Moore.
Sisters Elizabeth and Jean.
Exs.: Robert Whitehill and Samuel Wallace.
Wit.: James Whitehill, Robert Whitehill, Junr.   G. 38.

LOVE, JAMES. 17 July 1804. 20 Aug 1804.
Mother Margaret Love.
Deceased father John Love.
Exs.: Mother Margaret Love and James Carothers, Esq.
Wit.: Nancy Clark, Jean Clark, Elizabeth Maghy.   G. 38.

HUGHES, JOHN, Middleton. 7 Sept 1804. 10 Sept 1804.
Dau. Elizabeth and son in law Hugh H. Potts.
Children of said dau. Elizabeth.
Exs.: Son in law Hugh H. Potts.
Wit.: Thos. Duncan, D. Watts, Ja. Duncan.   G. 39.

DOUGLASS, MARGARET, Carlisle. 3 Sept 1804. 10 Sept 1804.
Joseph Knox intermarried with dau. Hannah.
Grandson John R. Knox, son of dau. Hannah.
Lot near the New College purchased by late husband of William Thompson.
Daus. Hannah Knox and Isabella Douglass.
Exs.: Samuel Postlethwaite, Samuel A. McCoskey and James Duncan.
Wit.: Ann Mahon, John Creigh.   G. 39-40.

BRICKER, PETER, yeoman, Allen. 14 April 1804. 13 Sept 1804.
Wife Mary.
Son Peter Bricker.
Land bought of Jacob Weise.
Land bought of William Hameroley.
Six daus., viz., Elizabeth wife of George Brindle, Barbara wife David
Brenizer, Magdalen wife of Jacob Miller, Mary wife John Beshor, Catherine
Bricker and Susanna Bricker.
Exs.: Adam Brandt and John Barr.
Wit.: Jacob Crever, Jacob Weise. G. 40-41.

REINNECK, JOHN, Eastpennsboro. 24 May 1799. 22 Sept 1804.
Dau. Nancy Cairns.
Grandsons Reinick and Jacob Angeny.
To Lutheran Church at Martin Longstaffs.
To Lutheran Church at Carlisle.
Exs.: John Lamb and son in law Richard Cairns.
Wit.: Andw. Galbreath, Michael Dill. G. 42.

MUSSELMAN, BARBARA, Rye. 24 Aug 1804. 6 Oct 1804.
George Cleas, Senr., sole heir and Ex.
Wit.: Gottleib Westfall, John Fritz, Fras. McCown. G. 42.

EVERLY, HENRY, Allen. 19 July 1804. 9 Oct 1804.
Wife Mary.
Sons Henry and Samuel.
Daus., viz., Catherine, Elizabeth and Barbara.
Minor children, viz., Joseph, Peter and John.
Exs.: George Brindle and Thomas Wise.
Wit.: James Gustine, William Black. G. 43-44.

DEYERMOND, HENRY, Newville. 7 Aug 1804. 10 Oct 1804.
Wife Deborah.
Son in law Hugh Wallace and his wife Margaret.
Grandson Thomas Wallace, son of Hugh Wallace.
Son in law John Love and his wife Elizabeth.
Son in law John Highlands and Sarah his wife.
Son in law John Murphy and Anne his wife.
Exs.: Major James Woodburn and James Ross, both of Newville.
Wit.: William McCandlish, William T. Hays, William Richey.
G. 45.

CLAUDY, MARTIN, Shippensburgh. 20 Sept 1804. 12 Oct 1804.
Son Abraham.
Dau. Mary Claudy.
Two youngest sons,George and Jacob.
Other six children, viz., Elizabeth, Margaret, Catherine, Martin, William and John.
Exs.: Son Abraham Claudy.
Wit.: William Devor, John Bailey.   G. 46.

HERR, ABRAHAM, Allen. 16 May 1804. 13 Oct 1804.
Wife Elizabeth.
Four children, viz., John, Abraham, Henry, a minor, and Barbara.
Children of dau. Barbara.
Henry Buckwalter husband of said dau. Barbara.
Exs.: Sons John Herr and Abraham Herr.
Wit.: A. P. Lyon, Samuel Martin, Junr.   G. 47.

CRANE (CREAN), ESPY, Middleton. 22 Sept 1804. 15 Oct 1804.
Sister Elizabeth Crane.
Sister's son Espy Vanhorn, son of Joseph Vanhorn.
Bros. William and George.
Three sisters Mary intermarried with James Hamilton, Jane widow of Joseph Vanhorn, and Anne intermarried with Matthew Dill.
Children of said sister Anne.
Bro. Richard Crane.
Sister's dau. Mary Vanhorn.
Father Richard Crane.
Exs.: George McMullen and Patrick Davidson.
Wit.: Richard Crean, Geo. Logue.   G. 69-70.

MOORE, WILLIAM, yeoman, Southampton. 16 March 1802. 20 Oct 1804.
Wife Ann.
Son James.
Dau. Rachel wife of Andrew Hunter.
Grandsons John and William Hunter, sons of sd. dau. Rachel.
Sons Andrew and John Moore.
Grandson William Craig Moore.
Daus. Elizabeth and Sarah Moore, minors.
Land purchased from Robert Culberton, adjoining lands of John Caldwell, Samuel Caldwell, Francis Campbell, Ebenezer Campbell and James Hamilton Wallace.

Dau. Agness wife of James Hamilton Wallace.
Exs.: Wife Ann Moore and son James Moore.
Wit.: Samuel Colwell, John Colwell, John Heap.   G. 70-73.

SEIRAH, GEORGE, Eastpennsborough. 26 Oct 1803. 25 Oct 1804.
Wife Catherine Elizabeth.
Sons John, Jacob, Adam and Daniel.
Daus. Elizabeth, Mary and Margaret.
Son in law John Hank.
Exs.: John Orr and Jonas Rupp.
Wit.: John Houk, William Orr.   G. 74.

BRICKLEY, PETER, Tyrone. 18 Sept 1804. 25 Oct 1804.
Wife.
Sons Valentine, Andrew, William and John.
Dau. Mary.
Other daus. names not given.
Exs.: Son Valentine Brickley and John Wingert.
Wit.: William Gamber, John Waggoner.   G. 75.

WAGGONER, JACOB, Senr., yeoman, Greenwood. 16 Oct 1804. 29 Oct
1804.
Granddau. Polly Waggoner (Smithly), a minor.
Son John Waggoner.
Dau. Elizabeth, now Elizabeth Long.
Son Jacob Waggoner, decd.
Dau. in law Magdalena Waggoner.
Other children, viz., Michael Waggoner, Catherine Reamer, Anna Kainee,
Margareth Deal, Susannah wife of Daniel Blocker, Polly married to Leonard
Kline and youngest dau. Magdalene Waggoner.
Exs.: John Reamer and Frederick Wendt.
Wit.: John Ottley, David Derickson.   G. 76.

CURTZ, LUDWICK, blacksmith, Greenwood. 8 Sept 1804. 5 Nov 1804.
Dau. Anne wife of David Pfoutz.
House and lot in Millerstown.
Sons Lawrence, Thomas, Abraham, Christly and William Curtz.
Daus. Margaret, Hannah Curtz and Sarah wife of Richard Custard.
Son Lewes Curtz.
Exs.: George Neagle and George Hoffman.
Wit.: Isaac Craven, David Rumbaugh.   G. 77-78.

118

SOUR, BARNHART, farmer, Hopewell. 11 Oct 1804. 8 Nov 1804.
Wife Barbara.
Son Barnhart and other children, minors.
Plantation in Lurgan Township.
Exs.: Wife Barbara Sour and Ludwick Miller.
Wit.: James Henderson, William Morrow.   G. 79.

ACKERMAN, PAUL, yeoman, Eastpennsborough. 28 Oct 1804. 17 Nov
1804.
Wife Margaret.
Children John, Paul, Margaret and Catherine.
Three youngest children George, Henry and Abraham.
Exs.: George Mann and John Rupley.
Wit.: Michael Hebison, Abraham Neidick.   G. 80.

MUSTA, GEORGE, yeoman, Tyrone. 22 Aug 1804. 19 Nov 1804.
Wife Martha.
Two minor children, son John, and a dau., name not given.
Exs.: Wife Martha Musta.
Wit.: Henry Titsel, John Jumper, John McClure.   G. 81.

KITCH, MICHAEL, Allen. 23 May 1800. 19 Nov 1804.
Wife Barbara.
Six children George, John, Henry, Martin, Catherine and Mary.
Son in law Andrew Erminger.
Trustee: Adam Brandt.
Exs.: Andrew Erminger and John Lamb.
Wit.: Jacob Lesher, Erfort Miller.   G. 82.

HENDERSON, MARY, Toboyre. Non cupative will. 21 Sept 1804. 21 Nov
1804.
Son Richard Henderson.
Daus. Ann Patterson, Letuce Sanderson and Mary Widney.
Son James Henderson.
Husband Saml. Henderson, decd.
Wit.: John Rodgers, Isabella Brown, Margey Mevier.
Adtor: John Patterson.   G. 83.

JORDAN, FRANCIS, farmer, Juniata. 14 April 1804. 26 Nov 1804.
Wife Catherine.
Sons Amos and John.

Dau. Elizabeth North.
Son Jeremiah Jordan.
Exs.: Sons Amos Jordan and John Jordan.
Wit.: Abigail North, James Beaty, Isaac Craven.   G. 84-85.

DONALDSON, THOMAS, Eastpennsborough. 24 March 1804. 29 Nov 1804.
Sons Alexander and John.
Grandson Thomas Donaldson, a minor.
Son Robert.
Dau. Patsey Donaldson.
Wife, name not given.
Exs.: Son Alexander and son in law James Cunningham.
Wit.: Robert Bell, Robert McKean.
Son Alexander Donaldson, decd. at time of proving the will.
                                                                  G. 86.

ROBESON, JOHN, yeoman, Hopewell. 30 Sept 1803. 3 Dec 1804.
Wife Easter.
Three younger sons, viz., William, John and James, when last named is of age.
Daus. Sarah intermarried with Joseph Combs, Mary Robeson and Agness intermarried with William Early.
Son Hug(h) Robison.
Exs.: John Duncan and son in law William Early.
Wit.: John McCune, Robert McIntyre.   G. 86-87.

COPE, CONRAD, now of Springfield. 5 Nov 1804. 4 Dec 1804.
Wife Catherine.
Seven sons, viz., George, John, Jacob, Daniel, Peter, Benjamin and Philip.
Exs.: Wife Catherine Cope.
Wit.: Joseph McKee, Wm. McDonald.   G. 88.

RODGERS, RICHARD, farmer, Hopewell. 11 Sept 1804. 4 Dec 1804.
Wife Rachel.
Eldest son William.
Sons James, Andrew and Denny Rodgers.
Daus. Rachel, Margaret intermarried with John Peebles, and Fanny intermarried with Samuel Sturgeon.
Exs.: Two eldest sons, William and James Rodgers.
Wit.: James Quigley, John Bolton, John Woods.   G. 88-89.

REES, JEREMIAH, Eastpennsborough. 9 Feb 1803. 11 Dec 1804.
Wife Mary.
Sons Richard, Jeremiah, Samuel and David.
Daus. Barbara Rees and Catey Rees.
Plantation in Northumberland Co., *White Deer Hole Valley*.
Land with Benjamin Patterson.
Exs.: Sons Richard and Jeremiah Rees and Samuel Jacobs of Dauphin Co.
Wit.: Abraham Neidick, Andrew Galbreath.   G. 90.

CAROTHERS, ALICE, East Pennsbro. 21 Nov 1804. 17 Dec 1804.
Two sons William and John.
Son James decd.
Dau. Jane.
Daus. Mary and Alice.
Exs.: Sons William Carothers and John Carothers.
Wit.: John Orr, William Orr.   G. 91.

HERMAN, MARTIN, Eastpennsborough. 27 Jan 1801. 21 Dec 1804.
Wife Dolly.
Sons Martin and Jacob.
Dau. Elizabeth Bower.
Grandchildren Martin Eichelberger and Mary Eichelberger.
Son Christopher Herman.
Exs.: Son Christopher and son in law Martin Bower.
Wit.: Joseph Junkin, John Junkin, Eleanor Junkin.   G. 92.

MOORE, JOHN, Rye. 18 Sept 1804. 22 Dec 1804.
Wife Nelly.
Sons William and James.
Daus. Margaret Findley and Nelly Wallace.
Exs.: Son James Moore.
Wit.: John Sterret, John Sweifshelm.   G. 93.

GILFILLEN (GILLFILON), JAMES, farmer, Greenwood. 3 Aug 1804. 22
Dec 1804.
Wife Nancy.
Dau. Polly wife of Thomas McLin.
Daus. Ann and Hannah.
Son James.
Youngest child Sally, a minor.

Daus. Betsy married to Philip Quigly, Margaret wife to Robert Jones, Rebecca, Dorcas, Matty and Jean.
Exs.: Wife Nancy and Samuel Utter of Millerstown.
Wit.: Daniel Staubb, Jacob Coffman.   G. 94-95.

RIPPEY, SAMUEL, Senr., farmer, Shippensburgh. 8 Sept 1804. 3 Jan 1805.
Wife Mary.
Son John.
Land to Mr. Hammill's farms at Mt. Rock Road on the Pittsburg Road and on the Roxbury and Strasburg Road in partnership with Judge Yeates, called the *Stuart's Tracts*.
Lott in Pittsburg purchased from Capt. John Peebles of near Shippensburgh.
Dau. Isabella wife of William Bailey.
Grandson Samuel Bailey, minor.
Houses &c. adjoining John Heap, Esq.
Son Armstrong.
Unmarried daus. Peggy, Harriet and Molly.
Granddau. Marion Smith, dau. of deceased dau. Elizabeth and Hugh Smith decd.
Exs.: Wife Mary Rippy, son John Rippy and Doctor John Simpson of Shippensburgh.
Wit.: Wm. Rippey, John Shipen.   G. 96-98.

BLEAN, DAVID, farmer, Westpennsborough. 9 Oct 1801. 19 Jan 1805.
Wife Isabella.
Son Robert Blean.
Grandchildren John, David and William Blean, children of son Robert, the son of Isabella Hill, now my wife aforesaid.
Exs.: Son Robert Blean.
Wit.: William Duncan, Jno. Geddis, John Carson.   G. 99.

ELLIOTT, DAVID, Middleton. Non Cupative Will. 21 Sept 1804. 26 Jan 1805.
Wife.
Sons Robert, George and David.
To each of daus., names not given.
Wit.: William Drennon, William Sanderson.
Adtor: Son David Elliott and William Drennon.   G. 100.

MC ELROY, JOHN, yeoman, Newton. 15 Nov 1804. 1 Feb 1805.
Wife Sarah.
Dau. Mary Hawthorn.
Other six children John, James, Hugh, Abraham, Martha and Joseph.
Some of the children, minors.
Exs.: Joseph McKee and David McKee.
Wit.: William Ramsey, Hugh Stuart.   G. 101.

RICHEY, ADAM. Middleton. 18 July 1804. 9 Feb 1805.
Wife.
Sons James, John, William and Adam.
William Leester, minor, son of son in law David Leester.
Thomas Dickey, son of son in law Robert Dickey.
Dau. Elizabeth wife of said David Leester.
Jain O'Hail wife of Edward O'Hail.
Dau. Nancy wife of Matthew Egnew.
Dau. in law Jain Richey widow of son Thomas Richey decd.
Grandson Thomas Richey, minor, son of son Thomas Richey decd.
Exs.: Edward O'Hail, Matthew Egnew and Samuel Irwin.
Wit.: Saml. Irwin, Gol. Reighter, Henry Woolf.   G. 102-104.

PATTON, JOHN, Westpennsborough. 17 Aug 1796. 16 Feb 1805.
Wife Elizabeth.
Dau. Mary, a minor.
A child not yet born.
Sister Margaret Gibson.
Bro. Thomas.
Land joining James Kirkpatrick's.
Exs.: John Purdy and Jared Graham.
Wit.: James Kirkpatrick, Wm. McKean, Junr.   G. 105-106.

CULBERTSON, AGNESS, widow of Wm. Culbertson, Eastpennsbro. 21
Aug 1801. 20 Feb 1805.
Older son, John Culbertson.
Daus. Sarah Culbertson and Margaret Culbertson.
Mother Sarah Bell.
Two other children, names not given.
Exs.: Thomas Urie and Andrew Parker.
Wit.: Samuel Culbertson, Henry Kellar.   G. 107.

MC CALLISTER, ANDREW, Westpennsbro. 26 Aug 1804. 20 Feb 1805.

Sons Archibald and James.

Daus. Elizabeth Parker, Jane Peirce, Mary McIntyre and Margaret Calhoon.

Minor children Eleanor, Lydia, Leacey and Sarah.

Exs.: Sons Archibald McCallister and James McCallister.

Wit.: Jane Pierce, Paul S. Pierce, Saml. Laird.   G. 108.

MC CORD, JAMES, Tyrone. 17 Aug 1802. 22 March 1805.

Wife Katherine.

Son James.

Daus. Margaret and Agness.

Sons Samuel, Benjamin and John.

Land on Buffalo Creek settlement adjoining land of Thomas Simonton.

Exs.: Sons Samuel McCord and James McCord.

Wit.: Edward West, Enoch Lewes.   G. 109.

RAMSEY, SAMUEL, farmer, Middleton. 13 Sept 1804. 27 Feb 1805.

Wife Esther.

Daus. Esther, Margaret, Elizabeth and Catherine.

Son Searight Ramsey.

Dau. Jane wife of William Searight.

Sons Samuel and Archibald Ramsey.

Exs.: Dau. Esther and son Searight Ramsey.

Wit.: John McCoy, Geo. Logue.   G. 110.

CAMPBLE, JOHN, Frankford. 25 Jan 1804. 30 March 1805.

Sons Robert and James.

Grandchildren minor sons of son William.

Grandson Robert, son of son John.

Son Joseph.

Grandson John Christie.

Granddau. Margaret.

Guardians of sons of son William.

Exs.: Son Robert, John Logan and Wm. Lindsay.

Wit.: William Connelly, Joseph Connelly, James Laird.   G. 111.

MORTON, EDWARD, East Pennsborough. 15 Oct 1802. 15 April 1805.

Son William and his children.

Dau. Mary wife of John McConnell and her children.

Dau. Jean wife of James Silver and her children.

John McMeen son of William McMeen.

Jean Cottingham (Cunningham).
Apprentice George Green.
Exs.: Son William Morton, Andrew Galbreath and Robert Whitehill, Senr.
Wit.: John Orr, William Orr, Andw. Galbreath.
Codicil: 20 Sept 1804.
Wit.: Richard Cairns, Francis Silver, John Armstrong.

G. 112-113.

KILGORE, HUGH, farmer, Tyrone. 5 April 1805. 23 April 1805.
Wife Jean.
Dau. Rebecca.
Sons David and James.
Daus. Elizabeth Kelly, Mary Kilgore and Margaret and Jean.
Exs.: Wife Jean Kilgore and nephew Wm. McClure.
Wit.: Edward West. James Wilson.   G. 114.

COPE (COP), ADAM, Carlisle. 20 April 1805. 7 May 1805.
Wife Catherine.
To building a church for the German Lutheran Society and maintaining a
clergyman.
Exs.: Jacob Hendel, Esq. and Leonard Keller.
Wit.: Frederick Uhler, Saml. Postlethwaite.   G. 114.

SHEELEY, MICHAEL, Eastpennsborough. 8 May 1805. 3 June 1805.
Wife Martelena.
Son Michael.
Sons and daus. David, Andrew, Molly, Sophia, Barbara and Elizabeth
Sheeley.
Granddau. Catey dau. of John Grouse.
Exs.: Bro. Andrew Sheeley and Jacob Miller.
Wit.: John Grouse, Martin Seliars.   G. 115.

JORDAN, JOHN, farmer, Juniata. 25 May 1805. 4 June 1805.
Wife Sophia.
Six children, viz., Amos, Nancy, Rebecka, Sarah, Lydia and Nathan, all
minors.
Exs.: Wife Sophia and bro. Amos Jordan.
Wit.: Martha Wallace, Saml. Utter.   G. 116.

MC DONALD, JAMES, Allen. 19 July 1805. 30 July 1805.

Bro. John McDonald and his three sons, viz., John, James and Jeremiah, minors.

Sister's son James Quigley.

Bro. John's dau. Martha.

To each of bro. John's daus.

Exs.: Bro.John McDonald, William Bryson and Benjamin Anderson.

Wit.: John Walker.   G. 117.

PRATZ, SIMON, Eastpennsborough. 10 Feb 1805. 17 Aug 1805.

Wife Chatarina.

Children Frederick, John, Simon, Conrad, Philip, Jacob, Daniel and Elizabeth.

Grandchildren, the children of son Abraham, viz., Jacob, Chatarina, John, Abraham and Thomas.

Exs.: Son John Pratz and John Mumma.

Wit.: Frederick Mumma, Jacob Ansberger.   G. 118-119.

ORNER, DAVID, farmer, Greenwood. 6 July 1805. 24 Aug 1805.

Wife Elizabeth.

Son Abraham.

Daus. Elizabeth, Mary, Susan, Sarah, Ann and Margaret, some of the children minors.

Lot of ground in Millerstown.

Exs.: Wife Elizabeth Orner and Jacob Caufman.

Wit.: Christian Mitchal, Christion Stemak.   G. 120.

CLARK, JOHN, yeoman, Allen. 3 March 1804. 27 Sept 1805.

Wife Margaret.

Dau. Mary widow of William Camlin, decd.

Dau. Agness wife of James Abernethy.

Sons John and James Clark.

Dau. Sarah wife of Alexander Gordon.

Son William Clark.

Minor children of son Thomas Clark, decd.

Land joining lands of Michael Ege.

Land in Monaghan Township, York Co. bounded by lands of John Bailey and heirs of Hugh McMullen.

Exs.: Wife Margaret Clark.

Wit.: Edward O'Hail, Adam Troudt.   G. 121.

BURKHOLDER, CHRISTTY, Middleton. 6 Aug 1805. 18 Oct 1805.

Wife Catherine.
Six children, minors, none named.
Exs.: Bro. John Burkholder and Daniel Wonderlick.
Wit.: John Craighead, Geo. Logue.   G. 122.

SNIVELY, HENRY, yeoman, East Pennsborough. 10 Oct 1805. 24 Oct 1805.
Wife Fanny.
Plantation adjoining lands of Edward Morton, Nicholas Kritzer and George Snively.
Sons John, George and Henry.
Daus. Nancy, Elizabeth and Polly.
Exs.: George Coover and Jacob Miller.
Wit.: John Bobb, George Shusoely.   G. 123.

MILLER, ABRAHAM, millwright, Allen. 8 April 1800. 26 Oct 1805.
Wife Rebecca.
Four sons, viz., Joseph, Abraham, Isaac and Jacob Miller.
Lot of ground in Harrisburgh.
Land in York Co.
Another disobedient son of my wife, Andrew Miller.
Exs.: Wife Rebecca Miller and son Joseph Miller.
Wit.: William Jones, Benjamin McMurray.   G. 124.

MC KINZIE, DOROTHEA. 13 May 1805. 6 Nov 1805.
Niece Rachel Jago and her son George Washington Jones.
Exs.: Saml. A. McCoskey and James Duncan.
Wit.: John Creigh, Hr. Wilson.   G. 125.

MC BRIDE, MATTHEW, blacksmith, Juniatta. 12 Oct 1805. 7 Nov 1805.
Bro. John McBride.
Deputed son William, when sixteen years of age.
Niece Margaret Chisholm.
John Chisholm.
Exs.: Bro. John McBride and Meredith Darlinton.
Wit.: George Wiseman, Meredith Darlinton.   G. 126.

KINSLOW, PATRICK. 16 April 1792. 23 Sept 1805.
Dau. Mary.
Land I now live on called *Chestnut Ridge*.
Son Thomas.

Son Michael.
Dau. Margaret.
Granddaus. Phoebe and Margaret.
Plantation in tenure of Philip Jones.
Exs.: Sons Thomas Kinslow and Michael Kinslow.
Wit.: James Diven, Edward West.   G. 126-127.

GUSTINE, LEMUEL, (Doctor), Carlisle. 27 May 1807. 28 Nov 1805.
Wife Rebecca.
Minor children Samuel, Richard, Lemuel P. and Mariah.
Son James.
Dau. Sally Snowdon.
Exs.: Wife Rebecca Gustine, son James Gustine and Andrew Parker.
Wit.: Wm. Drevish, Eph. Steel, J. Hughes.   G. 127.

CAIRNS, RICHARD, Eastpennsborugh. 22 Aug 1805. 6 Dec 1805.
Wife Nancy.
Two daus. Mary and Jane.
Two sons John and Robert, minors.
Exs.: John Carothers and John Lamb.
Wit.: Joseph Junkin, Jno. Anderson, John Sample.   G. 128-129.

GRAHAM, WILLIAM, Tyrone. 28 Aug 1805. 13 Dec 1805.
Eldest son James Graham.
Estate in Racoon Valley.
James Robinson of said place.
3rd dau. Susanna Robinson.
2nd dau. Sarah Robinson.
Dau. Margaret Black.
Eldest dau. Elizabeth Marshall.
Youngest dau. Jane Milligan.
Son William.
Exs.: James Black of Juniatta and Robert Robinson of Tyrone Township.
Wit.: Richard Jameson, Charles Elliott, Robert Elliott.   G. 130.

MORRISON, NOBLE, farmer, Tobogue. 24 Sept 1805. 18 Dec 1805.
Son James Morrison.
Daus. Jean Morrison and Mary Morrison.
Son Noble Morrison.
Exs.: James Morrison, Senr. and dau. Jean Morrison.
Wit.: John Cook, James Carson.   G. 131.

CALHOON, MARY, widow, East Pennsborough. 21 Dec 1805. 26 Dec 1805.
Eight living children, none named.
Estate of John Clendenin decd.
Exs.: Andrew Carothers and John Clendenin.
Wit.: Polly Fisher, William Clendenin.   G. 132.

TRIMBLE, JOHN, farmer, East Pennsboro. 21 Oct 1803. 31 Dec 1805.
Wife Mary.
Sons George and John.
Dau. Rebecca.
Granddaus. Jean Dickey and Jean Freiser.
Grandchildren John Trimble and Jean Trimble, children of son Thomas
decd.
Exs.: Sons George Trimble and John Trimble.
Wit.: John Dea, Robert Bell.   G. 132-133.

PATTERSON, ROBERT, Senr., farmer, Dickinson. 3 Oct 1805. 16 Jan
1806.
Sons John, Josiah and Ezra.
Heirs of son Obidiah Patterson decd.
Son Zacheus Patterson.
Heirs of son in law Alexander McBride and dau. Tabitha decd.
Son in law John Huston in light of his wife Deborah.
Son Josiah's son Robert.
Grandson Robert Patterson, son of Obidiah.
Lands to John Harper's and Alexander Glenn's lines.
Grandson John Patterson, son of Obidiah Patterson.
Exs.: Son John Patterson.
Wit.: Alexr. Smith, William Harper, John Harper.   G. 133-134.

BELL, WILLIAM, Hopewell. 17 March 1799. 18 Jan 1806.
Dau. Margaret wife of Andrew McLean.
Dau. in law Rosanna Bell.
Grandchildren William and Walter Bell, sons of son William Bell decd.
Lot of ground in Shippensburgh, adjoining lots of David McKnight and
James McClintock.
Exs.: James Henderson and Walter Bell.
Wit.: Samuel Henderson, Adam Harkson, James Waddel.   G. 135.

HECKERNELL, DAVID, Allen. 22 March 1803. 20 Jan 1806.
Wife Mary.

Son Henry.
Other children, names not given.
Exs.: Wife Mary and son Henry Heckerrell.
Wit.: Benjamin Anderson, James Legget, Junr.   G. 136.

HOLMES, JOHN, Carlisle. 11 Sept 1804. 30 Jan 1806.
Wife Mary.
Granddaus. Mary Offley, Jean Agnew and Jean Holmes dau. of son William Holmes, decd.
Catharine and Ann, daus. of son John.
Sons Garrad and Jonathan.
Children of decd. dau. Mary Stevenson.
Granddau. Juliana Holmes, dau. of son John.
children of son Andrew Holmes, decd.
Son John Holmes.
Exs.: Sons John Holmes, Jonathan Holmes and John Creigh, Dr. James Armstrong and James Duncan.
Wit.: James McCormick, W. Moore, Englehard Rheem.   G. 136-137.

SMITH, JEAN, Middleton. 10 Feb 1801. 7 Feb 1806.
Sons Robert Smith, Brice Smith, William Smith and Hugh Smith.
Dau. Mary Williams and her heirs.
Son James Smith.
Granddaus. Jean Christy, Jean Smith and Nancy Smith.
Exs.: Son Hugh Smith.
Wit.: James Lamberton, Ursula Lamberton.   G. 138.

LIGGET, PATRICK, Carlisle. 14 Oct 1805. 17 Feb 1806.
Wife Jane.
Sons, viz., Jacob, Peter, Stephen and Daniel.
Daus. Mary Filson, Sarah Ligget (Haymaker), Jane Burns and Elizabeth Heft.
David Carnes, a child now living with me.
Exs.: John Miller of Carlisle, merchant, and William Alexander also of Carlisle.
Wit.: Robert Wright, Adam Johnston.   G. 139-140.

VAN CAMP, JOHN, Buffaloe. 20 Feb 1805. 24 Feb 1806.
Wife Abigail.
Four daus., viz., Ann, Elizabeth, Deborah and Catherine Van Camp, minors.
(Wife Abigail, step-mother to three daus.)

To bros.

Exs.: Bro. James Van Camp and bro. in law Thos. Eagles.

Wit.: Andrew Van Camp, Frederick Nepple.

Codicil: 21 Feb 1806.

Land called Snyder's adjoining Carnaghan's and Philip Price's.

G. 141-142.

BORALL, JACOB, mason, Tyrone. 11 Nov 1805. 27 Feb 1806.

Wife Ann Mary.

Sons Nicholas and Jacob.

Daus. Elizabeth, Barbara wife of George Miller and Sarah wife of George Flesher.

Sons Paul and Valintine.

Dau. Catherine.

Exs.: George Miller and George Flesher.

Wit.: George Haller, Abraham Fulwiler.   G. 143-144.

MARLIN, JOHN, Juniata. 13 Aug 1798. 1 March 1806.

Wife Jane.

Children, minors, names not given.

Exs.: Wife Jane Marlin and George Dickson.

Wit.: John James, James Leonard.

Codicil:

Names son and dau. John Marlin and Sarah Marlin.   G. 145.

JOHNSTON, ISABELLA (ISABELA). 28 Feb 1806. 5 March 1806.

Son Richard Reece, minor.

Dau. Rebecka Kelso, under twenty one years of age.

Bro. John's children.

Sister Polly's children.

Exs.: Frederick May.

Wit.: Adam Kritzer, John Stoner.   G. 146.

IRWIN, SAMUEL, Middleton. 4 Dec 1805. 17 March 1806.

Wife Mary.

Five daus., viz., Mary Green, Jeney Murphy, Eloner McKinney, Ruth and Catherine.

Son Samuel.

Bro. James and his wife.

Lands at Casawago.

Mills and lands at Big Spring.

Granddau. Elizabeth, a minor.
Sum for use of the poor.
For use of propogating the Gospel.
J. Beard, sister Margaret Beard's son.
Bro. Robert's heirs.
Other bros. and sisters in North Carolina.
Grandsons Samuel Murphy and Samuel McKinney, minors.
Exs.: Son Samuel Irwin and James Duncan.
Wit.: Adam Brandt, J. Beard, John Brindle.
Codicil: 21 Jan 1806.
Matthew Miller.   G. 147-151.

WARD, JAMES, blacksmith, Rye. 18 Nov 1805. 27 March 1806.
Sons John Ward and Jonathan Ward of Carlisle.
Dau. Ann Wood.
Plantation whereon Benj. Jones lives.
Exs.: Hugh Smith of Middleton Township.
Wit.: Nathan Templeton, Edward Roberts.   G. 152.

GALBREATH, ANDREW, East Pennsborough. 17 Feb 1805. 3 April 1806.
Wife Barbara.
Eight daus., viz., Jean wife of Matthew Miller, Elizabeth, Juliana, Molly,
Sally, Barbara, Dorcas and Nancy.
Grandson Andrew Galbreath Miller.
Exs.: Wife Barbara Galbreath, Matthew Miller and William Alexander,
Esq.
Wit.: None.   G. 152.

PATTERSON, MARY, widow, Dickinson. 18 Dec 1801. 5 April 1806.
Seven children, viz., Jane, Grisald, Mary, Esther, Ann, Sarah and Thomas.
Exs.: Son Thomas Patterson.
Wit.: James McCormick, Margaret McCormick.   G. 153.

ALEXANDER, ELIZABETH, Southampton. 11 Feb 1803. 6 Aug 1810.
Sister Amelia.
Land held in partnership with said sister on Mount Rock Road where we
now live.
Niece Ann Highlands, dau. of sister Amelia.
Thomas Moore Highlands, husband of sd. niece.
Exs.: Sister Amelia and Robert McCune.
Wit.: Robert Quigley, John McCollam, James Simpson.   G. 154.

132

GERBER, CHRISTIAN, yeoman, Allen. 31 March 1806. 14 April 1806.
Bro. Benjamin Gerber.
Other bros. and sisters.
Exs.: Henry Brindle of Allen Town and Benjamin Kutz of Harrisburg.
Wit.: Benjamin Gerber, John Black. G. 154.

QUIGLEY, HENRY, Allen. 25 July 1805. 21 April 1806.
Wife Jane.
Sons James and Alexander.
Place called Anderson's Place called *Castle Rag*.
Two daus. Martha and Fanny.
Son Christy Quigley.
Some of those children minors.
Christopher Quigley.
Exs.: Son James Quigley and William Bryson.
Wit.: C. Quigley, Isaac McKniley. G.155-156.

OGLE, WILLIAM, yeoman, Rye. 14 Sept 1802. 24 May 1806.
Wife Sarah.
Oldest child Jane.
Son Alexander.
The children of last wife, minors, names not given.
Exs.: David Ogle and Frederick Myer of Rye Township.
Wit.: John Fry, Andrew Fry. G. 157.

FLICKINGER, GEORGE, Juniata. 14 April 1806. 30 May 1806.
Wife Christiana.
Two daus. Betsy and Bodlina and son Abraham, minors.
Exs.: Nicholas Lyon.
Wit.: Matthew London, Wm. Kerr. G. 157-158.

QUIGLEY, MOLLY, Eastpennsborough. 7 Sept 1803. 4 June 1806.
Son John.
Late husband John Quigley, Senr., decd.
Estate purchased of Thomas Trimble.
Dau. Rosana late the wife of Saml. Mateer.
Jean Bigger decd. of Allen Township.
Granddau. Jean Trimble, dau. of sd. Thomas Trimble.
William Irwin, Trustee, for sd. granddau.
William Bryson.
Dau. Molly Quigley.

Son James.
Granddau. Molly Flower.
Grandson James Flower.
Exs.: Sons James Quigley and John Quigley.
Wit.: Samuel Waugh, Andw. Galbreath.   G. 158.

SANDERSON, MARY, Middleton. 9 Oct 1805. 6 Aug 1806.
Dau. Jane Holley.
Granddau. Maria McLean.
Mary Campbell.
Son John.
Isabel Hamilton.
Exs.: Joseph Hays of Carlisle.
Wit.: Isabella Hamilton, Saml. Laird, Charles Rowan.   G. 159.

WALLACE, JOSEPH, Carlisle. 18 April 1804. 9 June 1806.
Wife Agness.
Sons James, Jonathan, Joseph, William and Thomas.
Dau. Elizabeth McCord.
Dau. Abigail.
Exs.: Wife Agness Wallace.
Writing sworn to by Saml. Criswell and Geo. Logue.   G. 160.

ALLEMAN, CHRISTOPHER, farmer, Swatara, Dauphin Co. 6 Sept 1802.
11 June 1806.
Wife Barbara.
Her five children, viz., Peter Sheets, Catherine Swartz, George Sheets,
Elizabeth Sheets and Anne Alleman.
Mills in Cumberland Co.
Sons Martin, Stophel, Jacob and George, a minor.
Land in Harrison Co., Va.
Dau. Barbara and her husband, George Shiley.
Five other daus., viz., Elizabeth, Christiana, Mottena, Mary and Anne.
Decd. son's two children, Christina and Catharine.
Exs.: Sons Stophel and Jacob.
Wit.: Henry Webber, Elisha Green.   G. 160-161.

DUNLAP, MARY, Westpennsboro. 16 Dec 1798. 14 June 1806.
Daus. Isabella Cunningham and Polly Adair.
Son John Dunlap.
Granddaus. Mary Cunningham, Margaret Cunningham and Polly Adair.

Granddau. Polly, dau. of William Dunlap.
Dau. Esther Dunlap.
James Dunlap decd.
Daus. Sarah Patrick and Nancy Glenn.
Children of dau. Sarah Patrick, when youngest comes of age.
Son William.
James Patrick.
Granddau. Polly Patrick.
Exs.: Rannell Blair and Robert Patterson.
Wit.: Robert Patterson, James Turner, Andrew Mitchel.   G. 162.

KRISHER, JOHN, Southampton. 31 May 1806. 17 June 1806.
Wife Ketren.
Land purchased from Jacob Young and Patrick Dillon.
Son Jacob and his sisters and bros., Mary, Elizabeth, David, John, Daniel,
Rosana and Rudolph, boys to be bound to trades and schooled.
Exs.: Bro. David and George Mower, Senr.
Wit.: Samuel McLean, James Hendrecks.   G. 163.

CUNNINGHAM, ADAM, yeoman, Hopewell. 25 June 1806. 29 July 1806.
Daus. Agness wife of John Young, Mary wife of David English, Margaret
wife of Moses Kirkpatrick, Isabella wife of Thomas Brittan, Elizabeth wife
of Thomas Smith and Ruth Cunningham.
Granddau. Sarah Kirkpatrick.
Grandson Adam Britton.
Son Adam Cunningham.
Exs.: John McCune and dau. Ruth Cunningham.
Wit.: David Duncan, John McCune.   G. 164.

COOPER, ROBERT, D. D., Pastor of Middle Spring Congregaton. 3 Aug
1795. 5 Aug 1806.
Wife Elizabeth.
Two daus. Jane Nicholson and Elizabeth Grier.
Only son John, a minor.
Exs.: Wife Elizabeth and bro. in law Mattw. Henderson.
Wit.: John Henderson, James Lowry, John Simpson.   G. 165.

LIGHTNER, WILLIAM, yeoman, Shippensburgh. 10 April 1806. 27 Sept
1806.
Three daus., viz., Jane, Margaret and Kesia.
Exs.: Dau. Jane Lightner and George Patterson of Carlisle.

Wit.: John Simpson, William Barr, Robert Hamill, Junr.   G. 166.

SPROUT, JOHN, farmer, Dickinson. 18 Oct 1796. 6 Aug 1806.
Eldest son Alexander.
Dau. Isabella.
Dau. in law Eve wife of son William decd.
Children of said son William decd., viz., Jean, Mary, Elizabeth, Isabella and Agness, minors.
Letters to Eve Sprout and William Gracey.
Exs.: Robert Blain and Robert Patterson.
Wit.: None.   G. 167.

ORRIS, WILLIAM, Tyrone. 21 July 1806. 6 Aug 1806.
Sons Henry, George, Joseph, Adam and John.
Daus. Catherine married to Godfrey Arbaugh, Mary married to Joseph Cough, Susannah married to William Bitner, Agness married to John Creslip.
Children of dau. Catherine Arbaugh, minors.
Dau. Elizabeth wife of Thomas Batts.
Exs.: Henry orris and Nicholas Ickes.
Wit.: Chas. Elliott, James Sanderson.   G. 168-169.

MC PHERSON, WILLIAM, Carlisle. 11 May 1805. 9 Aug 1806.
Bro. Alexander McPherson's son, Robert McPherson.
Bro. Alexander's dau, Mary McPherson.
Exs.: Nephew said Robert McPherson and Danl. Dunlap.
Wit.: William Smith, John Smith, John Crain.   G. 170.

JONES, JOHN, blacksmith, Juniata. Proved 14 Aug 1806.
Wife Ann.
Sons Joseph and John.
Daus. Nancy Vincent, Mary Harvey, Rebecca Jones and Sarah Jones.
Sons Thomas, Benjamin and Joshua.
Exs.: William Bull of Juniata and Isaac Craven of Greenwood Townships.
Wit.: Alexander Garret, Robert Garret.   G. 171-172.

COOPER, JOHN, Newton.
Wife Jane.
Her father, James Jack decd.
Son James.
Minor children Jane, Sarah, Margaret and Andrew.

Sons John and Robert.
Exs.: Son John Cooper.
Wit.: Wm. Montgomery, Ann Montgomery.   G. 173-174.

BECHTEL, JACOB, Westpennsborough. 25 July 1806. 2 Sept 1806.
Wife Veronia.
Sons Henry, Samuel, Martin and John.
Daus. Elizabeth, Maria and Magdalena.
Exs.: Son in law Henry Shenk and Henry Bowman.
Wit.: John Leidy, John Bear.   G. 175-177.

MC CORD, WILLIAM, Teboine. 27 Nov 1805. 24 Sept 1806.
Wife Sarah.
Sons and daus., viz., Joseph, John, Alexander, minor, Robert, minor, Isaac,
minor, Mary wife of Thomas Robinson and Anna wife of Alexander Blaine.
Agness Morrison, James Morrison and Anna Morrison, minor children of
decd. dau. Grizzel Morrison.
Sally McCord, dau. of son William decd.
To children of natural dau. Elizabeth decd., minors.
Exs.: John Patterson and son Samuel McCord, both of Teboine Township.
Wit.: John Linn, Robert Clark, Thomas Clark.   G. 178-179.

SWANGER, PAUL, yeoman, Middleton. 30 Aug 1806. 25 Sept 1806.
Children, viz., Christty decd., Nicholas, Jacob, Margaret wife of John Nagle,
David, Catherine wife of John Long, Christiana decd. wife of Valentine Wolf
and Michael Swanger.
Children of son Christty Swanger decd., minors.
Mary wife of said son Christty.
Children of dau. Christiana decd.
Exs.: Joseph Throm of Carlisle and Jacob Wise of Middleton Township.
Wit.: David Brandt, Geo. Stine.   G. 180-181.

RUFF, CATHERINE, Carlisle. Non Cupative Will. 24 Aug 1806. 1 Oct
1806.
Dau. Catherine Morrison's two children, William and Catharine.
Son Daniel Ruff's two children, Joseph and John.
Dau. Catherine Ruff.
Wit.: James Rowney, Mary Morrison, Mary Ann Gould, Catherine
Levinger.   G. 182.

GORDON, AGNESS, Frankford. 1 Sept 1806. 7 Oct 1806.

Bro. James Douglass.
Sister Jean Kilgore.
William Douglass son of bro. George Douglass decd.
Nancy, Mary and Anne Douglass, daus. of bro. William.
Jean Lindsay and Jean French.
Exs.: Bro. William Douglass and James Geddis.
Wit.: James Geddis, George Douglass.   G. 183.

FISHER, LEONARD, Eastpennsborough. 4 Sept 1806. 11 Oct 1806.
Dau. Catharine wife of John Shisler and his son Leonard.
Son John.
Matey, Elizabeth and Barbara.
Letters issued to Conrad Emmiger.
Exs.: Andrew Emmiger.
Wit.: Saml. Rees, John Erford.   G. 184.

REES, RICHARD, Eastpennsboro. 1 May 1806. 11 Oct 1806.
Son Ross, a minor.
To be put to tanning trade.
Exs.: Bro. Samuel Rees.
Wit.: Sarah Miller, William Neil.
Codicil: 8 July 1806.
To mother and to Elizabeth.
Wit.: James Brooks, William Murray.   G. 185.

LAIRD, SAMUEL, Carlisle. 13 May 1793. 15 Oct 1806.
Wife Mary.
Rachel Laird dau. of Matthew Laird and Betsy Brown her niece.
Three bros. Hugh, William and Matthew Laird.
Exs.: Wife Mary Laird, James Laird son of Hugh Laird and Samuel Laird
son of William Laird.
Wit.: James Brown, James Kenneday.   G. 186.

HENRY, MATHIAS, Greenwood. 27 June 1805. 29 Oct 1806.
Wife Lizzy.
Apprentice George Atkinson, alias Jesse Atkinson, a minor.
Exs.: George Rumbaugh of Greenwood Township.
Wit.: Christopher Walter, David Rumbaugh.   G. 187.

DAVIDSON, GEORGE, West Pennsborough. 8 Dec 1797. 3 Nov 1806.
Wife Prudence.

Sons John and Benjamin.
Dau. Elizabeth.
Heirs of son Samuel decd.
Sons William, George and Patrick.
Grandson George son of Samuel decd.
Exs.: Sons William and George Davidson.
Wit.: John Davidson, Matthew Davidson.   G. 188.

HEARST, JAMES, Juniata. 24 April 1806. 4 Nov 1806.
Wife Molly.
Sons and daus., names not given.
Exs.: Wife Molly Hearst and John Cambell.
Wit.: George Wiseman, James Humes.   G. 189.

BLOGHER, MATHIAS, mason, Greenwood. 10 Jan 1805. 13 Nov 1806.
Wife Sophia.
Eleven children, viz., Christian, Jacob, Catherine wife of Michael Riddle,
Susana widow of Andrew Sneisgood, Peter, John, George, Mathias, Daniel,
David and Elizabeth wife of Jacob Haist.
Five children of dau. Susana and Andrew Sneisgood decd.
Exs.: Wife Sophia Blogher and John Burns.
Wit.: Catherine Blogher, Albert Rule, Fredk. Wendt.   G. 189-190.

MC CLINTOCK, SARAH, Mifflin. 10 Oct 1806. 25 Oct 1806.
Alexander Weist son of Jacob Weist, now of Mifflin Township.
Three half sisters, viz., Margera Huston, Ann Clark and Jane Blair.
Sister in law Mary McFarlin.
Two bros., viz., James and Hugh Torrance.
Jane Buchanan the poor child bound to me and to her father Robert
Buchanan.
Friend Agness Drudge.
Exs.: Thomas McCormick and Samuel Fenton.
Wit.: James Harper, Henry Krettle.   G. 191.

ROSS, JAMES, Town of Newville. 26 Dec 1805. 18 Nov 1806.
Wife Sarah.
Sons William, James and John Ross, minors under fourteen years of age.
Exs.: Wife Sarah Ross and Atchison Laughlin of West Pennsborough.
Wit.: Hugh Rathford, Nicholas Howard.   G. 192-193.

REDER, PAUL, Senr., Juniata. 6 Aug 1804. 19 Dec 1806.

Wife Christiana.
Eldest son Paul.
Other sons John, Daniel, Abraham, Ephraim and Henry.
Daus. Elizabeth, Christiana and Rebecca.
Exs.: Sons Paul Reder and John Reder.
Wit.: G. Monroe, Abraham Worley.   G. 194-195.

JONSTON, JOHN, Eastpennsborough. 13 Dec 1806. 30 Dec 1806
Four children, viz., John, Ellick, Peggy and Polly, minors.
Letters issued to William Jonston.
Exs.: John Orr.
Wit.: George Mason, John Ackerman.   G. 196.

SMITH, JAMES, farmer. 3 Nov 1806. 31 Dec 1806.
Children, dau. Mary and minor sons James and George.
Exs.: Bro. George Smith.
Wit.: Andw. Holmes, Thos. Craighead.   G. 197.

CRAIG, JAMES, Carlisle. 31 Dec 1806. 2 Jan 1807.
To mother and brother and sisters.
Exs.: Mr. Robert Taylor and Moses Kulick.
Wit.: John Underwood, Joseph Porter, Mary McWhorta.   G. 198.

RANDOLPH, ANN, Widow. 19 March 1806. 15 Jan 1807.
Son Job Randolph,.
Daus. Rebecca intermarried with William Sanderson and Nancy Randolph.
Letters to Job Randolph, Paul Randolph and Jas. Fleming.
Exs.: Patrick Davidson.
Wit.: Sarah Davidson.   G. 199.

ADAMS, JEAN. 20 Dec 1806. 19 March 1807.
Sisters Betsy, Nancy, Polly and Mariah.
Bro. Isaac Adams.
Exs.: Samuel Adams.
Wit.: James McGuire, Willm. Quigley.   G. 200.

PARSEL, JOHN, Dickinson. 18 March 1805. 20 Jan 1807.
Wife Rachel.
Children, names not given.
Exs.: Sons in law James Love and Garret Dimmored.
Wit.: Philip Ebbert, John Clapper.   G. 200.

CAMPBELL, ROBERT, yeoman, Tyrone. 24 May 1806. 17 Feb 1807.
Two children Charles Campbell and Elizabeth Campbell.
Exs.: John Crever and Jacob Crever of Carlisle.
Wit.: William Melester, Ludwig Carman.   G. 201-202.

MONTGOMERY, WILLIAM. 15 Nov 1806. 21 Feb 1807.
Wife Margaret.
Five daus., viz. Susana, Ann, Rebecca, Ellenor and Elizabeth.
Grandson William Montgomery Holmes.
Contract with David Stereatt, Senr., decd.
Land in tenure of George Peters sold to James Pettigrew.
Robert Bell, decd.
Exs.: Daniel Sterrett and Walter Bell.
Wit.: Brice I. Sterrett, William Stevenson, John Laird.
                                                         G. 203-205.

HAMILTON, JAMES, Mifflin. 10 Oct 1806. 21 Feb 1807.
Bro. John Hamilton and his children.
Bro. Hugh Hamilton and his family.
Bro. William Hamilton and his family.
Sister Martha and her children.
Two nephews William and James Allen.
Niece Martha Glasford and her children, viz., Elizabeth, Alexander, Jennet
and Ann, minors.
Bro. George.
Sister in law Ruth Hamilton.
Nephew Samuel Hamilton and niece Nancy Hamilton, minors.
Nephew James Hamilton.
Niece Martha Hamilton.
Exs.: Brice I. Sterrett and David Sterrett.
Wit.: William Montgomery, Benjamin Hamberger.   G. 206-207.

FAHNSTOCK, DANIEL, Juniata. 6 Dec 1800. 21 Feb 1807.
Wife Catharine.
Sons William and David.
Daus. Mary, Esther, Margareth and Barbara.
Minor children, Eleanor and Joseph.
Guardians for said two children Boreas Fahnstock and Samuel Fahnestock
(Peter's son).
Dau. Salome.
Exs.: Sons William and Daniel.

Wit.: Delwick Fahnstock, John H. Souter.   G. 208-210.

MC DOWELL, JOHN, Frankford. 15 March 1806. 5 March 1807.
Wife Mary.
Sons John and Samuel.
Daus. Rachel Espy, Margaret Mitchel and Mary Armstrong.
Son James McDowell.
Dau. Nancy Douglass.
Exs.: Son John McDowell.
Wit.: James Laird, Alexander Logan.   G. 211-212.

MITCHELL, SAMUEL, Shippensburgh. 5 Nov 1805. 9 March 1807.
Friend Samuel Cooper, son of John Cooper of Kishicoquilas.
Friend John McWhorry, minor son of Samuel McWhorry.
To nurse and friend Hannah Brown.
Nephew John Mitchell.
John Beatty, son in law of Samuel Whorry.
Samuel Whorry (the elder).
Exs.: Alexander Pebles of Southampton and Thomas McClellan, Junr., of Lurgan.
Wit.: William McConnell, John Scott. Robert Smith sworn to signature of John Scott.   G. 213-214.

CAMPBELL, JAMES, Frankford. 16 Feb 1807. 16 March 1807.
Niece Margaret Campbell, dau. of Robert Campbell.
Bro. Joseph Campbell.
Children of decd. bro. John.
Sister Mary Chrisher's children.
James Campbell, son of bro. Robert.
Bro. William Campbell's children.
Ex.: Bro. Robert Campbell.
Wit.: William Lindsay, James Laird, James Geddis.   G. 225.

POLLOCK, JOHN, Carlisle. 7 Jan 1807. 18 March 1807.
Wife Grace.
Eldest grandsons, John Pollock Morrison and Lucas Morrison, sons of Hance Morrison intermarried with dau. Margaret.
Ex.: Wife Grace Pollock.
Wit.: Geo. Logue, James Mitchell.   G. 226.

CULBERTSON, SAMUEL, Eastpennsborough. 24 Aug 1803. 4 April 1807.

Two sons, viz., William and James, minors.
Nephews William, James and John Johnston, minors.
Nieces Jean Johnston and Sally and Peggy Culbertson.
Friend John Culbertson (Fuller).
Exs.: Andrew Parker and Thomas Urie.
Wit.: Michl. Haak, Robert Anderson.   G. 227.

PHILIPS, MARY, East Pennsborough. 28 Jan 1807. 18 April 1807.
Sons John Philips and Peter Philips.
Land purchased by son Michael Philips, from Joseph and Catty Orris.
Daus., viz., Mary Orris, Catty Orris, Molly Clerk and Barbara Hopple, for use of their children.
Exs.: Andrew and Conrad Emminger.
Wit.: William Jameson, Thomas Walker.   G. 228.

DONALDSON, ALEXANDER, farmer, Eastpennsboro. 14 April 1807. 21 April 1807.
Wife Jean, sole heir.
Exs.: Wife Jean, bro. in law Alexander Cunningham and Robert Bell.
Wit.: Adam Beidleman, Elis Woodward.   G. 229.

MOFFITT, MARY, East Pennsborough. 1 July 1800. 7 May 1807.
Dau. Sidney intermarried with John Chain.
Land in Middleton Township in tenure of Wm. Armstrong, Andrew Armstrong and John Armstrong, the property of bro. Thomas Armstrong, decd., and two sisters Margaret Irvine decd. and Jane Moore decd.
Exs.: Dau. Sidney Chain and her husband John Chain.
Wit.: Jane Chambers, Wm. Chambers, Senr.   G. 230.

SCOULLER, JOHN, Mifflin. 3 Oct 1805. 17 May 1807.
Eldest dau. Agness, wife of John Wallace, plantation in Frankford Township called *Hickory Valley* where she now lives.
Land bought of Thomas Kenneday.
Land bought of Elenor Porter.
Dau. Margaret wife of James Young.
Son John.
Plantation and mills called *Big Run Mill* whereon we now live.
Dau. Mary wife of Joseph McKee.
Ex.: Son John Scouller.
Wit.: John Brown, Thomas Jacob, Joseph Jacob.   G. 231-232.

PINCHSMITH, HENRY, Juniatta. 5 Feb 1807. 22 May 1807.
Wife Charity.
Dau. Rebecca Pinchsmith married woman.
Ex.: Wife Charity Pinchsmith.
Wit.: John Holepeter, Thomas Gibson.   G. 233-234.

FOGLESONG, JACOB, Hopewell. 11 March 1807. 29 May 1807.
Wife Elizabeth.
Son Jacob.
Dau. Mary wife of Jacob Preeker.
Plantation in Hopewell Township bounded by lands of John Woods, John
Ober, John Myers, John Gibb, John Duncan and Casper Leisure.
Ex.: Son Jacob Foglesong.
Wit.: Caspar Lesure, David Lesher, John Woods.   G. 235.

KELSO, WILLIAM, yeoman, East Pennsborough. 7 April 1807. 6 June
1807.
Wife Elizabeth.
Three children, viz., William, Elinor and John Joseph, minors.
Land purchased of Thomas Fisher on Susquehanna River.
House in Harrisburg to be occupied by wife and children.
Sister Rebecca Kelso.
Bro. Joseph.
Guardian of children Robert Harris of Harrisburg, Esq.
Exs.: Wife Elizabeth Kelso and Robert Harris.
Wit.: Charles Rowan, Robert Harris.   G. 236-240.

GREGG, JOHN, Middleton. 21 June 1804. 9 June 1807.
Wife Elizabeth.
Dau. Sarah.
Sons Andrew and John.
Dau. Margery Curtin.
Grandsons Alexander Gregg, John McEwin and John McKee.
Dau. Mary Hackett.
Exs.: Wife Elizabeth and sons Andrew and John.
Wit.: Andrew Gregg, Geo. Loas, Danl. Yoh, Junr.   G. 241-242.

BLYTH, BENJAMIN, Senr., Southampton. 20 Oct 1801. 12 June 1807.
Son Benjamin, his sons and daus. and his present wife.
Son in law William Leeper, dau. Hannah Leeper, his wife and their children.
Son in law William Boyd, dau. Elizabeth, his wife.

Grandson Benjamin Boyd, minor son of dau. Elizabeth.
Granddau. Hannah Reynolus Blyth, minor dau. of son Jacob Blyth decd.
Grandsons Patrick Watson and Benjamin Blyth Watson, minor sons of dau.
Abigail Watson decd.
Granddaus. Margaret McCall and Abigail Watson, minor daus. of dau.
Abigail Watson decd.
Sons John and Samuel.
Estate of son in law John Reynolds, Esq., decd.
Exs.: Friends Samuel Mathers and David McKnight and grand son in law
John Shippen.
Wit.: Robert Peebles, John Shippen.   G. 243-249.

CRYSHER, JOHN, Southampton. 31 May 1806. 17 June 1807.
Wife Ketren.
Land purchased from Jacob Young and Patrick Diller.
Son Jacob and his brothers and sisters, viz., Mary, Elizabeth, David, John,
Daniel, Rosana and Rudolph, boys to be bound to trades.
Exs.: Bros. Daniel and George Mowers, Senr.
Wit.: Saml. McLean, James Hendricks.   G. 250.

STAGGERS, CONRAD, Greenwood. 3 May 1797. 29 June 1807.
Wife Mary.
Bro. John Staggers.
Bro. John's eldest son Jacob Staggers.
Rest of bro. John's children.
Exs.: Wife Mary Staggers and George Mitchell.
Wit.: William North, Adam Ruppert.   G. 251-252.

KNOX, JOHN. ---. 7 July 1807.
Wife Elizabeth, sole heir.
Exs.: Wife Elizabeth Knox and cousin Jonathan Walker, Esq.
Wit.: Jonathan Walker, Isaac Grier, James Williams.   G. 253.

RUNNELLS, RUTH, widow of John Runnells, Esq., Carlisle. 28 Feb 1807.
28 July 1807.
Sons Doctor William McCaskry and Dr. Samuel A. McCaskey.
James Duncan, Esq.
Ex.: Son Dr. Samuel A. McCaskry.
Wit.: James Duncan, George Clark.   G. 254-255.

COLLIER, HANNAH, Carlisle. 25 Oct 1804. 28 Sept 1807.

Niece Ann Herwick.
Bro. James Davis.
Ex.: Sd. niece Ann Herwick.
Wit.: Saml. Criswell, Hetty Criswell.   G. 256.

ROGERS, WILLIAM, farmer, Buffaloe. 25 Sept 1807. 1 Oct 1807.
Wife Margaret.
Son John Rogers and Jane Rogers.
Other heirs, names not given.
Ex.: Son John Rogers.
Wit.: Jame Porter, James Maxwell, Jacob Leidy.   G. 257.

HANNA, WILLIAM, Frankford. 14 March 1803. 7 Oct 1807.
Wife Mary.
Sons John, James and Samuel.
Daus. Elizabeth wife of John Reid, Sarah wife of William Gilmore, Lydia
married to Isaac Plunket and Ruth.
Dau. Sarah's son William.
Exs.: Son John Hanna and Alexander Leckey.
Wit.: John King, James Glendenning.   G. 258.

BOYD, WILLIAM, Newton. 26 Sept 1807. 7 Oct 1807.
Wife Abigail.
Minor children, names not given.
Exs.: Matthew Thompson and Adam Boyd.
Wit.: Hugh Thompson, William Thompson.   G. 259.

GRAHAM, JAMES, farmer, West Pennsborough. 25 Sept 1807. 7 Oct
1807.
Wife Susanna.
Granddau. Susanna Graham, dau. of son Jared Graham.
Sons James, Jared, Arthur and Isaiah.
Grandson James Arthur Graham's son.
Isaiah Graham's young son, if called James.
Exs.: Sons Jared, Arthur and Isaiah Graham.
Wit.: Richard Woods, Robt. McFarland, Junr., Jno. Dunbar.
                                                        G. 261-262.

ARMSTRONG, MARGARET, widow of Andrew Armstrong. 12 Feb 1805.
13 Oct 1807.
Son William Armstrong.

Grandson Andrew Armstrong, natural son of son Andrew Armstrong decd.
Exs.: Son John Armstrong and William Irvine of East Pennsborough
Township.
Wit.: George Wereheim, Conrad Wereheim, Joseph Junkin.   G. 263.

GOOD, PETER, West Pennsboro. 5 Sept 1807. 21 Oct 1807.
Wife Christine.
Son John.
Dau. Christine.
Other children, not named.
Children of decd. son Henry Good.
Exs.: Son in law Abraham Diller and John Bear.
Wit.: Andrew Heikes, Henry Rhein.   G. 264-265.

SILVER, JAMES, East Pennsboro. 10 Sept 1807. 3 Nov 1807.
Wife Jane.
Sons Francis and Morton.
Other children, names not given.
Exs.: Wife and John Carothers.
Wit.: James McGuire, Jane Story.   G. 266.

JUNKIN, BENJAMIN, East Pennsboro. 12 Oct 1805. 9 Nov 1807.
Wife.
Agreement with Samuel Feree for sale of plantation on which I now live.
Sons John and Joseph Junkin, now living with me, and Benjamin Junkin,
all minors.
Mary Davidson, mother of sd. sons, now living in Carlisle.
Agness Junkin, dau. of sd. Mary Davidson.
Bro. Joseph Junkin.
Exs.: Thomas Urie and Thomas Bell.
Wit.: James Lamberton, Geo. Wise, James Given.   G. 267-269.

BAUMAN, SAMUEL, East Pennsboro. 5 June 1802. 18 Nov 1807.
Wife Catherine.
Ground in Harrisburg, Dauphin Co.
Son Henry.
Plantation on Susquehanna River, Buffaloe Township.
Dau. Susanna, her husband and children.
Son John.
Exs.: Son John Bauman and Christian Mohler.
Wit.: Danl. Fahnestock, Obed Fahnestock, Benjn. Kutz.

147

G. 270-273.

SPADE, RACHEL, widow, Carlisle. 5 June 1807. 1 Dec 1807.
Son in law Frederick Shupp, and his dau. Elizabeth Shupp.
Grandson Samuel Miller, minor.
Three daus., viz., Mary wife of Frederick Shupp, Elizabeth wife of Jacob
Spong, Eve wife of Danl. Metsker.
Ex.: Frederick Shupp of Allen Township.
Wit.: Charles Taylor, William Bryson.   G. 274-275.

CRAIGHEAD, THOMAS, Middleton. 2 March 1805. 3 Dec 1807.
Wife Margaret.
Sons Richard and William, James, Thomas Craighead.
Land purchased of Saml. Postlethwaite, late Sheriff, the property of John
Patterson.
Dau. Rachel, wife of John Cooper.
Son John Craighead and his children.
Son George Craighead.
Bro. Revd. John Craighead, decd.
Exs.: Sons Richard and William Craighead.
Wit.: Jno. Miller, James Duncan.   G. 276-279.

HUNTER, WILLIAM, Allen. 16 June 1807. 19 Dec 1807.
Son Thomas.
Daus. Polly, Jane and Juliann.
Land bought of Christy Bowman, paper maker.
Exs.: Son Thomas Hunter and James Dunlap.
Wit.: C. Quigley, John McDaniel.   G. 280-281.

IRVIN, EGNESS, East Pennsborough. 24 Feb 1806. 26 Dec 1807.
Granddau. Egness Irvin, dau. to John Irvin and her sister Jane Irvin.
Son Armstrong Irvin.
Exs.: John Armstrong and John Douglass.
Wit.: William Armstrong, Francis Johnston.   G. 282.

WITMORE, JOHN, Middleton. 23 Dec 1806. 2 Jan 1808.
Son Jacob.
Dau. Elizabeth wife of Isaac Young.
Daus. Esther and Anne.
Son Abraham.
Exs.: Son Abraham and dau. Esther.

148

Wit.: Peter Hetrick, George Logue. G. 283.

MAXWELL, WILLIAM. 16 Feb 1807. 4 Jan 1808.
Wife Sarah.
Son David Maxwell, a minor.
Sons George, William, John and James Maxwell.
Daus. Catherine Maxwell, Mary Maxwell, Sarah Maxwell and Elizabeth Maxwell.
Grandchildren William Johnston and Sarah Johnston.
Son in law George Johnston.
Grandson Samuel McKey, minor.
Exs.: Wife Sarah Maxwell and son William Maxwell.
Wit.: William Hunter, Robt. Quigley, Wm. Sheilds. G. 284-285.

JONES, ISAAC, yeoman, Rye. 10 Nov 1806. 27 Jan 1808.
Wife Priecla.
Dau. Sarah, a minor.
Son Robert.
Dau. Martha.
Son Cadawalader.
Exs.: Wife, son Robert and Robert Wallace.
Wit.: Robert Fulton, Esq., (Rev.) Joseph Brady, b.D.M.

G. 286-287.

BROWN, MARY, widow, Carlisle. ---. 28 Jan 1808.
Dau. Lucy Brown.
Sons William and Thompson.
Exs.: James Duncan, Esq., and son William Brown.
Wit.: Philip Wiant, John B. Gibson. G. 288.

MC ALLISTER, JOHN, Tyrone. 12 Jan 1808. 8 Feb 1808.
Sons John and Hugh.
Daus. Betty Gormly and Sarah McAllister.
Grandchildren the children of dau. Betsy intermarried with Abraham Gormly and the children of sons Hugh.
Exs.: Son Hugh McAllister, David Roble and John McClure, all of Tyrone Township.
Wit.: Peter Stroup, William Bitner, Wilson McClure. G. 289-290.

LONDON, WILLIAM, Buffalo. 18 Sept 1807. 16 Feb 1808.
Sons John and Jacob.

149

Daus. Elizabeth, now Elizabeth Gray, Catherine, now Catherine Steele.
Sons Thomas, Stophel and Henry.
Exs.: Son Henry Lowdon.
Wit.: Samuel Campbell, Peter Williamson.   G. 292-293.

CAMPBELL, WILLIAM, weaver, Toboyne. 27 April 1807. 16 Feb 1808.
Son William.
Isabella Holliday, Margaret Nickle (Nichols), Elizabeth Doke and Jane
Campbell, my granddaus. daus. to son William Campbell.
Exs.: Sons John Campbell and William Campbell.
Wit.: William Anderson, Elizabeth Campbell, William Thompson.
                                                            G. 291.

WERNS, JACOB, Dickenson. 5 March 1805. 18 March 1808.
Children, viz., George Werns and Catherine Painter.
Children of dau. Barbara, decd., wife of Abram Andrews, viz., Peggy
Andrews, Abraham, Samuel, Joseph, Jacob, George and Catherine
Andrews.
Trustee for sd. children Adam Houke.
Mary Werns, widow of son Philip, decd.
Three daus. of sd. son Philip Werns, decd.
Ex.: George Gilbert.
Wit.: John Moore, Junr., Matthew Moore.
Codicil: 11 April 1807.
Wit.: Peter Duey, D. Watts.   G. 294-296.

MC CLINTOCK, WILLIAM, Toboyne. 1 Jan 1800. 25 April 1808.
Dau. Elizabeth Huffard.
Sons William McClintock and Joseph McClintock.
Dau. Jean Buchanan.
Ex.: Son Joseph McClintock.
Wit.: William Adams, Enoch Anderson.   G. 297-298.

HUNTER, JANE, Frankford. 7 June 1805. 31 March 1808.
Dau. Mary Walker.
Son John Graham.
Son William Hunter.
Dau. Jane Baird and her dau. Jane Trotter.
Son Joseph Hunter.
Dau. Sarah McIntire, her father the late Wm. Hunter, decd.
Ex.: Son William Hunter of Southampton Township.

Wit.: William Richey, John Dunbar.   G. 299-300.

FISHER, PHILIP, Mifflin. 29 Dec 1806. 4 April 1808.
Children, viz., Elizabeth Bell, Kitty Wolf, Maryann, John Fisher, Maria Elouser and Christiana Fisher.
Exs.: John Fisher and Walter Bell.
Wit.: Hugh Smith, James Pettigrew.   G. 301.

MC FARLANE, JAMES, farmer, West Pennsborough. 5 Dec 1807. 16 Jan 1808.
Wife Elizabeth.
Son Robert.
Dau. Jane intermarried with James Davidson.
Other children, viz., John, William, Margaret, James, Samuel, Clemence, Eliza and Polly.
Some of children minors.
Exs.: Wife Elizabeth, son Robert McFarlane and son in law James Davidson.
Wit.: John Geddis, John Davidson.   G. 302-303.

EICHELBERGER, CHRISTOPHER, Allen. 26 Feb 1807. 1 May 1808.
Wife Barbara.
Sons George, Adam and John.
Daus. Barbara and Sarah.
Plantation adjoining lands of late Ludwig Weaver, Frederick Long, Gideon Coover, Christopher Cromlick, Martin Houser, Joseph and Hays Brooks and Nicholas Kifeike.
Son Jacob.
Daus. Anna, Maria, Elizabeth, Catherine and Eve.
Exs.: Sons Jacob, George and Adam Eichelberger.
Wit.: Soloman Gorgas, Christopher Gromlick, J. Eichelberger.
                                                      G. 304-307.

SMITH, HUGH, Middleton. 16 March 1808. 4 April 1808.
Bro. James Smith.
Niece Jane Criswell wife of James Criswell.
Niece Mary McCoy wife of William McCoy.
Bro. Dr. William Smith of Montgomery Co.
Niece Nancy wife of Michael Ruppert of Middleton Township.
Nephew William Smith son of bro. Robert Smith.
Niece Jane Smith dau. of bro. Robert.

Silver sugar tongs to be made by Robert Guthrie.
Apprentice girl, Matilda Moore.
Bros. Robert Smith and Brice Smith.
Sister Mary Williams widow of Edward Williams decd.
James Driswell and Wm. McCoy, both off Lewestown, Penna.
Exs.: Bro. Robert Smith and Joseph Clark and John Irvine, both of
Middleton Township.
Wit.: Andrew Carothers, William Drennon, David Elliott.

G. 308-311.

HULINGS, THOMAS, farmer, Buffaloe. 1 March 1808. 5 April 1808.
Wife Rebecca.
Son Mack (Mark) Hulings. Other children, viz., Rebecca, Mary, Frederick,
David, Elinor and Elizabeth Hulings and a child unborn.
Exs.: Wife Rebecca Hulings and David Watts.
Wit.: William Irvine, Joseph Duncan, Andrew Herster, James Elliott.

G. 312.

NEIL, JAMES. 25 Feb 1803. 6 April 1808.
Wife Sarah.
Two sons John and James.
Daus. Sarah, Marion and Peggy.
Exs.: Wife Sarah Neil and son John Neil.
Wit.: Robert Criswell, John Woodburn.   G. 313-315.

MC CULLOCK, JOHN, West Pennsborough. 20 Feb 1807. 8 April 1808.
Wife.
Sons William, James and John.
Land in Dickenson Township, known by name of *Union*, on Yellow
Breeches Creek, joining lands of John Arthur and Thomas Patterson.
Place known as *McCullock's Fancy* where I now live, adjoining Jacob
Myers.
Dau. Elizabeth wife of Robert McCormick.
Land in Southampton Township adjoining James Clark bought from
Honorable John Penn.
Dau. Margaret married to James Hill.
Dau. Sarah married to Richard Patton.
Dau. Jean married to James McKinstrey.
Granddaus. Isabella and Sarah Mitchell.
Zekiel Mitchell.
Jean Fisher.

Exs.: Sons James McCullock and William McCullock.
Wit.: Atcheson Laughlin, John Davidson, James Luaghlin.

G. 316-318.

PATTERSON, JAMES, yeoman, Newton. 9 June 1807. 19 April 1808.
Wife Catherine.
Son in law and dau. Matthew Kyle and Jemima Kyle.
Land to line of Michael Seever, John Moore, Senr., Balzar Whitman, Francis Fulton.
Steve and Joseph Goard.
Children of sd. Matthew and Jemima Kyle, minors.
Grandson Joseph Kyle.
Granddau. Elizabeth Kyle.
Son Robert Patterson.
Exs.: Nephews John Means and James Means.
Wit.: Joseph Goard, Wm. McDonald.

G. 319-322.

ESPY, THOMAS, Frankford. 1 Dec 1807. 16 May 1808.
Wife Anne.
Sons William and James.
Daus. Margaret Wilson and Rachel Bell.
Son Robert.
Daus. Elizabeth and Jane.
Exs.: Wife Anna and son Robert.
Wit.: James Laird, Joseph Crawford.

G. 323-324.

WAGGONER, JACOB, Middleton. 2 May 1808. 31 May 1808.
Wife Catherine.
Sons Jacob and Abraham.
Daus. Catherine married to Christian Hake, Mary married to Jacob Wolf and Margaret married to Philip Wolf.
Sons Philip and George Waggoner.
Exs.: Son Jacob Waggoner and Christian Hackedorn.
Wit.: Wm. Brown, Saml. Postlethwaite.

G. 325.

ROSS, SIMON (the Elder), Newton. 27 April 1808. 18 June 1808.
Wife Margaret.
Son James.
Daus. Jane married to Samuel Barber, Sarah wife of James Garret, Ruth wife to John Patterson and Mary wife to William Ramsey.
Sons Robert, Simon, Samuel and Ebenezer, a minor.

Dau. Peggy.
Step dau. Elinor Garret.
Exs.: Son Simon Ross and John Woodburn.
Wit.: James Paxton, Charles Gray.   G. 326-328.

WALKER, WILLIAM, farmer, Newton. 10 Sept 1804. 4 Aug 1808.
Wife Jane.
Daus. Elizabeth, Isabella wife of Samuel Walker, Mary wife of James
Walker, Rachel wife of William Brown and Jane.
Grandson William Walker son of above mentioned James Walker.
Three sons James, William and Samuel.
Exs.: Said sons James Walker, William Walker, Saml. Walker.
Wit.: William Richey, Thomas Jacob.   G. 329.

SMITH, CATHERINE, widow, Middleton. 4 Jan 1808. 16 June 1808.
Bro. Luke Shalley.
Nephew Valentine Shalley son of sd. Luke.
John Ludwig Boyer, minor son of Elizabeth Shalley.
Nephew Adam Shalley son of Christian Shalley.
Exs.: Jacob Crever and Jacob Whitmore.
Wit.: John Jinkins, Thomas Harwood.   G. 330-331.

QUIGLEY, WILLIAM, East Pennsborough. 15 Feb 1808. 6 Aug 1808.
Wife.
Children Polly Adams, Andrew, Betsy, and Anna Quigley.
Exs.: Son Andrew Quigley and John Orr.
Wit.: David Bell, Wm. Jameson.   G. 332.

HYDE, ELIZABETH, Allen. 28 May 1808. 22 Aug 1808.
Sons Adam Hyde and Abraham Hyde.
Dau. Juliann Fleming.
Grandson John Smith.
Other heirs Elizabeth Weaver, Catherine Gromlick, Margaret Rosh, John
Hyde, Mary Hailman, Michael Hyde, Christiana Weaver and Abraham
Hyde.
Exs.: Jacob Gromlick and Abraham Smith.
Wit.: John Wallace, Jacob Meyer.   G. 333-334.

HANNA, SAMUEL, Hopewell. 27 July 1808. 6 Sept 1808.
Wife Agness.
Dau. Jean White.

Son Samuel.

Two grandsons James and Samuel Sterrett, dau. Polly's sons.

Other children, Elizabeth Sterrett, David's wife, Rachel Trimble, Nancy Williamson, Martha Sharp and Sarah White.

Exs.: Wife Agness Hanna, son Samuel Hanna and son in law James Sharp.
Wit.: Ludw. Miller, James Pettigrew.   G. 335-336.

MC DONALD, MARGARET, Big Spring. 24 May 1805. 13 Sept 1808.
Dau. Sarah McDonald.
Son James McDonald.
Exs.: None named.
Wit.: James McCandlish, Saml. McDonald.
Adtor: William Reed.   G. 337.

CLARK, JOHN, farmer, Toboyne. 25 Sept 1807. 4 Oct 1808.
Wife Sarah.
Sons John, James and dau. Susanna, minors.
Exs.: Robert Adams and William McGuire.
Wit.: Bailey Long, Thomas Wallace.   G. 338-339.

MONTGOMERY, JOHN, Carlisle. 18 Sept 1800. 10 Oct 1808.
Wife Sarah.
Daus. Sidney Montgomery, Esther married to James Morrison, Jean married to Saml. Edmiston, Sarah married to David Harris.
Sons Doctr. William Montgomery and John Montgomery, Esq.
Grandson John, son of Samuel Edmiston.
Place called *Happy Retreat*.
Daus. Mary and Margaret.
Minor sons Thomas and James.
Exs.: Son John Montgomery, John Creigh, Robert Miller and James Duncan, Esqs.
Wit.: Robert Davidson, Saml. Laird, Thomas Duncan.   G. 340-342.

ARMPRESTOR, JACOB, yeoman, Middleton. 7 July 1807. 11 Oct 1808.
Eldest son William.
Granddau. Catherine dau. of son William Armprestor.
Exs.: Jacob Wetzel.
Wit.: John Goudy, Jacob Cornman, John Cornman.   G. 343-344.

MITCHELL, SAMUEL, Mifflin. 28 Sept MDCCCVIII. 27 Oct 1808.
Wife Mary.

155

Oldest son John.
Youngest son James.
Dau. Margaret.
Exs.: None given.
Wit.: None given.
Adtor: John Mitchell.   G. 345-346.

ENGLISH, ANDREW, Rye. 10 Jan 1788. 7 Nov 1808.
To son.
To dau. Elizabeth.
To the old woman and her dau. Ketren.
Exs.: Robert Burns and John McBride.
Wit.: Robert Burns, John McBride.   G. 347.

MC KINZEY, JOHN, Rye. 27 Sept 1808. 8 Nov 1808.
Wife Elizabeth.
Sons John and Thomas.
Other children Samuel, Daniel, Margaret, Ann, Mary and Betsy Brady, all
under twenty-one yrs. of age.
Exs.: Wife Elizabeth and son John.
Wit.: Moses Kirkpatrick,, Alexander Rodgers.   G. 348-349.

REDETT, JOHN, tanner, Shippensburgh. 1 Nov 1804. 9 Nov 1808.
Wife Catherine.
Sons Samuel and John, minors.
Daus. Elizabeth Duncan, Sophia and Catherine.
Farm in Franklin Co.
Land in Buffalo Valley, Northumberland Co.
Exs.: Wife, son in law John Duncan and son in law Abraham Beidleman, all
of Shippensburgh.
Wit.: John Rippey, William Bailey.   G. 350-351.

ROSS, ELIZABETH, Tyrone. 11 April 1807. 30 Nov 1808.
Dau. Elizabeth.
Dau. Mary Ross.
Ex.: Robert Robb of Tyrone Township.
Wit.: Wilson McClure.   G. 352-353.

HENRY, GODFRIED, Carlisle. Non Cupative Will. 10 Oct 1808. 16 Dec
1808.
Only heir, Elizabeth Woodward.

156

Sd. Godfried Henry, died 27 Oct 1808.
Wit.: Jacob Keigley, Stophel Gould. G. 354.

FULWILER, MARY, Tyrone. 15 Nov 1803. 3 Jan 1809.
Sons John and William.
Dau. Mary.
Dau. Mary Lefever, a minor (granddau.?)
Exs.: Son Abraham.
Wit.: Thomas Simonton, Abraham Kistler. G. 355-356.

RIPPEY, MARGARET, single woman, Shippensburg. 3 Dec 1808. 5 Jan 1809.
Father Samuel Rippey, decd.
To mother, farm in Franklin Co.
Niece Margaret Rippey, dau. of bro. John Rippey.
Niece Mary Ann Rippey, dau. of bro. Armstrong Rippey.
Niece Mary Findley Bailey, dau. of sister Isabella Bailey.
Aunt Elizabeth Rippey, widow of Uncle Elijah Rippey.
Land near Strasburgh.
Bro. Armstrong Rippey.
Sisters Harriott and Molly Rippey.
Ex.: William Scott of Southampton Township, Franklin Co.
Wit.: William Devor, John Rippey. G. 357-358.

BLACK, JAMES, Juniatta. 30 Dec 1808. 12 Jan 1809.
Sons John and William.
Daus. Mary, Jane, Rebecca, Abigail, a minor, and Sally, a minor.
Three youngest sons, minors, viz., James, Jonathan and George.
Dau. Nancy intermarried with Robert Elliott.
Dau. Jane, decd.
Exs.: Sons John Black, William Black and Thomas Simonton.
Wit.: Amos Jordan, Francis Jordan. G. 359-361.

REED, JAMES, Carlisle. 27 Dec 1808. 21 Jan 1809.
Wife Hannah.
Son John Reed.
Sons in law Levi Hollingsworth and Jacob Weaver, Junr.
Three sons, viz., James, George and Robert Reed.
Exs.: Wife Hannah, Levi Hollingsworth and Jacob Weaver.
Wit.: Geo. Crean, Geo. Logue. H. 1.

LYON, SAMUEL, farmer, Middleton. ---. 8 Feb 1809.
Eldest dau. Margaret Blaine married woman.
Second dau. Isabella Hoge married woman.
Eldest son John.
Daus. Agness Lyon and Rebecca Lyon.
Son Samuel or his guardian.
Exs.: Son John Lyon and friend Wm. Alexander, Esq.
Wit.: None given.
Handwriting sworn to be David Watts, Esq. and William Ramsey, Esq.
H. 1-2.

ELLIOTT, MARY, Carlisle, formerly of Maguire's Bridge in the Kingdom
of Ireland. 27 Jan 1809. 15 Feb 1809.
To Mary Crumer wife of John Crumer.
Anne and Elizabeth Maguaran. Henry Magauran.
Margaret Noble widow of the late John Noble and her daus. Marget,
Elizabeth and Anne.
Mary Noble niece of sd. John Noble.
Two nieces Margaret and Jane Johnston and nephew, their bro., Gustavus
Johnston.
Exs.: Edward Maugausan of Carlisle.
Wit.: Francis C. Campbell, Ags. Jordan, Alexr. Woods. H. 3.

WILSON, GRIZZEL, Allen. 8 Feb 1809. 17 Feb 1809.
Dau. Isabella Sterret.
Son Hugh.
Dau. Jane Wilson.
Exs.: Son Hugh Wilson and nephew John Black.
Wit.: A. Wills, Isable Wilson. H. 3-4.

MORRISON, ROBERT, farmer, Middleton. 27 May 1806. 20 Feb 1809.
Wife Mary.
Friend John Steel, Senr.
Amelia Given wife of James Given, merchant in Carlisle.
Nephew William Jackson.
To Lydia Sanderson.
Martha Huston.
James Lamberton.
To Nancy Dodds indentured girl.
Son John, decd.
Dau. Lydia, decd.

William Steel and John Steel, Junr., sons of John Steel, Esq.
Joseph Given minor son of James Given.
Exs.: James Lamberton, Esq. and James Given of Carlisle.
Wit.: Andrew Crocket, Thos. Foster, Jacob Hendel.   H. 5-6.

HOUSER, MARTIN, farmer, Allen. 1 Nov 1807. 11 March 1809.
Wife Mary.
Seven children, viz., Jacob, John a minor, Elizabeth married to Joseph
Pesh, Catherine, Anna, Sarah and Barbara.
Plantation in York Co. known as *Conrey's Place.*
Plantation in Cumberland Co. known as *Wallace's Place.*
Where I now live known by name of *Freidley's.*
Exs.:   Son Jacob Houser, Joseph Pesh and George Snevely of East
Pennsbro., son of John Snevely decd.
Wit.: Jno. Downey, Daniel Houser.   H. 7-9.

LYON, WILLIAM, Carlisle. 3 Oct 1805. 16 March 1809.
Son Alexander.
Daus. Mary and Alice Lyon.
Other sons James, John, William, Samuel and George A. Lyon.
Dau. Margaret Denny wife of Rev. David Denny.
Exs.: Sons John, Samuel, Alexander and George A. Lyon.
Wit.: George Pattison, Chas. Pattison.   H. 9-11.

WISE, GEORGE, yeoman, Mifflin. 1 Feb 1809. 23 March 1809.
Children, viz., Catherine wife of Henry Railing, George Wise, Elizabeth
Wise, Mary Wise and Michael Wise, a minor.
Exs.: Friend Felix Wise and Yost Railing.
Wit.: John Railing, John Houser.   H. 11-12.

CANNING, CHARLES, Dickinson. 11 Nov 1802. 5 April 1809.
Wife Jean.
Minor children, names not given.
Exs.: Wife Jean Canning.
Wit.: Andw. Huston, Wm. McDonald.   H. 13.

SMITH, JOHN, Mifflin. 2 Feb ---. 5 April 1809.
Daus. Hannah Hanna and Sarah Williams.
Son John Thomas Smith, a minor.
John C. Hanna.
To Jane B. Falkner her mother's wearing apparel.

To John Steen of Carlisle my wearing apparel.
Exs.: James Lamberton, William Levis and John C. Hanna.
Wit.: William Meffit (Maffit), John Mitchell.
Codicil: 22 Feb 1809.
Wit.: John Thompson.   H. 14-15.

MC CORMICK, ROBERT, Eastpennsbro. 23 March 1808. 22 April 1809.
Bro. James McCormick, Esq.
Children of bro. William McCormick, decd., viz., James and Margaret when
sixteen years of age.
Exs.: Bro. James McCormick.
Wit.: John Walker.   H. 16.

MC CLELLAND, THOMAS, Hopewell. 19 March 1808. 30 May 1809.
Wife Jannet.
Dau. Margaret.
Sons Thomas, Robert, William and Joseph.
Daus. Susanna and Elizabeth.
Ex.: Son Joseph McClelland.
Wit.: John Whorry, David McKinney, Junr.
Codicil: 14 April 1809.
Heirs of son James McClelland, decd.
Heirs of dau. Jean Mitchell, decd.
Wit.: John Whorry, Joseph Shannon.   H. 16-17.

WALKER, JOHN, farmer, Newton. 4 Dec 1808. 23 May 1809.
Sister Peggy Walker.
Bro. Robert Walker.
Sisters Polly Crowell and Betsy Enslow.
Exs.: Friends Thomas Jacob of Mifflin and Atcheson Laughlin of West
Pennsborough Townships.
Wit.: Jno. Geddis, William Brown.   H. 18.

REES, SIMON, Shippensburgh. 1 May 1807. 12 June 1809.
Wife Barbara.
Jacob Kerer son of dau. Sarah.
Daus. Anna, Mary, Elizabeth, Sarah and Margaret.
Exs.: John Shetler and Jacob Rhaum of Shippensburg.
Wit.: John Snider, John Kayler.   H. 19.

BROTHERTON, ELISHA, brazier, Donington in the Co. of Lincoln. 3 April 1801. 17 Aug 1809.
Wife Jane.
Freehold and copyhold, messauges, lands &c. situate and being in Donington, aforesd.
Ex.: Wife Jane Brotherton.
Wit.: J. Gleed, Rd. Gleed, Elizabeth Hickenbotham.
The will of Elisha Brotherton, late of Carlisle, legally proved on the principles of lasting "legal proof," as all the subscribing witnesses resided in England. H. 20.

BROWN, LUCY, Carlisle. 10 Aug 1809. 22 Aug 1809.
Bros. Arthur, George, William and Thompson.
Exs.: Bros. William Brown and Thompson Brown and friend James Duncan.
Wit.: Philip Wiant, Andrew Boden. H. 21.

KIMMEL, MARGARET, Tyrone. 1 March 1806. 12 Sept 1809.
Son Anthony.
Dau. Catherine Elizabeth Kimmel wife of Daniel Clark.
Granddau. Molly Foulk dau. of Peter Foulk.
Son Jacob Kimmel.
Dau. Margaret Kimmel wife of Peter Martin.
Ex.: Son Anthony Kimmel
Wit.: Wilson McClure. H. 21-22.

ORNER, ELIZABETH, widow, Greenwood. 7 March 1807. 10 Oct 1809.
Three sons, viz., Abraham Orner, Martin Orner, and John Orner.
Six daus., viz., Elizabeth, Mary, Susan, Sarah, Ann and Margaret.
Three children of dau. Mary by her first husband John Fryberger.
Exs.: George Rombaugh and Jacob Caufman.
Wit.: Christian Stemah, Fredk. Harter. H. 22.

RAUM, JACOB, Shippensburgh. 9 May 1808. 6 Nov 1809.
Wife Barbara.
Son John.
Ex.: Son John Raum.
Wit.: Saml. McClure, George Croft, John Scott. H. 23-24.

COOMBE, SAMUEL, of Co. Seneca, State of New York, presently in Borough of Carlisle. 23 Nov 1809. 12 Dec 1809.

Wife Hannah.
Son Peter.
Dau. Hannah intermarried with Daniel Jennings.
Exs.: Son Peter Coombe and friend Peter Smith, Junr., both of Seneca Co.,
New York.
Wit.: John Boden, Andrew Boden.   H. 25.

LAIRD, ANN, Allen. 6 Dec 1805. 28 Dec 1809.
Son William Laird.
Granddau. Ann McMeen.
Son Arthur Laird.
Dau. Jenny McMeen and granddau. Grizzel McMeen.
Exs.: Son James Laird and Benjamin Anderson.
Wit.: John Lutes, James Legget, Junr.   H. 26.

STAHL, ABRAHAM, Toboyne. 23 June 1808. 6 Nov 1809.
Dau. Margaret Stahl.
Four sons Peter, John, Abraham and William Stahl, two youngest minors.
Sons in law Peter Salsbury and George Geese.
Exs.: John Fusselman and Peter Salsbury.
Wit.: John Wack, Daniel Bloom.   H. 27-28.

WOLFF, CONRAD, Mifflin. 11 Nov 1809. 5 Dec 1809.
Son Jacob.
Dau. Mary wife of John Zellner.
Sons Peter, John Conrad and John.
Other children, viz., Mary Barbara wife of John Houser, Ann Mary wife of
John Reinert, Ann Elizabeth wife of Frederick Hoover, sons Michael,
Joseph and John Henry, dau. Ann Catherine and son Daniel.
Ex.: Son in law Henry Dalhousen.
Wit.: Thomas McCormick, James McFarlin.   H. 29.

MC FARLAND, MARGARET, West Pennsbro. 25 Nov 1809. 3 Jan 1810.
Dau. Mary married to John Scot.
Dau. Ann married to John Johnston.
Nees Peggy McFarlane.
Daus. Jenny married to William Thompson, Margaret married to Hugh
McClelland and Elizabeth wife of Thomas Walleis (Wallace).
Dau. in law Elizabeth McFarland.
To Samuel Myers for heirs of James McFarlane decd.
Exs.: William Thompson and James Davidson.

Wit.: John Dunbar, Isa. Graham.
Codicil: 17 Dec 1809.
Now of Newton Township.
Nephew Arthur Graham one of Exs.
Wit.: Hugh Thompson, Isaiah Graham.   H. 30-31.

POLLOCK, ELLINOR, widow of John Pollock, Carlisle. 29 Aug 1809. 5 Jan 1810.
Sister Elizabeth McDonnel widow of John McDonnel decd.
Daus. in law, viz., Ellinor Armstrong wife of James Armstrong and Jean Pollock wife of Alexander Pollock.
Exs.: James Duncan and Edward Magauran.
Wit.: Geo. Crean, Joseph Egolf.   H. 32.

TAYLOR, SUSANNAH, Juniata. 13 May 1809. 17 Feb 1810.
Dau. Elizabeth intermarried with Edward O'Donnall.
Son Mordecai Dougherty.
Dau. Nancy intermarried with Michael Robinson.
Exs.: Son Mordecai Dougherty and Edward O'Donnall.
Wit.: Thomas Simonton, Cloud Donnelly.   H. 32-33.

HOLMES, ANDREW, Carlisle. 20 May 1809. 12 March 1810.
Wife Jane.
Daus. Sarah Blair and Mary Holmes as long as they remain unmarried.
Sons Thomas and Andrew.
Grandchildren William Blair, Andrew Blair, Henry Blair and Jane Blair.
Granddaus. Elizabeth and Jane Patterson.
Grandsons Holmes and George Patterson.
Children of son Thompson Holmes.
Children of late dau. Margaret Thompson.
James son of son Abraham Holmes decd.
Children of son Thomas Holmes.
Dau. Nancy and her husband George Patterson.
Son in law John Thompson of Frederick Town.
Exs.: Friends Samuel Postlethwaite and Jno. McClure.
Wit.: John Miller, Chas. Patterson.   H. 33-35.

JONES, THOMAS, bricklayer, Carlisle. 12 Feb 1810. 13 March 1810.
Wife Agness.
Nephew Thomas Jones.

Exs.: John Gray, merchant and tallow chandler, and Melchor Hoffer, cooper, Carlisle.
Wit.: James Elliott, George Coffman, Valentine Wengert. H. 35.

CRAVEN, ISAAC, Millerstown, Greenwood. 22 Jan 1810. 3 April 1810.
Sarah Craven and Edith Craven, minor daus. of James and Rachel Craven of Millerstown.
Their aunt Anna Wright.
Thomas son of sd. James and Rachel Craven.
His uncle Azzar Wright.
Friend Ephraim Williams.
Uncle James Craven.
Exs.: Caleb North and Henry Leyman.
Wit.: Anthony Brandt, David Foutz, James Beaty. H. 36.

KENNEDAY, JOHN, Teboin. 13 Dec 1808. 7 April 1810.
Wife.
Daus. Isabel and Ketty.
Sons Richard, Thomas, John and William.
Daus. Ann, Betty and Peggy.
Exs.: Wife and friend David Bell.
Wit.: William Martin, George Bryner. H. 37.

WOLF, GEORGE, East Pennsborough. 24 Jan 1810. 10 April 1810.
Wife Leah.
Two daus. Mary Wolf and Elizabeth Wolf.
Another child, name not given.
All minors.
Ex.: Friend John Mumma.
Wit.: Saml. McHarry, Jacob Eppley. H. 38.

COOVER, GIDEON, yeoman, Allen. 6 Aug 1803. 3 May 1810.
Wife Freany.
Dau. Salome wife of Martin Brenizer.
Sons George, Samuel, Adam, David and Jacob.
Dau. Catherine.
Exs.: Sons George Coover and Adam Coover.
Wit.: James Whitehill, Adam Long. H. 39-41.

SCOTT, WILLIAM, Carlisle. 23 April 1810. 5 May 1810.
Wife Mary.

Son Joseph Scott, a minor.
Ex.: Wife Mary Scott.
Wit.: James Cameron, James Love, Saml. Postlethwaite.   H. 41.

MOLTZS, GEORGE, yeoman, East Pennsborough.
Sons George and Daniel.
Land in Westmoreland Co.
Dau. Elizabeth wife of John Stoner.
Grandsons Christian Stoner and John Stoner, minors.
Sons John, David and Henry.
Dau. Barbara wife of Barnet Mass.
Exs.: Jacob Wormly and sons Jacob and John Moltzs.
Wit.: John Rupley, Jacob Eichelberger.   H. 42.

DUNBAR, JOHN, Carlisle. 4 Dec 1809. 5 June 1810.
Wife Jane.
Plantation in West Pennsborough.
Son William.
Children of son William Dunbar.
Children of dau. Margaret who intermarried with Thomas Urie.
Dau. Eleanor wife of Dr. John Creigh.
Exs.: Wife, son in law John Creigh and Andrew Carothers, Esq., of Carlisle.
Wit.: William Alexander, Saml. Postlethwaite.   H. 43.

CHAIN, SIDNEY, widow, Middleton. 10 May 1810. 16 June 1810.
Son John chain, minor.
Land in Middleton Township adjoining lands of John Hetrick, John Armstrong and the Courdrguinet Creek.
To Miss Jane Chambers.
Exs. and Guardians of son John: Friends John Chambers and John Irvine of Middleton.
Wit.: Yofan Miller, Christian Coble.   H. 44-46.

CRISWELL, SAMUEL, Carlisle. 11 June 1810. 26 June 1810.
Wife Marget.
Children Mary, Robert and Ginny.
Other children, viz., Hetty, Betsy and Wilhelmina.
Exs.: Wife Marget and dau. Mary.
Wit.: Charles Patterson, Moses Bullock.   H. 46.

CAROTHERS, REBECCA. 18 June 1810. 2 July 1810.

Isabella Dinnen dau. of Francis Dinnen.
To sd. Francis Dinnen.
Rebecca Workman dau. of Saml. and Margery Workman, minor.
Rebecca Noble dau. of sister Isabella Noble, minor.
Sister Mary Greason wife of James Greason.
Exs.: James Greason and John Carothers of West Pennsborough.
Wit.: Mary Carothers, Jean Carothers, Agness Gresson.   H. 47.

RHINE, JOHN, innkeeper, Carlisle. 11 Feb 1809. 19 July 1810.
Wife Margaret.
Margaret Cart, minor dau. of Jacob Cart (butcher) of Carlisle.
Daus. of Catherine Miller wife of Jacob Miller.
Daus. of Philippina Smith wife of Tobias Smith.
Daus. of Catherine Phit wife of --- Phit.
Daus. of Henry Grice.
Exs.: Wife Margaret, George Hendel and Wm. Ramsey.
Wit.: Thompson Brown, Joseph Hays, Geo. Brown.   H. 48-49.

SULENBERGER, JOSEPH, Tyrone. 17 March 1803. 27 July 1810.
Wife Anna Elizabeth.
Son Henry.
Dau. Elizabeth wife of Peter Bens (Bentz).
Dau. Catherine wife of John McGlocklin.
Children of son Jacob decd.
Exs.: Adam Markle and Jacob Smith.
Wit.: George Stroop, George Olfingher.   H. 50.

LEE, THOMAS, Dickinson. 25 March 1808. 28 July 1810.
Wife Mary.
Son Thomas.
Daus. Elizabeth, Margaret and Mary.
Thomas McIntire.
Exs.: Son Thomas Lee and nephew Holliday Lee.
Wit.: Abraham Line, William Line, John Lee.   H. 51.

WASHMUTH, MARTIN, West Pennsbro. 15 June 1810. 28 July 1810.
Wife Elizabeth.
Children, minors, names not given.
Exs.: Andrew Hickes and John Bear.
Wit.: Samuel Reslor, Henry Weigle.   H. 52-54.

ROBINSON, WILLIAM, Juniatta. 26 April 1810. 2 Aug 1810.
Wife Sarah.
Son George.
Daus. Nancy and Hannah Robinson.
Sons John, William, Joseph, Michael, Robert and James.
Sarah Davis.
Dau. Mary Minshall.
Ex.: Son George Robinson.
Wit.: Wm. Linn, Jerh. Jordan, James Beatty.   H. 54-55.

MC COY, ALEXANDER, yeoman, Rye. 7 March 1810. 6 Aug 1810.
Wife Sarah.
Children, names not given.
Exs.: Wife Sarah and bro. in law Robert Fulton of Rye.
Wit.: Robert Thompson, James McCoy.   H. 56.

BECKER (BAKER), JOHN, Middleton. 29 Sept 1806. 15 Aug 1810.
Wife Catharina.
Four sons William, George, Philip and Martin, minors.
Plantation purchased from John Creigh, Esq., and Ross Mitchell.
Plantation in Rapho Township, Lancaster Co., adjoining land of Widow
Reigh, Jacob Meshey and others.
Daus. Catherine wife of John Finkly, Margaret wife of Henry Matthews and
Elizabeth.
Exs.: Wife Catharina, Wm. Becker and Philip Beeker.
Wit.: James Cameron, Jacob Eyler, Geo. Logue.   H. 57-59.

FRANK, JACOB. 16 Nov 1809. 28 Aug 1810.
Wife Mary.
Three daus., viz., Margaret Davis, Sarah Frank and Mary Frank.
Exs.: George Kline and Melchor Hoffer.
Wit.: Hugh Reed, John Kenneday.
Codicil: 22 July 1810.
House occupied by Jno. Trimble.   H. 59.

PINKERTON, THOMAS, East Pennsboro. 14 March 1810. 11 Oct 1810.
Four children, viz., Elizabeth Hoover, John, Polly and Margaret Pinkerton.
Exs.: John Carothers, Esq., and George Hoover.
Wit.: Wm. Jameson, John Goehlin.   H. 60.

BROWER, WILLIAM, Carlisle. 29 Oct 1810. 12 Nov 1810.

Wife Nancy.
Dau. Emily.
Robert Parkinson.
John Byers of Carlisle.
Exs.: Sd. John Byers and Robert Parkinson.
Wit.: Thomas McMurray, John L. Hays. H. 61.

WILSON, ELEANOR, Shippensburgh. 11 May 1809. 11 Jan 1811.
Dau. Maria, sole heir.
Exs.: Friend William Scott of Southampton Township, Franklin Co.
Wit.: John Scott, Jos. Scott. H. 62.

POSTLETHWAITE, SAMUEL, Carlisle. 1 May 1791. 30 Jan 1811.
Wife Matilda.
Son Joseph.
Dau. Sarah wife of John Duncan.
Exs.: Sons Joseph, John and Samuel and son in law John Duncan.
Wit.: None given.
Letters issued to Andrew Carothers, Esq. H. 63.

SCOTT, ANDREW, storekeeper, Carlisle. 4 May 1808. 31 Jan 1811.
Margaret McElrevy.
Plantation in Middleton Township adjoining Matthew Miller.
Natural dau. Jane Scott and son Andrew Scott, children of Jane McMichael,
minors.
Natural son Robert Scott, son of Margaret McElreoy, minor, and his bro.
Frederick McElreoy.
Exs.: John Miller, merchant of Carlisle, and Thomas Urie of Middleton.
Guardians of sd. children: James Lamberton and James Noble.
Wit.: Michael Miller, William Levis. H. 64-65.

MC CLURE, CHARLES, Middleton. 4 Feb 1807. 12 Feb 1811.
Wife Rebecca.
Home in Carlisle.
Children Charlotte, Rebecca, Charles and William, minors.
Dau. Mary.
Plantation near Boiling Springs.
Son John.
Lands conveyed to Revd. John Steel and Ephraim Blain.
Land bought by Clymen and Meredith joining Borough of Carlisle.
Land conveyed by Joseph Thornburg.

Land in West Pennsbro.
Exs.: Son John McClure and David Watts, also Guardians over minor children.
Wit.: Geo. A. Lyon, George Pattison.   H. 66-68.

MC BRIDE, ALEXANDER, Dickinson. 30 Nov 1807. 27 Feb 1811.
Daus. Mary Boyd, Jean Ewing and Sarah Reed.
Son Robert McBride.
Exs.: Friends Samuel Weakley, Esq., William Ewing and John Arthur, Esq.
Wit.: Henry Ocker, John Gray, Junr.   H. 69-71.

WALLACE, CHRISTIANA, single woman, Shippensburg. 12 Sept 1810. 1 April 1811.
Bro. James Wallace and his wife Agness Wallace.
Ex.: Bro. James Wallace.
Wit.: James Devor, John Bratton.   H. 71.

STERRETT, JOHN, Allen. 27 Jan 1811. 2 April 1811.
Wife Agness.
Son Robert Chambers.
Two daus., viz., Rachel and Margaret.
Exs.: Wife, bro. Brice Innes Sterrett and Thos. Urie.
Wit.: Robert Starrett, David Sterrett.   H. 72.

KRITZER, ADAM, Eastpensborough. 17 Feb 1807. 9 April 1811.
Wife Elizabeth.
Five children, viz., Barbary, Eve, Rosina, John and Andrews when youngest son comes of age.
Dau. Elizabeth and her husband Jehu Jacobs.
Exs.: John Bowman, Jacob Wormly and Fredk. Mays.
Wit.: John Weiser, Michael Heibeson.   H. 73-75.

FORNEY, GEORGE, Eastpennsborough. ---. 13 April 1811.
Wife.
Children, minors, not named.
Exs.: Andrew Emmiger, Senr., and John Carothers, Esq.
Wit.: Wm. Jameson, Nesbit Walkub.   H. 76.

SPROAT, EVES, Dickinson. 20 Oct 1810. 13 April 1811.
Elder dau. Elizabeth.
Dau. Isabella and her husband.

Daus. Nancy and Betsy.
Exs.: William Dunlap and Joseph Shaw.
Wit.: Mary Dunlap, James Stitt.   H. 77.

THOMPSON, WILLIAM, Buffalo. 19 July 1810. 6 May 1811.
Wife Margaret.
Son John.
Line to lands of late Richard Colhran and Morris Steel.
Dau. Nancy Thompson.
Son Samuel.
William Colhran, Polly Colhran, George Colhran and Betsy Colhran, minor
children of dau. Betsy Colhran, also her other minor son Samuel Colhran.
Exs.: Wife Margaret and Rev. Joseph Brady of Rye.
Wit.: James Porter, Peter Williamson.   H. 78-80.

IRVINE, JAMES, Middleton. 14 April 1810. 18 May 1811.
Wife Sarah.
Son John.
Dau. Catherine Ross.
Daus. Mary McClelland, Nancy Holmes and Jane Irvine.
Sons William and Robert.
Lot in Carlisle joining lot of William Miller.
Grandsons James Irvine McClelland and Robert Harris McClelland,
minors.
Exs.: Wife Sarah and sons John and William.
Wit.: Peter Hetrick, James Lamberton.   H. 81.

SHOWER, PETER, Tyrone. 9 April 1811. 30 May 1811.
Son David.
Daus. Catherine Ullrick and Mary Weaver.
Ex.: Son David Shower.
Wit.: James Wilson, Frederick Briner.   H. 82-83.

LOWRY, JAMES, Esq., Shippensburg. 9 May 1811. 5 Aug 1811.
Wife Nancy.
Daus. Mary Lowry, Peggy Lowry and Sally McKnight wife of Samuel
McKnight.
Sons John and James.
Minor children Thomas, Hannah Eliza and Henry Lowry.
Caroline minor dau. of Mary Lowry.
Exs.: John Duncan of Shippensburg and James Smith, Esq.

Wit.: Robert Porter, John McCarrell. H. 84-85.

KILGORE, JANE, Tyrone. 13 July 1811. 23 Aug 1811.
Eldest dau. Margaret.
Only son James.
Other daus. Mary and Jane.
Granddau. Sinthey Gowdey.
Exs.: Arthur Graham, Frankford, and John A. Scroggs of Tyrone Township.
Wit.: Christian Bigler, John Creigh, Junr. H. 86.

YOUNG, ELEANOR, widow of John Young, late of West Pennsborough Township, farmer, Newton. 11 March 1811. 29 Aug 1811.
Son William Young's oldest children.
Dau. Sally McKinney's two eldest children.
Dau. Elizabeth Davidson.
Grandchildren, John Young Davidson, Eleanor Davidson, Samuel and William Davidson and Nancy Davidson.
Exs.: Alexander Thompson and Atcheson Laughlin.
Wit.: Jno. Geddis, Andrew McCord. H. 87-88.

WORK, WILLIAM, Allen. 20 July 1811. 16 Sept 1811.
William Work, son of old friend William Work of Adams Co.
Elizabeth Crawford, my housekeeper.
Polly Crawford dau. of Elizabeth Crawford.
Nephew John Donaldson.
Michael McFall, the young man who lives with me.
Exs.: David Watts and Andrew Carothers.
Wit.: Chas. Taylor, William Wierman. H. 89-90.

WILSON, JOSEPH, Newton. 15 Aug 1793. 20 Sept 1811.
Wife Mary.
Sons William and James Wilson.
Ex.: Wife Mary Wilson.
Wit.: Joseph Wilson, William Wilson. H. 91.

HUME, JAMES, East Pennsbro. 25 June 1811. 6 Oct 1811.
Wife Frances.
Six sons, viz., Samuel, William, James, Andrew, John and David.
Four daus. Ann Swiler, Isabella McClintock, Frances and Jane Hume.
Exs.: Wife Frances, James Hume and Saml. Hume.

Wit.: James McGuire, George Swartz, George Parker.   H. 92.

OFFICER, WILLIAM, farmer, Tyrone. 10 Nov 1805. 19 Oct 1811.
Wife Elizabeth.
Land bounded by Michael Loy's, Briner's, Henry Rickett, George Loy's and
Haskett's land.
Four children, viz., John (in another place called James), Mary Officer wife
of George Sharp, Jenny Officer wife of John McClure and Martha Officer
wife of James Hackett.
Exs.: Son in law James Hackett and Henry Rickett.
Wit.: Wilson McClure, Adam Bernhisle.   H. 93.

WOLF, JACOB, Middleton. 18 Oct 1804. 26 Oct 1811.
Sons Jacob, John and Philip.
Daus. Barbara wife of George Lose, Elizabeth wife of Philip Waggoner, and
Christiana wife of Christian Failor.
Exs.: Sons Jacob Wolf and John Wolf.
Wit.: Leonard Failor, Saml. Postlethwaite.   H. 94.

MC COY, JAMES, miller, Rye. 8 Sept 1811. 4 Nov 1811.
Sister Mary, now Mary Harper.
Nonmarried sisters, eldest Nancy, Elizabeth and Margaret.
Nephew James McCoy, Junr., son of bro. Alexr. McCoy decd.
Exs.: Uncle Moses Kirkpatrick and Robert Thompson, both of Rye
Township.
Wit.: David McCoy, John Woodburn.   H. 95.

DELANCEY, FRANCIS, Toboine. 3 July 1811. 16 Nov 1811.
Wife Catherine.
Oldest son John.
Sons Philip and Christopher.
Dau. Mary Anderson.
Five other sons Francis, George, Jacob, Peter and William.
When youngest, William, is twenty one years of age.
Three daus. Barbara, Susannah and Sarah.
Exs.: John Urie and Daniel Bloom.
Wit.: George Anderson, William Campbell.   H. 96.

MARTIN, THOMAS, Shippensburgh. 22 Oct 1811. 21 Nov 1811.
Wife Elizabeth.
Dau. Nancy.

House where Paul Murphy lives.

Daus. Rosanna, Margaret (now Margaret Mitchell), Mary (now Mary Thompson) and Rachel (now Rachel McGaffin).

Sons Paul, Thomas and William.

Daus. Jane and youngest Hannah.

Some of the children minors.

Two children of decd. dau. Elinor, viz., Thomas Martin McCandlish and Agness, minors.

Exs.: Sons in law James McGuffin of Newton and Alexander Mitchell of Melat Township, Franklin Co., and son Paul.

Wit.: Alexr. Stewart, John Scott, Wm. McConnell. H. 97-99.

POWER, JOHN, Landisburgh. 25 Sept 1811. 28 Nov 1811.

To Fatima Power, dau. of James Power of Juniatta.

John Power, son of Captain William Power, Senr. of Juniatta.

Eliza Elliott, dau. of widow Jane Elliott of Juniatta Township.

Exs.: Meredith Darlington of Juniatta and Dr. John Creigh, Junr., of Landisburgh.

Wit.: Isaiah Carl, Wm. Wilson. H. 100.

SEMPLE, JOSEPH, farmer, Middleton. 14 July 1810. 28 Dec 1811.

Son Joseph.

Daus. Jane Semple and Elizabeth Semple.

Grandchildren James Beatty and Elizabeth Semple, minors.

Five grandchildren Hannah Beatty, Sarah Beatty, Margaret Beatty, Joseph and John Beatty, minor children of Robert and Martha Beatty.

Grandchildren Martha Sterrett and Elizabeth Sterrett, children of dau. Sarah Sterrett, decd., and John Sterrett.

Son David.

Dau. Martha Beatty.

Exs.: Son Joseph Semple and James McCormick, Esq. of Carlisle.

Wit.: John Officer, Jeremiah Miller. H. 101-102.

LOUTHER, JAMES, Tyrone. 9 March 1797. 17 Jan 1812.

Wife Elizabeth.

Sons John Louther and James Louther.

Dau. Margaret Kelly.

Exs.: Wife Elizabeth Louther and Enoch Lewis.

Wit.: Wm. Rogers, Margt. Rogers. H. 103.

ROSS, THOMAS. 25 July 1785. 5 Feb 1812.

Wife Jane.
Eldest son John.
Son Samuel.
Daus. Margaret and Mary.
Grandson Thomas Ross, son of son John.
Grandson Ross Buchanan.
Exs.: Sons John Ross and Samuel Ross.
Wit.: Hugh Kilgore, Samuel Harper, John Sharp. H. 103.

MILLER, JOHN, Middleton. 13 Dec 1811. 10 Feb 1812.
Wife Ann.
Son Joseph.
Daus. Elizabeth and Ann intermarried with Thomas Lindsey.
Exs.: Son Joseph Miller, David Watts and Thos. Urie.
Wit.: George Stubbs, Matthew Miller.
Codicil: 14 Dec 1811.
Plantation joining that of late Saml. Irwin on Trindle's Road.
Wit.: Michael Ege. H. 104-105.

GROSS, GEORGE, tenant, East Pennsborough. 3 Feb 1812. 12 Feb 1812.
Wife Barbara.
Children fourteen in number, Molly married to Jacob Kefer, Barbara married to Peter Shelley, George, Michael, Peggy, Jenney, John, Henry, Jacob, Daniel, Catherine, Elizabeth, Susanna and Sally, when minors come of age.
Ex.: Thomas Urie.
Wit.: John Spess, Abraham Thrush. H. 106.

SHUEBELY, GEORGE, East Pennsborough. 19 Jan 1812. 12 Feb 1812.
Wife Mary Magdalene.
Land joining land of John Rupp and Isaac Merkle.
Five children, none named.
Ex.: David Sherben.
Wit.: John Shop, David Everly. H. 107.

MC FEELY, ROGER. 3 Oct 1804. 4 April 1812.
Son in law and dau. John and Eleanor McKinley.
Ex.: John McKinley.
Attorneys: Gibson Craighead and Andrew Dunn, both of Cumberland Co.
Wit.: Hance Kenneday. H. 108.

KELLY, ALEXANDER, Toboine. 28 Feb 1812. 7 April 1812.
Sister Jennet Brown and Thomas Brown, her son.
Margaret Rodgers and Thomas Rodgers, her son.
Jean Hammaker.
John Ross, sister Mary's son.
Mary Gallaspey.
Exs.: William Anderson and James Johnston.
Wit.: John Long, John Brown.   H. 109.

SHARP, JAMES, yeoman, Hopewell. 21 Dec 1811. 28 May 1812.
Wife Mary.
Son Robert.
Plantation purchased from a Mr. Johnston, now in Beaver Co.
Four daus. Margaret wife of James Fullerton, Mary wife of Joseph Quigley,
Martha wife of William McClelland and Agness unmarried.
Son James.
Exs.: Bro. in law John McCane and son in law Jos. Quigley.
Wit.: David H. Woods, John Woods, William Green.   H. 110-112.

PELSE, JAMES, Southampton. 8 April 1812. 30 May 1812.
Beloved and beautiful children Christian, Catherine and Mary.
Exs.: Robert Peebles and son Christian Pelse.
Wit.: Andrew Moore, George Mower.   H. 113.

SOUDER, JACOB, farmer, Frankford. 5 March 1812. 13 July 1812.
Wife Catherine.
Daus. Caty and Polly.
Dau. Elizabeth and her children, viz., Joseph Jumper, Junr., Elizabeth
Jumper and John Jumper.
Exs.: Son in law John Leport and William Lehman.
Wit.: Martin George, Junr., William Lindsay.   H. 114.

WOODS, NATHAN, Dickinson. 7 Aug 1812. 22Aug 1812.
Wife Jane.
Son Samuel when twenty-one years of age, which will be on 23rd of June
1822.
Other children minors.
Exs.: Wife Jane, Andrew Boden of Carlisle and Thomas Patterson of
Dickinson.
Wit.: David Souder, James Weakley.
Codicil: 14 Aug 1812.

Wit.: Adam Houk.   H. 116-118.

BACHMAN, CHRISTIAN, Carlisle. 2 April 1811. 10 Sept 1812.
Wife Nancy.
Lots adjoining lots of H. H. Brackinridge and James Givin.
My mother who lives with me.
Sons John and Jacob.
Dau. Nancy.
All minors.
Exs.: William Alexander, John Boden and William Ramsey, Esq.
Wit.: Andrew Boden, Robt. McCoy.   H. 119-122.

ABRAHAMS, ENOCH, West Pennsborough. 7 June 1812. 12 Sept 1812.
Wife Hannah.
Land joining land of Andrew.
Nine children.
Son Michael Shower and dau. Catherine.
Names of other children not given.
Guardians over minor children: Andrew Heikes, Andrew Shower and
Michael Bear.
Exs.: Wife Hannah, son Michael Abraham and friend John Bear.
Wit.: Andrew Shower, Michael Bear.   H. 123-126.

STURM, GEORGE, merchant, Carlisle. 3 Aug 1812. 20 Sept 1812.
Wife Elizabeth.
Son George, minor.
Bro. David Sturm.
Guardian of son: George Hendel, Carlisle, silversmith.
Exs.: Jacob Hendel, Esq. and Jacob Cart.
Wit.: Samuel Stokes, John D. Haverstick.   H. 127.

POLLOCK, ANN, Carlisle. 17 April 1812. 2 Oct 1812.
Sister Elizabeth Hunt.
Niece Eliza Seely.
Exs.: Said sister Elizabeth and niece Eliza Seely.
Wit.: John Gray, James Gustine.   H. 128-129.

STUMBAUGH, PETER, Shippensburgh. 10 Feb 1807. 20 Oct 1812.
My seven daus.
The children of those who are decd.
Exs.: David McKnight and Alexander Stewart, Doctor.

Wit.: Jacob Dewalt, John Scott, John Shelter.   H. 130.

MEYER, GEORGE, Dickinson. 24 Sept 1812. 3 Nov 1812.
Wife Mary.
Sons Jacob, John and George.
Daus. Mary, Christine and Catherine.
Daus. Nancy wife of Wm. Myers and Barbara.
Children of dau. Barbara.
Another dau. name not given.
Son George Myer and son in law Abm. Myers, guardian of dau. Mary who is unable to act for herself.
Exs.: Son George, Abm. Myer and bro. Jacob Myer.
Wit.: Abraham Stievick, John Bear.   H. 131-135.

THOMPSON, JOHN, South Middleton. 12 May 1812. 4 Nov 1812.
Wife Jane.
Said wife Jane one of heirs of William Moore decd.
Dau. Eliza unmarried.
Son James, minor.
House and lot in Carlisle joining lots of Jacob Keigley and William Keith.
Sons Andrew and John.
Land on big Hatchey River in State of Tennessee.
Real estate in City of Baltimore.
Sons in law Standish Berry, John Franciscus and David McCormick.
Son William.
Daus. Agness Berry, Mary Franciscus and Jane McCormick.
Land sold to son in law David McCormick on Jones Creek, Tennessee.
Exs.: Son William Thompson and Standish Berry and friend James Giffen (Given).
Wit.: Geo. Metzgar, Hugh McCormick.   H. 136-138.

WALLACE, ROBERT, Junr., Rye. 9 Oct 1812. 11 Nov 1812.
Wife Mary.
Son John Swishelm Wallace.
Daus. Sarah and Eliza Wallace.
Exs.: Wife Mary, James Wallace and John Owens.
Wit.: Robert Wallace, Senr., Sarah Milligan.   H. 139.

RICHARDS, ALEXANDER, Shippensburgh. 13 Oct 1812. 25 Nov 1812.
Wife Sarah.
Only son James.

Grandson Alexander Richards.
Lot in tenure of Joseph Johnston.
Exs.: Wife Sarah Richards and John Means.
Wit.: Thomas McGaw, William Burd (Bard).   H. 140-141.

BAXTER, JAMES, Tyrone. 9 Aug 1808. 2 Dec 1812.
Nephew William Baxter's youngest dau. Martha, a minor, his sons John,
Robert and James and sd. nephew.
William's other daus. Jenny and Elizabeth.
Nephew James Baxter.
Niece Margaret Baxter.
Exs.: Thomas Simonton, James Baxter and Jno. Baxter.
Wit.: Abraham Kistler, Henry Shoemaker.   H. 142.

HUSTON, JAMES, blacksmith, Westpennsborough. 9 Aug 1812. 15 Dec
1812.
Wife Isabella.
Minor son Jabus (Jabez).
Dau. Margaret married to Jacob Palm, Junr.
Other three daus. Martha, Mary and Isabella, minors.
Son Andrew.
Land at William Huston's line.
Exs.: Son Andrew and James Sharp of Frankford.
Wit.: Jno. Geddis, B. McKeehan.   H. 143-145.

MC FARLANE, ROSANNA, widow, Newton. 1 April 1812. 15 Dec 1812.
Son James McFarlane.
Dau. Margaret wife of Thomas Kenneday of Newville.
Daus. Polly Dunbar wife of John Dunbar of Newville and Rosanna wife of
William Glenn of Newville.
Decd. husband Patrick McFarlane.
Son Robert.
Grandson William Thompson.
Granddau. Rosanna Hamilton.
Ex.: Son Robert.
Wit.: Jas. Montgomery, Jno. Geddis, David Mickey.   H. 145-146.

DAVIDSON, ROBERT, D. D., Carlisle. 5 Nov 1812. 17 Dec 1812.
Wife Jane.
Son Robert when eighteen years of age.
Children of bro. John Davidson, decd., of the State of Maryland.

Children of Margaret Herrick of the State of Ohio.
Children of James Cameron of Cumberland Co.
Exs.: Wife Jane and David Harris of City of Baltimore.
Wit.: James McCormick, Simon Boyd, Sarah Montgomery.   H. 147-148.

STOUGH, NICHOLAS, Newton. 12 Oct 1812. 21 Jan 1813.
Wife Margaret.
Sons Jacob, William and Samuel.
Daus. Susanna, Elizabeth and Catherine.
Son Hanes.
Exs.: Son Hanes and Jacob Stough.
Wit.: John Rodes, Jacob Stough.   H. 149-152.

SANDS, GEORGE, Rye. 5 Nov 1804. 21 Jan 1813.
Whole estate to dau. Mary.
Son in law Wm. Bothwell.
Exs.: Dau. Mary and James Quigley.
Wit.: James Waugh, Jonathan Reese.   H. 152-153.

LINDSAY, WILLIAM, Frankford. 17 Dec 1812. 29 Jan 1813.
Wife Jane.
Sons William, Samuel and James.
Daus. Jean and Martha.
Exs.: Isaiah Graham and John McDowell.
Wit.: John French, William Connelly.   H. 154.

LINN, WILLIAM, Tyrone. 9 Feb 1813. 8 March 1813.
Wife Martha.
Sons John,Samuel and Andrew.
William McMillan, his wife, my dau. Elizabeth.
Children of Chas. Elliott by dau. Ann, decd.
David Coyle intermarried with dau. Martha.
Daniel Ross and his wife, dau. Eleanor.
Dau. Jean.
Dau. Sally lately intermarried with John Elliott.
Robert Elliott and dau. Polly, his wife.
Grandson William McMillan, a minor.
Exs.: Wife Martha and sons Saml. and Andw. Linn.
Wit.: John Linn, Frederick Shull.   H. 155-156.

ELLIOTT, JAMES, Tyrone. 22 Feb 1813. 23 March 1813.

Wife Elizabeth.
Sons John, James and Robert.
Dau. Betsy Nelson's oldest son James Nelson, a minor.
Son William Elliott, a minor.
Daus. Nancy Elliott, Peggy Elliott and Polly Elliott.
Exs.: Son John Elliott and William Irvine.
Wit.: David Beard, James Elliott.   H. 157.

ALLEN, MARY, East Pennsbro. 9 May 1805. 27 March 1813.
Miss Margret Irvine and Eliza Waugh, daus. of James Irvine decd. and
Revd. Samuel Waugh.
Andrew Irvine son of James Irvine decd.
Mr. Saml. Waugh's son John Waugh.
Exs.: John Irvine and William Irvine.
Wit.: James Bell, Francis Johnston.   H. 158-159.

BEAR, HENRY, West Pennsborough. 21 Feb 1810. 27 March 1813.
Two sons John and Samuel.
Daus. Susanna and Magdalene and her husband Martin Bowman.
Exs.: Sons John Bear, Samuel Bear and Michael Bear.
Wit.: Samuel Bear, John Bear, Junr.   H. 160-161.

MC GLOGLIN, PATRICK, Rye. 8 March 1813. 29 March 1813.
Wife Mary.
Son in law James White intermarried with dau. Margaret decd.
Three daus. of dau. Margaret decd., viz., Anny, Elizabeth and Mary White.
Son George.
Other sons Daniel, Joseph, John, Samuel and Anthony.
Ex.: Joseph Longnecker.
Wit.: Michael Hebeison, Thomas James.   H. 162-163.

LECKEY, ALEXANDER, West Pennsborough. 11 March 1813. 29 March
1813.
Wife Elizabeth.
House and land in Frankford Township occupied by William McCoy.
Eldest son Daniel, land where he now lives in Frankford Township.
Land in sd. Township adjoining lands of James Laird and Abraham Landis.
Son George.
House in Newville.
Eldest dau. Prudence Irvine.

180

Other daus. Sarah Leckey, Ann Leckey, Mary Leckey, Isabella and Emily Leckey.
Grandson William Alexander Leckey, son of son Daniel.
Seventh dau. Hetty Leckey.
Grandson Alexander Leckey Irvine, son of dau. Prudence Irvine.
Son Daniel Leckey and James Irvine guardians for their own children to whom bequests are made.
Exs.: Wife Elizabeth and Daniel Leckey and Geo. Leckey.
Wit.: John Davidson, James McKihan, Wm. Davidson.   H. 164-166.

RATHFON (REATHFON), JOHN, Rye. 10 June 1808. 1 April 1813.
Wife Catherine.
Seven children, viz., John, Elizabeth, Catherine, Christiana, Jacob, George and Mary when youngest child is twenty one years old.
Exs.: Wife Catherine and Joseph Schram.
Wit.: Felix Young, Abm. Young.   H. 167.

MATTER (MATTEER), JACOB, North Middleton. 18 June 1812. 3 April 1813.
Wife Elizabeth.
The minor children of dau. Molly intermarried with Peter Allison.
All my children, viz., Margaret wife of Daniel Rupert, Elizabeth wife of George Sponsler, Catherine, Mary Ann, Jane, Nancy and Rachell when eighteen years old.
Exs.: Wife Elizabeth, son in law David Rupert and John Wolf.
Wit.: Robert McCoy, Isaac Wynkoop.   H. 168-169.

WALKER, ROBERT, yeoman, Rye. 15 June 1801. 6 April 1813.
Heirs of dau. Susanna Fredericks.
Dau. Margery Swair.
Grandson William Walker.
Dau. Margaret.
Exs.: Thomas Hulings and dau. Margaret Walker.
Wit.: John Bear, Jno. Elliott, Jacob Bear.
Letter issued to Thomas Adams, Exs. having renounced.   H. 170-171.

EWIG, JOHN, Town of Liverpool. ---. 6 April 1813.
Eight children, viz., Catherine Shell, Barbara Ewig, George, Hanna Ewig, Margaret Ewig, Mary Ewig, John and Matilda Ewig, when son John comes of age.

Exs.: Dau. Barbara Ewig and Benjamin Burrell of Town of Liverpool, County of Cumberland, Penna.
Wit.: John Buchan, Jno. Huggins.   H. 172-173.

STANBRIDGE, JOHN, Millerstown on the Juniata. 24 Feb 1812. 7 April 1813.
Consort and friend Mary.
Share in stock of Farmers and Mechanics' Bank in city of Philadelphia in her maiden name of Mary Hodgets.
Plantation in Pfoutz's Valley, Greenwood Township.
Son Thomas Stanbridge.
Surviving children of dau. Mary Baty decd. of Warwick, Great Britain.
Son William and each of his three daus., viz., Elizabeth, Mary Ann and Sarah.
Dau. Elizabeth Terry.
Son Christopher Stanbridge, lease hold lands &c situate in Temple Street, town of Bermingham, Great Britain.
Children of son John Christr. Stanbridge, two named, viz., dau. Susan Mary and second son George Livingston Stanbridge.
Dau. Anna Maria Ryley and her infant son Thomas Ryley.
Exs.: Son John Christopher Stanbridge of Philadelphia and Mr. Caleb North of Millertown.
Wit.: David Rumbaugh, Elijah Davis.   H. 174-177.

POWER, JAMES, Juniata. 22 Feb 1813. 9 April 1813.
Wife Mary.
Son Edward, a minor.
Other sons, viz., William, Joseph and James.
Dau. Tamar Power.
Son Alexander.
Land on Big Comiat Creek where Daniel Myers lives.
Exs.: Sons William Power and Joseph Power.
Wit.: Francis Beelen, David Mitchell.   H. 177-179.

BROWN, ROGER, Juniata. 3 April 1810. 10 April 1813.
Wife Mary.
Son Robert.
Dau. Martha Wallace.
Granddau. Grace Wallace.
Dau. Eleanor.
Son Francis.

Son William decd.

Papers of estate of John Guthrie, decd., with Finlaw McCown decd., to Margaret Gustine, alias now Margaret Marchall.

Exs.: Son Robert Brown and Francis McCown.

Wit.: Henry Bull, Robert Bull. H. 180-181.

OFFICER, THOMAS, Frankford. 17 Dec 1810. 13 April 1813.

Dau. Mary as she is now growing old.

Seven remaining children or their heirs, viz., son James' heirs, sons Thomas, Robert and David, Thomas Rutledge son of dau. Jane Rutledge, at her request, dau. Sarah, dau. Ann and her children, land conveyed by son in law and dau. Joseph and Ann Keers.

Children of sons bearing name of Thomas Officer.

Ruth Ann Officer.

Exs.: Son Thomas Officer and son in law Patrick Wallace.

Wit.: James Laird, Thos. Wallace, John Officer. H. 182.

LONG, JOHN, Greenwood. 15 Dec 1808. 15 April 1813.

Son Henry.

Two daus. of son John, decd.

Children of dau. Magdalene wife of Jacob Waggoner.

Children of John Rafter and dau. Elizabeth, decd.

Henry Waggoner.

My other children.

Exs.: Jonathan Long and Henry Long.

Wit.: Joseph Fry, Henry Fry. H. 183.

STEVENS, JOHN, North Middleton. 1 April 1813. 19 April 1813.

Wife Hannah.

Plantation in Adams Co. where son Thomas Stevens now lives.

Children, viz., sons Thomas, Richard, James, John Jefferson and Arthur, daus. Sarah Chambers and Elizabeth Flemming, when youngest child arrives at full age.

Exs.: Wife Hannah and son Thomas of Adams Co.

Wit.: John Chambers, James Lamberton. H. 185-186.

MC KEEHAN, JOHN, farmer, West Pennsborough. 27 Nov 1812. 23 April 1813.

Wife Elizabeth.

Sons Benjamin, George and James.

Son in law Andrew Mitchell.

183

Grandson Mark.
Sons John, Samuel and Alexander.
Exs.: Bro. Benjamin McKeehan and Richard Woods, both of West Pennsborough Township.
In case of death of sd. Exs., James McKeehan son of bro. James and Samuel McKeehan, son of bro. George McKeehan decd. appointed Exs.
Wit.: Richard Woods, James McKeehan, William McKeehan.

H. 187-189.

HENDERSON, ELIZABETH, South Middleton. 3 May 1813. 10 May 1813.
Sole heir and Exs.: Two children, viz., William Laird and Mary Steel.
Wit.: John Russel, Jean Thompson.   H. 190.

MC MANAGLE, WILLIAM, Newville. 22 May 1813. 27 July 1813.
Two sons Andrew and William.
Land near the town of Wooster, County of Wean, State of Ohio.
Christian Armor, the prentice bound to me.
Tenants, Philip Duck, Andrew Maxwell, Robert Linck and Jacob Kitzen.
Warrant granted to Saml. Ireland by Capt. William Buchanan.
Exs.: Stophel Hoon and son Andrew McManagle.
Wit.: Robt. Lusk, John Dunbar, Stophel Hoon.   H. 191-192.

ROSS, JOHN, yeoman, Tyrone. 11 May 1813. 6 Aug 1813.
Wife Susanna.
Sons Jonathan, David, Thomas, Daniel and Samuel.
Daus. Mary married to John Linn, Susanna married to John McClure and Jane.
Granddau. Mary Ross dau. of Jonathan.
Exs.: Sons Samuel Ross and David Ross.
Wit.: John McClure, Samuel Linn, John Creigh.   H. 193-195.

LEAMAN, JOHN, Toboyne. 27 May 1813. 6 Aug 1813.
Wife Diannah.
Son Alexander.
Daus. Polly and Alsabeth.
Exs.: Son Alexander Leaman and David Moreland.
Wit.: John Abernuthy, Geo. Ebright.   H. 196.

IRVIN, JOHN, Tyrone. 30 July 1813. 13 Aug 1813.
Wife Elizabeth.
Four children Ann, Polly, Peggy and James Irvin, all minors.

Exs.: Thomas Mulligan and William Elliott, Junr.
Wit.: George Wallick, William Irvin.   H. 197-198.

WEST, EDWARD, Tyrone. 13 Aug 1813. 26 Aug 1813.
Wife Ann.
Sons William and George.
Step son Andrew McDowell.
Daus. Ann wife of Revd. David Elliott and Frances, a minor.
Other children, minors, viz., sons Armstrong, Henry and Edward and dau.
Mary.
Exs.: Sons William, George West and Andw. McDowell.
Wit.: Gilbert Moore, Wm. Power, John Creigh.   H. 199-200.

HAMILTON, WILLIAM, Toboine, Sherman's Valley. 25 May 1813. 14 Sept
1813.
Oldest dau. Sera McMasters.
Oldest son George Hamilton.
Other children Wallas, Meary, John and James Hamilton, when James is
of age.
Exs.: John Urie and William Andrews, Esqs.
Wit.: John Nelson, John Bryner.   H. 201.

THOMPSON, JOHN, West Hanover, Dauphin Co. 14 Jun 1811. 16 Sept
1813.
Joseph Hunter, the Elder, and James Hunter, the Elder, both bros. being
my nephews of Buffalo Township.
Exs.: Sd. nephews Joseph and James Hunter.
Wit.: Joseph Hunter, Peter Williamson.   H. 202.

SMITH, WILLIAM, the Elder, West Pennsbro. 2 Sept 1813. 1 Oct 1813.
Sons Robert, William, John, Matthew and James.
Land in Mercer County, donation lands.
Daus. Elizabeth Smith and Mary wife of Samuel McClean.
Land bought of heirs of Jonathan Hage decd.
Exs.: Sons Matthew Smith and James Smith.
Wit.: Benjamin Cope, William McDonald.   H. 203-205.

SEARIGHT, GILBERT, Middleton. 18 Aug 1810. 4 Oct 1813.
Sons Alexander, Francis, George and Gilbert.
Land purchased of William Denny.
Dau. Elizabeth married to William Glaney.

Son William.
Exs.: Son Francis Searight and Searight Ramsey.
Wit.: Saml. Postlethwaite, John Miller.   H. 205-208.

MAKON, DAVID, Shippensburgh. 15 Feb 1812. 20 Oct 1813.
Wife Sarah.
Three grandchildren, children of oldest son, Samuel decd., viz., Mary
Mahon, John and David Mahon.
Son Archibald.
Granddau. Jane, dau. of son Archibald.
Son Sarah married to Oliver Ormsby.
Daus. Jane wife of Samuel Creigh, Hannah wife of Robert McPherson and
Mary McConaghy.
Sons Alexander, William and David.
Dau. Elizabeth Mahon.
Exs.: Wife Sarah and sons David and Alexr. Mahon.
Wit.: David McKnight, Jno. Simpson.   H. 209-211.

KUNTZ, ABRAHAM, yeoman, Greenwood. 23 Aug 1800. 16 Oct 1813.
Wife Catharina.
Son in law Philip Hoffman and Anna Maria his wife.
Land joining Frederick Wendt, David Boal, Abraham Gingerich and Michael
Pfouts.
Children of Adam Michael, decd., viz., Jacob and Anna Maria Michael.
Sister Anna Maria Michael, widow.
Decd. father, John Kuntz, of York County.
Exs.: Philip Hoffman and George Hoffman, Junr.
Wit.: Philip Harter, Frederick Wendt, John Went.   H. 212-215.

QUIGLEY, CHRISTOPHER, Allen. 30 March 1811. 26 Oct 1813.
Wife Catherine.
Dau. Patsy, if she be dead, to her two children.
Sums charged to John Irvin and her.
Sons James, John, Henry and Christopher.
Daus. Mary, Nancy, Anne, Rosanna and Betsy.
Bro. Henry.
Husbands of daus. Jean, Nancy and Anne.
Appraisers of estate James Graham, Tedy Coover, Senr. and Benjamin
Anderson.
Bound boy James Lewis.
Exs.: Joseph Moody and Henry Quigley.

Wit.: James Graham, James Quigley.   H. 216-218.

KOSER, JOHN, Tyrone. 31 Aug 1813. 27 Oct 1813.
Wife Gertrout.
Eldest son George.
Seven other children, viz., Rosina Stroup, Cadarina Wining, Barbara Schop, Gertrout Kremer, Elizabeth Koser, Christina Koser and Jonathan Koser.
Exs.: Isaiah Coil (Coyle), Esq. and John Hipple.
Wit.: George Waggoner, Henry Wingert, Isaiah Coil.   H. 219-220.

HELLER, ELIAS, South Middleton. 2 Sept 1813. 3 Nov 1813.
Wife Anna.
Sons and daus., viz., Benjamin, Daniel, Sally, Mary, Susanna and Martha.
Children of dau. Sally.
Exs.: Daniel Eby and John Wolf, both of South Middleton.
Wit.: Abm. Emminger, William Line, Moses Eby.   H. 221-222.

KIRKPATRICK, JOSEPH, yeoman, Rye. 16 July 1804. 31 Dec 1812 and 20 Feb 1813.
Wife Margaret.
Son James.
House in Petersburgh in tenure of Wm. Beaty.
Sons Joseph, William and John.
Daus. Sarah, Jane, Betsy and Nancy.
Son Alexander, a minor.
Exs.: Edward West and Hugh Smith.
Wit.: John Sweishelm, John Owen.
Exs. renounced, letters to Joseph Kirkpatrick and Francis Gibson.
    H. 223-224.

SHALLE, LUCAS, East Pennsborough. 6 Oct 1813. 6 Nov 1813.
Son Valindine, a minor.
Legacy from his aunt Chatharina Smith.
Granddau. Mary Beasor.
All children, viz., Magdalena D. Boyers, Chatharina Beasor, Elizabeth Boor, Mary Stren, Margrate Knolka, Barbara Eversold and Valindine.
Ex.: William Boor.
Wit.: John Mumma, Martin Renninger.   H. 225.

LINN, MARTHA, widow, Tyrone. 2 Aug 1813. 6 Nov 1813.
Daus. Jane Linn, Eleanor Ross, Martha Coyl, Polly Elliott and Sally Elliott.

Two grandaus. Jane and Martha Linn, children of son William.
Grandson William McMillan, a minor.
Sons Samuel and Andrew.
Exs.: Sons Samuel Linn and Andrew Linn.
Wit.: Wm. Irvin, Robt. Kelly.   H. 226.

LAUGHLIN, ALEXANDER, Esq., Mifflin. 20 Oct 1813. 12 Nov 1813.
Children of dau. Nancy Patterson, decd., minors.
Dau. Prudence McCune.
Daus. Charity and Elizabeth when they live single.
Sons John and Alexander.
Exs.: Sd. sons John Loughlin and Alexr. Laughlin.
Wit.: Alexr. Thompson, Wm. Thompson, Hugh Thompson.   H. 227-228.

COFFMAN, ISAAC, Carlisle. 8 Oct 1813. 13 Nov 1813.
Wife Margaret.
Lot adjoining Jacob Fetter.
Two children Eliza and Jacob Coffman.
Maria Martin.
Exs.: Wife Margaret Coffman and Philip Roads.
Wit.: Wm. Wheeler, Jacob Cart.   H. 229-230.

SHALLY, JACOB, yeoman, Allen. 19 Feb 1813. 16 Nov 1813.
Wife Barbara.
Son Daniel.
Other sons Christian, Jacob and Peter.
Son in law John Everly and dau. Easter, his wife.
Exs.: Christian Mohler and John Rupley.
Wit.: Jacob Merkel, Jacob Dalmer.   H. 231.

MC FARLIN, JOHN, farmer, Mifflin. 2 Sept 1813. 16 Nov 1813.
Wife Mary.
Sons John, Alexander and James.
Three daus. Peggy, Rachel and Nancy McFarlin.
Heirs of Daniel McDonnel, decd.
Son William.
Dau. Elizabeth, a single woman.
Exs.: Sons John and Alexander McFarlin.
Wit.: John Kooken, George Christlip.   H. 232-233.

MOORE, JAMES, Dickinson. 6 Dec 1813. 30 Dec 1813.

Wife Nancy.

Two sons Johnston and John, minors.

Land purchased of Daniel Smith.

Children of decd. sister Nancy Galbreath.

Land purchased from Milhael Leven for use of my father.

Guardians of sons: James Duncan, Esq. of Carlisle, John Finley of Chambersburg and Andw. Carothers, Carlisle.

Exs.: Wife Nancy, James Duncan and Thos. Patterson.

Wit.: Thos. Johnston, Matthew Thompson, Jno. Simpson, Thompson Brown.   H. 234-236.

MC CUNE, SAMUEL, yeoman, Newton. 9 Nov 1813. 4 Jan 1814.

Wife Hanna.

Children, minors, names not given.

Exs.: Wife Hanna and cousin John McCune.

Wit.: Hugh McCune, Wm. McCune.   H. 237.

AUCHER, CASPAR, Greenwood. 10 Nov 1813. 10 Jan 1814.

Wife Mary.

Son Jacob.

Other children.

Exs.: Son Peter Aucher and Michael Brand of Milford.

Wit.: James Gilfillen, Daniel Stall.   H. 238-239.

HUSTON, ROBERT, Newton. 11 Aug 1813. 18 Jan 1814.

Wife Jane.

Three daus. Jane, Nancy and Isabella, all single.

Exs.: John Scouller and William Munro.

Wit.: John Sharp, Robert Cooper.   H. 240.

SHANK, SUSANNA, East Pennsbro. 24 Oct 1813. 24 Jan 1814.

Eldest dau. Elizabeth Kilheaffer and granddau. Barbara Kilheaffer.

Eldest son Conrad Leininger.

Youngest dau. Ann Meckey.

Youngest son Philip Leininger.

Grandson Jacob Hildebrand.

Exs.: Son Conrad Leininger and Philip Leininger.

Wit.: Jacob Wormley, Wm. Durborow.   H. 241-242.

MC FARLANE, SAMUEL, Juniata Township. 28 Jan 1814. 22 Feb 1814.

Wife.

Dau. Nelly McFarlane.
Title to donation lands in west part of the State in hands of Gen. Miller.
Exs.: Dau. Nelly and John Kiser of Juniata.
Wit.: Martha Barkley, Margaret Simonton.　　　　　　H. 243.

BOWER, CHRISTOPHER, farmer, Toboyne. 21 Jan 1814. 24 Feb 1814.
Wife Susannah.
Oldest dau. Hannah Beaver.
Son Abraham.
Land on Meeting House Ridge, adjoining Nicholas Loy and Azria Tousey.
Dau. Susannah Barnhidle.
Solomon Shively and his six children, minors, whom dau. Elizabeth bore to him.
Daus. Easter Creamer, Mary Stumbaugh and Liddy.
Granddau. Sally Beaver.
Rebecca Stumbaugh.
Exs.: Sons Abraham Bower, Solomon Bower and William Anderson, Esq.
Wit.: John Gardner, Stephen Cessna, Saml. McCord.　　　H. 244-246.

DILLER, FRANCIS, West Pennsborough. 3 Feb 1814. 3 March 1814.
Wife Elizabeth.
Son Francis.
My five children.
Exs.: Son Francis Diller and bro. Peter Diller.
Wit.: John Bear, Isaac Paul.　　　　　　　　　　　　H. 247-248.

LOGUE, GEORGE, Carlisle. 7 March 1811. 12 March 1814.
Wife Christiana.
Brothers' and sister's children (legitimate).
Bro. in law George Hendel.
Ex.: Christiana Logue.
Wit.: Geo. Hendel.
Codicil: 27 Dec 1812.
Children of bro. Joseph Logue, now decd., viz., Jane, George and Eliza.
Elizabeth Logue, dau. of Wm. Logue, land in Rye Township.
Wit.: Geo. Hendel, Moses Bullock.
Codicil: 14 Dec 1813.
Bro. Wm. Logue.
Wit.: Adam Wert, Jacob Hendel.　　　　　　　　　　H. 249-251.

GALBRAITH, WILLIAM, yeoman, Rye. 17 March 1814. 31 March 1814.

Bros. Elijah Galbraith and John Galbraith.
Sister Sarah Fenton.
Ex.: James Fenton, Junr.
Wit.: Isaac Kip, Geo. Baird. H. 252-253.

MATEER, MARY, Allen. 11 Jan 1808. 6 April 1814.
Son James.
Dau. Isabella.
Decd. husband, late John Mateer.
Dau. Mary Patterson.
Son Samuel Huston, decd.
Sons Andrew and John, decd.
Ex.: Son Andrew.
Wit.: Benjamin Anderson, William Mateer, Junr. H. 254-255.

MC FARLANE, ELIZABETH, widow of John McFarlane, Esq., West
Pennsboro.
Sons Robert and John.
Dau. Jane married to James Davidson.
Son William.
Minor children, viz., Samuel, James, Clemence, Eliza and Polly.
Ex.: Son Robert McFarlane.
Wit.: Jno. Geddis, John Green. H. 256-257.

PARKER, RICHARD. 18 April 1814. 3 May 1814.
To Mary Hacket.
George Hacket.
Charles Hacket, a minor.
Jane Blaine, dau. of James Blaine.
Heirs of bro. William Parker.
Exs.: Robert Blaine and George Hacket.
Wit.: Robert Blaine, Wm. C. Chambers. H. 258-259.

RUPERT, DANIEL, North Middleton. 18 April 1814. 10 May 1814.
Wife Margaret.
Dau. Catherine, a minor.
Exs.: Wife Margaret, John P. Helfenstein and Abraham Myers of North
Middleton Township.
Wit.: Andw. Boden, Jacob Richer. H. 260-261.

GRAHAM, JAMES, farmer, Allen. 29 Dec 18--. 31 May 1814.

Sons John and James.
Land purchased from Charles Taylor.
Samuel Hanna's heirs.
Daus. Eleanor McCue and Elizabeth Young and Pricilla Gracey.
Grandson John Orr.
Granddau. Ruth Ferguson, minor.
Dau. Esther Ferguson, Andrew Ferguson.
Ex.: Son James Graham of Allen Township.
Wit.: Wm. Bryson, John Hayes.   H. 262-264.

BRINDLE, HENRY, Allen. 15 Dec 1812. 31 May 1814.
Wife Susannah.
Bro. Abraham Brindle.
God children John and Susanna, minor children of said bro. Abraham Brindle.
Present dwelling and plantation sold to John Crist.
To church commonly called Mode Creek in Cocallico Township, Lancaster Co.
Exs.: Wife Susanna and relation Mathias Gerner of Huntingdon Co.
Wit.: Adam Vickman, Jacob Shelly.   H. 265.

MURRAY, ANN, Toboyne. 11 Feb 1809. 1 June 1814.
Daus. Margaret Nesbit and Jane McCray.
Granddau. Isabella Anderson.
Children of dau. Mary Fisher.
Grandson Alexander Nesbit, son of Allen Nesbit.
Henry Zimmerman.
Samuel McCord.
Ex.: Grandson Alexander Nesbit of Toboyne Township.
Wit.: John Ewing, John Nesbit.   H. 266-267.

LOVE, JOHN, South Middleton. 5 April 1814. 9 June 1814.
Wife Mary.
Son James and his son John Love.
William Johnson son of Samuel Johnson and dau. Rachel.
Ground in town of Westphalia on Susquehanna River.
Dau. Rachel Johnson and her dau. Ann.
Lot in Carlisle purchased of Simon Smith.
Exs.: Son James Love.
Wit.: John Moorhead, John Hershey.   H. 268-269.

RICHESON, JOHN, Dickinson. 7 Feb 1814. 7 April 1814.
Wife Mary.
Sons Joseph, Philip and John.
Daus. Jane, Sally, Mary and Catherine.
Exs.: Mary Richeson and Peter Anthony.
Wit.: Peter Miller, Christian Hoffer. H. 270-272.

PATTERSON, MARY, Carlisle. 16 May 1814. 23 June 1814.
Dau. Mary Ann, a minor, under the care of niece Mary Webber.
Sons Christopher, William and John, as they come of age.
My mother.
Exs.: John Elliott, Esq., Isaac Todd and son Christopher.
Exs. to be overseers of minor children.
Wit.: John Officer, Robert Wright. H. 273.

WOLF, MATHIAS, Shippensburgh. 29 June 1814. 1 Aug 1814.
Wife Mary.
Nephew John Redig, a minor.
Two bros. Jacob and Peter Wolf.
Friend Jacob Redig.
Lots joining lots of Robert Porter and Dr. John Simpson.
Exs.: Wife Mary Wolf and friend William Devor.
Wit.: Henry Davis, John Bowman. H. 274-275.

HAMILTON, GEORGE, Mifflin. 17 Sept 1813. 6 Aug 1814.
Wife Ruth.
Son Samuel and dau. Nancy, when married.
Son James.
Dau. Martha Brandt.
Ex.: Son Samuel Hamilton.
Wit.: Robert Lusk, Junr., Robert Lusk. H. 276-277.

MC LEAN, JOHN. 10 Jan 1801. 17 Aug 1814.
Wife Mary.
Dau. Jane wife of Robert Smith.
Dau. Margaret.
Five sons Samuel, William and minor sons, John, Ebenezer C. and James
McLean.
Daus. Ruth McLean and Mary McLean.
Mother in law Jane McLean.
Exs.: Wife Mary, son Samuel McLean and Alexr. Peebles, Esq.

Wit.: Allen McLane, Wm. McKnight. H. 278-280.

WAREHEIM, CHRISTIANA, South Middleton. 25 Aug 1814. 1 Sept 1814.
Only son Joseph, a minor.
Ex. and Guardian of son: Father Philip Wareheim.
Wit.: John Knisely, Thos. A. Bigham. H. 281.

MC GUFFIN, JAMES, farmer, Newton. 30 July 1814. 3 Sept 1814.
Wife Rachel.
Two children James Nicholson and William.
Exs.: John Laughlin, Junr. of Mifflin and Alexr. Thompson.
Wit.: John Geddis, David McGlouchlin, Junr. H. 282.

MC BRIDE, JOHN, Rye. 12 July 1814. 12 Sept 1814.
Wife Mary.
Two sons Matthew and John.
Land joining heirs of John Rathson.
William McBride.
Bro. Matthew, decd.
Son Joseph.
Daus. Margaret Chisholm, Mary Owens, Isabella, Elizabeth, Jane and Ann.
Exs.: Wife Mary and sons Matthew and John.
Wit.: John Rathson, Robert Clark. H. 283-284.

DAVIDSON, GEORGE, Mifflin. 28 Aug 1814. 10 Oct 1814.
Wife Mary.
Only dau. Jane Eliza Davidson, a minor.
Exs.: Uncle Richard Woods of West Pennsborough and bro. in law Samuel
Woods of Dickinson Township.
Wit.: Daniel Knettle, William Brown. H. 284-286.

REED, JOHN, Greenwood. 17 Aug 1813. 14 Oct 1814.
Wife Barbara.
Her son Henry Limpart.
Son Paul Reed.
Dau. Eleanor Eagley.
Step dau. Mary Rumbaugh.
Land in Turkey Valley, Mifflin Co., sold in name of Edward Quinn.
John Limpart, infant son of Henry Limpart.
Exs.: Step son Henry Limpart and Caleb North of Millerstown.
Wit.: Samuel Mealey, Abm. Adams. H. 287-289.

MC KEEHAN, BENJAMIN, farmer, Westpennsbro. 20 Oct 1814. 9 Nov 1814.
Wife Margaret.
Sons John and William.
Three daus., oldest wife of Samuel McKeehan, second wife of William Douglass and Peggy unmarried.
Exs.: Two sons John and William.
Wit.: Richard Woods, Samuel McKeehan, James McKeehan, Senr.

H. 290-291.

RODGERS, WILLIAM, Tyrone. 18 April ---. 28 Nov 1814.
Sister in law Rosannah and her son Jonathan Hoge providing he do not become a lawyer.
Bro. in law and sister in law Francis McCown and Eleanor Beatty.
Only dau. Mary Cook.
To the Sherman's Creek Presbyterian Church.
Ex.: Sister in law Rosannah Hoge.
Wit.: John Bready, Isaac Kirkpatrick.

H. 292-293.

MC KINSTRY, JAMES, (the Elder), Dickinson. 9 July 1811. 2 Jan 1815.
Wife Sarah.
Son Alexander.
Plantation in Wayne Township, Mifflin Co., joining lands of William Bratton, John Carlisle and Juniata River.
Children of dau. Mary who was intermarried with Alexander Murkland.
Daus. Rebecca wife of George Bratton, Sarah wife of Fran. Fulton and Susanna wife of Alexr. Glenn.
Grandsons John and James McKinstry, children of son James.
Dau. in law Jane wife of son James.
Land in Dickinson bounded by lands of John Harper, decd., Joseph Mathers, William Hennon and Baltzer Whitmer.
Exs.: Sons Alexander McKinstry and James McKinstry.
Wit.: Robert McBride, Robert McBride, Junr.

H. 294-296.

HUSTON, NANCY, widow of Christy Huston, Eastpennsboro. 27 Dec 1814. 6 Jan 1815.
Bro's. son William Smith.
Matty Woodard.
Ebbey Smith and Elizabeth Smith.
John Woodord, Polly Woodord and Cathrene Woodord.
Exs.: Matty Woodord and Benjamin Woodord.

Wit.: Richard Waugh, A. Wills. H. 297-298.

STROEH, JOSEPH, yeoman, Allen. -- 1810. 3 Feb 1815.
Sons Joseph Stroeh and Jacob Stroeh.
Exs.: Jacob Kennower and Jacob Wise.
Wit.: Jacob Goodyear, Frederick Goodyear. H. 299.

DENISTON, SAMUEL, laborer. 18 Feb 1814. 7 Feb 1815.
All my effects to James Patterson "as I am determined to go forth, the first expedition."
Exs.: None named.
Letters to Jas. Patterson.
Wit.: John Wormly, Peter Fahnestock. H. 300.

SCHNYDER, GEORGE, Greenwood. 4 July 1813. 11 Feb 1815.
Wife Susannah.
Children, minors.
Mother.
Exs.: Wife Susannah and John Schons of Greenwood.
Wit.: Jacob Long, Jacob Ulsh. H.301-302.

SNODY, JOHN. 1 Feb 1815. 14 Feb 1815.
Wife.
Dau. Mabel Donavan.
Rest of children, viz., Mathew, Adam, John, William, Polly, Johnston and Benjamin.
Exs.: Son Matthew Snody and William Johnston Snody.
Wit.: David McKinney, John Carson. H. 303-305.

WALLACE, JOHN, Frankford. 7 Oct 1814. 16 Feb 1815.
Wife Nancy.
Sons James, Thomas, John and William, when William is of age.
Daus. Nancy and Margaret.
Exs.: Son James Wallace and bro. in law John Scouller.
Wit.: John Brown, Senr., John Brown, Junr. H. 305-306.

DUEY, MARTIN, North Middleton. 4 Aug 1814. 23 Feb 1815.
Wife Jean.
Six children, viz., Jacob, John, James, Martin, George and Elizabeth Duey.
Oldest dau. Catherine Galbreath wife of William Galbraith.
Second dau. Isabella Cline.

Exs.: Wife Jean Duey and bro. Conrad Duey.
Wit.: Gilson Craighead, Conrad Duey. H. 307.

DIXON, THOMAS, Carlisle. 8 March 1815. 13 March 1815.
Jane Colwell married to Samuel Colwell.
Jane Colewell dau.. of sd. Samuel and Jane Colwell.
Thomas Dixon Colwell son of sd. Samuel and Jane.
Patrick Long.
Exs.: Robert Leyburn and Jane Colwell.
Wit.: John Wightman, Jas. Wightman, Plunkt. Hacket, Robt. Leyburn.
H. 308-309.

GOODYEAR, FREDERICK, yeoman, Allen. 4 Feb 1815. 14 March 1815.
Wife.
Sons Daniel, Frederick, Jacob and Abraham.
Daus. Rosannah wife of Rudolph Krysher and Elizabeth wife of David Cockey.
Son Samuel.
Land joining lands of Daniel Baker and Samuel Martin.
Exs.: Sons Daniel, Frederick, Jacob and Abraham.
Wit.: Jacob Strock, John Miller. H. 310-312.

WILSON, JOSEPH C., Cumberland Co., North Carolina. 15 March 1815.
16 March 1815.
Bounty land and money coming to me as a soldier in the United States Army.
Uncle Joseph Cooper's family.
Uncle John Butter of Bladen Co., N. C.
Aunt Mary Taylor and her two daus. Mary Locke and Eliza Taylor.
Cousin Joseph Wilson.
Exs.: James Anderson Bulneck of Cumberland Co., N. C. and Joseph Wilson of Bladen Co., N. C.
Wit.: Isaac McKeever, John Peace, Andrew Hall. H. 313.

LEWIS, MICHAEL, Carlisle. 11 March 1815. 16 March 1815.
Son Michael.
Daus. Elizabeth and Emelia.
Sheriff Leeper and Fredk. Speak, Exs. of George Logue decd.
Exs.: Dau. Elizabeth and John Delaney, Esq.
Wit.: C. Lamberton, Abm. Longhridge, Abm. Longhridge, Junr.
H. 314-315.

ADAMS, JAMES, yeoman, Tyrone. 16 Nov 1814. 20 March 1815.
Half bro. William Simpson of Huntingdon Co.
The children of William Foster of Tyrone Township, viz., Mary Foster,
Isabella Foster, Jane Foster and James Foster.
Exs.: Said William Foster and James Foster.
Wit.: Robert Kelly, John Creigh.   H. 316-317.

OLLINGER, GEORGE, Tyrone. 13 Sept 1813. 22 Nov 1813.
Wife Justina.
Step son John Goodlander.
Children of my first wife.
Dau. Sara, child of present wife, a minor under sixteen years of age.
Exs.: Wife Justina and John Goodlander.
Wit.: John Kitner, George Stroop.   H. 318-319.

ANDERSON, ALEXANDER M., private in Capt. Matthew S. Magee's Co.
2, Fourth Rifle Reg., U. S. Riflemen, Bedford place of enlistment, now of
Carlisle. 31 March 1815. 4 April 1815.
Sole heir and Ex.: Robert Leyburn.
Wit.: James Wightman, Robert Hutchinson.   H. 320.

SMITH, JOSEPH, yeoman, Juniata. 6 March 1815. 11 April 1815.
Son John.
Daus. Ann wife of William Ferguson, Mary wife of John White, Elizabeth
Smith, and Sarah wife of John Hanna.
Son Joseph.
Grandson Jesse Miller, minor son of dau. Ann Ferguson.
Exs.: Dau. Elizabeth Smith, son Joseph Smith and John Owen of Rye
Township.
Wit.: Thomas Marshall, Joseph Marshall.   H. 321.

GREIGOR, JOHN, Senr., yeoman, Allen. 21 Dec 1813. 15 April 1815.
Wife Margaret.
Sons John and Jacob.
Daus. Elizabeth married to John Shaffer, Mary and Magdalene.
Legal children of son George, decd.
Legal children of son Abraham.
Son David's children.
Children of dau. Catherine, decd.
Children of son Adam, decd.
Exs.: Friends Michael Hoover and Abraham Pollinger.

Wit.: John Hoover, Abraham Smith. H. 322-323.

RACHFORD, HUGH, weaver, Newville. 14 Dec 1810. 24 April 1815.
Wife Jane.
Old son Alexander Rachford of the State of Ohio.
Son Robert.
To none else of my children.
Exs.: John Brown, Senr. of Frankford Township and son Robert Rachford
of the town of Newville.
Wit.: William Richey, Ann Richey. H. 324-325.

ARMSTRONG, WILLIAM, Tyrone. 28 May 1813. 21 April 1815.
Sister in law Margaret Armstrong wife of bro John.
Two bros. and two sisters, viz., Alexander Armstrong, John Armstrong,
Jean Nelson and Elizabeth Hervey.
Exs.: Bro. John Armstrong and Andrew Carothers, Esq. of Carlisle.
Wit.: William Anderson, James Hackett. H. 326.

MATTER, ELIZABETH, widow, Carlisle. 13 April 1815. 9 May 1815.
Dau. Molly married to Peter Alison.
Children of sd. dau. Molly, minors.
Dau. Elizabeth married to George Sponsier and her son Alexander, a minor.
Dau. Jane married with Joseph Cauffman.
Children of sd. dau. Jane, minors.
Dau. Margaret Rupert, widow of Daniel Rupert, decd.
Daus. Catherine, Mary, Ann, Nancy and Rachel.
...? John.
Exs.: Dau. Nancy Matter and George Hendel of Carlisle, silversmith.
Wit.: George Pattison, Jacob Hendel. H. 327-328.

TRAUGH, ADAM, Carlisle. 27 Dec 1813. 10 May 1815.
Wife Eve.
Children Henry, Rudolph, Peter, Philip, Michael, John, Elizabeth and
Hannah.
Exs.: Sons Rudolph Trough and John Trough.
Wit.: Conrad Bollinger, Charles Bovard.
Codicil: 28 Dec 1814.
Wit.: John Peters, Charles Board. H. 329-331.

RENCHENBERGER, JACOB, Cordwinder, Allen. 15 March 1815. 22 May
1815.

Wife Elizabeth.
Exs.: Wife Elizabeth and Adam Leidick.
Wit.: Adam Brandt, David Brandt.   H. 332.

MC CONNELL, MERGERA, Mifflin. 26 March 1814. 25 May 1815.
Dau. Mergara.
Exs.: None given.
Letters to Margery Johnston.
Wit.: Samuel Hanna, James Pettigrew.   H. 333.

MURRAY, RICHARD, farmer, Toboyne. 21 Jan 1815. 16 June 1815.
Wife Elizabeth.
Nefew Richard Shields.
Nefew Richard Murray, son to bro. William Murray.
Bros. William Murray and Robert Murray.
Exs.: Wife Elizabeth Murray and Richard Shields.
Wit.: Philip Bergetressor, Wm. Anderson, Culbertson Clark.
                                                       H. 334.

DUNLAP, SARAH, widow of John Dunlap, late of Allen. 29 April 1809. 25
April 1815.
Sons John and James Dunlap.
Children of dau. Elizabeth wife of Craford White.
Sons William and Martin.
Daus. Anna Dunlap and youngest dau. Sarah Dunlap.
Exs.: Sons James Dunlap and William Dunlap.
Wit.: Edward O'Hail, John Mateer.   H. 335-336.

TATE, SAMUEL, Carlisle. 3 April 1815. 18 May 1815.
To respected friend, Mary Lyon dau. of late William Lyon, Esq.
Esteemed friend Mary Craig.
Jane McArthur wife of John McArthur.
Joseph Given son of James Given.
To the Bible Society.
Exs.: John Officer, Joseph Hays and James Given.
Wit.: Thos. Foster, George Pattison.   H. 337.

BASKIN, ROBERT, fuller, Buffaloe. 25 Aug 1813. 26 June 1815.
Wife Catherine.
Daus. Jane Watts and Mary Baskin.
Three sons John, Oliver and Robert.

Exs.: Son John Baskin and bro. Thomas Baskin.
Wit.: Geo. McGinnes, Wm. Montgomery.
Codicil: 25 Aug 1814.
Wit.: Frazer Montgomery.   H. 338-339.

WESTHAFFER, CHRISTIAN, yeoman, Allen. 9 March 1815. 5 July 1815.
Wife Susannah.
Son William.
Minor children.
Aged father.
Plantation joining lands of John Hoover and John Greigor.
Exs.: Wife Susannah and son William.
Wit.: David Boden, Abraham Smith.   H. 340-341.

JACOB, THOMAS, farmer, Mifflin. 5 Dec 1814. 1 Aug 1815.
Wife Jane.
Son in law Robert McFarlane.
Children of dau. Mary, decd., who was intermarried with Alexander Brown,
Esq.
Dau. Eliza wife of James Woodburn.
Sons David and Joseph and Thomas.
Exs.: Sons Joseph and David Jacob.
Wit.: Jno. Geddis, John Shannon, Junr.   H. 342.

DIMSEY, MARGARET, Allen. 16 April 1810. 8 Aug 1815.
Son Henry.
Dau. Nancy.
Son John's widow.
Exs.: Benjamin Anderson and Peter McCan, both of Lisburn, Allen
Township.
Wit.: Jacob Sherrick, Samuel Fisher, James Smith.   H. 343.

GOOD, EDWARD, Rye. 4 June 1815. 5 Aug 1815.
Children Edward, William, Elizabeth, Polly, Margareth and Anney.
Grandchildren William and Eliza, children of dau. Polly.
Ex.: Son Edward Good.
Wit.: Thomas Wharton, James Ellis.   H. 344.

QUIGLEY, ROBERT, yeoman, Hopewell. 8 Nov 1814. 28 Sept 1815.
Wife Mary.
Sons Joseph, John and James.

Four daus. Eleanor wife of David McKenny, Jannet wife of James Rodgers, Dina wife of Joseph McKenny and Mary wife of David Bell.
David King, an apprentice.
Exs.: Sons John Quigley and Joseph Quigley.
Wit.: Andrew Rodgers, John Wills, John Woods. H. 345-346.

BROWN, JOHN, the Elder, Westpennsbro. 16 April 1814. 13 Oct 1815.
Wife Elizabeth.
Sons Joseph and John.
Children and heirs at law of son Adam, decd.
Son in law John Reese in right of his wife Mary.
Plantation in Butler Co., now in occupancy of sd. John Reese.
Son in law George Boyd and his wife Elizabeth.
Son in law John Dods and his wife Hannah.
Part of said plantation in Butler Co. in occupancy of sd. John Dods.
Grandson Josiah Hood.
Exs.: Sons Joseph and John Brown.
Wit.: Peter Tritt, William McDonald. H. 347-348.

GOOSEWEILER, JOHN, farmer, Allen. 29 June 1810. 17 Oct 1815.
Present wife Maria Sarah.
Friend Andrew Emminger.
Three children of former wife, viz., John Gooseweiler, Catherine wife of William Messinger, and Elizabeth wife of Abraham Heckernell.
Ex.: Andrew Emminger.
Wit.: Leonard Kellar, Geo. Metzgar. H. 349-350.

ELLIOTT, THOMAS, Tyrone. 24 June 1815. 30 Oct 1815.
Sons Charles and Robert.
Daus. Mary intermarried with Andrew Patterson and Catherine.
Exs.: Sons Charles Elliott and Robert Elliott.
Wit.: Nicholas Ikass, Thomas Simonton, Peter Baker. H. 351-352.

MILLIGAN, SAMUEL, Tyrone. 2 March 1810. 3 Nov 1815.
Wife Sarah.
Son Thomas.
Dau. Margaret Wallace.
Dau. in law Betty Milligan.
Sons John, David, Joseph and Hugh.
Daus. Jane Bell and Elizabeth Boyd.
Sister Margaret Jameson.

202

Exs.: Son Thomas Milligan and William Irwin.
Wit.: David Coyle, James McMillen. H. 353.353.

SHARP, ROBERT. 8 Sept 1804. 7 Nov 1815.
Wife Margaret.
Three sons James, David and John, when John comes to full age.
Grandchildren Margaret, Jane and Mary Smith, minors.
Exs.: Three sons and Atcheson Laughlin.
Wit.: Thos. Kenneday, Soloman Lightcap, Thos. Lightcap. H. 354.

BAXTER, WILLIAM. 9 Dec 1801. 9 Nov 1815.
Wife Margret.
Sons and dau., when youngest child comes of age, names of children not given.
Exs.: Wife Margret Baxter and bro. James Baxter.
Wit.: William McClintock, Martha Hunter, Joseph Hunter.
H. 355-356.

SPROAT, NANCY. 21 Sept 1815. 21 Nov 1815.
Sisters Elizabeth Dunlap and Isabella Dallas.
Exs.: Bro. in law Wm. Dunlap and Joseph Shawn.
Wit.: Samuel Stanly, Martin Claudy. H. 357.

BOWMAN, CHRISTIAN, Eastpennsbro. 16 Dec 1807. 4 Dec 1815.
Nancy Seibert and Daniel Seibert, children of Jacob Seibert of Cocallico Township, Lancaster Co.
Bro. Benjamin Bowman.
Bro. in law Deitrick Fanestock of Lancaster Co.
Bro. Daniel Bowman.
The widow of bro. Samuel Bowman, decd., and his children.
Exs.: John Bowman son of bro. Benjamin of Lancaster Co. and John Bowman son of bro. Samuel, decd.
Wit.: John Rupley, Jacob Wormly. H. 358.

WISE, GEORGE, Carlisle. 6 July 1813. 9 Dec 1815.
Wife Rebeckah.
Son Jacob.
Dau. Elizabeth wife of James Quigley of Shippensburgh.
Son George Crop Wise, estate of his grandfather Gasper Crop.
Other five children, viz., Hendricks, John, James, Mary and Rachel Wise.

Exs.: Wife Rebeckah Wise, George Wise of South Middleton Township and Andrew Boden of Carlisle.
Wit.: Jacob Hendel, Jno. Boden. H. 359.

DONALDSON, JANE, widow, Eastpennsbro. ---. 9 Dec 1815.
Two bros. Samuel and John Cunningham.
Sister Martha Cunningham.
Bro. Alexander Cunningham.
Exs.: Bros. Samuel and John Cunningham.
Wit.: Wm. Jameson, Christian Haymaker. H. 360.

BORDNER, JACOB, East Pennsbro. 13 Jan 1815. 9 Dec 1815.
Wife Eve.
Sons Samuel, George and Jacob.
Land on which son Samuel lives adjoining lands of Leonard Buttorff, John Bossler.
Daus. Elizabeth wife of Philip Bretz and Barbara wife of Walter Linn.
Exs.: Wife Eve Bordner and John Bossler.
Wit.: John McHose, Christr. Coble. H. 361.

KRYSHER, JACOB, yeoman, Allen. 6 March 1815. 9 Dec 1815.
Wife Barbara.
Sons David and Rudolph.
Daus. Elizabeth, Mary and Catherine.
Exs.: Son Rudolph and David and son in law Jno. Wolf.
Wit.: David Boden, Adam Leidig. H. 362-364.

FRY, ADAM, Tyrone. 8 March 1815. 19 Dec 1815.
Wife Mary.
Five sons John, Peter, Abraham, George and Daniel.
Daus. Elizabeth Garllen, Catherine Bossler and Lavinia Fry.
Wit.: Sabastian Shober, Abraham Fry. H. 365-366.

SMITH, JAMES, Rye. 15 Feb 1815. 23 Dec 1815.
Wife Elizabeth.
Sons James, John and Alexander.
Daus. Barbara Martin, Rachel Watts, Agness Branyan, and Elizabeth Smith.
Sons Samuel, Joseph and Andrew.
Margaret Elliott.
Margaret Martin.

Elizabeth Elliott, James Elliott and Frances Elliott.
Exs.: Alexr. Shortes and John Owen, both of Rye.
Wit.: Andrew Gelly (Gaily), Joseph Dunbar.   H. 367.

HUSTON, ANDREW, farmer, West Pennsborough. 21 Dec 1815. 26 Dec 1815.
Mother.
Bro. Jabus and single sisters.
Exs.: James Sharp of Frankford Township and James Neel of Dickinson Township.
Wit.: Benjn. McKeehan, Jno. Geddis, James Rea.   H. 368.

GALBREIATH, WILLIAM, Frankford. 11 May 1813. 3 Jan 1816.
Wife Sarah.
Daus. Jane wife of Matthew Woods and Sarah Galbreiath.
Nieces Nancy and Jane Galbreiath, daus. of bro. John Galbreiath.
Dau. Nancy wife of Joseph Edmiston.
Exs.: Wife Sarah and son in law Joseph Edmiston.
Wit.: John Scouler, John Ernst.   H. 369-370.

MC NAUGHTON, PATRICK. 14 Aug 1809. 4 Jan 1816.
Daus. Mary and Jessy.
Exs.: Dau. Mary McNaughton.
To be directed by David Watts, Esq., Charles Smith, Esq., and T. Duncan, Esq.
Wit.: None given.
Writing sworn to by John Holland and Alexr. Rodgers.   H. 371.

HAMILTON, MARY, late of Toboyne. 22 Nov 1815. 1 Feb 1816.
Eldest sister Sarah McMasters.
Father William Hamilton, decd.
Bros. George Hamilton, William Wallace Hamilton, James and John Hamilton.
Exs.: Bro. John Hamilton.
Wit.: John Heap, Atcheson Laughlin.   H. 372.

PEDEN, JOHN, Tyrone. 14 Dec 1814. 5 June 1815.
Wife Mary.
Four sons, viz., William, Robert, Ross and John, a minor.
Daus. Jane wife of John Clark, Agness, Margaret, Mary and Sarah wife of John Hench.

Exs.: Son William, Charles Elliott and Thos. Simonton.
Wit.: Henry Long, Peter Long.   H. 373-374.

ROWNEY, JAMES, Carlisle. 2 Sept 1808. 3 Feb 1816.
Wife Mary.
Three children William, Charles and Mary Rowney.
Exs.: Sons William Rowney and Charles Rowney.
Wit.: John Underwood, James Underwood.   H. 375.

KNISELEY, GEORGE, Dickinson. 22 July 1815. 26 Feb 1816.
Wife Elizabeth.
Six children, viz., Samuel, Daniel, Abraham, George, John and Catherine
Swope.
John McCrory, tenant.
Land adjoining John Zeigler's, Weakley's, Dixon's and M. Ege's.
To Jacob Gehr's line.
Eleanor Moffit, tenant.
Exs.: Sons Daniel, George and John Kniseley.
Wit.: George Wilson, Samuel Weakley.   H. 386-378.

HARPER, JAMES, Mifflin. 4 July 1814. 28 Feb 1816.
Wife Mary.
Son John.
Daus. Jane Harper and Margaret Harper.
Plantation formerly William and Samuel Gillispie's down the Big Run.
Bro. William Harper, guardian of dau. Margaret.
Ex.: Son John Harper.
Wit.: Daniel McDonnell, James Purdy.   H. 379-380.

STUART, JOHN, Tyrone. 15 Jan 1816. 1 March 1816.
My housekeeper Isabella Stuart.
John Stuart, Robert Stuart and William Stuart, sons of above named
Isabella Stuart.
My dau. Elizabeth Arbuckle.
Exs.: Revd. Joseph Brady and Alexr. Rodgers, Esq.
Wit.: James Lamberton, Nathan Jones.   H. 381-382.

MOORE, WILLIAM, blacksmith, Carlisle. 22 Aug 1814. 11 March 1816.
Wife Elizabeth.
Son James.
Daus. to live with son James while they remain single.

Ex.: Son James Moore.
Wit.: Archibald London, Jno. Boden, Andrew Boden. H. 383.

WHITEHILL, ROBERT, Eastpennsborough. 29 Sept 1808. 27 March 1816.
Sons James and Robert.
Daus. Rachel, Elizabeth and Eleanor.
Alexander McBeth and Rachel his wife.
Children of said Rachel McBeth.
Grandson James Whitehill, a minor.
Exs.: Sons James Whitehill and Robert Whitehill.
Wit.: None given.
Sworn to by John Kean and William N. Irvin, both of Harissburgh, Dauphin
Co. H. 384-386.

MC FARLANE, ELIZABETH, Newton. 8 Sept 1815. 29 March 1816.
Bro. James McFarlane.
Sister Margaret married to Thomas Kenneday of Frankford Township.
Sister Mary married to John Dunbar of Newville.
William Thompson and his sister Rosanna wife of William Glenn, the
children of sister Ann, decd.
Rosanna Hamilton of Harrisburg, dau. of sister Jane, decd.
Rosanna Dunbar.
Bro. Robert's son and dau., viz., Thomas and Rosanna McFarlane.
Ex.: Bro. Robert McFarlane.
Wit.: Andw. Thompson, Samuel Kilgore, William Kilgore. H. 387.

WORST, HENRY, Frankford. 10 Oct 1812. 25 April 1816.
Wife Elizabeth.
Daus. Margaret and Elizabeth.
Son Henry.
Grandchildren, children of son Jacob, decd., viz., Jacob, David, Daniel,
Peter, Samuel, Elizabeth, Annamary and Catherine.
Exs.: Friends Peter Diller and Michael Line.
Wit.: John Bear, John Konig. H. 388-389.

HELBURNE (HEILUN), PETER, Revd., Carlisle. 22 April 1816. 29 April
1816.
To Mary Hagan, wife of Thomas Hagan, in trust for the Catholic Church of
Carlisle.
Ex.: Thomas Hagan of Carlisle.
Wit.: Wm. Ramsey, John A. Black. H. 390.

STEEL, MARY, Carlisle. Non Cupative Will. 1 April 1816. 6 May 1816.
Estate to four children of William Laird, viz., Steel Henderson, Lard,
William and Matthew Lard.
Wit.: Mary Harris, William Laird.   H. 391.

SHANLEY, ADAM, gentleman, Shippensburgh. 1 Feb 1814. 10 May 1816.
Granddau. Katherine Shanley, dau. of son Jacob.
Sons John and Valentine Shanley.
Daus. Elizabeth wife of Jacob Hay and Catherine.
House in which I now live, bought from heirs of James Lowry, Esq.
Exs.: John Means and Benjamin Reynolds, one of Shippensburgh, the other
of Franklin Co.
Wit.: Robert Piper, John Dewalt.   H. 392.

GLENN, SUSANNA, widow, Dickinson. 31 March 1816. 14 May 1816.
Children Thomas, Elizabeth and Sarah Glenn.
Bro. James McKinstry.
Ex.: William McDonald.
Wit.: David Evans, Jonathan Booth.   H. 393.

ELLIOTT, ROBERT, Toboyne, formerly of Mifflin Co. 5 Aug 1814. 14 May
1816.
Dau. Grizell Maxwell.
Sons Thomas and Robert Urie Elliott.
Youngest sons, George D., Alexander and William.
Exs.: John Maxwell and George D. Elliott.
Wit.: Henry Zimmerman, William Anderson.   H. 394-395.

BACKMAN, CATHERINE, widow, Derry, Dauphin Co. 2 Aug 1804. 24
April 1816.
Son Christian.
To my own children.
Step dau. Elizabeth wife of John Wilhelm.
Exs.: Friends Christian Coffman and John Risser, both of Derry Township,
Dauphin Co.
Wit.: William Hamilton, James Hamilton.   H. 396.

PATTERSON, CATHERINE, Newton. 14 May 1816. 20 May 1816.
To heirs of Robert Patterson and Jemima Kyle.
Polly Blaine.
Margaret Deizer.

208

One handkerchief each to Robert Blaine, Wm. Dunlap and his wife, Matthew Kyle and his wife, Francis Patterson, Martha Donaldson, Sarah Harper, Anne Patterson, Robert Blaine's wife, Catherine Kyle, Catherine Donaldson, Catherine Sprout and James Means.
Exs.: Matthew Kyle and Robert Blaine.
Wit.: Evan Davis, David Blean. H. 397.

JOHN, MARY, widow, Eastpennsborough. 28 Oct 1815. 23 May 1816.
Minor dau. Susanna in care of John Clendenin.
Other three children Margaret, David and William.
Ex.: Jonas Rupp, Senr.
Wit.: John Clendenin, George Williams. H. 398.

HUNTER, JOHN, Middleton. 18 Dec 1812. 22 May 1816.
Wife.
Sons William and James Hunter, both now living in State of South Carolina.
Sons John, Joseph and Cyrus, a minor.
Daus. Mary, Mandana and Ethelinda, a minor.
Niece Elizabeth Davis.
Exs.: Wife, son Joseph Hunter and Francis Searight.
Wit.: James Lamberton, Philip Swords. H. 399.

MC KINLEY, JAMES, now in service of United States. 28 Feb 1812. 9 Oct. 1815.
A brother.
Friends Francis Conner and Wm. Porter.
Exs.: None given.
Wit.: John Delancy, Conrad Wereham. H. 400-401.

MC KIBBEN, JEREMIAH, farmer, Newville. 13 Feb 1816. 3 June 1816.
Wife Mary.
Sons John and Joseph.
Land joining Carothers' land.
Daus. Rebeckah married to Andrew Pierce and Keziah, unmarried.
Minor son Chambers McKibben.
Grandchildren George and Mary Hays, children of dau. Polly, decd. and their father, William J. Hays.
Land in Harrison Co., Virginia, near Clarksburgh.
Exs.: Sons John McKibben and Joseph McKibben.
Wit.: John Geddis, James Huston. H. 402-404.

LEAMON, SAMUEL, farmer, Toboyne. 6 Nov 1815. 25 June 1816.
Wife Margaret.
Three sons John, Isaack and Samuel.
Dau. Susannah, a minor.
Exs.: David Moreland, Esq. and John Nelson, Junr.
Wit.: James Adams, Henry Wamper.   H. 405-406.

BRACKENRIDGE, H. H., Esq. 22 Feb 1813. 28 June 1816.
To wife Sabina, all estate in fee simple, that she may retain, control over to
children.
Sole Ex.: Wife Sabina.
Wit.: Archd. Lonond, wife Sabina and Robert McClan.
Memorandum: 19 May 1816.
Made and published.   H. 407-408.

BRANIZER, JOHN, Senr., Allen. 25 July 1805. 5 July 1816.
Nine children, viz., Peggy wife of Jonas Kline, John, Christiana widow of
Christian Beelman, Barbara Branizer, George, Mary wife of John
Dornbaugh, David, Adam and Michael.
Exs.: Sons Michael Branizer and David Branizer.
Wit.: Adam Brandt, David Brandt.   H. 409-411.

HOLMES, MARY, Carlisle. 3 May 1816. 12 July 1816.
Nephews William Blair and Andrew Blair, sons of William Blair, decd.
Niece Jane McClure, wife of John McClure.
Sister Sarah Blair, widow of Wm. Blair, decd.
Niece Elizabeth Patterson and nephews, Holmes Patterson and George
Patterson, dau. and sons of George Pattison, Esq.
Niece Margaret Thompson and nephew William Thompson, dau. and son of
John Thompson of Frederick Town, Maryland.
Nephew James Holmes, son of Abraham Holmes, decd.
Nephews Andrew Holmes and Thomas Holmes, sons of Thomas Holmes.
Mary Craig of Carlisle.
Exs.: Andrew Blair and John Boden, both of Carlisle.
Wit.: Joseph Hays, Geo. D. Foulke.   H. 412-413.

MAYBERRY, SILVANUS. 9 May 1816. 25 July 1816.
Wife Nancy.
Four children, viz., Elizabeth Gahene, William, David and Catrin Mayberry.
Exs.: Sons William Mayberry and David Mayberry.
Wit.: John Elliott, David McGowan.   H. 414.

FULTZ, ADAM, Rye. 14 June 1816. 29 July 1816.
Wife Mary.
Sons George, John, Daniel, William and Henry.
Daus. Eve Dehove (Dehuff), Caty Fultz and Susannah Fultz.
Exs.: Sons Daniel Fultz and William Fultz.
Wit.: Alexr. Rodgers, John Swisher. H. 415-416.

HIGHLANDS, ROBERT. 15 March 1816. 5 Aug 1816.
Heirs of oldest bro. John Highlands, Nathaniel, Margaret, Rebecka, Thomas, William Highlands, Elizabeth Cummins and Jane Maps.
Exs.: Robert Cummins and Adam Shoddy.
Wit.: Ashael Mapps, William Harrison. H. 417.

RODGERS, ALEXANDER, farmer, Toboyne. 5 April 1809. 5 Aug 1816.
Wife Jerusha.
Three sons Alexander, Robert and James.
Land at John Patterson's line to Martin Surmis.'
Daus. Margaret Boide, Elizabeth Rodgers, Ann Rodgers and Mary Rodgers.
Other sons Samuel and William.
Land to Michael Glutshalls.
Exs.: Son Alexander Rodgers and James McNeal.
Wit.: James Carson, Joseph Robinson. H. 418-420.

LEIDY, MICHAEL, Allen. ---. 6 Aug 1816.
Wife Sarah.
All surviving children.
Exs.: Henry Myers of Allen and Andw. Emminger, kinsbro.
Wit.: Joshua Myers, Peter Leitig. H. 421.

CLEVER, BARNEY (BARNHART), Southampton. ---. 6 Aug 1816.
Land to be divided in even shears.
Small children to be supported.
Conrad and his bro. Barney.
Exs.: None named.
Wit.: James Hendricks, Peggy Mier.
Adtors: George Clever, Conrad Clever. H. 422.

RUFSEL, RACHEL, Toboyne. 18 Dec 183. 22 Aug 1816.
Four daus., viz., Jean Wolf, Margaret Quin, decd., Sarah Douds, decd., and Margaret Bergetresser.
Children of decd. daus. Margaret Quin and Sarah Douds.

George Wilson.
Ex.: Son in law David Bergetressor.
Wit.: Frederick Bergstressor, Jacob Bergstressor, George Baxter, Solomon Baxter.   H. 423.

GRUBER, SILVESTER, Senr., South Middleton. 3 Sept 1816. 23 Sept 1816.
Bro. Christian Gruber.
Bro. in law Ludwick Gutjahr, decd., his two sons, viz., John Gutjahr and Jacob Gutjahr (Goodyear.)
Sisters Catherine, Rosanna, Regina and Margaret.
Exs.: Nephews John Gutsahr and Jacob Gutjahr.
Wit.: Peter Young, Jacob Myer.   H. 424-425.

MOOTZER, MARTIN, Toboyne. 31 Aug 1816. 4 Oct 1816.
Sons John and Daniel.
Land joining John Briner and Matthew Shanks.
Children of dau. Catherine Briner, minors.
Daus. Hannah Hedden and Catherine Briner.
Grandchildren, viz., Martin Mootzer, son of son Daniel and Hannah Briner.
Exs.: John Mootzer and Daniel Mootzer.
Wit.: David Grove, Frederick Kiser.   H. 426-427.

LONGNECKER, ABRAHAM, East Pennsborough. 5 Sept 1816. 5 Oct 1816.
Sons Joseph, Isick and Benjamin.
Daus. Elizabeth Gib, Susannah Livingston, Anna Dill and Fanny Oldwine.
Heirs of dau. Barbara.
Heirs of dau. Catherine Miller.
Exs.: Sons Isick and Benjamin.
Wit.: Martin Kenninger, John Mumma.   H. 428.

DILL, MICHAEL, Eastpennsboro. 15 June 1815. 5 Oct 1816.
Sons Michael, Jacob, John and Peter.
Daus. Elizabeth Bernhardt, Susanah Wharton, Eve Tronvinger and Christiana Snyder.
Grandson Jacob Arnsberger, minor son of Margaret Arnsberger, decd.
Exs.: Martin Kenninger and John Haltz.
Wit.: Jacob Bretz, Martin Benninger.   H. 429-430.

212

HELTRICK, CATHERINE, widow of George Heltrick, North Middleton.
17 Sept 1815. 11 Oct 1816.
Sons Peter and Abraham Hetrick.
Dau. Susanna Hettrick.
Dau. Mary Bakcr.
Son John Hettrick.
Ex.: Son Peter Hettrick.
Wit.: Henry Sailor, Wm. Ramsey. H. 431-432.

SHAFER, JOHN, Senr., yeoman, Eastpennsbro. 12 April 1815. 15 Oct
1816.
Wife Barbarah.
Children, viz., Elizabeth, Nicholas, Rozena, Mary, Catherine, Betsy and
Deborah.
Sons John Junr. and Henry.
Other children, David, Sarah, Susy and Petre, the youngest.
Exs.: Son John Shafer, Junr. and Jonas Rupp.
Wit.: Matthias Swiler, Christopher Swiler. H. 433.

MC CUNE, ROBERT, Southampton. 11 May 1816. 17 Oct 1816.
Wife Mary.
Three sons Thomas, John and Robert.
Four daus. Letticia, Kesiah, Elizabeth and Mary Ann.
Children not of age to choose guardians.
Exs.: Wife Mary and sons Thomas, John and Robert McCune.
Wit.: Thomas Highlands, John Chestnut, Henry Hock. H. 434-437.

KNETTLE, GEORGE, yeoman, Mifflin. 7 Aug 1813. 19 Oct 1816.
Wife Elizabeth Catharina.
Children, viz., George, Joseph, Henry, Jacob, Elizabeth wife of Christopher
Hoon, Catherine wife of Christian Wisler, Junr., Polly wife of George Wise,
Sarah a single woman and William, David, Daniel and Isaac.
Exs.: Son Isaac Knettle and Christian Wisler, Junr.
Wit.: John Houser, Joseph McDannil. H. 438-439.

BOYD, SIMON, Carlisle. 19 May 1814. 24 Oct 1816.
Sole Heir and Ex.: Wife Priscilla.
Wit.: Jeremiah Atwake, George Philips, George Murray. H. 440.

FINTON, JAMES, Buffaloe. 18 April 1812. 28 Oct 1816.
Wife Jane.

Sons William, John and James, youngest son.
Son in law Peter Kip in light of his wife, dau. Margaret Kip.
Daus. Jane and Elizabeth.
Ex.: Son James Fenton.
Wit.: Richard Baird, Peter Shaw.   H. 441.

WALKER, JAMES, Carlisle. 5 March 1816. 31 Oct 1816.
Wife Ann.
Sons William, James and John, minors.
Exs.: Bro. in law Alexr. Woods and Isaac Todd, Esq.
Wit.: Jacob Squier, Alexander McHaffey.   H. 442-443.

SHELLY, PETER, East Pennsborough. 21 Oct 1816. 2 Nov 1816.
Wife Barbara.
Wife's bros. and sisters, viz., John, Henry, Jacob and Daniel Gross, and
Jane Gross, Margaret, Catherine, Susannah and Sarah Gross.
Ex.: Andrew Emminger.
Wit.: Jacob Steair, John Philips.   H. 444.

COFFMAN, JOSEPH, Greenwood. 6 Sept 1816. 7 Nov 1816.
Wife Elizabeth.
Infant son.
Exs.: Wife Elizabeth Coffman and David Long.
Wit.: David Long, Junr., Peter Coffman.   H. 445.

RAMSEY, WILLIAM, Senr., farmer, South Middleton. 24 Oct 1816. 4 Nov
1816.
Wife Elizabeth.
Sons William and David.
Two daus., viz., Sarah and Elizabeth Ramsey when children are of age.
Exs.: Searight Ramsey and William Barber, Senr.
Wit.: Thomas Baker, David Davidson.   H. 445-446.

BULL, HENRY, Juniatta. 11 May 1816. 14 Nov 1816.
Wife Grace.
Daus. Elizabeth married to James Beaty, Jemimah married to Francis
Jordan, Rebecca married to John Okeson, Martha Bull and Eleanor Bull,
youngest dau.
Son Robert Bull, decd.
Grandsons Amos Jordan and Henry Beaty, minors.
Exs.: James Teaty and Francis Jordan.

214

Wit.: Willm. Bull, Jno. Bull, G. Monroe.   H. 448-449.

BRANDT, DANIEL, Mifflin. 2 July 1816. 14 Nov 1816.
Wife Elizabeth.
Three children, minors.
Jacob Moorhart.
To John Crim for service of Ann Crim.
Exs.: Wife Elizabeth Brandt and Christian Heckerdorn.
Wit.: John Senseborg, Philip Kamp.   H. 450.

MC ELWAIN, JAMES. 28 March 1816. 22 Nov 1816.
Wife Margaret.
Daus. Margaret, Mary Steel and Ruth Carnahan.
Grandson James, son of John McElwaine.
Two sons John and Richard.
Exs.: Sons John McElwain and Richard McElwain.
Wit.: Brice I. Sterret, Robert McElwain.   H. 451-453.

WOLF, ANDREW, Middleton. 27 Dec 1804. 26 Nov 1816.
Wife Margaret.
Sons Andrew, Christopher, George, John and Samuel.
Daus. Margaret, Katrene, Barbara, Eve, Elizabeth, Christina and Leah.
Exs.: Wife Margaret and Andw. Wolf.
Wit.: Johannes Appell, Abraham Thompson.   H. 454.

YAUNDERS, GODFREID, yeoman, Mifflin. 2 Sept 1816. 7 Jan 1817.
Wife Elizabeth.
Sons Christian, Elias and David.
Daus. Mary and Catherine.
Other sons Jacob and Henry.
Exs.: Thomas Macormick and John Barnet.
Wit.: Thomas Murray, Henry D. Dealhousen.   H. 455.

TOWSEY, AZARIAH, Tyrone. 28 March 1816. 7 Feb 1817.
Wife Sarah.
Son William.
Land in Toboyne Township.
Daus. Margaret, Juliana and Eliza.
Dau. Hannah Fitz Towsey, who has lived in New England with my father.
Ex.: Bro. Salmon Towsy (until son William comes of age).

Guardian of William: Margaret, Juliana and Eliza, bros. Thomas Towsey and Salmon Towsey.
Wit.: William Larned, Jacob Walker, John Creigh.   H. 456.

ALLEN, JOHN, Frankford. 4 Feb 1817. 26 Feb 1817.
Bro. James Williams Allen, lots on Eutaw Street, Baltimore.
Anna Laird, dau. of James Laird.
Bro. Samuel, houses and lots on Howard St., Baltimore.
Exs.: Bro. James Williams Allen.
Wit.: John McDowel, Thomas Wallace.   H. 458.

MARSHALL, JANE, South Middleton. Died 21 Jan 1817. 7 Feb 1817.
To Aunt Margaret.
Cousins Sally, Jame, Thomas, John and Andrew.
Ex.: Friend William Ramsey of Carlisle.
Wit.: None named.
Sworn to by David Ebey, Simon Ebey, Rebecca Richwine.   H. 459.

CAROTHERS, ANDREW, yeoman, Eastpennsbro. 24 Feb 1817. 14 March 1817.
Wife Mary.
Sons William and Andrew, plantation on Susquehanna River.
Son Samuel, plantation joining John Clendenin's and Samuel Fisher's.
Dau. Sarah Mickey.
Sons John and James, a minor.
Grandson Andrew Wayne Carothers.
Levitate (Letitia?), Mary and Maryann (Marian?).
Exs.: Wife, son Samuel and John Clendenin.
Wit.: Samuel Fought, Jesse Patterson.   H. 460-462.

WOODS, ELIZABETH. 26 Feb 1817. 15 March 1817.
Daus. Jean Woods, Margaret Holmes, Elizabeth Grier and Mary Woods.
Granddau. Elizabeth Holmes.
Andrew Boden, Esq.
Exs.: Grandson Samuel Woods and Nathan Woods.
Wit.: Jonathan Holmes, R. O'Brien, Isaac Todd.   H. 463-464.

LOVE, JAMES, Carlisle. 30 Dec 1813. 18 March 1817.
Wife Isabella.
Adopted son in law Jacob Duey and Ester his wife.
Exs.: Wife and James McNeal of Shermans Valley.

Wit.: Alexander Woods, George Murray.   H. 465.

UTTEY, SAMUEL, Tyrone. 2 March 1817. 22 March 1817.
Wife Barbara.
Children Peter, Susannah, Moses, Betsy and Samuel.
Exs.: Samuel Kitzel and Jacob Kinard.
Wit.: Valentine Hossinger, John Roth.   H. 466-468.

PORTER, ROBERT, Millerstown, Greenwood. 18 March 1817. 28 March 1817.
Wife Ann.
Son Moses Porter and Margaret Wilson, both of Ireland.
Dau. Sophia and her husband Thos. Cochran.
Mary Porter widow of George Porter, decd.
Granddau. Eliza Steel.
Step dau. Margaret Steel.
Grandchildren Robert Porter, William P. Cochran and George and Caroline
Porter, children of Geo. Porter, decd.
Andrew Trimmer.
Exs.: Wife, Abraham Adams and Caleb North.
Wit.: Jacob Bollinger, John Pursell.   H. 469-472.

LONG, HENRY, Greenwood. 21 March 1813. 28 April 1817.
Sole Heir and Ex.: Wife Eve.
Wit.: Abm. Adams, David Rumbaugh.   I. 1.

BOWER, MARGARET, Dickinson. 20 Nov 1816. 3 May 1817.
To Henry Bowers, William Bowers, Rebecca Harriott and Rachel Peffer.
David Bowers.
Ex.: Daniel Bowers.
Wit.: Philip Peffer, George Stevens.   I. 2.

MITCHELL, GEORGE, Greenwood. 2 April 1817. 12 May 1817.
Wife Hannah.
Dau. Polly.
John Anderson to be maintained while he lives.
When youngest son is of age.
Susannah Brothers.
Exs.: Wife Hannah and sons John, James and Geo. Mitchell.
Wit.: Samuel Mealy, Wm. Howe.   I. 3.

BURD, MATTHIAS, shoemaker, Tyrone. 26 April 1815. 27 May 1817.
Wife Catherine.
Estate in Tyrone and Juniatta Townships adjoining lands of Wm. Barkley,
George Smith and Joseph Sprigle.
Children, to wit, Jacob, George, Matthias, John, William, Margaret wife of
John Barrack and Elizabeth wife of Henry Folk.
Exs.: Son George Burd and John Holepeter of Juniatta.
Wit.: John Vincent, Wilson McClure.   I. 4-5.

SHOOP, FREDERICK, blacksmith, Allen. 8 Sept 1814. 25 March 1817.
Children Adam, Samuel, Elizabeth, Christopher, George and Jacob.
Exs.: Son Adam Shoop and Abraham Bollinger.
Wit.: David Brenizer, Wm. Bryson.   I. 6-7.

BOEH, JOHN GEORGE GODFREID, yeoman, Mifflin. 18 Feb 1812. 7
June 1817.
Step bro. Jacob Christlieb residing in Harnson Co., Virginia.
Nephews George, Samuel, Abraham, William, Isaac, John and Jacob
Christlieb, sons of said Jacob Christlieb.
Second step bro. Charles Christlieb.
Children of said Charles, viz., John, George, Charles, Isaac, Jacob, Sarah
and Solomon.
Exs.: Step bro. Charles Christlieb and Jacob Knettle.
Wit.: James Harper, Thomas McCormick.
Codicil: 21 Oct 1812.
To grand nephews John and George Christlieb, sons of nephew George
Christlieb and John Scouller, Ex. in place of Jacob Knettle.
                                                                       I. 8-11.

WEAKLEY, EDWARD. 21 March 1817. 11 June 1817.
Wife Margaret.
Sons Samuel, James, John, David and Thomas.
Dau. Margaret.
Friend Mary Lightcap, a minor.
Exs.: Wife Margaret and James and John Weakley.
Wit.: John Baldwin, Geo. Stevens.   I. 12-13.

COOPER, CHARLES, Carlisle. 25 Aug 1814. 14 June 1817.
Dau. Mary wife of James Noble.
Grandson Charles Cooper, son of son John A. Cooper.
Granddaus. Margaret and Ann Noble, daus. of sd. Mary Noble.

218

Son John A. Cooper.
Lots adjoining lots of Joseph Knox, James Noble and heirs of Genl. William Alexander, decd.
House on High St. joining James Hamilton's, Esq.
Dau. Jane Cooper.
Dau. in law Rachel Cooper wife of John A. Cooper.
Exs.: William Craighead of South Middleton.
Wit.: Joseph Knox, Andw. Carothers.   I. 14-17.

BOB, NICHOLAS, East Pennsborough. 11 June 1811. 17 June 1817.
Second son George.
Minor children of son John, decd., viz., George and John Bob and Margaret, Magdalena and Elizabeth Bob.
Son Michael.
Daus. Catherina wife of John Evers, Magdalena wife of William Free, Elizabeth wife of John Herman, Barbara and Margaret Bob.
Exs.: Son George Bob and friend John Sailor.
Wit.: Peter Phillips, John Greklin.   I. 18-20.

MILLER, JEREMIAH, innkeeper, Carlisle. 3 June 1817. 15 July 1815.
Wife Mary.
Son Jeremiah.
Daus. Sophia, Susanna, Catherine married to James McKim, Elizabeth married to James Boyd and Mary wife of John Herman.
Exs.: Son Jeremiah Miller and son in law James McKim.
Wit.: John Officer, Robert D. Guthrie.   I. 22.

LINN, SAMUEL, Tyrone. 18 June 1817. 29 July 1817.
Sister Jane Linn.
Nephew William McMillen.
Bros. John, William and Andrew Linn.
Other sisters Elizabeth McMillen, Martha Coyle, Elinor Ross and Polly Elliott.
Exs.: Bros. John Linn and Robert Elliott.
Wit.: William Irvin, Wm. Linn.   I. 22-24.

WEISE, JACOB, Senr., yeoman, Allen. 28 May 1817. 30 July 1817.
Wife Anna.
Son Samuel, a minor.
All surviving children.
Exs.: Joseph Bricker and Rudolph Krysher, Esq.

Wit.: Adam Ludig, Jacob Wolf. I. 25-27.

LUSK, ROBERT, Mifflin. 24 June 1817. 13 Aug 1817.
Dau. Jane Patterson.
Sons William, Thomas and Robert.
Unmarried daus. Martha and Betsy.
Mr. Whitton.
Exs.: Son Robert Lusk and son William Lusk.
Wit.: None named.
Sworn to by James Lamberton and Christen Wisler. I. 28.

FENTON, SAMUEL, farmer, Mifflin. 16 Dec 1816. 2 Sept 1817.
Wife Nancy.
My sickly son, Samuel Rippey Fenton.
Son Thomas.
Tract of land in Turnbull Co., Ohio.
Daus. Anne and Mary during their single life.
Son Robert and his son Samuel Fenton, a minor.
Sons James, John and David.
Little girl named Charlotte Fenton, now in my house.
Exs.: Sons James Fenton and John Fenton.
Wit.: John Mitchell, William Richey, John Scouller. I. 29-33.

JONES, SAMUEL, Shippensburgh. 12 April 1817. 9 Sept 1817.
Daus. Margaret now Margaret Davis, Mary now Mary Buckwalter and
Amelia widow of Samuel Brandeberry, decd.
Step dau. Mariah Owens.
Step sons James and William Owens, minors.
Four youngest children, minors, viz., Samuel Rees Jones, Robert Coleman
Jones, Sarah Jones and John Davis Jones.
Exs.: Son in law John Davis and friend Wm. Devor.
Wit.: Wm. Brookins, Henry Davis.
Codicil: 25 Aug 1817.
Nieces Mary Sturges and Elizabeth Burge. I. 34-36.

DOUGLASS, JOHN, East Pennsborough. 13 Aug 1817. 30 Sept 1817.
Three children, viz., Joseph Douglass, Martha Irvin and George Douglass.
Children of son John Douglass, decd.
Tract of land in Shearman's Valley where sd. George Douglass now lives.
Exs.: Son in law Wm. Irvin, John Armstrong and son George Douglass.
Wit.: Jno. Armstrong, Wm. Strong. I. 37.

MURPHY, WILLIAM, Rye. 29 July 1817. 27 Sept 1817.
Wife Elizabeth.
Sons John and William.
Heirs of son James Murphy.
Daus. Mary Flemming, Jane Mills and Nancy Moore.
William, son of James Murphy, decd.
Exs.: William Murphy, Junr. and Alexander Shortess.
Wit.: Joseph Dunbar, John Owen.   I. 38.

SPAHR, FREDERICK, yeoman, East Pennsbro. 2 Aug 1817. 4 Oct 1817.
Wife Nancy.
Eight children, viz., Polly, Samuel, Eliza, Susan, Isaac, John, Joseph and
Simon, all minors.
Exs.: Wife Nancy and David Emminger.
Wit.: Christian Haymaker, John Clendenin.   I. 39-40.

KEEFER, ADAM, North Middleton. 14 Sept 1817. 13 Oct 1817.
Wife Elizabeth.
Eldest son George.
Daus. Elizabeth and Sallehmay.
Sons Martin, John and David, if any die before of age.
Dau. Rosanna intermarried with Martin Stuckey and their children.
Exs.: Wife Elizabeth and sons George and John Keefer.
Wit.: Abraham Hettrick, Jms. Wightman.   I. 41-44.

DARLINGTON, JOHN, Juniatta. 2 Aug 1799. 28 Oct 1817.
Wife Mary.
Eldest dau. Sarah wife of William Bull.
Two sons Meredith and John.
Second dau. Mary wife of William McClure.
Exs.: Sons Meredith Darlington and John Darlington.
Wit.: David Mitchel, Benjamin Leas.   I. 45-46.

MC MANUS, CHARLES, Carlisle. 19 April 1817. 10 Nov 1817.
Son Thomas McManus.
Bro. Patrick McManus now residing in the State of Kentucky.
Children of decd. bro. Thomas, viz., Charles, Margaret, Mary Ann and
Naomi McManus.
Bro. Thomas, decd., lived in Kentucky.
Exs.: John Boden and Cormick McManus, both of Carlisle.
Wit.: Plunkt. Hackett, Andrew Martin.   I. 46-47.

PINKERTON, MARGARET, East Pennsborough. 11 Oct 1817. 14 Nov 1817.
Bro. John Pinkerton.
Nephew Matthew London, minor son of James London.
Sister Mary wife of sd. James London.
Sister Elizabeth Hoover.
Geo. Beidleman.
Exs.: Asa Hening.
Wit.: James Roberts, Margret Douglass.   I. 48-49.

THOMPSON, DAVID, yeoman, Hopewell. 1 Nov 1817. 24 Nov 1817.
Daus. Ann Kesia and Rachel Maria, minors.
Exs.: John Quigley, John Walls and Ludwick Webber.
Wit.: William Smith, David Green, Samuel Irvin.   I. 50-51.

WRIGHT, JOHN, Buffaloe. 31 Nov 1817. 2 Jan 1818.
To mother.
Bro. Samuel, in case of marriage.
Children of two sisters Jane Crozier and Ann Linton.
Exs.: John Steel of Buffaloe Township.
Wit.: Robt. Buchanan, John Davies.   I. 52-53.

CAMPBELL, DAVID, Rye. 6 May 1815. 31 Dec 1817.
Daus. Jane wife of Samuel Elliott, Margaret wife of James Elliott and Mary Campbell.
To John son of her that was my wife.
Exs.: James Wallace and Benjamin Owens.
Wit.: John Dunbarr, John Owens.   I. 54.

UTTEY, BARBARA, Tyrone. 20 Nov 1817. 24 Dec 1817.
Dau. Betsy Uttey.
Son John Kiser.
Son Samuel.
Ex.: Son John Kiser.
Wit.: Valentine Hossinger, Daniel Ritter.   I. 55.

ROWAN, STEWART, South Middleton. 29 Aug 1817. 31 Dec 1817.
To Margaret Moore, Catherine Moore, Stewart Moore and Robert Moore, minor children of sister Mary Rowan, decd., who was wife of Robert Moore.
Ex.: Michael Ege.
Wit.: Holmes A. Pattison, T. B. Parker.   I. 52-54.

PAGUE, JOHN, Shippensburgh. 9 Nov 1817. 6 Jan 1818.
Wife Molly.
Children, viz., Elizabeth Wheeler, Philip, Peter, James, Samuel, William, Jacob and Rebecca Pague.
Exs.: David Foglesonger and John Raum.
Wit.: Robert Porter, John Stewart.   I. 58.

HUSTON, JOHN, East Pennsbro. 17 May 1808. 10 Jan 1818.
All my children by four women, viz., Sidney, Ann and Isabela, by Nancy Carlos; John by Mary Hall; Jean and Jonathan by Mary Pea; and Sarah by Sarah Pea.
Bro. Samuel Huston.
Isabella Eckels.
Nephew Samuel Huston.
Exs.: Wm. Jameson and John Waugh.
Wit.: James McGuire, John Waugh, Elis Woodward.
Last witness decd. at time of probate; signature sworn to by his son, Benjamin Woodward.   I. 59-60.

DUNBAR, JOHN, Senr., Landisburgh. 8 Jan 1818. 20 Jan 1818.
Dau. Jane Trimble.
Son John.
Daus. Nancy wife of Charles McCoy and Sally wife of John Curry.
Sons George, David and William Dunbar.
Children of son Robert Dunbar, decd., viz., Margaret, John and Elizabeth Dunbar.
Peggy dau. of dau. Nancy.
Robert Welsh son of dau. Jane.
Exs.: Dau. Jane Trimble, John Boden, Esq. of Carlisle, and George Stroop, Esq.
Wit.: Henry Fetter, John Creigh.   I. 61.

WICK, CHRISTOPHER, yeoman, West Pennsborough. 31 Dec 1814. 17 Jan 1818.
Wife Margaret.
Son George Wick, now living in Stark Co., Ohio.
Wife Margaret who is his step mother.
Daus. Susannah wife of Jacob Failor of Mifflin Township and her heirs, Sally Wick now of State of Ohio, Catherine Wick and Elizabeth intermarried with Joseph McKill (Gill?).
Exs.: David Bricker, Senr. and William Duncan, Esq.

Wit.: Robert Bean, John Hiskey, John Bean.   I. 62-64.

HARRIS, GEORGE, Juniatta. 25 Jan 1818. 11 Feb 1818.
Wife Elizabeth.
Son Joseph.
Bro. in law Jacob Balsley.
Other sons Joshan and Samuel.
Wm. Bull.
Ex.: James Beatty.
Wit.: William Bull, Samuel Postlethwaite.   I. 65.

MICKEY, ANDREW, farmer, Newton. 7 Feb 1818. 17 March 1818.
Bro. Thomas Mickey of Newton Township.
Sister Polly Mickey and her heirs (she being intermarried with Hugh Hazelton of the City of Pittsburgh).
Bro. James Mickey a young man.
Sister Margaret Mickey intermarried with Patrick Hays of Dauphin Co.
Niece Nancy Huston, minor dau. of sister Nancey, decd., wife of Jonathan Huston.
Exs.: Hugh McCune farmer of Newton and Capt. John McCune of Township of Mifflin or Hopewell.
Wit.: Alexander Sharp, Matthew Thompson, William Richey.
     I. 66-68.

HAINZ, MAXIMILIAN, Petersburg, Rye Township. 11 March 1818. 30 March 1818.
Wife Elizabeth.
Son Peter.
Grandson John.
Rest of children.
Exs.: John Hainz of Dauphin Co. and his bro. Adam Hainz.
Wit.: John Chizholm, Philip Swisser.   I. 69.

HOUSER, JOHN, blacksmith, Mifflin. 9 Jan 1818. 31 March 1818.
Wife Mary Barbara.
Two children, viz., son John and dau. Mary Elizabeth wife of Peter Jacoby.
Exs.: Henry Knettle and bro. in law Reinert.
Wit.: Henry D. Daelhouser, Isaac Knettle.   I. 70.

RUPLEY, MICHAEL, yeoman, Eastpennsboro. 15 Feb 1818. 9 April 1818.
Wife Elizabeth.

Seven sons and two daus., none named.
Exs.: Wife Elizabeth Rupley and John Earford.
Wit.: Jacob Moll, John Rupley.   I. 71.

CLOUSER, JOHN, Juniatta. 2 Dec 1817. 24 April 1818.
Wife Mary.
Eight children, viz., John, George, Simon, Elizabeth wife of Elijah
McKeehan, Peggy wife of George Leonard, Barbara wife of Samuel
Kniseley, youngest dau. Catherine unmarried and son Philip.
Grandchildren, children of son Jacob Clouser, decd., viz., John, Peggy,
Nancy and Mary Clouser, all minors.
Exs.: Sons John and George Closer and Elijah McKeehan, all of Juniatta
Township.
Wit.: Joseph McNaughton, G. Monroe.   I. 72-74.

DEVIN, JAMES, farmer, Tyrone. 19 May 1818. 10 June 1818.
Wife Margaret.
Sons William, John and Joseph.
Daus. Margaret wife of Samuel Ross, Anna, and Mary wife of John Baxter.
Son in law Samuel Ross.
Granddau. Margaret Brewster.
Grandson Alexander Ross.
All children of dau. Margaret Ross.
Grandchildren James Devin and Sarah Williamson, son and dau. of son
Alexander Devin, decd.
Children of son James Devin, decd.
Son William, unmarried.
Land joining Joseph Neeley's and James Henderson's.
Exs.: Sons John Devin and Joseph Devin.
Wit.: Francis Gibson, Samuel Ickes.   I. 75-76.

YEATES, RICHARD, Senr., yeoman, Shippensburgh. 14 April 1814. 19
Aug 1818.
Wife Elizabeth.
Sons George, Thomas, John and Robert.
Dau. Margaret, now Margaret Askin.
Ex.: Son Robert Yeates.
Wit.: William Devor, Wm. McConnell.   I. 77.

PEA, MARY, East Pennsborough. 22 Feb 1818. 25 May 1818.
Son Jonathan Huston.

Samuel Rees' two children, viz., his son Jeremiah and dau. Mary Jean, minors.
Dau. Jean Ageney.
Son in law Samuel Rees.
Exs.: John Clendenin and Samuel Huston.
Wit.: James Huston, Nancy Pea. I. 79.

STEWART, JOHN, single man, Newton. 4 Aug 1818. 5 Sept 1818.
Bro. Robert Stewart.
Sister Elizabeth.
Cousin John McCune, son of uncle Hugh McCune.
Land purchased at Land Office at Vomcennes, Ohio, on 14 Nov 1817.
Exs.: Uncle Hugh McCune and cousin William McCune, both of Newton Township.
Wit.: Samuel Irwin, James McCune, John Woods. I. 80-81.

LEARD, ELIZABETH. 2 May 1818. 12 May 1818.
Archibald McAllister and Philip Roads to be guardians to children, Steel Leard, William Leard and Mary Leard.
Benjamin Henderson to keep and send to school said children.
Mary to be raised by her aunt Nancy Henderson.
Money divided between sd. children and Jno. McGinley.
Ex.: Benjamin Henderson.
Wit.: William Keath, Daniel Lyneh. I. 82.

BAKER, MAGDALENE, Frankford. 22 Feb 1814. 15 Aug 1818.
Son John Bock.
Dau. Machtelina Darr.
Exs.: Son John Bock and son in law Henry Darr.
Wit.: Henry Snyder, Daniel Reoe. I. 82-83.

STEPHENS, HANNAH, Carlisle. 7 Oct 1818. 16 Oct 1818.
Daus. Mary Stephens married to Jacob Kunkle and Elizabeth Henning Stephens.
Estate divided between all children.
Exs.: Son Thomas Stephens of Adams Co. and Jacob Konkle.
Wit.: Levi Wheaton, Robt. Blaine. I. 84.

CHESTNUT, WILLIAM, Southampton. 23 July 1817. 19 Oct 1818.
Sister Jane Chestnut.
Sister's son, William Clark son of John Clark.

William and Samuel Chestnut, sons of bro. John Chestnut.
Samuel Chestnut Clark, son of bro. in law John Clark.
Agness Clark, dau. of sister Livy Clark.
Bro. John Chestnut.
Exs.: William Devor and John Davis.
Wit.: Thomas M. Highlands, Henry Hock, Thomas McCune.   I. 85.

BUTDORFF, LEONARD, Eastpennsboro. 22 Aug 1818. 27 Oct 1818.
Wife Margaret.
Four sons, viz., George, Frederick, John and Leonard, a minor.
Wife of son John.
Exs.: George Butdorff and George Swartz.
Wit.: Samuel Rees, Jno. Clendenin.   I. 86-87.

CAMERON, JAMES, North Middleton. 19 Oct 1818. 3 Nov 1818.
Sons Robert, William and James.
Daus. Nancy and Abigail.
Exs.: Sons William and Robert.
Wit.: George Murray, Elisha Doyle.   I. 88.

ALEXANDER, ROBERT, Allen. 16 Aug 1818. 11 Nov 1818.
Wife Mary.
Bro. William Alexander of Washington Co. and his son Robert Alexander.
Step sons James Graham and Nathan Graham.
William Alexander Graham (son of sd. James Graham).
Niece Jane Robinson of Baltimore, Maryland.
Mary Graham wife of sd. James Graham and James Graham (son of
aforesaid James).
Exs.: Step son James Graham and John Bailey of Monaghan Township,
York Co.
Wit.: Thomas Carroll, John Bailey.   I. 89-90.

BITTNER, JOHN, Shippensburgh. 30 May 1818. 21 Aug 1818.
Children George, Margaret Bitner now a widow, Peter, Susannah wife of
Jonathan Bittner, Mary Bitner single woman, Jane now Jane Cobaugh,
Michael, Martha wife of Wm. Miller and Jacob Bitner.
Ex.: William Devor.
Wit.: George Smith, Jno. Ealy.
Codicil: 17 July 1818.
Wit.: Jacob Bitner, Sarah McBride.   I. 91.

STEVENSON, WILLIAM, Mifflin. 3 Dec 1816. 19 Jan 1818.
Wife Jane.
Dau. Elizabeth Bell and her son William, a minor.
Son James' son William, minor.
Daus. Mary, Jane and Margaret.
Sons James, John and William.
Exs.: Sons James and William.
Wit.: David Sterrett, Jno. S. Morrow.   I. 92.

LAUGHLIN, MARY, widow of Wm. Laughlin, West Pennsboro. 27 Dec
1815. 18 Nov 1818.
Son James Laughlin.
Decd. father John Atcheson.
Sons Atcheson and William Laughlin.
Dau. Mary Pollock, widow of Joseph Pollock.
Betsy Pollock, dau. of sd. Mary Pollock.
Exs.: None named.
Wit.: John Heap, Jane Heap, Jane Wilson.   I. 93.

WEAVER, ANN, Mifflin. 15 Dec 1818. 7 Jan 1819.
Children Samuel Houts and Mary Houts.
Exs.: Son Samuel Houts and David Steret, Senr.
Wit.: Robt. Lusk, Henry Anghenbaugh.   I. 94.

WOODS, MARGARET, widow, Carlisle. 31 Dec 1806. 24 Dec 1818.
Granddaus. Mary, Margaret and Eliza Lamberton, minors.
Their mother if she survives her husband James Lamberton, Esq.
Exs.: Samuel Postlethwaite and James Dunean.
Wit.: Ja. Duncan, Geo. Richeson.   I. 95-96.

CLARK, DAVID, yeoman, Southampton. 5 June 1818. 6 Jan 1819.
Bros. John Clark and Robert Clark.
Land conveyed by father Robert Clark.
Sister Catherine Roberts.
Bro. James Clark.
Half sister Elizabeth Clark.
Isabella.
Margaret.
Mr. Irvin's mill.
Exs.: Bro. George Clark and Samuel Clark.
Wit.: Wm. Rodgers, Danl. Henderson, John Woods.   I. 97.

CAMPBELL, WILLIAM, Newville, Newton Township. 6 May 1818. 9 Jan 1819.
Wife Rebecca.
Jane Bell, dau. of David Bell, decd. and his late wife, now Mary Rotz, and niece of wife Rebecca Campbell.
Exs.: Wife Rebecca and James Huston of Newville.
Wit.: James McCord, John Heap. I. 98-99.

WILSON, HENRY C., late a soldier in Army of U.S., Carlisle. 15 Feb 1817. 28 Jan 1819.
To Thomas Early of Carlisle all bounty land &c.
Exs.: None named.
Wit.: John Pool, Francis Smith. I. 100.

MITCHELL, DAVID, Juniata. 16 Sept 1814. 20 July 1818.
Wife Martha.
Son Robert.
Grandson David Michael English, a minor.
Other sons James, David and William.
Exs.: Sons Robert and James.
Wit.: Francis Beelen, Henry Beelen. I. 101-102.

COX, FRANCIS, Saville, Cumberland Co. 19 Feb 1819. 1 March 1819. Wife Mary.
Dau. Rachel Cox.
Son Francis, minor.
Ex.: James Beatty.
Wit.: Henry Pickard, William Graham. I. 103-104.

MAYBERRY, CATHERINE. 4 Jan 1819. 2 Feb 1819.
Sister Elizabeth Gahene.
Mother Nancy Mayberry.
Exs.: Bro. Davis Mayberry and Richard Mills.
Wit.: Alexr. Woods, William Keith. I. 105.

SNYDER, DAVID, West Pennsborough. 18 July 1818. 16 Feb 1819.
Wife Elizabeth.
Sally Congh who now lives with us.
Tenant Alexr. Sanders.
Rebecca Byerly.
Children of bro. Merchor, decd.

Children of bro. Philip Snyder.
Children of sister Margaret Kell, decd.
Children of sister Rosina Byerly, decd.
Children of sister Catherine Heiter, decd.
David Shellaberger, miller, son of Martin Shellaberger, decd.
Ephraim Bear of West Pennsborough.
Jacob, David, Isaac and John Shellaberger, sons of Isaac Shellaberger of West Pennsborough Township.
Exs.: Philip Roths of Newton and John Hicks.
Wit.: Jno. Geddis, Robt. Peebles.   I. 106-107.

HARMONY, JOHN, Tyrone. 23 March 1818. 28 April 1818.
Wife Elenor.
Youngest dau. Sally.
Molly Keck, wife of Stephen Keck.
Other children.
Land to John Dunkleberger's line.
Exs.: Elenor Harmony and Leonard Keck.
Wit.: Henry Kell, Jacob Fritz.   I. 108-110.

CREVER, JOHN, Carlisle. 17 Feb 1819. 23 Feb 1819.
Wife Eve.
Son Jacob.
Daus. Catherine Crever, Mary wife of Henry Rheen and Sarah wife of Alexander McGee.
Adjoining property of Frank McManus.
Exs.: Son Jacob Crever and John Boden.
Wit.: Joseph Shrom, James McKim, Francis McManus.   I. 111-112.

BILLO, PETER, Senr., Rye. 16 April 1816. 10 March 1819.
Sons Peter and George.
Daus. Elizabeth Newcomer, Margaret Swartz, Mary Shade, Caty, Lydia and Leina.
Son Jacob, a minor.
Dau. Sally.
Ex.: Son George Billo.
Wit.: Alexr. Rodgers, Christian Emminger.   I. 113-114.

MAYBERRY, DAVIS. 2 March 1819. 24 March 1819.
To mother all bequeathed by father Silvanus Mayberry and sister Catty Mayberry.

Sister Elizabeth Duhane[?].
Exs.: Mother and John Elliott, Esq.
Wit.: John Cauffman, Jacob Kauffman.   I. 115.

PATTERSON, WILLIAM, farmer, Rye. 11 March 1816. 17 March 1819.
Only son Alexander.
Land joining lands of Revd. Joseph Brady, Abraham Young &c.
Daus. Jane, Catherine, Margaret and Isabella.
Exs.: Son Alexander Patterson and Rev. Joseph Brady.
Wit.: Isaac Kirkpatrick, Junr., Thos. Foster, Junr.   I. 116.

MC QUOWN, JOSEPH, merchant, Toboyne. 30 Dec 1805. 7 April 1819.
Bro. James McQuown.
Friend Walker McQuown.
Land bought from John Morrison occupied by James Anderson.
Exs.: Wm. Anderson, Esq. and Walker McQuown.
Wit.: Henry Zimmerman, Abraham Bower.   I. 117.

GIBSON, WILLIAM C., Tyrone. 3 April 1818. 26 May 1819.
Bro. Francis, sole legatee.
Exs.: Bro. Francis Gibson and George S. West.
Wit.: David Miller, John Creigh.   I. 118-119.

GIS, CONRAD, Mifflin. 12 April 1819. 20 May 1819.
Wife Barbara.
Oldest son George estate in Frankford Township that he now occupies.
Son Abraham.
Sons in law Henry Becher and Philip Shoemaker.
Grandson John Gis, son of George Gis ground in Waterford, Lack
Township, Mifflin Co.
Exs.: Philip Shoemaker and George Gis.
Wit.: John Mitchell, Peter Deehl, John Bernet.   I. 120-121.

BAIR, SAMUEL, wheelright, Buffaloe. 7 April 1819. 12 May 1819.
Three sons John, Samuel and Jacob.
Youngest dau. Margaret Bair.
Other daus. Catherine Myers, Elizabeth Stephen and Mary Page.
Ex.: Oldest son John Bair.
Wit.: James Finton, Jacob Huggins.   I. 122.

SHEELY, ANDREW, yeoman, Eastpennsborough. ---. 24 May 1819.

Wife Barbary.

Six sons John, Michael, Andrew, Adam, Christian and Frederick.

Daus. Barbara wife of John Beelman and Marry wife of Frederick Smith.

Grandchildren, children of Frederick Smith.

Land purchased of Adam Alrick.

Exs.: Sons John Sheely and Andrew Sheely.

Wit.: Nicholas Kreitzer, Henry Sidle. I. 123.

HAMILTON, JAMES, Carlisle. At Gettysburg night of 16 Jan 1819. 25 May 1819.

Wife.

Children son James and three daus. Mary, Susan and Emmiline.

Lands and estate in Penna., Ohio and Kentucky.

Exs.: Bro. Thomas Hamilton and son James aforesd.

Wit.: None named.

Writing sworn to by Jacob Hendel and J. B. Parker. I. 125.

LONG, JONATHAN, yeoman, Greenwood. Non Cupative Will. 14 May 1819. 7 June 1819.

Wife Catherine.

Children, minors, names not given.

Adtrix: Wife Catherine Long.

Wit.: Henry Long, John Myer. I. 126.

BELL, SARAH, widow of James Bell, East Pennsbro. 15 April 1819. 21 June 1819.

Sons Thomas and William.

Daus. Polly, Jane Dunlap and Rebecca wife of Thomas Williamson.

Grandson John Culbertson.

Granddaus.

Rev. John Riley.

Exs.: Sons Thomas Bell and William Bell.

Wit.: John Davidson, Tho. Urie. I. 127.

HARRIS, JANE, North Middleton. 4 Feb 1818. 31 March 1819.

Sarah Wibley and George Wibley, dau. and son of Jacob Wibley.

Elizabeth wife of Jacob Wibley.

Son Joseph Harris.

Ex.: Jacob Wibley aforesd.

Wit.: John Kibler, Simon Clouser. I. 128.

LYDICK, NICHOLAS, Buffaloe. 26 Jan 1811. 5 Aug 1819.
Wife Rosana.
Sons John and Jacob land adjoining George Albright.
Three other sons, viz., Philip, Peter and Daniel.
Grandson Frederick Albright.
Exs.: Son John Lydick and John McGinness.
Wit.: George McGinness, William Hower.   I. 129.

ROBB, DAVID, Tyrone. 18 Oct 1818. 6 Aug 1819.
Wife Margaret.
Nephew David, minor son of William Robb of Lycoming Co.
Sister Isabella Irwin, wife of James Irwin of Cumberland Co.
Niece Susannah Tucker, dau. of bro. Robert Robb of Lycoming Co.
Niece Mary Feister, widow, dau. of bro. John Robb, and her children.
Sisters in law Martha Robb, widow of bro. James and Jerusha Robb, widow
of bro. John Robb.
Friend David Robb Buchanan son of George Buchanan of Washington Co.
Sd. George Buchanan guardian of his son David.
Thomas Ross son of Samuel Ross, Senr.
Exs.: John Ross and David Ross, sons of Samuel Ross, Senr., of Tyrone
Township.
Wit.: John Welsh, Ezekiel McMurray, John Creigh.   I. 130-131.

GANGEWER, GEORGE, Carlisle. 8 July 1819. 9 Sept 1819.
Wife Nancy.
Infant son Allen M. Gangewer.
Guardian of said son: Andrew Boden, Esq.
Exs.: Wife Nancy Gangewer and Robert McCoy.
Wit.: George Pattison, George Pattison, Junr.   I. 132.

MC TEER, WILLIAM, Allen. 23 July 1810. 13 Sept 1819.
Wife Jane.
Sons James and William.
Land adjoining John McCue and Christian Woist.
Land purchased from George Arnold in Harrison Co., Virginia.
Son in law William Ross and Alice his wife.
Dau. Jane, unmarried.
Land purchased of Wm. Byers.
Adam Hackman.
Brown & Morris.
Exs.: Two sons James McTeer and William McTeer.

Wit.: Benjn. Anderson, Andrew Mateer.   I. 134.

WATTS, DAVID, Carlisle. 3 July 1819. 18 Sept 1819.
Wife Julianna.
Plantation on the Juniatta on which Genl. Miller now lives.
Children, minors, not named.
Friend William Miles.
Henry Miller Campbell and John B. Alexander of Greensburgh.
Lands in counties of Armstrong, Indiana and Cambria.
Exs.: Wife Julianna, William Miles, George Lyon, Samuel Alexander and
Henry M. Campbell.
Wit.: James Duncan, H. Miller, Jno. Arthur.   I. 135-136.

KUTZ, DEWALD, North Middleton. 1 Nov 1814. 11 Oct 1819.
Wife Elizabeth.
Two eldest sons David and Jacob.
Plantation adjoining lands of Christian Keetzer, David Smith, Matthew
Miller and Richard O'Brien.
Other nine children, viz., Susannah Kutz and minor children Gideon, Mary,
George, William, Jacob, Benjamin, Josiah and Daniel.
Youngest, Elizabeth.
Ex.: Wife Elizabeth Kutz.
Wit.: Christian Crotzer, Jacob Crever.   I. 137-139.

ELLIOTT, ALEXANDER, Mifflin. 15 June 1811. 26 Oct 1819.
Two sons Thomas and James.
Daus. Jean Thompson, Mary Russell and Catherine Elliott.
Grandson Alexander Elliott Thompson, son of dau. Jean.
Exs.: Sons Thomas Elliott and James Elliott.
Wit.: John Scouller, William Mathers.   I. 140.

RIPPEY, WILLIAM, Shippensburgh. 26 Dec 1818. 26 Oct 1819.
Wife Elizabeth.
Grandsons William Rippey Duncan, John Duncan and David Duncan, sons
of Joseph Duncan, Esq., decd. and dau. Ruth.
William Rippey, son of Samuel A. Rippey, decd.
William Stewart, son of Dr. Alexander Stewart and dau. Jane, his wife.
William Raum, son of John Raum and dau. Catherine, his wife.
Son Dr. John C. Rippey.
Daus. Margaret Chambers and Ruth, widow of Jos.Duncan.
Heirs of Joseph Kerr, Esq. and dau. Isabella, late his wife.

Son William Rippey, Esq.
"My body to be interred beside that of deceased wife."
Exs.: Dr. Alexander Stewart and John Raum.
Wit.: David Nevin, Geo. Hamill.   I. 141-143.

GREGORY, CATHERINE, Allen. 29 April 1819. 27 Oct 1819.
Sole heir and Ex.: Bro. Walter Gregory.
Wit.: Andrew Carothers, William Cline.   I. 144.

DAVIDSON, JAMES, yeoman, West Pennsborough. 17 Sept 1819. 27 Oct 1819.
Five children, minors, viz., Nancy, Elizabeth, John, Margaret Jane and Mary Ann.
Exs.: Isaiah Graham, Esq. and Robert McFarlane.
Wit.: Arthur Graham, James Rea.   I. 144-145.

WILSON, JAMES, Tyrone. 6 Sept 1819. 2 Nov 1819.
Wife Margaret.
Sons William and John.
Land at Henry Sunday's and Jacob Sanders' lines.
Dau. Jean Allen.
John Ross, decd.
Widow Ross and her son David Ross.
Granddaus. Margaret Ross and Mary Ross.
Dau. Margaret Wilson.
Four young sons, viz., James, Samuel, Hugh and Benjamin.
Step dau. Cinthy Gandey.
Exs.: Sons William Wilson and John Wilson.
Wit.: Abraham Shively, Jacob Fritz.   I. 146-148.

HIGHLANDER, WILLIAM, Southampton. 23 Aug 1814. 13 Oct 1819.
Sons Robert, William, John, Nathan and Thomas.
Daus. Margaret Highlands, Rebecca Highlands, Isabella Cummins and Jane Maps.
William Reed, son of dau. Betty.
Exs.: Sons William and Robert and William Hunter.
Wit.: Alexander Pebles, William Hunter, Jos. Burd.   I. 149.

HAMILTON, SARAH. 14 Dec 1819.
Refusal on the bequest of her late husband, Hon. James Hamilton.
Wit.: Mary Hamilton, James Hamilton.   I. 150.

CLARK, ROBERT, Teboyne. 5 April 1813. 12 Nov 1819.
Wife Mary.
Sons Hugh, John, David, James, Andrew and Thomas.
Daus. Fanny and Peggy.
Robert Adams in right of his wife, dau. Martha.
Exs.: Wife Mary and sons Hugh and John Clark.
Wit.: Alexander McCord, Samuel McCord, William McClintock.
I. 150-151.

LOGAN, ALEXANDER, farmer, Frankford. 14 Nov 1819. 8 Dec 1819.
Wife Jane.
Three oldest sons William, John and Alexander.
Daus. Mary and minor daus. Jane, Elizabeth and Margaret.
Minor sons George and James Logan.
Exs.: Wife Jane and sons William, John and Alexander.
Wit.: John McDowell, Samuel Lindsey.
I. 152.

GORDON, JOHN, Carlisle. 13 Dec 1819. 20 Dec 1819.
Francis McManus, sole legatee.
Demands against the United States for pension.
Adam Houke, A. Martin Clark, John Boughman, Dennis McGowan, Patrick
McManus.
John Boden.
Wit.: John Gillen, Wm. Taylor.
Adtor.: Fearnus McManus.
I. 153.

MUNRO, MARGARET, Dickinson. 18 Dec 1818. 3 Jan 1820.
Bros. William and Ruben Monro, decd.
Exs.: Bro. William Munro.
Wit.: John Peffer, David Gilen.
I. 153.

WEAKLEY, JAMES, Dickinson. 6 April 1815. 31 Jan 1820.
Wife Rebecca.
Sons Isaac, Nathaniel and James.
Daus. Nancy Weakley, Elizabeth Weakley, Jane Woods and Rebecca Boden.
Exs.: Andrew Boden and son James Weakley.
Wit.: James Weakley, Junr., Samuel Weakley.
I. 154.

MILLER, HENRY, Allen. 1 Aug 1817. 8 Feb 1820.
Wife Ann.
Son John, unmarried.

236

The children of Barbara Moyer of Montgomery Co., viz., Henry, John, Jacob and Samuel Moyer.
Maria, wife of Abraham Geyenger.
Ann, wife of Abraham Kulp.
Elizabeth, wife of Michael Shelly.
The children of Christian Moyer, decd., and Isaac Moyer, decd., being the grandchildren of Barbara Moyer.
Ex.: David Martin of Allen Township.
Wit.: John Fahnestock, Geo. Metgar. I. 155-156.

RUMEL, FREDERICK, Carlisle. ---. 12 Feb 1820.
Wife Elizabeth.
Dau. Catherine Rumel.
Son George.
Dau. Leno Hening.
Remain of children.
Ex.: Joseph Shrom, Senr.
Wit.: George Pattison, John Crever. I. 157.

LAIRD, ELIZABETH, South Middleton. 25 Feb 1820. 2 March 1820.
Decd. husband Matthew Laird.
Dau. Elizabeth Burkholder.
Five sons Matthew, Samuel, William, Francis and John.
Son John to attend Medical Lectures in Philadelphia.
Appraisers and overseers: James Duncan, Dr. George Foulke, Andrew Carothers, John Wolf and Andw. Holmes.
Exs.: Gilson Craighead, Henry Burkholder, Matthew Laird and John Laird.
Wit.: James Duncan, John Mark. I. 158-159.

WHARTON, HENRY, Eastpennsborough. 19 Feb 1820. 4 March 1820.
Wife Susana.
Father Thomas Wharton.
Exs.: Wife Susana and William Stakemiller.
Wit.: John Mumma, John Dill. I. 160.

BEALMAN, CHRISTINA, Allen. 24 March 1820. 17 April 1820.
Decd. husband Christopher Bealman.
Dau. Sarah, decd. wife of Abraham Leamer.
Sons David Bealman, decd., and Jacob Bealman, decd.
Estate of father John Brenizer and bro. Michael Brenizer.

Daus. Elizabeth wife of John Smith, Christina wife of John Mumper, Barbara wife of George Brandt, Mary Bealman and Ammy Bealman.
Sons John, Christian and George.
Children of dau. Sarah Leamer, decd.
Children of dau. Catherine, now wife of Robert Heltrick.
Exs.: Son George Bealman.
Wit.: John Rode, Jno. Bailey.   I. 160-161.

PRATZ, FREDERICK, Eastpennsboro. 28 Dec 1819. 15 April 1820.
Wife Magdalena.
Sons John and Daniel, a minor.
Elizabeth McQueath's heirs, viz., Henry, Mary, Sussana, John, Daniel and Magdalena.
All my children.
Exs.: Son Henry Pratz and John Frees.
Wit.: Henry Remminger, John Mumma.   I. 162.

LANTZ, PHILIP, Eastpennsboro. 1 May 1820. 3 June 1820.
Son John.
Land joining John Weiser.
Sons Philip and Henry.
Dau. Elizabeth.
Heirs of dau. Chatarina Earnsberger, decd.
Ex.: Son Philip Lantz.
Wit.: Martin Remminger, Isaac Longnecker.   I. 163.

BRITTAIN, ADAM, Mifflin. 24 April 1820. 10 June 1820.
Wife Ann
Dau. Martha married to Isaac Weakley.
Unmarried daus. Nelly and Mary.
Sons George, Samuel and William.
Wit.: John Scouller, John Y. Davidson.   I. 164.

REIGHTER, PHILIP, Southmiddleton. 18 June 1820. 1 July 1820.
Wife Anna.
Son Philip and dau. Mary, minors.
Dau. Hannah.
Son George.
Son in law William Moore.
Infant son Thompson.
The Thompson estate.

Exs.: William Moore and Jacob Zug.
Wit.: Jacob Whitcomb, Jno. Moore, Jam. Feris.   I. 165.

THOMPSON, JAMES, Southmiddleton. 14 June 1820. 13 July 1820.
Wife Ann.
Property in or near City of Baltimore, Maryland, from late father John
Thompson.
Mother Jane Thompson.
Bros. and sisters.
Exs.: Friends Thomas Stansberry and John Franciscus of Baltimore and
wife Ann Thompson.
Wit.: Saml. Alexander, Thos. A. Bigham, Wm. Alexander.   I. 167.

DAVIDSON, WILLIAM, yeoman, Westpennsboro. 13 March 1820. 13 May
1820.
Wife.
Three children son William Gass Davidson, only named.
Sister Ann Crawford.
Land near bro. George's.
James Giffen's land.
Exs.: Richard Woods and nephew George Davidson.
Wit.: Jno. Geddis, John Davidson, Junr.   I. 168-169.

FINFEROCK, MICHAEL, Shippensburg. 2 July 1820. 7 Aug 1820.
Wife Sarah.
Children Daniel, Elizabeth, Anna and Mary Jane, minors.
Ex.: Joseph Creps of Shippensburg.
Wit.: Michael Hubley, David Waggoner.   I. 170.

CARSON, JOHN, Newton. 26 May 1820. 7 Aug 1820.
Bro. Elisha Carson.
Sisters Hannah and Priscilla Carson.
Ex.: Neighbor Capt. James Piper.
Wit.: Wm. McDonald, Robert Blean.   I. 171.

BLACK, JOHN, Juniatta. 14 May 1810. 22 Aug 1820.
Wife Mary.
Five sons, names not given.
Land in Racoon Valley.
Donation lands in Craford Co.

Daus. Mary Ramsey, Hester Wiseman, Jean Meredith, Abigail Carson and Rebecca Matteer.

Lands in Buffaloe Township and in French Creek bought from Francis Wadle.

Exs.: Wife Mary and son Robinson Black.

Wit.: Philip Klinger, William Black.

At time of probate, Philip Klinger being out of State of Penna., Abm. Fulwiler and Nicholas Ikass, witnesses to signature.

I. 172-173.

CRAIN, RICHARD, North Middleton. 3 April 1817. 5 Sept 1820.
Son Richard.
Margaret Crain, widow of George Crain.
Dau. Elizabeth Crain.
Son William.
Children and grandchildren, to wit, Mary Hamilton, Jane Vanhorn, Ann Dill, Elizabeth Crain, William Crain and Abner Crain.
Exs.: Patrick Davidson and Joseph Clark.
Wit.: Jas. Lamberton, Henry Stoffer.   I. 174.

LINN, JOHN, Minister of the Gospel, Tyrone. 12 Jan 1818. 8 Sept 1820.
Wife Mary.
Sons John, William, Samuel and James.
Daus. Anny married to John Diver and Polly married to Samuel Anderson.
Son Andrew.
Hugh Hamilton of Harrisburg.
Bro. David Linn.
Exs.: Sons Samuel, William and Andrew.
Wit.: John Linn, B.L., Andrew Linn, Senr.   I. 175-177.

ANDERSON, JAMES, Allen. 8 Feb 1820. 18 Sept 1820.
Wife Sarah.
Son Alexander.
Appraisers Michael Hart, Esq., Jonathan Lutes, Hugh Foster, Thomas Metzgar and Hugh M. Mullen.
Five of children, viz., Rennix Anderson, William Anderson, Mary Parker, Betsy Smith and John Anderson.
Granddau. Polly Oliver.
Exs.: Friend Benjamin Anderson of Allen and son Alexander Anderson.
Wit.: Andrew Mateer, Peter McCann.   I. 178.

ARMOR, WILLIAM, Carlisle. 22 Aug 1820. 21 Sept 1820.
Wife Rachel.
Seven children, viz., Samuel, Edward, John, James, Sarah, Jean and Susan (daus. unmarried).
Lot adjoining Adam Recsinger.
Exs.: Wife Rachel, Robert Irvine and Andw. Blair.
Wit.: James Thompson, George Pattison.   I. 179.

RESSLER, JOHN, Westpennsborough. 3 Aug 1820. 27 Sept 1820.
Wife Catherine, sole heir.
Exs.: Bro. Samuel Ressler and John Heiks.
Wit.: Philip Zeigler, Henry Rine.   I. 180.

FAHNESTOCK, BENJAMIN. 1 June 1820. 26 Sept 1820.
Wife Christina.
Heirs, viz., sons George, John, Henry, Peter and Benjamin, daus. Christina married to Peter Aughenbach, Joseba married to Dr. Jacob Bowman.
Joseph How, tenant.
Hanna How, wife of Joseph How.
Bound girl Rosy Egy.
Exs.: Sons George Fahnestock and Benjn. Fahnestock.
Wit.: Benjamin Konigmaker, J. Konigmaker, Dr. Jacob Konigmaker.
                                                                I. 181.

BOOR, WILLIAM, Westpennsborough. 2 Jun 1812. 19 Oct 1820.
Wife Elizabeth, formerly Elizabeth Shelly.
Sons Nicholas and William.
Other children, Michael, Henry, Jacob, Mary, Betsy, Catherine, Susannah and Margaret.
Guardians to have children properly educated.
Plantation in Greenwood Township.
Exs.: John Tailor and son Nicholas Boor.
Wit.: Elisha Doyle, Robt. McCoy.   I. 182.

WHITE, JAMES, Rye. 23 Sept 1820. 28 Sept 1820.
Wife Elizabeth.
Sons Thomas, William, John, Joseph, Right (Wright), Samuel and Robert.
Two daus. Margaret and Mary.
Some of children minors.
Place joining lands of Christian Ensminger, Wm. Hipple and Anthony Kimmel.

Exs.: Thomas Shortless, William Eckels, John White and wife Elizabeth White.
Wit.: John Ensminger, Daniel Ensminger.   I. 183.

TEMPLETON, JOHN, Frankford. 12 June 1820. 3 Nov 1820.
Wife Jane.
Mary McKee, minor.
Sally Kenneday, a girl that now lives with me.
Children of John Adair, my sister's son by his first wife.
Exs.: Wife Jane and neighbor James W. Allen.
Wit.: James Laird, John McDowell.   I. 184.

LEHMAN, ADAM, Frankford. 30 Oct 1820. 114 Nov 1820.
Wife Catherine.
To my lawful heirs.
Exs.: Sons Adam Lehman and William Lehman.
Wit.: Jacob Arter, Daniel Luckey, John Musser.   I. 185.

KLINE, GEORGE, Carlisle. 9 Nov 1820. 18 Nov 1820.
Wife Rebecca.
Son William.
Grandsons George Carothers and Charles Weaver.
Sons in law George Natcher and Philip Weaver.
Ex.: Wife Rebecca Kline.
Wit.: Abraham Stayman, S. Douglass.   I. 186.

COOVER, GEORGE, yeoman, Allen. 30 March 1818. 20 Nov 1820.
Wife Elizabeth.
Four children, viz., George, Henry, Elizabeth widow of Samuel Kimmel, and Ann wife of Peter Dill.
Grandchildren John Smith and Adam Smith, the children of dau. Ann, by her first husband.
Grandsons George Kunkel and Aaron Kunkel, children of dau. Susanna, decd., and John Kunkel.
Other sons Jacob, John and Michael.
Exs.: Sons Jacob Coover and John Coover, both of Allen.
Wit.: Soloman Gorgas, Joseph Best.   I. 188-189.

ROSS, HUGH, Mifflin. 14 Oct 1819. 29 Nov 1820.
Wife Jane.
Daus. Jane, Eliza and Kesia.

Son David.
The lawful children of son Hugh.
Exs.: John Scouller and William Lenney.
Wit.: John Scouller, Adam Jacobs.   I. 190.

FULTON, JAMES, Springfield, Newton. 3 Jan 1820. 1 Dec 1820.
Wife Polly.
Bros. and sisters, viz., Charles, William, Jean and Polly Fulton and Lydia McNeel.
Nephew James Clark, a minor.
Niece Lucinda Allen, a minor.
Place bought of Simon Ross.
Exs.: James McCullock and Jesse Kilgore.
Wit.: John McCullock, John Johnson.   I. 191-192.

BRANNIGER, BARBARA, Eastpennsbro. 24 Oct 1820. 9 Dec 1820.
Bro. David's son John Branniger.
Niece Christina Brenenizer, dau. of sd. bro. David.
All children of Bro. David.
Bro. Adam Brannizer.
All bros. and sistrs.
Ex.: Bro. David Branniger.
Wit.: A. Cunningham, John Bender.   I. 193.

HAGAN, MARY, wife of Thomas Hagan, Carlisle. 9 Nov 1820. 3 Jan 1821.
Son John Black.
Little grandson Thomas Hagan Black, a minor.
Husband Thomas Hagan.
Late decd. mother Catherine Fishbaugh.
Exs.: Joseph Blaine of Philadelphia, Peter Black and John D. Mahon.
Wit.: Thomas Hagan, John Creigh, James Duncan.   I. 194.

ORR, MARTHA, Eastpennsbro. 30 March 1819. 3 Jan 1821.
Daus. Mary, Rachel and Jane.
Son William and his wife Martha.
Granddau. Martha Jackson, Martha Gilchrist, Rebecca Orr and Martha Anderson.
Granddau. Jane Orr, dau. of son John Orr.
Exs.: Son William Orr and son in law Bejn. Anderson.
Wit.: Robert Young, Daniel Sharbon.   I. 195.

BRICKER, MARY, widow of Peter Bricker, Allen. 22 Aug 1820. 5 Feb 1821.
Sons Peter, Samuel and John.
Daus. Elizabeth Brindle, Mary Basehore, Catherine Searer and Susanna
Geary.
Granddau. Lucetta Geary.
Exs.: Son Peter Bricker and George Beltzhoover.
Wit.: Rudolph Krysher, David Norris, George Lutz.
Two other daus. Barbara Brennizer and Magdalena Miller.
I. 196-197.

HAWK, CHRISTOPHER, Frankford. 4 March 1819. 16 Feb 1821.
Wife Anna.
All my children.
Children of decd. dau. Barbara.
My children's children.
Exs.: Son John Hawk and son in law John Gring.
Wit.: John Bear, Henry Clay.
I. 198.

CAROTHERS, WILLIAM. 5 Nov 1786. 25 Jan 1794. Letters 16 Feb 1821.
Bro. John.
Honoured mother.
Bros. James, Martin, Andrew and Armstrong.
Sisters Margaret, Jean and Isabel.
Exs.: Wm. Clark, James Carothers, Junr. and Jno. Carothers.
Wit.: Armstrong Carothers, John Kean, James Carothers.
At time of probate, John Kean and James Carothers dead. Signature sworn
to by John Carothers, nephew of sd. James Carothers.
I. 199.

GALBREATH, MARY, widow of John Galbreath, Shippensburg. 18 Dec
1820. 7 March 1821.
Oldest dau. Elizabeth wife of Patrick Hays.
Oldest son James Galbreath.
Other sons John, Thomas, Robert and William Galbreath.
Daus. Agness wife of Robert Stockton and Mary wife of William Linn.
Heirs of dau. Dorcas, late deceased.
Mary Hays dau. of Patrick Hays.
Exs.: Son Thomas Galbreath, William Brookins, Esq. and John Cox, Esq.
Wit.: John Irwin, George R. Leeper.
I. 200-201.

BOWMAN, JACOB, Frankford. 15 May 1815. 30 March 1821.

Sons Abraham, Christian and Samuel.
Dau. Mary, decd.
Daus. Elizabeth, Magdalene and Catherine.
Children of dau. Mary, decd.
Dau. Rebecca who is not capable to care for herself under guardianship of sons.
Exs.: Son Christian Bowman and Martin George, Esq.
Wit.: John Bear, John Bear, Junr. I. 202.

MC GUIRE, JAMES, Eastpennsbro. 3 July 1809. 7 April 1821.
Son Francis.
Two daus. Peggy and Nancy.
Exs.: Son Francis McGuire and Samuel Sample.
Wit.: None named.
"No witnesses, but this my last will." I. 203.

DICKSON, JOHN, Dickinson. 29 March 1821. 23 April 1821.
Wife Margaret.
Son John.
Daus. Mary wife of Adam Sowers, and Sarah wife of George Deeme.
Children of dau. Ann Underwood, decd., viz., John Dickson Underwood, Margaret and Sarah Underwood, minors.
Minor son of decd. dau. Jane Rowan, viz., James Rowan.
Son in law Robt. Rowan.
Exs.: George Groop of Adams Co. and John Dickson.
Wit.: Philip Ebert, Peter Camp. I. 204-205.

STANDLEY, SAMUEL, teacher. Non Cupative Will. 15 March 1821. 18 May 1821.
To Sarah Dunlap, Senr., of West Pennsborough at whose house sd. Standley died, 30 March 1821.
Wit.: Joseph Shaw, Wm. Dunlap. I. 206.

GREIGER, JOHN, Allen. 23 March 1820. 30 April 1821.
To mother.
Elizabeth Beirmaster, sister's dau.
Sister's dau., Margaret Cochenower.
Bros. and sisters and the children of those bros. and sisters, who are dead.
Exs.: Michael Hoover and his son John.
Wit.: Abraham Smith, David Weaver. I. 206-207.

LEHMAN, JACOB, Frankford. 22 Oct 1817. 5 June 1821.
Wife Catherine.
Son Jacob.
Land joining John Clay, --- Kolb, George Kuhl and Abraham Heigenell.
Son in law Matthew Clay.
Four children of dau. Eve, viz., Elizabeth Mell, John Mell, Catherine Mell
and Sarah Mell, minors.
My eight children.
Exs.: Son Jacob Lehman and Matthew Clay.
Wit.: Conrad Snyder, Philip Clay.   I. 208.

ELLIOTT, MARY, North Middleton. 6 July 1820. 26 June 1821.
Three daus. Margaret Elliott, Martha Elliott and Sally Elliott wife of
Cadwalader Jones.
Sons David, Robert and George.
Living in home of George Sanders.
Land to Henry Singer's and Robert Sanderson's lines.
Exs.: Sons George Elliott and David Elliott.
Wit.: Jas. Lamberton, Ursula Lamberton.   I. 209-210.

HAGAN, THOMAS, Carlisle. 16 April 1821. 27 June 1821.
Dau. Elizabeth, a minor.
Sister Bridget wife of Barney Carney.
Trustees: James Breden, Andrew and Robert Irvine.
Guardians of dau. Elizabeth, Andrew Blair.
Sd. dau. to be sent to Sisterhood of Saint Joseph's.
Exs.: James Breden, Andrew Blair and Robt. Irvine.
Wit.: Robert McCoy, F. R. Kernan.   I. 211-212.

HACKETT, GEORGE, at Carlisle Barracks. 4 Feb 1821. 27 June 1821.
Wife Elizabeth.
Children when twenty-one years of age.
Ex.: Wife Elizabeth Hackett.
Wit.: Robt. McCoy, Plunkett Hackett.   I. 213.

TRINDLE, JOHN, Hopewell. 6 July 1821. 10 Aug 1821.
Nephews John Paxton and David Paxton.
Land in Lurgan Township, Franklin Co.
Children of eldest sister Ann Lamb, decd.
Sisters Jane Holmes and Agness Porer.
Bro. Alexander.

Bro. David Trindle's children, viz., Lucinda, John, David, William and Jane.
Sister Margery Johnston.
Niece Agness Miller.
Exs.: Nephews John Paxton and David Paxton.
Wit.: James Henderson, James Rodgers.   I. 214.

LONGHRIDGE, ABRAHAM, Carlisle. 8 Jan 1821. 5 Sept 1821.
Wife.
Son Abraham.
Abraham Brown son of dau. Nancy Brown.
Exs.: Son Abraham Longridge, Junr. and James Lamberton of Carlisle.
Wit.: James Lamberton, Neal McLaughlin.   I. 215.

REED, JOHN, Mifflin. 22 July 1818. 13 Oct 1821.
Wife Sarah.
My own relations, viz., Susannah wife of nephew David Blain, and children
of sd. nephew David.
Niece Jane Enslo and children of sd. Jane Enslo.
My wife's relations, viz., nephew James Blair Mitchell, sister in law Martha
Blair, nephews John Mitchell and James Blair son of Joseph Blair and niece
Sarah Blair, dau. of sd. Joseph Blair whom he had by Sarah McCumsey.
Niece Sarah Blair dau. of James Blair.
Bro in law Joseph Blair and bro. in law Andrew Blair.
Exs.: Wife Sarah Reed and friend John Scouller.
Wit.: James Sharp, John Sharp.   I. 216.

BAKER, JONATHAN, Westpennsbro. 5 Oct 1821. 31 Oct 1821.
Wife Catherine.
Father in law Andrew Heikes.
Children, minors.
Son to go to my father in Canada.
Exs. and Guardians of children: John Heikes and John Hawenstine.
Wit.: Samuel Allen, John Bear.   I. 217-218.

EICHELBERGER, GEORGE, Allen. 13 Oct 1821. 7 Nov 1821.
Bro. Adam.
Children of sister Sarah, decd.
Bro. Jacob.
Bro. in law Vernor Weitzel married to sister Elizabeth.
Catherine Eichelberger wife of bro. Adam.
All my bros. and sisters.

Land purchased of Jacob and John Hocker.
Exs.: Jacob Eichelberger and Adam Eichelberger.
Wit.: Richard M. Crain, Michael Long.   I. 219-220.

KEITH, JOHN, Carlisle. 23 Nov 1821. 27 Nov 1821.
To John Smith, Junr., son of John Smith, Senr., of Carlisle.
Robert Smith, shoemaker, of Carlisle.
James Given, Junr., son of James Given, Senr., Carlisle.
Mary Davis with whom I now live.
Agness Junkin dau. of Mary Davis.
Bro. William Keith.
Jane McGarrigal dau. of sister Elizabeth McGarrigal, decd.
Three nephews, viz., John, James, and Robert McGarrigal, sons of sd. sister
Elizabeth, decd.
Exs.: Friends James Given and Robert Smith.
Wit.: Jacob Squier, James Noble.   I. 221.

BARTON, VALENTINE, inn keeper, Eastpennsboro. 2 Nov 1821. 28 Nov
1821.
Wife Letty.
Father Joseph Barton.
Mother Feby Barton.
Bros. Isaac, James, Joseph and John and sister Polly Barton.
Exs.: Wife Letty and Alexander Wills, Esq.
Wit.: Joseph Kelso, William Kelso.   I. 222.

MITCHELL, JOHN, Hopewell. 16 Aug 1819. 28 Dec 1821.
Daus. Margaret Wherry, Mary Shannon and Elizabeth Beech and her
chldren.
Son William, unmarried.
Daus. Martha Mitchell and Jenny Mitchell.
Ex.: Son William Mitchell.
Wit.: Ebenezer McElwain, Andrew Robe.   I. 223-224.

MATTHEWS, MARY, Allen. 25 Sept 1811. 4 Jan 1822.
Sole Heir and Ex.: Only dau. Jane Starr.
Wit.: Janet Harris, Solomon Harris.   I. 225.

MUTERSPAUGH, PETER, Southampton. 1 Jan 1822. 20 Feb 1822.
Wife Elizabeth.
Sons Peter, John and Philip.

Daus. Katrine, Mary, Elizabeth, Nancy and Sarah.
Children of dau. Mary and her husband Alexander Wilson, decd.
Exs.: John Keppinger and David Edwards.
Wit.: John Steele, John Grubb.   I. 226.

ZINN, WILLIAM, West Pennsboro. ---. 26 Feb 1822.
Wife Hannah.
Children George, Mary Elizabeth and Hannah, minors.
Exs.: George Zinn, Senr., and Philip Spangler.
Wit.: Peter Spangler, Elijah Zinn, Saml. Woodburn.   I. 227.

PEFFER, EVE, widow, South Middleton. 17 Feb 1821. 14 March 1822.
Son in law David Norris of South Middleton Township.
Ex.: Friend William Moore of Allen Township.
Wit.: David Gartner, Jacob Zug.   I. 228.

HEIMERDINGER, JACOB, distiller, Carlisle. 7 Feb 1822. 18 March 1822.
Bro. John Heimerdinger.
Jacob Crone (son of sister Elizabeth).
William Baker of North Middleton, guardian of sd. minor, Jacob Crone.
Sd. Jacob to be apprenticed to Christian Fertig of Manheim, Lancaster Co.,
to learn boot and shoemaking.
Heirs of bro. Eberhard Heimerdinger.
Heirs of bro. George Heimerdinger.
Ex.: William Baker.
Wit.: Jacob Hendel, Abraham Barnett.   I. 229-230.

IRVIN, JOHN, innkeeper, North Middleton. 16 Jan 1819. 10 April 1822.
Wife Sarah.
Five daus., viz., Jane Adams, Agness Griffith, Sarah Irvin, Martha Irvin,
Margaret Irvine.
Exs.: Wife Sarah, Isaac Adams and Joseph Griffith.
Wit.: Jas. Lamberton, William Irvine.
Codicil: 14 Aug 1821.
Dau. Martha, late Martha Bell, died leaving one dau. named Martha Bell.
Wit.: William Crall, James Lamberton.   I. 231-233.

MC GOWAN, DAVID. 7 March 1822. 16 April 1822.
Wife Elizabeth.
Two sons James and Stewart.
Daus. Elizabeth, Emily and Mary.

Land to Michael Ege's line.
The husband of dau. Elizabeth McAlhanney.
Exs.: Sons James McGowan and Stewart McGowan.
Wit.: Michl. Ege, Philip Miller, Thomas Brown.   I. 235-236.

FAUST, JOHN, Carlisle. 21 April 1822. 30 April 1822.
Wife Mary Magdalene.
Dau. Mary Faust.
Other children.
Exs.: Wife Mary Magdalene and son Jacob Faust.
Wit.: C. Lamberton, Henry Leckler.   I. 237.

HUSTON, MARY, widow of William Huston, late of Newville. 20 April
1822. 8 May 1822.
Daus. of son James, viz., Eleanor, Mary, Martha and Agness Huston,
minors.
Granddau. Nancy Mathers, dau. of John Mathers and Agness Mathers,
decd. (a minor).
The two children of dau. Jane Johnson, decd., viz., William and Jane
Johnson, minors.
Lot adjoining James McCord.
Exs.: Son James Huston, Samuel Piper, Esq. and Dr. William M. Sharp of
Newton Township.
Wit.: John Heap, John York, Isaac Crowell.   I. 238-240.

YOUNG, MAY, widow of James Young, Eastpennsboro. 5 Jan 1822. 18
May 1822.
Daus. Maria McLean, Mary Carothers and Jane Armstrong.
Land in Fairview Township, York Co. (bequeathed by father).
Son in law Edward Matchet.
Exs.: None named.
Wit.: Peter Wm. Mathews, James Quigley.   I. 241.

HARKNESS, WILLIAM, Allen. 10 Jan 1808. 29 May 1822.
Wife Priscila.
Son William.
Daus. Elizabeth and Mary.
Granddaus. Priscila Bryson and Elizabeth Bryson, minors.
Grandson Robert Bryson, a minor.
Prentice boy, George Hoge.
Ex.: Son William Harkness.

250

Wit.: James Brown, Ephraim Brown.   I. 242.

MC ELWAIN, JOSEPH, Mifflin. 10 Jan 1814. 1 June 1822.
Sons George, Alexander and Ebenezer.
Son in law George Crow married to dau. Margaret.
Son Andrew McElwain, decd.
Son in law Joseph Graham married to dau. Jane.
Land in Flemming Co., State of Kentucky, near the Waters Locust.
Exs.: Friends Robert Lusk, Esq., and John Scouller.
Wit.: John Boden, John Cooper.
Time of probate, Robert Lusk, decd. Letters to Ebenezer McElwain.
                                                              I. 243-244.

HOFFMAN, WILLIAM, Carlisle. 28 March 1822. 25 May 1822.
Son in law Jacob.
Dau. Barbara, "to take her choice as Charlotte and Catherine did."
Exs.: None named.
Wit.: None named.
Adtors: Jacob Hoffman and Robert McClan.
Sworn to by John Peters and Christian Humrick.   I. 245.

MC CORMICK, JOSEPH, Mifflin. 17 April 1822. 12 July 1822.
Son Samuel.
Daus. Leacy and Eliza.
Other children Joseph A. and Thomas.
Late father in law Joseph Connelly.
Exs.: Son Samuel McCormick and John Harper.
Wit.: Samuel J. McCormick, James Purdy, Thomas McCormick.
                                                              I. 246.

MARTIN, DAVID, Allen. 22 July 1822. 1 Aug 1822.
Wife Magdalena.
Sons David, Christian, Abraham and Henry.
Dau. Maria.
Unmarried daus. Barbara and Susannah.
David Neidig and Polly and David Neidig.
David Snyder.
Exs.: Neighbors Daniel Sheely and Peter Zimmerman.
Wit.: Henry Weaver, Henry Martin.   I. 247.

MC LAIN, MARY, widow of John McLain, Southampton. 8 May 1822. 5
Aug 1822.
Sons William and Ebenezer Chambers McLain.
Daus. Jenny Smith and Peggy Wilson.
Granddau. Anna Maria, dau. of son John decd.
Eliza, widow of son John.
Children of dau. Peggy, her present husband.
All son John's children.
Exs.: Son William McLain and John Duncan.
Wit.: George Croft, John Craft, Jno. Livingston.   I. 248.

BRANDT, MARY, Allen. 8 April 1821. 31 Aug 1822.
Two daus., viz., Elizabeth wife of George Shenk, and Catherine wife of John
Shellar.
Children of son Martin Brandt, decd.
Son David Brandt and his dau. Molly Brandt.
Granddau. Elizabeth Pence, dau. of Philip Pence.
Two granddaus. and one grandson, children of George Pence.
Exs.: Jacob Strock and Benjn. Kibbler of Allen.
Wit.: David Seiser, Henry Croll.
Codicil: 18 Aug 1822.
Wit.: Elizabeth Rheem.   I. 249-250.

BRICKER, JOSEPH, Allen. 28 July 1822. 4 Sept 1822.
Wife Barbara.
Sons Samuel, John, Joseph, George, William and Moses.
Four daus. Margaret, Julia Ann, Eve Ann and Mary Ann.
Samuel Buchanan, tenant.
Peter Sholl, tenant.
Land partly in Cumberland and partly in York Co.
House in Lewistown, Mifflin Co.
Exs.: Son Samuel Bricker and Wm. Line of Carlisle.
Wit.: Samuel Young, George Smith.   I. 251-254.

JUMPER, EVA, Carlisle. 16 July 1822. 21 Sept 1822.
To Mary Smith, wife of George Smith of the state of Ohio.
Rosanna Hendel wife of George Hendel.
Elizabeth Jumper and Barbara Stone, my granddaus.
House and ground in Carlisle adjoining that in tenure of Revd. Dr. Mason
and the property of John Delaney, Esq.
Son in law George Hendel.

All my daus., viz., Christiana Logue, Mary Smith, Elizabeth McDaniel, Nancy Logue and Rosanna Hendel.
Ex.: Dau. Christiana Logue.
Wit.: John Thompson, Geo. Metzgar.   I. 255-256.

LAMBERTON, JAMES, farmer, North Middleton. 2 Aug 1822. 21 Sept 1822.
Wife Ursula.
Dau. Mary Elliott, her husband John Elliott.
Grandson James Lamberton Elliott, a minor.
Dau. Margaret Lamberton.
Granddau. Eliza Irvine, a minor.
Two sons Abraham and Ross Lamberton.
Land in Tyrone Township, Perry Co. bought from Samuel Dean.
Alexander McBeth.
Simon Lamberton.
Exs.: Wife Ursula and son Abraham.
Wit.: James Griffen, David Elliott.   I. 257-258.

CAROTHERS, JOHN, Westpennsborough. ---. 7 Oct 1822.
Wife Mary.
Son William.
Dau. Jane Conly.
James Geason.
William Carothers, Armstrong Carothers.
Land known by name of *Irish Town*.
Exs.: James Neal, son William Carothers and son in law Joseph Conly.
Wit.: George Davidson, Senr., John Fleck.
Codicil: 12 Aug 1822.
Names dau. Mary Carothers.
Wit.: James Carothers, John Davidson.   I. 259-260.

THOMPSON, JOHN, South Middleton. 1 May 1822. 8 Oct 1822.
Wife.
Children.
Son William and dau. Agness to care of sister Eliza.
Lands in West Tennessee and North Carolina.
Exs.: Thomas Weakley and John Franciscus.
Wit.: Samuel Alexander, Thos. Weakley.   I. 261.

CORREL, ABRAHAM, farmer, Allen Township. Non Cupative Will. 18 - 19 Aug 1822. 19 Oct 1822.
Wife Ann.
Minor children.
Wit.: Daniel Markly, Henry Martin.
Sd. Correl died 22 Aug 1822.
Adtor: Abraham Hartzler. I. 262.

MC KEEHAN, ELIZABETH, widow, West Pennsborough. 22 Feb 1820. 26 Oct 1822.
Mark McKeehan.
Sons George McKeehan and Benjamin McKeehan.
Late husband John McKeehan.
Exs.: Son Benjamin McKeehan.
Wit.: Isa. Graham, Richd. Woods. I. 263.

RAILING, YOST, yeoman, Mifflin. 24 Aug 1816. 5 Nov 1822.
Wife Catherine.
Eight children, viz., Magdalena wife of Balthazar Loas, Eve wife of Joseph Eden, John, Yost, Henry, Adam, George and Jacob Railing.
Exs.: Son John Railing and Henry Daniel Dalhousen.
Wit.: Henry Knettle, Isaac Knettle. I. 264-266.

MORRET, HORTENAN, yeoman, Allen. 5 Dec 1821. 5 Nov 1822.
Wife Gertrout.
Sons John, Michael and Jacob.
Daus., names not given.
Exs.: John Morret and son in law Jacob Coover.
Wit.: Rudolph Krgsher, Adam Leidy. I. 267-268.

ELLIOTT, JAMES, farmer, North Middleton. 3 Dec 1817. 30 Nov 1822.
Wife Margaret.
Son John.
Daus. Margaret and Elizabeth, unmarried.
Land joining lands of Mr. Zeigler and Henry Hock, Senr.
Dau. Mary intermarried with John Goudy.
Surviving Exs. of James Elliott, decd.
Son George.
Wife's bro. John Sanderson, decd.
Exs.: Son John Elliott and son in law James Giffen.
Wit.: Isaac Angrey, Geo. Metzgar.

Dau. Martha intermarried with James Giffen.   I. 269-270.

GIVLERD, ANNA MARY, Allen. 1 Nov 1822. 21 Dec 1822.
Two daus. Elizabeth and Susanna.
Exs.: Adam Brandt and Daniel Baker.
Wit.: John McCanel, John Baker.   I. 271.

SOWERS, JACOB, Westpennsborough. 8 Nov 1822. 7 Jan 1823.
Wife Sarah.
All my children.
Exs.: Bro. in law Henry Albert.
Wit.: James D. Summers, Elizabeth Sowers.   I. 271-272.

MITCHELL, JOHN, Senr., Mifflin. 24 Dec 1820. 20 Feb 1823.
Wife Susanna.
Son John, a minor.
Four daus. Margery, Rachel, Polly and Susanna, when any one of them
marry.
John Mitchell of Mifflin Township, cooper.
John Snyder.
Exs.: Wife Susanna and Col. James Finton.
Wit.: James Mitchell, John Finton.   I. 273.

MUMMA, JOHN, Senr. 22 July 1821. 30 Jan 1823.
Wife Margaret.
Grandchildren Joseph and Mary Rife.
John Mumma, Esq.
Grandchildren Samuel, Frederick and Mary Mumma, a minor.
Ex.: Loving friend John Mumma, Esq.
Wit.: John Noble, Mary Noble.   I. 273-274.

RUPP, JONAS, Eastpennsboro. 14 Nov 1820. 17 Feb 1823.
Wife Catherine.
All my heirs, viz., Jonas, George, David, daus. Elizabeth married to Jacob
Eichelberger, Catherine married to Adam Eichelberger and Ann.
(David and Ann, not married.)
Exs.: Martin Rupp, Esq. and Martin Kennenger.
Wit.: Frederick Shomberger, Lewis Zeaning.
Codicil: 3 Feb 1823.
Land purchased of Mathias Swiler.   I. 275-276.

FLEMMING, JAMES, North Middleton. 22 Feb 1823. 26 Feb 1823.
Wife Margaret.
Sons William and John.
Daus. Ann Shrom wife of Joseph Shrom, Junr. and Margaret Flemming, a minor.
John Moody, tenant.
Appriasers Job Randolph and Joseph Clark.
Exs.: Son William Flemming and son in law Jos. Shrom.
Wit.: Geo. A. Lyon, Robert Clark. I. 278.

WOODS, RICHARD, Westpennsborough. 5 Oct 1822. 22Feb 1823.
William and John Kere, Lilly Woods, their sister wife of Samuel Woods, Junr., and Mary Kerr, all children of sister Mary who was intermarried with William Kerr, Senr.
William Woods and Samuel Woods, Junr., sons of bro. Thomas Woods, decd. Former property of Samuel White.
Nathan Woods, son of bro. William Woods, decd.
Mary Davidson, widow of George Davidson and dau. of bro. Thos. Woods, decd., and her dau.
Elizabeth Means, dau. of sd. bro. Thomas, decd. and intermarried with John Means of Alleghany Co.
Jean Cowan who now lives with me.
Bro. Samuel Woods and his sons William, James and Richard and his dau. Jane Woods.
Jean Woods dau. of bro. William, decd.
Thomas Trimble's three children, minors.
William Agnew Kerr, minor son of John Kerr.
Appraisers David Sterret, Thomas Patterson, John Harper and Samuel McKechan, Junr.
Exs.: William Kerr, Junr., Nathan Woods and Isaiah Graham.
Wit.: David Shellaberger, George McBride. I. 280-282.

GRIER, JANE. 5 April 1821. 21 Feb 1823.
Son John.
Two duas. Elizabeth Wilson and Catherine Grier.
Grandchild Margaret.
Exs.: Son John John[?].
Wit.: John McKinley, William Morrison. I. 283.

GIBSON, JANE, Carlisle. 25 Oct 1820. 28 Feb 1823.
Sole Heir and Ex.: Samuel Hill, sadler, of Carlisle.

Wit.: Robert McCord, Hugh Reed. I. 284.

WUNDERLICK, CHRISTOPHER, North Middleton. 21 Dec 1822. 1 March 1823.
Wife Eleanor.
Sister Rosanna Miller, wife of Melchor Miller.
Heirs of sister Susanna Rheem, Polly Wetzel and Susannah Rheem, minor.
Moses Wetzel husband of sd. Polly.
Two bros., viz., Detrick Wunderlick and Daniel Wunderlick.
Land in Clearfield Co. held with John Carmeny.
Christian Howard of Millersburg, Dauphin Co.
Ann Howard wife of Christian Howard.
John Solander.
John, William, Daniel and Jacob Rheem, children of sister Susanna Rheem, decd.
Exs.: Wife Eleanor Wunderlick, John Wunderlick of South Middleton and Jacob Wetzel.
Wit.: Jacob Wehrie, John Boden. I. 285-286.

SHARP, JAMES, Frankford. 25 Feb 1823. 3 March 1823.
Wife Martha.
Dau. Nancy Maria.
Son Samuel Hanna.
Other sons and daus., all children minors.
A child not yet born.
Exs.: Wife Martha Sharp, cousin Dr. William Sharp of Newville and Thos. Wallace, son of Patrick Wallace.
Wit.: Samuel McDowel, James Laird, James Wallace. I. 287.

VANDERBELT, ELIZABETH, Newville. 15 Oct 1822. 27 Feb 1823.
Son John Vanderbelt, a minor.
Daus. Eliza Vanderbelt and Eleanor Derr.
Son David.
Exs.: William R. Malroy and John McCullough.
Wit.: Robert McLaughlin, George Lightner. I. 288.

DAVIDSON, JOHN, farmer, Westpennsboro. 18 Feb 1823. 4 March 1823.
Wife Leacy.
Grandsons, the sons of son John, decd., and the sons of dau. Margaret who was intermarried with James Herron.
Land in Lycoming Co.

Grandchildren, children of son James, decd.
Sons Hugh and Alexander.
Children of dau. Susannah who was intermarried with James McCord.
Dau. Leacy wife of Robert McCord.
Son William.
Granddau. Leacy dau. of said dau. Susannah.
Exs.: Sons Alexander and William and son in law Robert McCord.
Wit.: Alexr. Thompson, Jno. Davidson, Junr. I. 289-290.

CORNMAN, VALENTINE, North Middleton. 6 Feb 1823. 4 March 1823.
Dau. Eve.
Son John.
Children of dau. Catherine.
Other daus. Elizabeth, Sarah, Christina and Margaret.
Renneck Angerey to have charge of dau. Margaret's share, "she being incapable of managing her own concerns."
Exs.: Son John Cornman and son in law John Wetzel, both of North Middleton.
Wit.: John Cornman, David Braugt, Renick Angrey. I. 291.

WALLACE, THOMAS, weaver, Newville. 7 Oct 1822. 7 Jan 1823.
Wife Sally or Sarah.
Only son Thomas Wallace, now a soldier in the British Army, reported to belong to the train of Artillery serving in West Indies.
Dau. Mary intermarried with a man named McCuley in Parish of Clogne, County tyrone, Province of Ulster, Ireland.
Dau. Sally or Sarah married to a man of name of Irwin living in Newville.
Exs.: William Richey, Esq. and Dr. John Geddis, both of Newville.
Wit.: Jno. Moore, George Davidson. I. 292-293.

ADAMS, SAMUEL, Eastpennsbro. 12 Nov 1822. 13 March 1823.
Wife Elizabeth.
Son William who will be of age in May next.
The London place purchased in partnership with William Harkness.
Sons Abraham and Harkness, minors.
Daus. Eliza, Mary and Priscilla, minors.
Exs.: Wife Elizabeth Adams and William Harkness.
Wit.: James Lamberton, R. Lamberton. I. 294-296.

MULLIN, JOHN, East Pennsborough. 31 March 1823. 4 April 1823.
To Patrick McQuire in whose house I now live.

Mr. Harris, Attorney at Law in Harrisburg.
Mr. George Ricket, Attorney at Law in Lancaster City.
Mr. John Carothers.
Pastor of Roman Catholic Church in Carlisle.
To be interred in that graveyard.
Exs.: None named.
Wit.: James Johnson, Henry Brown.   I. 297.

STEPHENSON, MARGARET, Middleton. Non Cupative Will. 18 March
1823. 9 April 1823.
Thomas Stephenson.
Son John Stephenson.
Daus. Elizabeth Feloon and Jane Hays.
Wit.: Searight Ramsey, Esq., Daniel Denny.   I. 298.

DANNING, JOHN, East Pennsboro. 21 March 1823. 13 May 1823.
Bro. in law Martin Cupper, if living, his dau. Polly Cupper (Clopper?)
Exs.: John Bowman and John Rupley.
Wit.: Charles Briner, Joseph Benger (Burger).   I. 299.

SMITH, HUGH, Hopewell. 26 June 1821. 18 April 1823.
Wife Elizabeth.
Sons Thomas, John and Joseph.
Daus. Eliza and Jane.
Children of dau. Nancy, decd., viz., Elizabeth, Nancy, James and John
Colwell.
Sons Samuel and James.
Exs.: Thomas McCormick and sons Samuel Smith and James Smith.
Wit.: Joseph McCormick, Samuel J. McCormick.
Since termination of son James Smith's studies at Princeton.

                                                                     I. 300.

WALLACE, PATRICK, Frankford. 13 March 1813. 29 April 1823.
Wife Sarah.
Dau. Rachel Bovard.
Son John who lives in Washington Co.
Thomas Officer of Washington Co., trustee.
Son Thomas.
Dau. Ann.
Exs.: Wife Sarah Wallace and son Thomas Wallace.
Wit.: Thomas Connelly, James Laird, John McDowel.   I. 301.

CONAWAY, MARY, Frankford. 3 May 1823. 2 June 1823.
Sons George, William and Andrew Conaway.
Son Ezekiel Conaway if he returns to this part of the country.
Dau. Elizabeth Diller.
Granddau. Martha Diller.
John Diller trustee for sons William and Andrew Conaway.
Exs.: Son George Conaway and John Diller.
Wit.: John McDowell, John Wise.   I. 302.

WICKERT, JACOB, North Middleton. 9 June 1823. 25 June 1823.
Wife Barbara.
Step dau. Elizabeth Kelly.
Exs.: Wife Barbara and Reinneck Angney.
Wit.: Henry Coruman, Job Randolph.   I. 303.

SPEAR, WILLIAM, blacksmith, Carlisle. 13 Nov 1822. 6 Aug 1823.
Wife Elizabeth.
Son William.
Other children.
Exs.: Wife Elizabeth and Geo. McGinnis of Shippensburg.
Wit.: Adams Nimmon, John Woods.   I. 304.

SHUGHART, JOHN, shoemaker, North Middleton. Non Cupative Will.
11 July 1823. 17 July 1823.
Wife Sabina.
Four children, viz., Rachel, William, John and George, minors.
Wit.: Jacob Shughart, Martin Cornman.
Adtors: Widow Sabina Shughart and Henry Swiger.   I. 305.

KING, DAVID, Dickinson. 6 March 1822. 22 July 1823.
Dau. Sarah Reed.
Four grandchildren, viz., William, Jean, John and Sidney Boden, minors.
Dau. Martha Caldwell.
Other four daus. Jane, Rebecca, Sidney and Nancy King.
Niece Esther Caldwell.
Harriot Weakley.
Exs.: Four daus. Jane, Rebecca, Sidney and Nancy King.
Wit.: Nathan Ramsey, Saml. Weakley.   I. 305-306.

HUFF, WILLIAM, Newville. 22 Aug 1823. 1 Sept 1823.
To Trustees of Roman Catholic Church of Carlisle.

260

Elizabeth Lynch of Newville.
Polly Neil of Newton Township.
Ruth Rowan of Newville.
James Shannon.
Robert Prebles of Newville.
Saml. McKeehan, Junr.
Exs.: Robert Peebles.
Wit.: None named.   I. 307.

LONGNECKER, BENJAMIN.
Appeal in light of his wife Mary, late Mary Rife. One of heirs of John
Mumma, decd., late of Eastpennsborough.   I. 310.

KAUFFMAN, CHRISTIAN, Eastpennsborough. 15 March 1823. 4 Sept
1823.
Wife Elizabeth.
Son Isaac.
Daus. Elizabeth Rupp and Barbara Eberly and their children.
Children of son John.
Grandson John Kauffman and his two bros. and sister.
Wm. Snively.
Exs.: George Rupp, Senr., and Benjn. Eberley.
Wit.: Samuel Fisher, Jno. Clendenin.   I. 311.

GREIGER, MARGARET, widow of John Greiger, Allen. 8 July 1823. 15
Sept 1823.
Son Jacob Greiger.
Daus. Magdalena wife of Melchor Prindle (Brindle), Elizabeth wife of John
Sheffer, Margaret wife of George Bowermaster.
Catherine Smith intermarried with Michael Hide.
Ex.: Martin Brandt, merchant.
Wit.: Michael Hoover, Lewis Zearing.   I. 313-314.

FISTER, CASPAR, North Middleton. 9 Aug 1823. 20 Sept 1823.
Wife Barbara.
Daus. Catherine wife of John Swartz and Mary.
Son John, a minor.
Ex.: Son in law John Swartz.
Wit.: Abraham Sigler, John Sigler.   I. 314.

MC ELWAIN, MARGARET, Mifflin. 31 July 1823. 26 Sept 1823.

Dau. Margaret, sole heir.
Ex.: David Ralston.
Wit.: Wm. Lusk, Richard McElwain. I. 315.

MC ELHENNY, HUGH, yeoman, Mifflin. 13 Sept 1823. 7 Oct 1823.
Son Samuel.
Two daus. Jane and Rebecca.
Land adjoining Jacob High and Widow McElwain.
Son Hugh.
Heirs of son Robert, decd.
Land near Samuel Hamilton's bought of John Weaver, decd.
Landed property in State of Ohio.
Sons James and Joseph.
Margaret Shannon, minor dau.
Jos. Shannon.
To Peter Weaver's heir.
Exs.: Son Samuel McElhenny and Robt. Lusk, Esq.
Wit.: Henry Dalhouser, John Weaver. I. 316.

BELL, SAMUEL, Shippensburg. 2 Oct 1823. 9 Oct 1823.
Sisters Elizabeth married to James Jones, Martha married to James
McCausland, Rosanna married to Andrew McCord and Sarah married to
Samuel Redett, Esq.
Friend Ebenezer Wills of Shippensburg.
Miss Rebecca Mull of Shippensburg.
Exs.: Samuel Redett, Esq., of Shippensburg.
Wit.: Peter Hertzler, George Croft.
Codicil: 3 Oct 1823.
Step sister Nancy Bell.
Natural daus. Polly Bell dau. of Charlotte Bailey in or near Rockingham Co.,
Va., Charlotte Kessler, minor dau. of Betty Kessler and Eliza Beaver minor
dau. of Sarah Beaver.
Wit.: Ebenezer Wills. I. 317-318.

MC KEE, JOHN, Shippensburg. 29 March 1823. 16 Oct 1823.
Wife Agness.
Grandson John Irwin, minor.
Guardian of sd. grandson George McQinnes of Shippensburg.
Grandson John Shannon son of dau. Isabella Shannon, decd.
Granddaus. Jane McElwain, Margaret McClelland and Elizabeth Robeson,
all children of dau. Isabella Shannon, decd.

Son in law James Irwin.

Grandchildren by dau. Mary Shannon, decd., viz., Robert, John, Samuel and Mary Shannon and Jane McElhainny.

Exs.: Wife Agness McKee, son in law James Irwin and nephew James McKee.

Wit.: John Irwin, George Bates.   I. 319-320.

THOMPSON, MATTHEW, farmer, Mifflin. 7 March 1821. 28 Oct 1823.
Wife Ruth.

Sons Samuel and William, minors.

Land in Harrison Co., Virginia.

Dau. Rosanna Glenn.

Exs.: Wife Ruth and William Glenn of Newville.

Wit.: Alex Thompson, Jno. Geddis, Wm. Thompson.

Codicil: 9 Oct 1823.

John Davidson, Esq. of West Pennsborough and Hugh L. Kenneday.
                                                            I.321-323.

TAYLOR, ROBERT, Carlisle. 21 April 1817. 3 Nov 1823.

Children John, Robert and Grace Taylor, minors.

Bro. John Taylor.

Land joining Jacob Waggoner and William Brown in North Middleton.

Exs.: John Boden and Robert McCoy.

Guardians of sd. three children: Robert Irvine, James Lamberton and James Noble.

Wit.: John Hastey, Robert Taylor.   I. 324-325.

MOORE, NANCY, widow of James Moore, Dickinson. 24 Sept 1823. 19 Nov 1823.

Sister Elizabeth McLanahan.

Margarette McConnell who lives with me.

Nancy Johnston Beatty dau. James Beatty, Esq., a minor.

Bro. Robert Johnston.

Nephews Johnston McLanahan and John McLanahan.

Bro. Robert Johnston's wife.

Bro. Thomas Johnston.

Margaretta Johnston dau. of bro. James.

Minor son Johnston Moore.

Exs.: Bro. Robert Johnston, David Fullerton, Esq. and nefew Johnston McLanahan.

Wit.: Samuel Potts, Andrew McConnell, Margaret McConnell, Amelia Given.
Codicil: 6 - 7 Nov 1823.
Eleanor Galbreath dau. of Samuel Galbreath.
Former named Exs. revoked and appoint Thompson Brown and James Neal of Carlisle.
Wit.: R. Lambuton, Andw. Carothers.   I. 326-328.

FORBES, JOHN, Westpennsborough. 25 June 1822. 14 Oct 1823.
Wife Jane.
Sons Andrew, John P. and Richard.
Daus. Elizabeth Dunbar, Rebecca Agnew, Mary Lindsey and Margaret Forbes.
Land joining John and Richard Woodland.
Niece Ann Black.
Exs.: Son Andrew Forbes, John P. Forbes and Richard Forbes.
Wit.: John Black, Geo. Joyce, John Creigh.   I. 329-330.

REIFSNYDER, ABRAHAM, Westpennsborough. 1 Sept 1823. 19 Nov 1823.
Wife Catherine.
My children, names not given.
Exs.: Wife Catherine and son in law Jacob Plank.
Wit.: Jo. Haverly (Eberly), David Bear.   I. 331.

ALEXANDER, AMELIA. 1802. 20 Nov 1823.
Land in partnership with sister Elizabeth, where we now live on Mount Rock Road.
Dau. Ann Highlands, her husband Thomas Moore Highlands.
Exs.: Sister Elizabeth and Robert McCune.
Wit.: Robert Quigley, John McElroy.
Signature of witnesses sworn to by Robert McBride, Jr. and Joseph Magee.
                                                                  I. 332.

REED, HUGH, Newville. 2 Sept 1823. 22 Nov 1823.
Wife Jean.
Sons John, James and William, minors.
My aged mother.
Exs.: Wife Jean Reed and friend John Hasina.
Wit.: Alexander Cox, William Gilmore.
Signature of Wm. Gilmore sworn to by Alex. R. Gilmore.

I. 333-334.

WOODBURN, JAMES, innkeeper, Newville. 20 July 1822. 25 Nov 1823.
Wife Agness.
Oldest son George.
Plantation purchased from John Morrow in Newton Township.
Son William Henry.
Land purchased from heirs of Joseph Walker, decd.
Daus. Margaret Woodburn and Jane, a minor.
Minor sons John and James.
Land in Harrison Co., Virginia.
Thomas Glenn.
Christian Shullers.
Exs.: Son George, Wm. McCullough and Wm. McCandlish.
Wit.: Joseph McKibben, Wm. Laughlin, William Richey.

I. 335-338.

SWARTZ, GEORGE, yeoman, East Pennsborough. 23 Oct 1823. 25 Nov 1823.
Wife Elizabeth.
Two sons Gasper and Peter.
Daus. Mary and Elizabeth.
Two grandsons George and Isaac Fireoved.
Sons John and Jacob.
Exs.: Son John Swartz and nephew George Buttorf.
Wit.: Jno. Clendenin, John Ultz.   I. 339.

URIE, GRIZZLE, North Middleton. 29 Dec 1819. 25 Nov 1823.
Son Thomas Urie, Esq.
Dau. Catherine Jacobs.
Exs.: Sd. son Thomas Urie.
Wit.: John Davidson, James Keyes, Andw. Carothers.   I. 340.

MICKEY, DAVID, Newton. 30 Aug 1823. 1 Dec 1823.
Nieces Rebecca Mickey and Elizabeth Mickey.
Nancy Gray whom I have raised from a child.
Exs.: Ezekiel Kilgore and niece Rebecca Mickey.
Wit.: Alexr. Thompson, R. C. Kilgore, Jesse Kilgore.   I. 341.

SNYDER, CONRAD, Frankford. 11 June 1823. 3 Dec 1823.
Wife Susanna.

Dau. Elizabeth.
Minor children.
Exs.: Son John Snyder and bro. John Snyder of Frankford.
Wit.: Jacob George, Adam Mountz.   I. 342.

GLENDENNING, JAMES, weaver, Mifflin. 1820. 10 Dec 1823.
Wife Elizabeth.
Dau. Elizabeth intermarried with John Hanna.
Daus. Jean Given and Sarah McMonagle.
Little granddau. Eliza Hanna.
Grandson William Hanna.
Daus. Molly Glendenning and Martha Dixon.
Exs.: Son in law John Hanna and step son Hugh Barr.
Wit.: Robert Middleton, Henry Brehm.   I. 343-344.

HANNA, JOHN, Esq., Frankford. 3 Oct 1823. 12 Dec 1823.
Wife Elizabeth.
Nine children, minors, viz., William, James, Jean, Polly, John, Andrew and
three youngest, names not given.
Exs.: Isaac Shellaberger and Hugh Reed.
Wit.: Robert Middleton, Sophia Shulenberger.   I. 345.

EBERLY, ELIZABETH, widow of John Eberley, Eastpennsbro. 29 Nov
1823. 13 Dec 1823.
Five daus. Elizabeth married to John Snively, Catherine married to Joseph
Whitmer, Anna married to Jno. Martin, and Mary married to Daniel Coble.
Sons John, David, Benjamin, Samuel, Henry, Joseph and Peter.
Exs.: Son John Eberley.
Wit.: Nicholas Kritoes, Saml. Ruby.   I. 346-347.

YOUNG, RUDOLPH, Allen. 25 Feb 1822. 15 Dec 1823.
Bro. Mathias Young.
Weise's church near Jacob Stroek's.
Exs.: John Goodyear.
Wit.: David Boden, Jacob Goodyear.   I. 348.

COOVER, TEDRICK, Senr., Allen. 8 Oct 1823. 16 Dec 1823.
Wife Salmy.
Son Solomon.

Other children Mary married to John Wolf, Tederick, Nelly married to Philip Waggoner, Catherine married to Tederick Cocklin, Jacob and Samuel.

Exs.: Wife Salmy Coover, son Tederick Coover and son in law Tederick Cocklin.

Wit.: Samuel Flickinger, Philip Rohland, Patrick Laverty.

I. 349.

BOUGHER, LUDWICK, North Middleton. 18 Dec 1823. 22 Dec 1823.
To my mothr.
John Diller son of Benjamin Diller.
John Jacob who now lives with me.
Exs.: Jacob Bishop and George McFeeley.
W.Ramsey, Benjamin Diller.
16 Jan 1824.
Appeal of Elizabeth Shelby, mother of Ludwick Bougher, decd.

I. 350-351.

LIPPERT, HENRY, Frankford, 14 Oct 1823. 12 Jan 1824.
Wife Catherine and her granddau. Elizabeth Shoff.
Sd. granddau.'s two children which she had before she married Gamfres.
Grandson Daniel Sites.
Dau. Susan Snyder, widow, and her children.
Sons Henry and Jacob Lippert.
Dau. Mary married to Philip Gran.
Exs.: Son Henry Lippert and John Snyder.
Wit.: Joseph Connelly, Philip Zeigler.   I. 351.

QUIGLEY, HENRY, Allen. 20 Jan 1824. 11 Feb 1824.
Wife Anne.
Son Henry.
Exs.: Benjamin Anderson and James Graham.
Wit.: George F. Cain, Samuel Starr.   I. 352.

SAMPLE, JOHN, yeoman, East Pennsborough. 1 Feb 1824. 21 Feb 1824.
Nephew Henry Ewalt.
Sister in law Agness Sample.
Bro. Samuel Sample.
Step mother.
Niece Elizabeth Monasmith.
Half bro. James Sample, if dead, to his two sons.

Ex.: Thomas Anderson.
Wit.: Jno. Clendenin, Alexander McConnel. I. 353.

CARNEY, BRIDGET, wife of B. Carney, Carlisle. 24 Dec 1823. 6 March 1824.
Four children, minors, names not given.
Bro. Thomas Hagan, decd.
Ex. and Guardian of Children: Revd. Patrick Diven, the present pastor of Catholic Church of Carlisle.
Wit.: Sebastian Zeigler, B. Hagan. I. 354.

BIXLER, JACOB, West Pennsborough. 30 Oct 1823. 10 March 1824.
Wife Mary.
Five children, viz., Leah, Samuel, Mary and Jacob.
Land adjoining Samuel Bear.
Exs.: Daniel Dener and John Heikes.
Wit.: Charles Knettlewell, Ephraim Bear. I. 355.

SHARP, JOHN, Frankford. 14 Feb 1824. 13 March 1824.
Heirs of son James, decd.
Three daus., viz., Mary, Margaret and Martha.
Exs.: John Brown, Junr. and Thomas Wallace, son of Patrick Wallace, decd.
Wit.: James Logan, William Blosser. I. 357.

MERCK, CONRAD, North Middleton. 8 June 1815. 10 April 1824.
Son George.
Bros. in law, viz., George Merck, Christian Crotzer, Christian Ruhl.
My three children.
Exs.: Son George Merck.
Wit.: John King, Jacob Stonaker.
Son George dead at time of probate. I. 358.

KESSLER, DAVID, Revd., Allen. 5 April 1822. 13 April 1824.
Elizabeth wife of Adam Ernst for services rendered me.
Catherine dau. of sd. Adam Ernst.
Catherine McCroskry.
Bro. Adam Kessler.
Exs.: Adam Leitig and David Drysher.
Wit.: John Ernst, Adam Ernst. I. 359.

DAVIDSON, HUGH, West Pennsboro. 29 March 1824. 13 April 1824.

Bros. Alexander and William.
Sister Lacy McCord.
Sisters in law Jane Davidson and Polly Davidson.
Exs.: John Davidson, Esq. and Samuel D. Greason.
Wit.: John Davidson, Thomas Miller, Joseph Trego.   I. 360.

MC KINNEY, ELIZABETH, South Middleton. 2 April 1824. 1 May 1824.
Granddaus. Dolly Conly and Polly Harris.
Dau. Eleanor Harris with her two daus.
Exs.: Two granddaus. Dolly Donly and Mary Harris.
Wit.: Saml. Woodburn, James Weakley.   I. 362.

WILSON, JOSEPH, East Pennsboro. 15 Jan 1824. 15 May 1824.
Two sisters in Ireland, viz., Ann Quinn and Martha Griffen.
Ann Simpson dau of sd. Ann Quinn, her bros. and sisters.
Children of sister Martha Griffen.
Joseph Quinn son of sd. Ann Quinn, now in this country.
Exs.: Countryman and friend Matthew Irwin.
Wit.: Thomas Rodgers.
Sworn to by Mattw. Irwin, the subscribing witness, Thomas Rodgers being
in City of Philadelphia.   I. 362.

MILLER, JOHN, Eastpennsborough. 29 Oct 1822. 17 May 1824.
Wife Ester.
Five sons, viz., Christian, Henry, David and Abraham.
Exs.: Sons David and Abraham and Jacob Kreider.
Wit.: Jno. Williamson, Thos. Bell.   I. 363-364.

TOBIAS, BENJAMIN, Frankford. 5 April 1824. 17 May 1824.
Wife Sarah.
Children, viz., Catherine, Peter, Simon, Maryann, Abraham and Elizann,
when him or her arrives at age of twenty one years.
Exs.: Leonard Minnich and Joseph Werth.
Wit.: Leonard Minnich, Joseph Werth.   I. 365.

HARPER, WILLIAM, Mifflin. 5 July 1823. 31 May 1824.
Wife Esther.
Oldest son John.
Daus. Mary intermarried with Thomas Wallace, Jane and Margaret.
Sons Andrew and William.
Grandson William Harper Wallace, a minor.

Share of estate of Thomas Patterson, decd. of Dickinson Township.
Exs.: Three sons John, Andrew and William.
Wit.: John Harper, Samuel McCormick.
Codicil: 24 Feb 1824.
Wit.: John Harper, Jno. Harper, Junr.   I. 366-367.

WILSON, MATTHEW, Frankford. 7 May 1824. 10 June 1824.
John Cook, a sister's son.
Bro. John Wilson's children, William and Ann.
Bro. Samuel Wilson.
David Gibson's children by sister Jane.
Jane Legget a girl that formerly lived with me.
Exs.: John Bower, the elder and John Diller.
Wit.: Martha Roberts, James Laird, David Gagman.
Codicil: 9 May 1824.
Nancy Fulton dau. of Jane Ligget.
John McDowell appointed an Ex.   I. 368.

HUSTON, JAMES, Newville. 3 May 1824. 16 June 1824.
Wife Sally.
Daus. Eleanor, Mary, Martha and Agness, minors.
John McWilliams and Jacob Boil, tenants.
Land purchased of Joseph Walker of Newton Township.
House in occupancy of James McFarlane.
Exs.: Wife Sally, bro. in law Thomas McCullock and friend William
McCullock.
Wit.: Jno. Geddis, Jo. Sruoyer.
Refusal of Sarah Huston to accept bequest of late husband James Huston.
Wit.: Jno. Geddis, John Harper.   I. 369-370.

TRIMBLE, JANE, Dickinson. 17 Jan. 1824. 28 July 1824.
Sons Joseph and Thomas.
Dau. Jane Barr.
Exs.: Son John Trimble.
Wit.: Andrew Davidson, Richard Woods.   I. 371.

WOLF, JOHN, North Middleton. 24 July 1824. 29 July 1824.
Wife Elizabeth.
Sons John and David (when David is of age).
To son Jacob, place where he now lives adjoining lands of D. Elliott and
James Lamberton.

Mountain lands adjoining lands of M. Miller, J. Cornman and James Given.
Dau. Christina wife of Henry Jacobs.
Exs.: Son Jacob Wolf and son in law Henry Jacobs.
Wit.: Christian Wolf, Daniel Handshoe, John Wolf, Jacob Hendel.

I. 372-374.

LEARIGHT, FRANCIS, Esq., Southampton. 17 June 1824. 5 Aug 1824.
Wife Ann.
Sons Gilbert and Walter when they are twenty two years of age.
Daus. Sarah Ann, Elizabeth and Esther Ann.
Exs.: Thomas Lee and Searight Ramsey.
Wit.: Gilbert Searight, Wm. Line.   I. 375-376.

FLEMING, JAMES. 27 Sept 1823. 9 Aug 1824.
Sole heir and Ex. James Fleming Linn, nephew.
Wit.: James Hamilton, William Irvine.   I. 377.

SHUGART, JACOB, North Middleton. Non Cupative Will. 23 Aug 1824.
14 Sept 1824.
Wife and minor children.
Exs.: Philip Zeigler and Philip Shamburgh.
Wit.: Dr. Henry Cole, John Cornman, Junr., and Mary Cornman wife of
John Cornman, Jr.   I. 377.

KNETTLE, JACOB, yeoman, Mifflin. 2 Aug 1824. 1 Oct 1824.
Sole Heir and Ex.: Wife Susannah.
Wit.: Henry D. Dalhousen, Andrew Heister.
Note: 22 Nov 1838.
The widow having died.
Adtor: Henry Knettle.   I. 378.

CLOUSER, MARGARET. ---. 29 Oct 1824.
Dau. Catherine and granddau. Margaret Culp.
All my daus.
Son Simon.
Wit.: William Drennon, Elizabeth Armstrong.
Adtor: Joseph Clark.   I. 379.

HUSTON, WILLIAM, farmer, Newville. 9 Dec 1820. 19 Nov 1824.
Wife Mary.
Granddau. Nancy Mathers, minor.

Grandchildren William B. Johnson and Jane Johnson, minors.
Son James Huston, to each of his children.
Exs.: Wife Mary, son James and William McCullock.
Wit.: Jno. Geddis, John Mathers.
Note: 8 May 1822.
"The will of Mary Huston, widow of said William Huston" was proven.

I. 379-380.

MC CULLOCK, WILLIAM, farmer, Westpennsboro. 6 Sept 1824. 19 Nov 1824.
Wife Sally.
Daus. Tabitha married to Joseph McKibben of Newville and Elizabeth, a minor.
Fivesons, viz., John, Alexander, James, William and Samuel when youngest is twenty one years of age.
Christopher Schuler of Dickinson Township.
Exs.: Wife Sally, son John and John McKeehan of West Pennsborough Township.
Wit.: James Dunlap, John Geddis, John Dunlap.   I. 381.

HUNTER, ELIZABETH, widow, Southampton. 6 July 1824. 3 Dec 1824.
To second cousin John Crocket.
John Hunter, bro. in law.
Sister in law Jane Beard.
Sister in law Sally McIntire.
William Hunter Trotter.
Elizabeth Trotter.
John Russell, Senr.
Jacob Heller's children.
Peggy Elliott.
John Elliott, his wife and four children.
Philip Miller, blacksmith.
John Filey, carpenter.
John Wallsbach's children.
Margaret Crocket, sister of James Crocket.
Jane Smith, widow, her two children.
Cousin Elizabeth Smith.
Trustees of Middle Spring Church.
Conrad Struckler's children.
Presbyterian Church at Shippensburg.
Jacob Cooper's children (for schooling).

William Hunter Heppeneteil.
John McConaughy's children.
James Hendricks.
To old Mr. Chronister.
Nancy Russell (widow).
John Russell, Junr.
William Arbuckle.
David and John Miller, children of Thomas Miller.
Thomas Miller's wife.
Mrs. Eleanor Walker, wife of Rev. James Walker.
George Mathews to school his children.
Children of Alexander Peebles, Junr.
Robert Peebles' children.
Jonathan Eagle, Senr. and his wife.
Catherine Eagle.
John Eagle's children.
Henry Zeller's children.
Crowley, the blacksmith.
Adam Reest.
Andrew Halter.
Elizabeth Peebles, wife of Alexander.
George Lee's children.
Molly Ann Cloud, dau. of Sally Wingley.
Henry Chronister.
Thomas Grimes.
James Crocket.
Kitty Crocket (widow).
Samuel Cooper, son of Jacob Cooper.
Exs.: Alexander Peebles, Junr. and John Nevin.
Wit.: Robert Peebles, James Kelso, Junr.   I. 382-384.

SHARP, ALEXANDER, farmer, Newton. 17 Sept 1822. 24 Dec 1824.
Wife Isabella.
Sons John, Alexander, Dr. William M., Andrew and Thomas.
Dau. Mrs. Eleanor McCune.
Land called James Laughlin tract.
Exs.: Sons John Sharp, Dr. Wm. M. Sharp, Andrew Sharp and Thomas
Sharp.
Wit.: Willm. McCandlish, William Richey.   I. 385-387.

PEEBLES, ALEXANDER, Senr., Esq., Southampton. 13 Feb 1820. 24 & 28 Dec 1824.
Sons Alexander and Robert.
Son in law John McGee.
Dau. Elizabeth, now Elizabeth Highlands.
Grandsons Thomas McClelland and Alexander McClelland, minors.
Son in law Robert McClelland.
Dau. Ann, wife of James McMullin.
Grandson Alexander Highlands.
Exs.: Son Alexander Peebles and John McKee of Shippensburg.
Codicil: 22 July 1824.
Appoints John North in place of John McKee.
Wit.: Patrick Rebuck, Johnston Williamson, James Devor.
I. 388-389.

HERRIOTT, ELIAS, shoemaker, Allen. 16 Nov 1824. 12 Jan 1825.
Wife Rebecca Herriott.
Exs.: Bro. in law Daniel Bower and wife Rebecca Herriott.
Wit.: Rudolph Krysher, Jane Herriott.
I. 390.

CAROTHERS, ELIZABETH, Westpennsboro. 8 March 1824. 26 Jan 1825.
Three daus. Margery Workman, Elizabeth Holsaple and Mary Grayson.
Erasmus Holsaple, James D. Grayson.
James Neel.
Son James Carothers of Carlisle.
Exs.: Son James Carothers and Saml. Douglass, Esq.
Wit.: Michael Sanno, Bernard Hendel.
Codicil: 17 May 1824.
I. 390-391.

MC ELWAIN, EBENEZER, Mifflin. 3 Jan 1825. 8 Feb 1825.
Wife Elizabeth.
Children, until youngest dau. Margaret, be eighteen years of age.
Ex.: William Stephenson of Mifflin Township.
Wit.: John Ferguson, William Mitchell, James Morron.
I. 392.

HANNA, SAMUEL, Mifflin. 30 June 1824. 17 Feb 1825.
Wife Eals.
Sons William and John.
Daus. Mary Mitchell and Eliza Hanna.
Exs.: Sons William Hanna and William Mitchell.
Wit.: John Ferguson, James Morrow.
I. 393.

HOLSAPLE, MARGARET, Westpennsborough. 10 Dec 1824. 19 Feb 1825.
Three daus. Mary, Elizabeth and Lydia Holsaple.
Sons Erasmus and John.
Daus. Catherine McManus, Margaret Miller and Esther Eby and her husband Abraham Eby.
Exs.: Sons Erasmus Holsaple and John Holsaple.
Wit.: James Greason, George Neiler.   I. 394.

DILLER, DAVID, Monroe. 19 Feb 1825. 23 Feb 1825.
Bros. Martin and Benjamin.
Sister Elizabeth.
Bro. Martin's seven children, viz., Martin, Peter, Joseph, Catherine, Leah, Rebecca and Julian.
Abe Bollinger.
George Foster.
Casper Diller.
Julian Rider.
Christina Myers.
Ex.: George Foster.
Wit.: William Henwood, John Morret.   I. 395.

FISHBURN, PETER, Westpennsboro. 7 March 1824. 27 March 1825.
Wife Catherine.
Son John.
Land in Frankford Township adjoining land of Peter Wax and John Snider.
Daus. Catherine married to George Myer, Polly married to Jacob Musselman and Elizabeth married to Jno. Myer.
Exs.: Wife Catherine, son John and John Howenstine.
Wit.: George Stubbs, Wm. Line.   I. 396-398.

MC KIBBEN, MARY, widow of Jeremiah McKibben, Newton. 5 Nov 1823. 8 March 1823.
Daus. Rebecca intermarried with Andrew Pierce of West Pennsborough township and Keziah McKibben.
Sons Joseph, John and Chambers.
Granddau. Mary Chambers Pierce.
Granddau. Mary Chambers Hays.
Son in law Andrew Pierce.
Children of son John.
Exs.: Son Chambers McKibben and Andrew Pierce.
Wit.: Jas. McCormick, Jno. Geddis.   I. 399.

LAMBERTON, SIMON, North Middleton. 24 Dec 1824. 23 March 1825.
Land joining heirs of bro. James Lamberton and Fireobend.
Dau. Louisa Lamberton (the mother of whom was Mary Steelman).
James Lamberton.
Exs.: Thomas Bell and James Lamberton of Carlisle.
Wit.: Robert D. Guthrie, Francis Noble.
Codicil: 13 Feb 1825.
Wit.: William McClintock.   I. 400.

SEVERS, MICHAEL, Newton. 22 March 1825. 1 April 1825.
Wife Mary.
Sons Abraham, John and George.
Plantation joining Samuel Caldwell and Joseph Goard.
Four daus. Elizabeth, Sally, Leah and Rachel.
Two youngest sons, Jacob and David.
Where John Ross now resides.
Exs.: Four sons Abraham, John, George and Jacob Severs.
Wit.: William Dagarman, Henry Buchman, Nicholas Sheetz.
                                                                 I. 401-402.

BROWN, PHILIP, Shippensburg. 11 Oct 1824. 12 April 1825.
Philip Wanamaker, only son of dau. Elizabeth.
House and lot near Halafax, Dauphin Co.
Ex.: Dau. Elizabeth Wanamaker.
Wit.: Stephen Cochran, Stephen Colp.   I. 403.

STEEL, ESTHER, widow of Ephraim Steel of Carlisle, and one of the daus.
of Robert Smith, decd., formerly of the City of Philadelphia. 28 March
1825. 12 May 1825.
Sons Robert Smith, John and Ephraim Steel.
Decd. step mother Mary Smith.
Ground rent lot at S. E. corner High and Third Streets, Philadelphia.
Dau. Mary wife of Dr. George D. Foulke.
Exs.: Benjamin Childs and Jacob Bishop.
Wit.: Margaret McFeely, James Duncan.   I. 403-404.

STOCKDALE, JOHN, Carlisle. 17 May 1825. 24 May 1825.
Wife Elizabeth.
Son John.
Children, noned others named.
Adtrix: Elizabeth Stockdale.

Wit.: Samuel Thompson and R. Lamberton.
Jas. Underwood swears to signatures.   I. 405.

SHELL, HENRY, Carlisle. 18 March 1825. 25 May 1825.
Wife Margretta.
Daus. Elizabeth Weaver and Rachel Byers.
Son Henry.
John Bigler of Harrisburg.
George Alspaugh.
Exs.: Wife Margaretta Shell and John Lane of North Middleton Township.
Wit.: Thos. McMurray, Walter Bell.   I. 406-407.

DAVIDSON, MATTHEW, Senr., Westpennsboro. 18 May 1825. 27 May 1825.
Sons John and Matthew, Junr.
Two daus. Isabella Davidson and Ann Leckey.
Land adjoining John Myers and John Bucher, also William Davidson's heirs.
Dau. Mary McIntire.
Exs.: Sons John Davidson, Esq. and Matthew Davidson, Junr.
Wit.: Saml. Alexander, Wm. Davidson.   I. 408.

KELSO, WILLIAM. 16 March 1825. 28 May 1825.
Bro. John Joseph.
Aunts Jane Chambers and Margaret Chambers.
Uncle William Chambers.
Father William Kelso, decd.
Place called *Kelso's Ferry* in Cumberland Co.
Aunt Mary McKinney.
Exs.: Bro. John Joseph Kelso and Dr. Wm. E. Chambers of Carlisle.
Wit.: M. McKinney, Junr., A. Graydon.
Codicil: 28 March 1825.
Wit.: Jeremiah Rees.   I. 409-410.

RIDSECKER, NICHOLAS, yeoman, East Pennsborough. 28 Dec 1824. 10 June 1825.
John Ulch and his children.
Nieces Elizabeth Myer and Catherine Palmer.
Nephew George Ridsecker.
German Presbyterian Church near Mr. Nicholas Kritzer's.
Ex.: Christopher Seviler.
Wit.: John Seviler, Jno. Clendenin.   I. 411.

FUNCK, ABRAHAM, yeoman, East Pennsborough. 14 April 1824. 14 June 1825.
Samuel Nicolas, son of sister's daughter.
Maria Nicolas, sister of sd. Samuel Nicolas.
Heirs of John Steigleman.
Wilkenson Steigleman, son of John Steigleman.
Other children of sd. John Steigleman, a son of my sister, viz., John, Mary, Sarah, Elizabeth and Rachel Steigleman.
The children of my sister, viz., the children of Jacob Hocheteler.
Sister's children, viz., the children of Henry Strickler.
Peter Fahnestock heirs.
Exs.: John Snivley and Benjamin Gibler.
Wit.: William Kirtland, Jonas Grubb.   I. 412.

DUNCAN, JOHN, Hopewell. 29 Jan 1825. 19 July 1825.
Son David.
Land bounded by lands of David Foglesonger, William McIntire, Samuel Duncan, James Hemphill, Jacob Foglesonger and David Duncan, Senr. in Hopewell Township.
Dau. Catherine intermarried with John Wiley of Franklin Co.
Sons William and Samuel.
Son John should he never return or be dead.
Daus. of son John Duncan, viz., Mary and Eliza Ann.
Exs.: Son Samuel Duncan and John Cox.
Wit.: William McIntire, Daniel Ressler, Saml. Cox.   I. 413.

RINE, MARGARET, widow, Carlisle. 17 May 1823. 29 July 1825.
Cyrus Rine and Hannah Rine, son and dau. of Daniel Rine.
Catherine Plitt and Mary Crise.
Father George Rine, decd., late of Lancaster Co.
Davis Rine (son of Daniel Rine).
Exs.: David Smith of Carlisle and William Baker of North Middleton Township.
Wit.: J. Sheilds, Jacob Hendel.
Codicil: 1 Dec 1824.
To Elizabeth Rine, who now lives with me.
George Rine.
Wit.: Wm. Ramsey, Saml. C. Smith.   I. 414-415.

SANDERSON, REBECCAH, Carlisle. 7 Feb 1824. 30 July 1825.
Dau. Mary, sole heir.

278

Ex.: Bro. Paul Randolph of North Middleton Township.
Wit.: Alexander C. Gregg, John Creigh. I. 416.

KREITZER, NICHOLAS, Eastpennsborough. 29 Jan 1824. 6 Aug 1825.
Wife Elizabeth.
Sons Andrew and John, a minor.
Dau. Mary intermarried with Sidle.
Land in Rye Township.
Daus. Catherine married to John Swiler, Eve married to Joel Kimmel,
Susanna married to William Brenizer, now decd., Henrietta and Wilamina.
Land joining Robert Young's and Martin's.
Exs.: Son Andrew Kreitzer and neighbor Jno. Shiveley.
Wit.: Andrew Sheely, Saml. Ruby.
Codicil: 5 June 1825.
Dau. Catherine, wife of John Swiler, died since above will was executed.
Heirs of sd. dau., viz., Elizabeth Swiler and Susanna Swiler, minors.
Plantation adjoining lands of George Renner, Andrew Sheetz, Joseph
Briller and Samuel Eberly.
Wit.: John Wise, Saml. Ruby. I. 416-421.

STERRETT, DAVID, Mifflin. 25 July 1825. 11 Aug 1825.
Wife Isabella.
Son David.
Land joining lands of John Laughlin, Junr., and William Montgomery's
heirs.
Land adjoining Peter Weaver's and Andrew Bell's.
Late property of Robert Cummins in Southampton Township.
Minor children Jane, Brice Innes and Alexander Wilson Sterrett.
Dau. Eliza Kerr.
Sister Elizabeth Stevenson.
Charlotte Danford to be provided for.
Peter Geeseman tenant of land in Lurgan Township.
Land in Fairfield Co., Ohio.
Exs. and Guardians of minor children: William Greacy of Mifflin and John
Wherry of Hopewell Townships.
Wit.: James McElhenny, Saml. Woods, Junr., John Laughlin, Junr.
I. 422-425.

MILLER, JACOB, East Pennsboro. 30 June 1820. 18 Aug 1825.
Wife Elizabeth.
Sons John and Jacob.

Land adjoining lands of Balser Tedlar, Sheely's heirs, Martin Kellar and Houser's heirs.
Son Tobias.
Land in Harrison Co., Virginia, adjoining Hackett's Creek.
Daus. Barbara, Elizabeth, Cathrine and Molly.
Grandchildren, the children of son Peter Miller, decd., viz., Jane, Elizabeth, Sally, Tobias and Peter Miller.
Wit.: John Eberly, Saml. Ruby.
Codicil: 12 June 1825.
Son John Miller, decd.
Land in East Pennsboro bounded by Jacob Miller's and Frederick Smith's sold to George Stonebring.   I. 426-427.

STEVENSON, MARGARET, Mifflin. 12 March 1821. 24 Aug 1825.
Bros. and sisters that are at home, viz., John Stevenson, Mary and Jane Stevenson and William Stevenson.
Exs.: Sister Jane Stevenson and Wm. Stevenson.
Wit.: Peter Hershey, Eleanor Morrow.   I. 428.

FRENCH, JOHN, Frankford. 8 April 1825. 26 Aug 1825.
Two sisters Mary and Jane, who now live with me.
Bro. Samuel.
Exs.: Bro. William French and Saml. Lindsey.
Wit.: John Showalter, Wm. Lindsay.   I. 429.

MC CULLOCK, JAMES, Newton. 11 Aug 1825. 13 Sept 1825.
Wife Mary.
Three sons John, Thomas and William.
Dau. Sarah Huston.
Daus. Mary Jane, Eliza and Margaret Ann.
Son James when seventeen years of age.
Exs.: Sons John, Thomas and Wm. McCullock.
Wit.: James Piper, John Sharp, Wm. Allen.   I. 430-431.

SMITH, DAVID, shoemaker, Carlisle. 6 Sept 1822. 20 Sept 1825.
Wife Mary.
Sons David and Samuel.
Ex.: Wife Mary Smith of Carlisle.
Wit.: Wm. Ramsey.
Codicil: 5 Sept 1825.
Appoints Daniel Fisher, Esq., co-Exec. with wife Mary Smith.

I. 432.

DIDLLER, CASPAR, yeoman, Monroe. 8 Aug 1825. 26 Sept 1825.
Wife Christiana.
Five sons, viz., Daniel, Leonard, Solomon, Samuel and David.
Four daus. Sally married to Christian Richwine, Rachel married to
Frederick Goodyear, Margaret married to William Derr and Catherine.
Exs.: Son Davd Diller and son in law Fredk. Goodyear.
Wit.: Rudolph Krysher, Peter Bricker.   I. 433.

WIBLEY, CATHERINE, North Middleton. 8 Jan 1824. 14 Nov 1825.
To Sarah Wibley.
Elizabeth Wibley.
Sons Jacob and Adam Wibley.
Late husband Jacob Wibley, decd.
Ex.: Son Jacob Wibley.
Wit.: Peter Duey, David Angrey.   I. 434.

SCHWENDT, JOHN NCHOLAS, Senr., cordwainer, North Middleton. 30
April 1821. 14 Nov 1825.
Sons John, Philp, George and Peter.
Daus. Magdalena and Maria.
Ten heirs, names of other children not given.
Exs.: Sons George Schwendt and Peter Schwendt.
Sworn to by three sons Nicholas Schwendt, John Schwendt and Philip
Schwendt.   I. 435-436.

HERMAN, DOROTHEA, widow, Eastpennsbro. 12 April 1810. 15 Nov
1825.
Sons Martin, Jacob and Christian. Dau. Elizabeth wife of Philip Alspaugh.
Heirs of late dau. Barbara who was intermarried with Henry Eichelberger.
Exs.: Son Martin Herman and Philp Alspaugh.
Wit.: Chrisn. Coble, Christian Wissler.
Signature of Christian Coble, decd., sworn to by his son David Coble.
          I. 437.

COOPER, JANE, relict of John Cooper, Esq., decd., Newton. 28 Dec 1821.
21 June 1825.
Dau. Margaret sole heir.
Late father James Jack, decd., late of Newton Township.
Exs.: William Carnahan and James Hemphill.

Wit.: James A. Mitchell, David Wills. I. 438.

CLEVER, MARTIN, Senr., Westpennsboro. 23 Sept 1823. 23 Nov 1825.
Wife Catherine.
Son Martin and dau. Catherine.
Son in law Jacob Lehman.
Exs.: Son Martin Clever and Jacob Lehman.
Wit.: John Bear, Philip Zeigler. I. 439-441.

CURYEA, JOHN, North Middleton. 21 Oct 1825. 6 Dec 1825.
Wife Margaret.
Bro. Adam and sister Mary.
Bro. Philip if he is still living.
Henry, eldest son of bro. Philip Curyea.
Heirs of bro. Henry, viz., John and George Curyea and Elizabeth and Mary.
Exs.: Jacob Wetzel and bro. Adam Curyea.
Wit.: Henry Edendburn, David Braught. I. 441-442.

MAGAURAN, EDWARD, Saville, Perry Co. 15 May 1823. 6 Dec 1825.
Wife Margaret.
Two children of sd. wife, viz., Sophia and David Sturm.
Daus. Elizabeth Magauran and Margaretta Magauran.
Lotts in Carlisle in possession of James Bredin.
Dau. Mary Crummer, now Mary Eckel.
Her dau. Catherine Crummer, who lives with me, incapable of taking care
of herself.
Son Henry who lives with his sister in Baltimore.
Ex.: Wife Margaret Magauran.
Wit.: None named.
Sworn to by Walter Bell and Andw. Boden. K. 1.
Dau. Ester Blackburn, her half bro. William Foulk.
Children of Ester Blackburn.
Dau. Susannah Sheldon and her children.
Houses occupied by William Hacal and Jacob Fry.
Son Eneas, a minor.
Land in Alleghany Co. bought from John W. Hatarah.
Frederick Kowar.
Exs.: Son-in-law Samuel Blackburn, son John Foulk and Thomas Foster.
Wit.: Saml. Irwin, Eleanor Roseberry. F. 201-203.

INDEX

-A-

ABERCROMBIE, John, 103
ABERNETHY, Agness, 125; James, 125
ABERNUTHY, John, 183
ABRAHAMS, Andrew, 175; Enoch, 175; Hannah, 175
ACKERMAN, Abraham, 118;
Catherine, 118; George, 118;
Henry, 118; John, 118, 139;
Margaret, 118; Paul, 118
ADAIR, Elizabeth, 16; Elsey, 105; Isable, 105; James, 15, 105; John, 16, 241; Joseph, 9, 16; Polly, 105, 133;
Rosana, 7; Sinny, 105;
William, 16, 105
ADAMS, Abm., 193, 216; Abraham, 25, 36, 107, 216, 257; Ann, 17, 39; Betsy, 101, 139;
Eliza, 257; Elizabeth, 107, 257; Hanna, 101; Harkness, 257; Isaac, 107, 139, 248;
James, 6, 17, 24, 28, 30, 59, 197, 209; Jane, 39, 248;
Jean, 107, 139; Letty, 101;
Maria, 107; Mariah, 139;
Martha, 235; Mary, 107, 257;
Matthew, 59, 103; Nancy, 107, 139; Polly, 101, 139, 153;
Priscilla, 257; Richard, 59;
Robert, 29, 34, 101, 154, 235; Samuel, 107, 139, 257;
Terra, 101; Thomas, 34, 36, 101, 180; William, 17, 59, 68, 107, 149, 257
ADDAMS, Abraham, 111; W., 107
AGENEY, Jean, 225
AGNES, John, 25
AGNEW, Elizabeth, 77; Isaac, 77; James, 27, 77; Jean, 129;
John, 27, 77; Matthew, 77;
Nancy, 77; Rebecca, 263;
Samuel N., 77
ALBERT, Andrew, 36; Henry, 254
ALBRIGHT, Barbara, 5; George, 5, 232
ALENBERGER, Peter, 9; Rebecca, 9
ALEXANDER, Amelia, 131, 263;
Amey, 8; David, 8; Elizabeth, 8, 131, 263; John, 18, 59;
John B., 233; Joseph, 8;
Margaret, 8; Mary, 8, 226;
Robert, 226; Samuel, 233, 238, 252, 276; Thomas, 8; W., 69; William, 1, 8, 27, 33, 50, 52, 76, 129, 131, 157, 164, 175, 218, 226, 238
ALISON, Molly, 198; Peter, 198

ALLEMAN, Anne, 133; Barbara, 133; Catharine, 133;
Christaiana, 133; Christina, 133; Christopher, 133;
Elizabeth, 133; George, 133;
Jacob, 133; Martin, 133;
Mary, 133; Mottena, 133;
Stophel, 133
ALLEN, Catherine, 98; David, 44, 45; Elizabeth, 79; Hugh, 79; James, 44, 45, 140; James W., 241; James Williams, 215;
Jean, 79, 234; Jenny, 79;
John, 44, 52, 79, 215;
Joseph, 44, 45; Lucinda, 242;
Mary, 28, 79, 179; Rachel, 79; Robert, 28, 45; Samuel, 215, 246; Sarah, 44, 45, 52;
Watson, 52; William, 44, 140, 279
ALLISON, John, 4; Molly, 180;
Peter, 180; Thomas, 4
ALREIGHT, James, 20
ALRICK, Adam, 231
ALSPAUGH, Elizabeth, 280;
George, 276; Philip, 280
ANDERSON, Alexander, 95, 239;
Alexander M., 197; Allen, 6;
Bejn., 242; Benjamin, 125, 129, 161, 185, 190, 200, 239, 266; Benjn., 233; Betsy, 104;
Enoch, 92, 149; George, 95, 171; Isabella, 191; James, 55, 95, 196, 230, 239; John, 6, 9, 15, 25, 65, 70, 127.
216, 239; Martha, 242; Mary, 6, 95, 171; Oliver, 67;
Polly, 239; Rennix, 239;
Robert, 102, 104, 142; Ruth, 95; Samuel, 95, 239; Sarah, 239; Thomas, 267; William, 67, 81, 87, 95, 149, 174, 189, 198, 199, 207, 230, 239
ANDREWS, Abraham, 88; Andrew, 149; Barbara, 149; Catherine, 149; George, 88, 149; Jacob, 149; Joseph, 149; Peggy, 149;
Samuel, 149; William, 184
ANGENY, Jacob, 115; Reincik, 115
ANGEREY, Renneck, 257
ANGHENSBAUGH, Henry, 227
ANGNEY, Reinneck, 259
ANGREY, David, 280; Isaac, 253
ANSBERGER, Henry, 111; Jacob, 125
ANTHONY, Peter, 192
APPELL, Johannes, 214
ARBAUGH, Catherine, 135;
Godfrey, 135

146; John, 146; Samuel, 146;
Susanna, 146
BAUR, Catherine, 8; Elizabeth,
8; Elizabeth Catherine, 8;
Martin, 8; Mary, 8
BAXTER, Elizabeth, 177; George,
211; James, 18, 92, 177, 202;
Jenny, 92, 177; John, 92,
177, 224; Margaret, 177;
Margret, 202; Martha, 177;
Mary, 224; Robert, 177;
Solomon, 211; William, 92,
177, 202
BEAL, Thomas, 7
BEALMAN, Ammy, 237; Christian,
237; Christina, 236;
Christopher, 236; David, 236;
George, 237; Jacob, 236;
John, 237; Mary, 237
BEAMER, Conrad, 28
BEAN, John, 223; Robert, 223
BEAR, David, 263; Ephraim, 229,
267; Henry, 179; Jacob, 180;
John, 136, 146, 165, 175,
176, 179, 180, 189, 206, 243,
244, 246, 281; Michael, 175,
179; Samuel, 179, 267;
Susanna, 179
BEARD, David, 89, 90, 179; J.,
131; James, 3; Jane, 271;
Jennet, 90; John, 3, 41, 90;
Margaret, 131; Robert, 3, 83
BEASLEY, William, 88
BEASOR, Chatharina, 186; Mary,
186
BEATTY, Eleanor, 194; Elinor,
84; Finlaw, 84; Hannah, 172;
Isabella, 103; James, 52, 56,
103, 166, 172, 223, 228, 262;
John, 12, 56, 84, 103, 141,
172; Joseph, 51, 56, 64, 172;
Margaret, 172; Martha, 172;
Nancy, 103; Nancy Johnston,
262; Robert, 56, 64, 103,
172; Samuel, 51; Sarah, 172;
William, 56, 103
BEATY, Alexander, 32; Andrew,
32; Elizabeth, 32, 213;
Esquire, 93; Henry, 213;
James, 32, 119, 163, 213;
John, 32; Joseph, 32;
Margaret, 32; Robert, 32;
Samuel, 32; William, 32, 186
BEAVER, Eliza, 261; Hannah,
189; Sally, 189; Sarah, 261
BECHER, Henry, 230
BECHTEL, Elizabeth, 136; Henry,
136; Jacob, 136; John, 136;
Magdalena, 136; Maria, 136;
Martin, 136; Samuel, 136;
Veronia, 136
BECK (Beek), John, 28

BECKER (Baker), Elizabeth, 166,
Catharina, 166; Elizabeth,
166; George, 166; John, 166;
Martin, 166; Philip, 166;
William, 166
BEDCOM, ----, 53
BEECH, Elizabeth, 247
BEEKER, Philip, 166
BEELEN, Francis, 181, 228;
Henry, 228
BEELMAN, Barbara, 231;
Christian, 209; Christiana,
209; John, 231
BEIDLEMAN, Abraham, 155; Adam,
142; George, 221
BEIRMASTER, Elizabeth, 244
BEITLEMAN, Abraham, 28
BELL, Andrew, 278; David, 1,
113, 153, 163, 201, 228;
Elizabeth, 150, 227; James,
113, 179, 231; Jane, 201,
228; Janet, 6; Martha, 248;
Mary, 201; Nancy, 261; Polly,
231, 261; Rachel, 102, 152;
Robert, 41, 102, 113, 119,
128, 140, 142; Rosanna, 128;
Samuel, 261; Sarah, 113, 122,
231; Thomas, 110, 146, 231,
268, 275; Walter, 99, 128,
140, 150, 276, 281; William,
7, 8, 11, 128, 227, 231
BELTZHOOVER, George, 243
BENDER, John, 242
BENEZET, James, 74
BENGER (Burger), Joseph, 258
BENS (Bentz), Elizabeth, 165;
Peter, 165
BERGETRESER, Jacob, 61
BERGETRESOR, David, 211;
Frederick, 211; Jacob, 211
BERGETRESSER, Margaret, 210
BERGETRESSOR, Philip, 199
BERNET, John, 230
BERNHARDT, Elizabeth, 211
BERNHISLE, Adam, 171
BERRY, Agness, 176; Standish,
176
BERRYHILL, Alexr., 66
BESAN, Peter, 26
BESHOR, John, 115; Mary, 115
BESOR, John, 106
BEST, Joseph, 241; Mathias, 111
BEYENER, Elizabeth, 92; Jacob,
92; John, 92
BEYER, William, 64
BIELMAN (Beilman), John, 60
BIGGAR (Biggert), Jane, 109;
William, 109
BIGGER, Jean, 132
BIGHAM, Thomas A., 193, 238
BIGLER, Christian, 170; John,
276

BORALL, Ann Mary, 130;
  Catherine, 130; Elizabeth,
  130; Jacob, 130; Nicholas,
  130; Paul, 130; Valintine,
  130
BORDEN, John, 102
BORDNER, Eve, 203; George, 203;
  Jacob, 203; Samuel, 203
BORE, William, 58
BORLAND, Joseph, 70; Mary, 40,
  70; Samuel, 70; Thomas, 70
BORTNEER, Jacob, 73
BOSSERMAN, Philip, 84
BOSSLER, Catherine, 203; John,
  203
BOTHWELL, William, 178
BOUGHER, Ludwick, 266
BOUGHMAN, John, 235
BOVARD, Charles, 98, 198;
  Rachel, 258
BOW, Andrew, 33; Catherine, 33;
  Michael, 33; Nancy, 33
BOWEN, Rosana, 49
BOWER, Abraham, 189, 230;
  Catherine, 8; Christopher,
  61, 189; Daniel, 107, 273;
  David, 48; Elizabeth, 8, 45,
  120; Henry, 107, 216; John,
  269; Liddy, 189; Margaret,
  107, 216; Martin, 8, 13, 45,
  63, 97; Peter, 74; Rebecka,
  107; Solomon, 189; Susannah,
  189; William, 216
BOWERMASTER, George, 260;
  Margaret, 260
BOWERS, Daniel, 216; David, 216
BOWLY, Danl., 30
BOWMAN, Abraham, 244; Benjamin,
  202; Catherine, 244;
  Christian, 202, 244; Christy,
  147; Daniel, 202; Dr. Jacob,
  240; Elizabeth, 244; Henry,
  87, 136; Jacob, 243; John,
  87, 107, 168, 192, 202, 258;
  Joseba, 240; Magdalene, 179,
  244; Martin, 179; Mary, 244;
  Rebecca, 244; Samuel, 202,
  244
BOYCE, Ann, 48; John, 48; Mary,
  48; Robert, 48; William, 48
BOYD, Abigail, 145; Abraham,
  58; Adam, 145; Alexander, 59;
  Benjamin, 144; David, 71;
  Elinor, 37; Elizabeth, 1,
  143, 144, 201, 218; George,
  201; Hugh, 59; James, 59;
  218; John, 30; Martha, 59;
  Mary, 168; Priscilla, 212;
  Robert, 59; Samuel, 33;
  Simon, 178, 212; William, 9,
  57, 143, 145
BOYER, John Ludwig, 153

BOYERS, Magdalena D., 186
BOYLE, Daniel, 20; James, 7;
  Samuel, 7
BRACKENRIDGE, H. H., 209; John,
  93; Nancy, 93; Sabina, 209
BRACKINRIDGE, H. H., 175
BRADLEY, Joseph, 58
BRADY, Betsy, 155; Ebenezer,
  15; Elizabeth, 16; Hannah,
  15, 16; Hugh, 15, 16; James,
  15; Jean, 15, 16; John, 15;
  Joseph, 15, 16, 22, 148, 169,
  205, 230; Marget, 16; Mary,
  15, 16, 31; Rebeccah, 15;
  Samuel, 15
BRAND, Adam, 10; Michael, 188
BRANDEBERRY, Amelia, 219;
  Samuel, 219
BRANDON, Martha, 95
BRANDT (Branet), Abraham, 106;
  Adam, 84, 87, 92, 98, 106,
  115, 118, 131, 199, 209, 254;
  Anthony, 163; Barbara, 106,
  237; Catherine, 106; Daniel,
  214; David, 105, 106, 136,
  199, 209, 251; Elizabeth,
  106, 214; George, 237;
  Martha, 192; Martin, 105,
  106, 251, 260; Mary, 105,
  251; Molly, 251; Philip, 105
BRANIZER, Adam, 209; Barbara,
  209; David, 209; George, 209;
  Henry, 77; John, 209;
  Michael, 209
BRANNIGER, Barbara, 242; David,
  242; John, 242
BRANNIZER, Adam, 242
BRANYAN, Agness, 203
BRATTON, Adam, 74; Elizabeth,
  12; George, 12, 194; Horas,
  74; Issable, 12; James, 12;
  Jean, 12; Jenny, 74; John,
  168; Phebe, 12; Rebecca, 74,
  194; Robert, 12; Samuel, 74;
  William, 12, 194
BRAUGHT, David, 281
BRAUGT, David, 257
BREADY, John, 194
BREDEN, Agness, 18; Elder, 18;
  Hugh, 21; James, 245;
  Margaret, 18; Robert, 18;
  Sarah, 18; William, 18
BREDIN, James, 281
BREHM, Henry, 265
BRENENIZER, Christina, 242
BRENIZER, Barbara, 115; David,
  115, 217; Henry, 55; John,
  84, 236; Martin, 163;
  Michael, 236; Salome, 163;
  Susanna, 278; William, 278
BRENNIZER, Barbara, 243
BRETZ, Elizabeth, 203; Jacob,

288

211; Philip, 203
BREWES, James, 88
BREWSTER, Charles, 73;
Margaret, 224
BRICE, Elizabeth, 11; Samuel,
11
BRICKER, Barbara, 251;
Catherine, 115; David, 222;
Eve Ann, 251; George, 251;
John, 243, 251; Joseph, 218,
251; Julia Ann], 251;
Margaret, 251; Mary, 115,
243; Mary Ann, 251; Moses,
251; Peter, 115, 243, 280;
Samuel, 243, 251; Susanna,
115; William, 251
BRICKLEY, Andrew, 117; John,
117; Mary, 117; Peter, 117;
Valentine, 117; William, 117
BRIGGS, Anna, 110, 111;
Benjamin, 110; David, 110,
111; Joseph, 110
BRILLER, Joseph, 278
BRINDLE, Abraham, 191;
Elizabeth, 115, 243; George,
115; Henry, 132, 191; John,
60, 131, 191; Mark, 75;
Sophia Margaret, 75;
Susannah, 191
BRINER, ---, 171; Catherine,
211; Charles, 258; Frederick,
169; John, 211
BRINES, Sarah, 74
BRINGHAM, Jean, 4
BRITTAIN, Adam, 237; Ann, 237;
George, 237; Mary, 237;
Nelly, 237; Samuel, 237;
William, 237
BRITTAN, Isabella, 134; Thomas,
134
BRITTON, Adam, 134; James, 96;
John, 96; Thomas, 96
BRODRICK, Mary, 33
BROOKINS, William, 219, 243
BROOKS, Abraham, 43; Elizabeth,
69; Hays, 69, 150; James, 69,
137; Jean, 69; Joseph, 69,
150; Margaret, 78; Martha,
69; Matthew, 69; Samuel, 69;
Sarah, 78; Susanna, 69;
William, 69
BROTHERS, Susannah, 216
BROTHERTON, Elisha, 160; Jane,
160; John, 93; Martha, 83;
Mr., 51; Patty, 93
BROWER, Emily, 167; Nancy, 167;
William, 166
BROWN, ---, 232; Abraham, 246;
Adam, 201; Alexander, 200;
Alexr., 70; Andrew, 70;
Arthur, 98, 160; Betsy, 137;
Daniel, 58; Eleanor, 181;

Elizabeth, 9, 201; Ephraim,
32, 70, 250; Francis, 181;
George, 56, 98, 160, 165;
Hannah, 37, 141; Henry, 258;
Isabella, 118; Jacob, 47;
James, 29, 44, 70, 86, 137,
250; Jennet, 174; John, 2, 4,
7, 11, 59, 74, 142, 174, 195,
198, 201, 267; Joseph, 201;
Josias, 34, 35, 37, 38, 63;
Lucy, 98, 148, 160; Martha,
70; Mary, 7, 70, 98, 148,
181, 200; Michael, 64; Nancy,
246; Peter, 106; Philip, 275;
Pitt, 98; Rachel, 153;
Robert, 81, 181, 182; Roger,
58, 82, 84, 181; Thomas, 174,
249; Thompson, 98, 148, 160,
165, 188, 263; William, 6,
11, 76, 98, 106, 112, 148,
152, 153, 159, 160, 182, 193,
262
BROWNFIELD, Elizabeth, 20, 21;
James, 21; Jean, 21; John,
20; Maryann, 21
BROWNLEE, John, 77
BRYNER, George, 163; John, 96,
184
BRYSON, Elizabeth, 249; Esther,
110; James, 110; Jane, 110;
Pricillah, 110; Priscila,
249; Robert, 110, 249;
Samuel, 79; William, 89, 109,
110, 125, 132, 147, 191, 217;
William Biggert, 110
BUCANAN, Elizabeth, 107
BUCHAN, John, 181
BUCHANAN, Ann, 15; Capt.
William, 183; David Robb,
232; Dorcas, 10, 81; George,
232; Isabella, 53; Jane, 138;
Jean, 149; John, 10, 15, 16,
26, 35; Margery, 31; Robert,
3, 138, 221; Ross, 173;
Samuel, 251; Thomas, 2, 4,
19, 45; Walter, 1, 71
BUCHER, John, 276
BUCHMAN, Henry, 275
BUCHOLDER, Willary, 21
BUCK, George, 35; Jacob, 59
BUCKWALTER, Barbara, 116;
Henry, 116; Mary, 219
BULL, Eleanor, 213; Grace, 213;
Henry, 82, 182, 213; John,
82, 214; Martha, 213;
Richard, 82; Robert, 182,
213; Sarah, 220; Thomas, 82;
William, 82, 135, 214, 220,
223
BULLEN, Thomas, 8
BULLOCK, Mary, 164; Moses, 189
BUMBERGER, Hannah, 79

51, 70, 77, 112, 125, 225, 243

CLAUDY, Abraham, 116; Catherine, 116; Elizabeth, 116; George, 116; Jacob, 116; John, 116; Margaret, 116; Martin, 116, 202; Mary, 116; William, 116

CLAY, Henry, 243; John, 245; Matthew, 245; Philip, 245

CLAYTON, James, 42

CLEAS, George, 115

CLENDENEN, Agness, 100; Catherine, 100; Elizabeth, 100; Isabella, 100; Janet, 100; Jean, 100; John, 100, 101; Mary, 100; Samuel, 100; William, 100, 101

CLENDENIN, Elizabeth, 57; James, 71; Janet, 71; John, 57, 71, 89, 128, 208, 215, 220, 225, 226, 260, 264, 267, 276; Samuel, 57, 71; William, 128

CLERK, Joseph, 48; Mary, 48; Molly, 142

CLEVER, Barney (Barnhart), 210; Catherine, 281; Conrad, 210; George, 210; Martin., 281

CLEVERSOLE, Peter, 15

CLINE, Isabella, 195; William, 234

CLIPPENGER, Frederick, 78

CLIPPINGER, Anthony, 97; Barbara, 97; Elizabeth, 97; Frederick, 97; George, 97; John, 97; Susanna, 97

CLOPPER, Elizabeth, 113; John, 113

CLOSER, George, 224; John, 224

CLOUD, Molly Ann, 272

CLOUSER, Catherine, 224, 270; Elizabeth, 51; George, 51, 224; John, 12, 51, 224; Margaret, 12, 51, 270; Mary, 224; Michael, 51; Nancy, 224; Peggy, 224; Peter, 51; Philip, 224; Simon, 12, 224, 231, 270; Sydney, 51

CLYD, Solomon, 49

CLYMEN, ---, 167

COBAUGH, Jane, 226

COBLE, Chrisn., 280; Christian, 164, 280; Christr., 203; Daniel, 265; David, 280; Mary, 265

COBURN, William, 67

COCHENOWER, Margaret, 244

COCHRAN, John, 49; Martha, 78; Patrick, 45, 78; Sophia, 216; Stephen, 275; Thomas, 216; William P., 216

COCKEY, David, 196; Elizabeth, 196

COCKLIN, Barbara, 92; Catherine, 266; David, 84, 92; Elizabeth, 84; Fanny, 92; Jacob, 84; John, 84, 92; Peter, 92; Tederick, 266; Tedry, 92

COFFEY, George, 62; James, 62; Jean, 62; John, 35, 62; Martha, 62; Mary, 62, 63; Robert, 35, 62; Thomas, 62; William, 62

COFFMAN, Christian, 207; Christopher, 111; Eliza, 187; Elizabeth, 213; George, 163; Isaac, 187; Jacob, 121, 187; John, 108; Joseph, 213; Margaret, 187; Peter, 213

COIL (Coyle), Isaiah, 186

COLE, Henry, 270

COLHOON, Andrew, 54; Elizabeth, 54; Esther, 54, 55; Lydia, 54; Rebecca, 54; Sarah, 54

COLHRAN, Betsy, 169; George, 169; Polly, 169; Richard, 169; Samuel, 169; William, 169

COLLIER, Hannah, 33, 48, 144; Joseph, 33

COLP, Stephen, 275

COLWELL, Abdiel, 45, 83, 92; Agness, 45, 83, 93; Ann, 45; Betsy, 45; Elizabeth, 258; James, 45, 83, 92, 258; Jane, 196; John, 45, 83, 92, 103, 117, 258; Joseph, 45, 83, 92; Martha, 45; Mary, 45; Nancy, 45, 83, 258; Polly, 83, 93; Robert, 45; Samuel, 45, 83, 92, 93, 117, 196; Thomas Dixon, 196; William, 57

COMBS, Joseph, 119; Sarah, 119

CONAWAY, Andrew, 259; Ezekiel, 259; George, 259; Mary, 259; William, 259

CONGH, Sally, 228

CONKEL, Adam, 58

CONLY, Dolly, 268; Jane, 252; Joseph, 252

CONNELLY, Adam, 22; John, 57; Joseph, 22, 88, 123, 250, 266; Lacey, 22; Thomas, 258; William, 88, 123, 178

CONNER, Francis, 208

COOK, George, 21; Isaac, 57; John, 21, 127, 269; Margaret, 77; Mary, 194; Robert, 21; Ruth, 48; William, 5

COOMBE, Hannah, 161; Peter, 161; Samuel, 160

COOPER, Andrew, 135; Charles,

Martha, 265; Thomas, 16, 196
DODDS, Elizabeth, 37; James,
37; Nancy, 37, 157
DODS, Betsy, 102; Hannah, 201;
John, 201; Mary, 102
DOKE, Elizabeth, 149
DONAHD, Francis, 48
DONALDSON, Alexander, 119, 142;
Catherine, 208; Jane, 203;
Janet, 42; Jean, 142; John,
119, 170; Joseph, 30; Martha,
80, 208; Patsey, 119; Robert,
119; Thomas, 80, 119;
William, 43
DONALY, Easter, 16; Elianor,
16; Hugh, 16; James, 16;
Margaret, 16; Philip, 16;
Rosana, 16
DONATH, Herman, 104
DONAVAN, Mabel, 195; Robert, 10
DONNALD, Alexander, 5
DONNELLY, Cloud, 162; James, 57
DONOVAN, Robert, 23
DORAN, Sarah, 63
DORBREY, Jane, 99
DORNBAUGH, John, 209; Mary, 209
DOUDS, Sarah, 210
DOUGHERTY, Mordecai, 162;
Sarah, 17
DOUGHTER, Margaret, 102
DOUGLASS, Ann, 95; Anne, 137;
Elizabeth, 91; George, 91,
102, 137, 219; Isabella, 106,
114; James, 13, 137; Jennet,
13; John, 37, 71, 106, 147,
219; Joseph, 219; Margaret,
106, 114; Margret, 221;
Martha, 91; Mary, 13, 137;
Nancy, 137, 141; S., 241;
Samuel, 273; Watson, 91;
William, 13, 17, 84, 91, 137,
194
DOUTY, Elizabeth, 24
DOWDEN, James, 95
DOWNEY, John, 158
DOYLE, Elisha, 226, 240;
Elizabeth, 98; Richard, 98
DREANER, William, 49
DRENNON, William, 12, 70, 121,
151, 270
DREVISH, Maria Elizabetta, 110;
William, 110, 127
DRIMMORED, Garret, 139
DRIWELL, James, 151
DRUDGE, Agness, 138
DRYSHER, David, 267
DUCK, Catharina, 88; Elizabeth,
88; Eve, 88; George, 88;
Margratha, 88; Philip, 88,
183; Poly, 88
DUEY, Catherine, 25; Conrad,
196; Elizabeth, 195; Ester,

215; George, 195; Jacob, 195,
215; James, 195; Jean, 195,
196; John, 195; Martin, 195;
Peter, 149, 280
DUGAN, Catherine, 54;
Elizabeth, 54; George, 54;
Margaret, 54; Phoebe, 54;
William, 54
DUHANE, Elizabeth, 230
DUN, Richard, 13
DUNB--, John, 75
DUNBAN, Rosanna, 206
DUNBAR, David, 222; Elizabeth,
30, 222, 263; George, 222;
Jane, 164; John, 44, 100,
145, 150, 162, 164, 177, 183,
206, 222; Joseph, 204, 220;
Margaret, 222; Mary, 206;
Polly, 96, 177; Robert, 44,
222; William, 164, 222
DUNBARR, John, 221
DUNCAN, Amelia, 56; Ann, 56;
Bery, 87; Calender, 27;
Daniel, 23, 40, 53; David,
53, 134, 233, 277; Eliza Ann,
277; Elizabeth, 155; Ja., 89,
101, 103, 104, 110, 114, 227;
James (Jas.), 22, 53, 56, 67,
98, 106, 111, 114, 126, 129,
131, 144, 147, 148, 154, 160,
162, 188, 233, 236, 242, 275;
John, 56, 119, 143, 155, 167,
169, 233, 251, 277; Joseph
(Jos.), 53, 151, 233; Mary,
53, 56, 277; Mary Ann, 56;
Matilda, 56; Robert, 56, 103,
111; Ruth, 233; Samuel, 56,
277; Sarah, 167; Stephen, 2,
53, 56; T., 204; Thomas, 27,
56, 101, 114, 154; William,
53, 121, 222, 277; William
Rippey, 233
DUNEAN, James, 227
DUNKLEBERGER, John, 229
DUNLAP, Ann, 199; Craford, 199;
Daniel, 114; Danl., 135;
Elizabeth, 202; Esther, 134;
George, 244; James, 63, 134,
147, 199, 271; Jane, 231;
John, 113, 133, 199, 271;
Martin, 199; Mary, 133, 169;
Polly, 134; Sarah, 199;
William, 105, 109, 134, 169,
199, 202, 208, 244
DUNLOP, Easter, 45; Isbel, 45;
James, 45; John, 45; Mary,
45; Nancy, 45; Sarah, 30, 45;
William, 45
DUNN, Andrew, 173; John, 17;
Liddy, 2
DUNNING, Ann, 45; Ez., 45;
Ezekiel, 45

Philip, 150; Polly, 128;
Samuel, 25, 26, 28, 74, 83,
200, 215, 260; Sarah, 25;
Susanah, 2; Thomas, 25, 74,
143; William, 39, 48
FISSELL, Philip, 113
FISTER, Barbara, 260; Caspar,
260; John, 260; Mary, 260
FITZGERALD, William, 106
FITZPATRICK, William, 65
FLAGHART, George, 39
FLECK, Frederick, 104; John,
252
FLEICHER, John, 39
FLEMING, James, 76, 270; Jas.,
139; Juliann, 153; Rebecca,
97; Samuel, 48; William, 14
FLEMMING, Elizabeth, 182;
James, 42, 255; John, 255;
Margaret, 255; Mary, 42, 220;
William, 255
FLESHER, George, 130; Sarah,
130
FLICKINGER, Abraham, 132;
Betsy, 132; Bodlina, 132;
Christiana, 132; George, 132;
Samuel, 266
FLORENTINA, Carolina, 110
FLOWER, James, 133; Molly, 133
FOGLESONG, Elizabeth, 143;
Jacob, 143
FOGLESONGER, David, 222, 277;
Jacob, 277
FOLK, Christiana, 101;
Elizabeth, 217; Henry, 217;
James, 101; Jean, 101;
Richard, 101; William, 101
FONDERAN, Adam, 47; Margaret,
47
FORBES, Andrew, 263; Jane, 263;
John, 85, 263; John P., 263;
Margaret, 263; Richard, 263
FORDIG, Nicholas, 80
FORDIG (Fordick), Nicholas, 112
FORGGY, Marg., 20
FORNEY, George, 168
FOSSLER, George, 67; Molly, 67
FOSTER, Arthur, 36; George,
113, 274; Hugh, 239;
Isabella, 113, 197; James,
197; Jane, 197; Jean, 113;
John, 103; Mary, 113, 197;
Thomas, 22, 27, 94, 158, 199,
230, 281; William, 6, 17, 25,
113, 197
FOUGHT, Samuel, 215
FOULK, Isabella, 98; John, 281;
Lewis, 27, 98; Margret, 89;
Molly, 160; Moses, 89; Peter,
160; Priscilla, 89; Sarah,
89; Stephen, 89; William,
281; Willis, 89

FOULKE, George D., 209, 236,
275; Mary, 275
FOUTZ, David, 163
FRANCISCUS, John, 176, 238,
252; Mary, 176
FRANK, Daniel, 47; Dorothea,
47; Jacob, 166; Jane, 87;
Mary, 166; Sarah, 166
FRAZER, Alexander, 15; Aron,
15; Jane, 15; John, 10, 15;
Ruth, 15
FREDERICK, Samuel, 254
FREDERICKS, Susanna, 180
FREE, Magdalena, 218; William,
218
FREES, John, 237
FREISER, Jean, 128
FRENCH, Jane, 279; Jean, 137;
John, 178, 279; Martha, 31;
Mary, 279; Samuel, 279;
William, 45, 279
FRITLE, Jacob, 5
FRITZ, Jacob, 229, 234; John,
115
FRY, Abraham, 203; Adam, 203;
Andrew, 132; Daniel, 203;
George, 203; Henry, 182;
Jacob, 281; John, 132, 203;
Joseph, 182; Lavinia, 203;
Mary, 203; Peter, 203
FRYBERGER, John, 160; Mary, 160
FULLERTON, David, 262; James,
174; Margaret, 174
FULTON, Charles, 242; Fran.,
194; Francis, 152; George
Washington, 65; Henry, 65,
66; Isabella, 66; James, 242;
Jean, 242; Jenny, 65; Mr.,
66; Nancy, 269; Polly, 242;
Robert, 148, 166; Sarah, 194;
William, 242
FULTZ, Adam, 210; Caty, 210;
Daniel, 210; George, 210;
Henry, 210; John, 210; Mary,
210; Susannah, 210; William,
210
FULWILER, Abm., 239; Abraham,
130, 156; John, 156; Mary,
156; William, 156
FUNCK, Abraham, 277
FUNK, David, 101
FURRY, Henry, 43; Jane, 43
FUSSELMAN, John, 161

-G-
GABEY, Robert, 66
GAGMAN, David, 269
GAHENE, Elizabeth, 209, 228
GALBRAITH, Andrew, 85; Elijah,
190; Elizabeth, 16; Hannah,
16; James, 16, 62; John, 16,
190; Nancy, 16; Robert, 16;

Samuel, 16, 62, 72; Sarah, 16; William, 16, 62, 189
GALBREATH, Agness, 10; Andrew, 10, 93, 108, 111, 120, 124, 131; Andw., 81, 115, 133; Barbara, 131; Bartram, 10; Catherine, 195; Dorcas, 131, 243; Eleanor, 263; Elizabeth, 10, 81, 131; James, 10, 243; John, 81, 243; Juliana, 131; Mary, 10, 81, 243; Molly, 131; Nancy, 131, 188; Robert, 10, 243; Sally, 131; Samuel, 263; Sarah, 108; Thomas, 10, 81, 243; William, 108, 195, 243
GALBREIATH, Jane, 204; John, 204; Nancy, 204; Sarah, 204; William, 204
GALLASPEY, Mary, 174
GALLESPIE, James, 30; Jenny, 30; Mary, 79; Matthew Miller, 30
GAMBER, Valentine, 102; William, 117
GAMBLE, Benjamin, 46
GAMFRES, ---, 266
GANDEY, Cinthy, 234
GANETS, Andrew, 49
GANGEWER, Allen M., 232; George, 232; Nancy, 232
GANSEE, John, 112
GARDNER, John, 35, 189; Rebecca, 35; William, 35
GARELT, Jean, 93
GARETSON, John, 15
GARLLEN, Elizabeth, 203
GARRET, Alexander, 13, 135; Elinor, 153; James, 152; Jean, 13; Robert, 13, 135; Sarah, 152
GARTNER, David, 248
GARVIN, David, 14; Easter, 14; Elizabeth, 14; James, 14; John, 14, 81; Margaret, 14, 40; Mary, 14; Thomas, 14
GASS, Henry, 3
GATZ, Mary, 66; Susannah, 66
GAW, Catherine, 33; John, 33
GEARY, Lucetta, 243; Susanna, 243
GEASON, James, 252
GEDDIS, Cathrine, 25; James, 25, 58, 137, 141; John, 25, 86, 95, 121, 150, 159, 170, 177, 190, 193, 200, 204, 208, 229, 238, 257, 262, 269, 271; Margaret, 25; Paul, 25; Robert, 25; Samuel, 107; Thomas, 25; William, 10, 25, 26, 57
GEESE, George, 161

GEESEMAN, Peter, 278
GEHR, Jacob, 205
GEIGOR, Jacob, 197; John, 197; Margaret, 197
GELLY (Gaily), Andrew, 204
GEMMILL, Elizabeth, 4; John, 4; Mary Ann, 4; William, 4
GENET, B., 89
GENSIUL, Jacob, 60
GEOBLE, Henry, 94; John Andrew, 94; John Conrad, 94
GEOOP, Philip, 95
GEORGE, Jacob, 265; Martin, 174, 244; Robert, 41
GERBER, Benjamin, 132; Christian, 132
GERNER, Mathias, 191
GESHAM, John, 27
GEYENGER, Abraham, 236; Maria, 236
GIB, Elizabeth, 211
GIBB, John, 143
GIBLER, Benjamin, 277
GIBSON, Andrew, 40; David, 269; Francis, 186, 224, 230; George, 28, 76; Isaac, 25; James, 76; Jane, 255; Jean, 79; John, 76; John B., 148; Margaret, 76, 122; Mary Fitzgerald, 76; Robert, 76; Thomas, 143; William, 76; William C., 230
GIDDIS, John, 274
GIFFEN, James, 176, 238, 253, 254; Martha, 254
GILBERT, George, 68, 149
GILCHRIST, Martha, 242
GILEN, David, 235
GILFILLEN, Ann, 120; Dorcas, 121; Hannah, 120; James, 25, 188; Jean, 121; Matty, 121; Nancy, 121; Rebecca, 121; Sally, 120
GILFILLEN (Gillfilon), James, 120; Nancy, 120
GILL, John, 13
GILLEN, John, 235
GILLESPIE, Jain, 58; James, 58; Jean, 49; Nathaniel, 96; Nathl., 58; Robert, 58
GILLISPIE, Samuel, 205; William, 205
GILMOR, Moses, 22
GILMORE, Alex. R., 263; Charity, 61; Hugh, 61; James, 61; Jean, 61; John, 61; Joseph, 61; Margaret, 55; Moses, 81; Robert, 61; Sarah, 145; Thomas, 61; William, 61, 145, 263
GINGERICH, Abraham, 185
GIS, Abraham, 230; Barbara,

230; Conrad, 230; George,
230; John, 230
GIVEN, Amelia, 157, 263;
Benjamin, 38; James, 38, 87,
94, 110, 146, 157, 158, 199,
247, 270; Jean, 265; John,
38; Joseph, 38, 158, 199;
Robert, 38; Samuel, 38
GIVIN, James, 175
GIVLERD, Anna Mary, 254;
Elizabeth, 254; Susanna, 254
GLADEN, William, 32
GLADSTEN, David, 97; Elizabeth,
97; Jean, 97; William, 97
GLANEY, Elizabeth, 184;
William, 184
GLASFORD, Alexander, 140; Ann,
140; Elizabeth, 140; Jennet,
140; Martha, 140
GLASS, Daniel, 110; Margaret,
110
GLEAN, David, 105
GLEED, J., 160; Rd., 160
GLEMING, James, 97; John, 97;
William, 97
GLEN, Alexander, 47; David, 47;
Gabrael, 47; Jane, 47; Moses,
28; Rachel, 47; Rebecca, 47;
William, 47
GLENDENNING, Elizabeth, 265;
James, 145, 265; Molly, 265
GLENN, Alexander, 72, 128;
Alexr., 194; Ann, 206;
Elizabeth, 72, 207; Lettice,
72; Matthew, 72; Moses, 72;
Nancy, 134; Peggy, 72;
Robert, 72; Rosanna, 177,
206, 262; Sarah, 207;
Susanna, 194, 207; Thomas,
72, 207, 263; William, 177,
206, 262
GLUTSHALLS, Michael, 210
GOARD, Joseph, 152, 275; Steve,
152
GOEHLIN, John, 166
GOLKLIN, Jacop, 92
GOOD, Anney, 200; Christine,
146; Edward, 200; Elizabeth,
200; Henry, 146; John, 146;
Margareth, 200; Peter, 81,
82, 146; Polly, 200; William,
200
GOODLANDER, John, 197
GOODYEAR, Abraham, 196; Daniel,
196; Frederick, 195, 196,
280; Jacob, 195, 196, 265;
John, 265; Rachel, 280;
Samuel, 196
GOORLEY, Agness, 103;
Elizabeth, 103; Isabella,
103; Jean, 103; John, 103;
Margret, 103

GOOSEWEILER, John, 201; Maria
Sarah, 201
GORDON, Agness, 13; Alexander,
125; Angess, 136; James, 13;
John, 13, 74, 235; Mary, 63;
Nancy, 13; Samuel, 13; Sarah,
125
GORGAS, Soloman, 150, 241
GORMELY, Hugh, 108
GORMLY, Abraham, 148; Betty,
148; Hugh, 6, 7
GOUDY, John, 154, 253; Mary,
253
GOULD, Mary Ann, 136; Stophel,
156
GOUNT, Jacob, 108
GOWDEY, Sinthey, 170
GOWDY, James, 66; Samuel, 66;
Sarah, 66
GRACEY, Pricilla, 191; William,
135
GRAHAM, Arthur, 145, 162, 170,
234; Gared, 105; Isa., 162,
253; Isaiah, 88, 145, 162,
178, 234, 255; James, 32, 56,
59, 70, 71, 81, 110, 127,
145, 185, 186, 190, 191, 226,
266; James Arthur, 145; Jane,
250; Jared, 68, 122, 145;
John, 71, 149, 191; Joseph,
250; Mary, 226; Nancy, 88;
Nathan, 226; Sarah, 105;
Susanna, 145; William, 127,
228; William Alexander, 226
GRAME, Frederick, 89
GRAN, Mary, 266; Philip, 266
GRAY, Charles, 153; Elizabeth,
149; John, 18, 163, 168, 175;
Nancy, 264; Robert, 74;
Thomas, 19; William, 15
GRAYBILL, Jane, 74
GRAYDON, A., 276
GRAYSON, Jain, 85; James D.,
273; Mary, 273
GREACY, William, 278
GREAEY, William, 103
GREASON, James, 165, 274; Mary,
165; Samuel D., 268
GREAVER, Anna Maria, 2; Jacob,
2
GREEN, David, 221; Elisha, 133;
George, 124; John, 190; Mary,
14, 130; William, 14, 174
GREER, Samuel, 43, 69
GREGG, Alexander, 97; 143;
Alexander C., 278; Andrew, 1,
31, 143; Ann, 30; Charles,
97; Elizabeth, 1, 143; James,
1, 31, 114; Jean, 1; Jennet,
1; John, 1, 31, 143; Leah, 1;
Margaret, 1; Margery, 1;
Mary, 1; Matthew, 1, 31, 49;

Nancy, 97; Sarah, 143; Smith, 31
GREGORY, Catherine, 234; Elizabeth, 87; James, 84, 87; John, 87; Richard, 87; Walter, 234
GREIGER, Jacob, 260; John, 244, 260; Margaret, 260
GREIGOR, Abraham, 197; Adam, 197; Catherine, 197; David, 197; George, 197; John, 197, 200; Magadalene, 197; Mary, 197
GREKLIN, John, 218
GRESSON, Agness, 165
GRICE, Henry, 165
GRIER, Catherine, 255; Elizabeth, 134, 215; Isaac, 144; Jane, 255; John, 255; John John, 255; Margaret, 255
GRIFFEN, Andrew, 94; James, 252; Jane, 94; Josiah, 10; Martha, 268
GRIFFITH, Agness, 248; Joseph, 248; William, 5
GRIMES, John Adam, 28; Thomas, 272
GRING, John, 243
GRIZZEL, Hugh, 157
GROMLICH, Frederick, 91
GROMLICK, Adam, 94; Anna Mary, 94; Catherine, 153; Christopher, 94; Jacob, 153; John, 94; Magdelena, 94; Peter, 94
GROOP, George, 244
GROSS, Barbara, 173; Catherine, 173, 213; Daniel, 173, 213; Elizabeth, 173; George, 173; Henry, 173, 213; Jacob, 173, 213; Jane, 213; Jenney, 173; John, 173, 213; Margaret, 213; Michael, 173; Peggy, 173; Sally, 173; Sarah, 213; Susanna, 173; Susannah, 213
GROUSE, Catey, 124; John, 124
GROVE, Abraham, 79, 107; David, 79, 211; Jacob, 79; Martha, 107
GRUBB, John, 248; Jonas, 277
GRUBER, Catherine, 211; Christian, 211; Margaret, 211; Regina, 211; Rosanna, 211; Silvester, 211
GUDLANDER, Catherine, 102; Elizabeth, 102; George William, 102; Jacob, 102; John, 102; Justina, 102; Margaret, 102; Susannah, 102
GUMMERY, Rachel, 32
GUNKEL, Adam, 95; Ann, 95; Jacob, 95; Michael, 95

GUNSALUS, Benjamin, 14; Daniel, 14; James, 14, 20; Manuel, 14; Richard, 14; Sarah, 14
GUSTINE, Dr., 55; James, 55, 115, 127, 175; Lemuel, 38, 42, 45, 52, 79. 86, 127; Lemuel P., 127; Margaret, 182; Mariah, 127; Rebecca, 127; Richard, 127; Samuel, 98, 127
GUTERY (Guthrie?), Robert, 13
GUTHRIE, John, 182; Robert, 151; Robert D., 218, 275
GUTJAHR, John, 211; Ludwick, 211
GUTJAHR (Goodyear), Jacob, 211
GUTSAHR, John, 211

-H-
HAAK, Michl., 142
HACAL, William, 281
HACKEDORN, Christian, 152
HACKET, Charles, 190; Eleanor, 87; Elizabeth, 87; George, 87, 190; Henry, 87; Isabella, 87; James, 87; Mary, 190; Plunkt., 196; Robert, 87; William, 87
HACKETT, Elizabeth, 245; George, 245; James, 22, 171, 198; Martha, 171; Mary, 143; Plunkett, 245; Plunkt., 220
HACKMAN, Adam, 232
HAFT, Elizabeth, 86
HAGAN, B., 267; Elizabeth, 245; Mary, 206, 242; Thomas, 206, 242, 245, 267
HAGE, Jonathan, 184
HAILMAN, Mary, 153
HAINZ, Adam, 223; Elizabeth, 223; John, 223; Maximilian, 223; Peter, 223
HAIST, Elizabeth, 138; Jacob, 138
HAKE, Catherine, 152; Christian, 152
HALE, Matthew, 108
HALL, Andrew, 196; Hugh, 48; Isabella, 48; Margaret, 66; Mary, 222; Susannah, 25
HALLER, George, 130
HALSHER, Jacob, 9
HALTER, Andrew, 272
HALTZ, John, 211
HAMBERGER, Benjamin, 140
HAMEROLEY, William, 115
HAMIL, William, 77
HAMILL, George, 234; Robert, 135
HAMILTON, Archibald, 76; Elizabeth, 65; Emmiline, 231; George, 13, 65, 140, 184,

192, 204; Hon. James, 234;
Hugh, 65, 140, 239; Isabel,
133; James, 26, 65, 116, 140,
184, 192, 204, 207, 218, 231,
234, 270; John, 140, 184,
204; Martha, 65, 140; Mary,
116, 204, 231, 234, 239;
Meary, 184; Nancy, 140, 192;
Patrick, 80; Rosanna, 177,
206; Ruth, 140, 192; Samuel,
140, 192, 261; Sarah, 234;
Susan, 231; Thomas, 231;
Wallas, 184; William, 65, 79,
140, 184, 204, 207; William
Wallace, 204
HAMMAKER, Jean, 174
HAMMILL, Mr., 121
HAMMON, Margaret, 39, 88
HANDSHOE, Daniel, 270
HANK, John, 117
HANNA, Agness, 153, 154;
Andrew, 265; Eals, 273;
Eliza, 265, 273; Elizabeth,
265; Hannah, 158; James, 145,
265; Jean, 265; John, 145,
265, 273; John A., 22; John
C., 158, 159; Mary, 145;
Polly, 265; Ruth, 145;
Samuel, 16, 29, 145, 153,
154, 191, 199, 273; William,
145, 265, 273
HANNAH, Ebenezer, 22;
Elizabeth, 22; John, 197;
Joseph, 22; Margaret, 22;
Mary, 22; Samuel, 16, 22, 77;
Sarah, 197
HARDY, Hugh, 7; John, 84;
Margret, 7; Rachel, 84;
Sally, 84
HARE, Jacob, 27; Joseph, 58
HARKINS, Daniel, 67
HARKNESS, David, 32; Elizabeth,
249; Jain, 32; Margaret, 32;
Mary, 249; Priscila, 249;
William, 32, 70, 81, 249, 257
HARKSON, Adam, 128
HARMON, Martin, 104
HARMONY, Elenor, 229; John,
229; Sally, 229
HARPER, Andrew, 268, 269;
Esther, 268; James, 34, 99,
107, 138, 205, 217; Jane,
205, 268; John, 99, 128, 194,
205, 250, 255, 268, 269;
Margaret, 205, 268; Mary,
171, 205; Robert, 99; Samuel,
99, 173; Sarah, 99, 208;
William, 99, 128, 205, 268,
269
HARRIOTT, Rebecca, 216
HARRIS, ---, 258; David, 154,
178; Eleanor, 268; Elizabeth,

223; George, 223; Jane, 231;
Janet, 247; John, 22, 61;
Joseph, 223, 231; Joshan,
223; Mary, 207, 268; Polly,
268; Robert, 61, 143; Samuel,
223; Sarah, 154; Solomon, 247
HARRISON, William, 210
HART, Epinetas, 2; John, 49;
Mary, 2; Matthew, 49;
Michael, 239
HARTER, Fredk., 160; Philip,
185
HARTER (Houter), Fredk., 98
HARTMAN, Henry, 82, 95
HARTZLER, Abraham, 253
HARVEY, Mary, 135
HARVY, William, 1
HARWOOD, Thomas, 153
HASHEY, Jane, 49
HASINA, John, 263
HASKETT, ----, 171
HASLETT, James, 99
HASTEY, John, 262
HATARAH, John W., 281
HATHORN, Alexander, 59; James,
21, 58, 59, 103; Martha, 58
HAUCK, Adam, 43, 49
HAVERLY (Eberly), Jo., 263
HAVERSTICK, John D., 175
HAWENSTINE, John, 246
HAWITT, Mary, 29; Thomas, 29
HAWK, Anna, 243; Barbara, 243;
Christopher, 243; John, 107,
243; Michael, 43
HAWKINS, Lydia, 87
HAWLING, Jane, 112; William,
112
HAWTHORN, Mary, 122; Robert,
28; Sarah, 28
HAWTHORNE, Adam, 28
HAY, Elizabeth, 207; Jacob,
207; Joseph, 133
HAYMAKER, Christian, 203, 220;
Sarah Ligget, 129
HAYS, Adam, 22; Charity, 22,
31; Denniston, 31; Elizabeth,
52, 243; George, 22, 208;
Henry, 22; Isabella, 92;
Jane, 258; Jean, 31; John,
22, 191; John L., 167;
Joseph, 22, 39, 165, 199,
209; Margaret, 223; Mary, 31,
208, 243; Mary Chambers, 274;
Moses, 53; Nancy, 39; Nathan,
22; Patrick, 223, 243; Polly,
208; Richard, 2; Sarah, 31;
William, 52, 60; William J.,
208; William T., 115
HAZELTON, Hugh, 223; Polly, 223
HAZLETT, Mary, 43
HEACK, Catherine, 57; Jacob,
57; John, 57; Mary Elizabeth,

KISLEY, George, 108
KISLEY (Knisley), Samuel, 108
KISSLER, John, 10
KISTLER, Abraham, 156, 177;
    Frederick, 73
KITCH, Barbara, 118; Catherine,
    118; George, 118; Henry, 118;
    John, 118; Martin, 118; Mary,
    118; Michael, 118
KITNER, John, 197
KITZEL, Samuel, 216
KITZEN, Jacob, 183
KLEE, John, 109; Matthias, 109
KLINE, George, 166, 241; Jonas,
    209; Leonard, 117; Peggy,
    209; Polly, 117; Rebecca,
    241; William, 241
KLINGER, Philip, 239
KNETTLE, Daniel, 193, 212;
    David, 212; Elizabeth
    Catharina, 212; George, 212;
    Henry, 212, 223, 253, 270;
    Isaac, 212, 223, 253; Jacob,
    212, 217, 270; Joseph, 212;
    Sarah, 212; Susannah, 270;
    William, 212
KNETTLEWELL, Charles, 267
KNISELEY, Abraham, 205;
    Barbara, 224; Daniel, 205;
    Elizabeth, 205; George, 205;
    John, 205; Samuel, 205, 224
KNISELY, John, 193
KNISLEY, Samuel, 108
KNOBLER, Jacob, 64
KNOLKA, Margrate, 186
KNOP, Jacob, 13
KNOPF, Anely, 23; Annely, 23;
    Benjamin, 23; Christian, 23;
    David, 23; Elizabeth, 23;
    Jacob, 23; John, 23; Mary,
    23; Michael, 23
KNOX, Elizabeth, 144; Hannah,
    106, 114; John, 144; John R.,
    114; Joseph, 106, 114, 218
KOACH (Kock), Christiana, 58;
    John, 58; Margaret, 58;
    Peter, 58; Sally, 58
KOCK, Philip, 57
KOLB, ----, 245
KONIG, John, 94, 206
KONIGMAKER, Benjamin, 240;
    Jacob, 240; J., 240
KONKLE, Jacob, 225
KOOKEN, John, 187
KOSER, Christina, 186;
    Elizabeth, 186; George, 186;
    Gertrout, 186; John, 186;
    Jonathan, 186
KOWAR, Frederick, 281
KREHL, N., 92
KREIDER, Jacob, 268
KREITZER, Andrew, 278;

Elizabeth, 278; Henrietta,
    278; John, 278; Nicholas,
    231, 278; Wilamina, 278
KREMER, Gertrout, 186
KRETTLE, Henry, 138
KRGSHER, Rudolph, 253
KRISHER, Daniel, 134; David,
    134; Elizabeth, 134; Jacob,
    134; John, 134; Ketren, 134;
    Mary, 134; Rosana, 134;
    Rudolph, 134
KRITOES, Nicholas, 265
KRITZER, Adam, 130, 168;
    Andrews, 168; Barbary, 168;
    Elizabeth, 168; Eve, 168;
    John, 168; Nicholas, 126,
    276; Rosina, 168
KRYSHER, Barbara, 203;
    Catherine, 203; David, 203;
    Elizabeth, 203; Jacob, 203;
    Mary, 203; Rosannah, 196;
    Rudolph, 196, 203, 218, 243,
    273, 280
KUHL, George, 245
KULICK, Moses, 139
KULP, Abraham, 236; Ann, 236
KUNKEL, Aaron, 241; George,
    241; John, 241; Susanna, 241
KUNKLE, Jacob, 225; Mary, 225
KUNTZ, Abraham, 185; Catharina,
    185; Isaac, 55; John, 185;
    Margaret, 73
KUTZ, Benjamin, 132, 233;
    Benjn., 146; Daniel, 233;
    David, 233; Dewald, 233;
    Elizabeth, 233; George, 233;
    Gideon, 233; Jacob, 233;
    Josiah, 233; Mary, 233;
    Samuel, 233; William, 233
KYLE, Catherine, 208;
    Elizabeth, 152; Jemima, 152,
    207; Joseph, 152; Matthew,
    152, 208
KYSER, David, 47; Jacob, 53

-L-

LACKEY, Elizabeth, 43
LAFEVER, Jacob, 105
LAING, Nicholas, 51
LAIRD, Ann, 161; Anna, 93, 215;
    Arthur, 93, 161; Elizabeth,
    236; Francis, 236; Hugh, 1,
    3, 12, 93, 137; James, 44,
    58, 79, 94, 108, 123, 137,
    141, 152, 161, 179, 182, 215,
    241, 256, 258, 269; Jane, 94;
    John, 140, 236; Lard, 207;
    Mary, 137; Matthew, 26, 137,
    236; Matthew Lard, 207;
    Rachel, 137; Sam., 18;
    Samuel, 11, 26, 27, 44, 49,
    54, 93, 94, 104, 123, 133,

MCCREARY, Robert, 103
MCCREE, Eleanor, 57; Elonar,
 48; James, 48; Jean, 48
MCCRORY, John, 205
MCCROSKRY, Catherine, 267
MCCUE, Abraham, 26; Anthony,
 26; Eleanor, 191; Jane, 26;
 John, 26, 232; Thomas, 26
MCCULEY, Mary, 257
MCCULLOCH, John, 104; Mary, 104
MCCULLOCK, Alexander, 271;
 Eliza, 279; Elizabeth, 271;
 James, 151, 152, 242, 271,
 279; John, 151, 242, 271,
 279; Margaret Ann, 279; Mary,
 279; Mary Jane, 279; Sally,
 271; Samuel, 271; Thomas,
 269, 279; William, 151, 152,
 269, 271, 279
MCCULLOGH, Archibald, 7;
 Elizabeth, 7; James, 7;
 Robert, 7
MCCULLOUGH, John, 256; Samuel,
 28; William, 263
MCCULLY, George, 41
MCCUMSEY, Sarah, 246
MCCUNE, Andrew, 46; David, 46;
 Eleanor, 272; Elenor, 12;
 Elizabeth, 12, 212; Hanna,
 188; Hugh, 76, 188, 223, 225;
 James, 12, 31, 225; John, 12,
 46, 76, 119, 134, 188, 212,
 223, 225; Kesiah, 212; Kezia,
 12; Letticia, 212; Mary, 46,
 75, 212; Mary Ann, 212;
 Nelly, 12; Peggy, 12;
 Prudence, 187; Robert, 28,
 46, 59, 72, 103, 131, 263,
 212; Rosanna, 12; Samuel, 12,
 46, 76, 188; Thomas, 212,
 226; William, 46, 188, 225
MCCURDY, John, 50; Robert, 64
MCCUTCHEN, Hugh, 3
MCDANEL, John, 89
MCDANIEL, Daniel, 23; David,
 23; Elizabeth, 252; Jean, 23;
 John, 147; Joseph, 23
MCDANIELS, Daniel, 4
MCDANNIL, Joseph, 212
MCDONALD, Daniel, 109; James,
 124, 125, 154; Jeremiah, 125;
 John, 125; Margaret, 154;
 Martha, 125; Saml., 154;
 Sarah, 154; William, 119,
 152, 158, 184, 201, 207, 238
MCDONNEL, Daniel, 187;
 Elizabeth, 162; John, 162
MCDONNELL, Daniel, 86, 205;
 Elizabeth, 86; John, 86
MCDOUD, Agness, 45
MCDOWEL, John, 215, 258;
 Samuel, 59, 256

MCDOWELL, Andrew, 184; Andw.,
 184; James, 141; John, 41,
 141, 178, 235, 241, 259, 269;
 Mary, 141; Samuel, 56, 83,
 141
MCELHAINNY, Jane, 262
MCELHENNY, Hugh, 62, 261;
 James, 261, 278; Jane, 261;
 Joseph, 261; Rebecca, 261;
 Robert, 62, 261; Samuel, 261
MCELREOY, Frederick, 167
MCELREVY, Margaret, 167
MCELROY, Abraham, 122; Ann, 63;
 Hugh, 63, 122; James, 122;
 John, 122, 263; Joseph, 122;
 Martha, 122; Sarah, 122
MCELWAIN, Alexander, 250;
 Andrew, 62, 250; Ebenezer,
 247, 250, 273; Elizabeth,
 273; George, 250; James, 214;
 Jane, 261; Jennet, 63; Jeny,
 62; John, 46, 214; Joseph,
 63, 250; Margaret, 214, 260,
 261, 273; Mary, 46; Richard,
 46, 214, 261; Robert, 62;
 Ruth, 46; Widow, 261
MCENAIR, Alexander, 40; David,
 40; Dening, 40; Mary, 40;
 Robert, 40
MCEWEN, James, 31; Maryann, 31
MCEWIN, John, 143
MCFADDEN, Hugh, 104
MCFALL, Michael, 170
MCFARLAND, Elizabeth, 161;
 James, 90; John, 107;
 Margaret, 161; Robert, 96,
 145; William, 17
MCFARLANE, Andrew, 45; Ann, 15;
 Clemence, 150, 190; Eliza,
 150, 190; Elizabeth, 47, 96,
 150, 190, 206; James, 15, 47,
 96, 150, 161, 177, 190, 206,
 269; Jennet, 15; John, 15,
 150, 190; Margaret, 15, 47,
 150; Mary, 47; Nelly, 189;
 Patrick, 47, 177; Peggy, 161;
 Polly, 150, 190; Robert, 15,
 47, 96, 150, 177, 190, 200,
 206, 234; Rosanah, 47;
 Rosanna, 177, 206; Samuel,
 150, 188, 190; Thomas, 206;
 William, 4, 15, 47, 51, 57,
 96, 150, 190
MCFARLIN, Alexander, 187;
 Elizabeth, 187; James, 161,
 187; Jean, 6; John, 187;
 Mary, 138, 187; Nancy, 187;
 Peggy, 187; Rachel, 187;
 William, 2, 187
MCFARLINE, Mary, 89
MCFEELEY, George, 266; John, 97
MCFEELY, Margaret, 275; Roger,

316

MAGAURAN, Edward, 89, 162, 281;
Elizabeth, 281; Eneas, 281;
Henry, 281; Margaret, 281;
Margaretta, 281
MAGAW, Elizabeth, 26; Marietta,
26; Robert, 10, 22, 26;
Vanbrunt, 26
MAGEE, Alexander, 90; Ebenezer,
90; Eleanor, 61; James, 90;
John, 90; Joseph, 263;
Morison, 90
MAGHY, Elizabeth, 114
MAGOVENEY, Agness, 33; James,
33
MAGUARAN, Anne, 157; Elizabeth,
157; Henry, 157
MAHON, Ann, 56, 114; David, 63;
Elizabeth, 185; John D., 242;
Samuel, 56
MAKEHAN (Mahon), Alexander, 52
MAKON, Alexander, 185;
Archibald, 185; David, 185;
Jane, 185; John, 185; Mary,
185; Samuel, 185; Sarah, 185;
William, 185
MALKOLM, Roddy, 106
MALROY, William R., 256
MANN, George, 118
MAPPAN, John, 19
MAPPS, Ashael, 210
MAPS, Jane, 210, 234
MARCHALL, Margaret, 182
MAREDY (McCready?), David, 82
MARK, John, 236
MARKLE, Adam, 165
MARKLY, Daniel, 253
MARLIN, Jane, 130; John, 130;
Joshua, 7; Sarah, 130
MARSCHALK, A., 89
MARSHALL, Andrew, 215;
Catherine, 5; David, 5;
Elinor, 5; Elizabeth, 56,
127; Jame, 215; James, 67;
Jane, 215; Jean, 5; John, 5,
52, 67, 215; Joseph, 5, 107,
197; Letitia, 52; Margaret,
215; Mary, 5; Michael, 5, 25,
52, 74, 107; Sally, 215;
Samuel, 52; Thomas, 197, 215;
William, 67
MARTIN, ---, 278; Abraham, 250;
Agness, 172; Alexander, 29;
Andrew, 4, 220; Anna, 265;
Barbara, 82, 203, 250;
Charles, 99; Christian, 250;
David, 113, 236, 250; Elinor,
172; Elizabeth, 171; Hannah,
172; Henry, 250, 253; Jane,
172; John, 99, 113, 265;
Joshua, 52; Magdalena, 250;
Margaret, 75, 203; Maria,
187, 250; Nancy, 171;

Patrick, 17; Paul, 99, 172;
Peter, 160; Robert, 1, 29;
Rosana, 99; Rosanna, 172;
Saml., 77; Samuel, 4, 116,
196; Susannah, 250; Thomas,
1, 4, 99, 113, 171, 172;
William, 57, 65, 163, 172
MASON, George, 139; Revd. Dr.,
251
MASONER, Elizabeth, 95
MASS, Barbara, 164; Barnet, 164
MATCHET, Edward, 249
MATEER, Andrew, 190, 233, 239;
Isabella, 190; James, 107,
108, 190; John, 108, 190,
199; Mary, 190; Rosana, 132;
Saml., 132; William, 190
MATHERS, Agness, 249; Eleanor,
103; Jane, 86; John, 249,
271; Joseph, 194; Mary, 86;
Nancy, 249, 270; Samuel
(Saml.), 23, 86, 105, 144;
Thomas, 86; William, 86, 233
MATHEWS, David, 20; George,
272; Jane, 54; Peter William,
249; Philip, 5; Richard, 54;
Susannah, 53
MATHIAS, Henry, 137; Lizzy, 137
MATIER, Thomas, 25
MATTEER, Rebecca, 239
MATTER, Ann, 198; Catherine,
180, 198; Elizabeth, 198;
Jane, 180; Mary, 198; Mary
Ann, 180; Nancy, 180, 198;
Rachel, 198; Rachell, 180
MATTER (Matteer), Elizabeth,
180; Jacob, 180
MATTHEWS, Esther, 53; Henry,
166; James, 54; Margaret,
166; Mary, 247
MAUGAUSON, Edward, 157
MAVINS, George, 78
MAXWELL, Albert, 22; Alexander,
22; Andrew, 22, 183; Ann, 22;
Catherine, 148; David, 148;
Elizabeth, 148; George, 148;
Grizell, 207; James, 22, 86,
92, 145, 148; John, 148, 207;
Margaret, 22; Mary, 22, 148;
Robert, 22; Sarah, 148;
William, 22, 148
MAY, Frederick, 130
MAYBERRY, Catherine, 228;
Catrin, 209; Catty, 229;
David, 209; Davis, 228, 229;
Nancy, 209, 228; Silvanus,
209, 229; William, 209
MAYS, Fredk., 168
MEALEY, Samuel, 193
MEALY, Laurence, 7; Samuel, 216
MEANS, Elizabeth, 255; James,
90, 152, 208; John, 152, 177,

318

75, 141, 154; Susanah, 37;
Susanna, 254; William, 228,
247, 273
MITHCELL, Isabella, 151; Sarah,
151; Zekiel, 151
MITTEN, Joseph, 60
MOFFIT, Eleanor, 205
MOFFITT, Mary, 142
MOHLER, Christian, 146, 187;
Jacob, 106
MOLEN, Christiana, 60
MOLL, Jacob, 224
MOLTZS, Daniel, 164; David,
164; George, 164; Henry, 164;
Jacob, 164; John, 164
MONASMITH, Elizabeth, 266
MONROE, G., 139, 214, 224;
George, 108
MONTGOMERY, Ann, 140; ann, 136;
Dr. William, 154; Elizabeth,
140; Ellenor, 140; Frazer,
200; James (Jas.), 154, 177;
John, 1, 18, 154; Margaret,
140, 154; Mary, 154; Rebecca,
140; Sarah, 48, 154, 178;
Sidney, 154; Susana, 140;
Thomas, 154; William, 29, 35,
37, 41, 68, 77, 136, 140,
200, 278
MOODY, John, 255; Joseph, 185
MOON, Andrew, 55
MOORE, Andrew, 55, 114, 116,
174; Ann, 116, 117;
Archibald, 14; Catherine,
221; Elizabeth, 114, 116,
205; George, 114; Gilbert,
184; Howard, 114; James, 101,
102, 116, 117, 120, 187, 205,
206, 262; Jane, 142; Jean,
114; Job, 80; John, 25, 50,
73, 116, 120, 149, 152, 188,
238, 257; Johnston, 188, 262;
Margaret, 104, 221; Matilda,
151; Matthew, 149; Nancy, 50,
188, 220, 262; Nelly, 120;
Robert, 114, 221; Sarah, 116;
Stewart, 221; W., 129;
William, 114, 116, 120, 176,
205, 237, 238, 248; William
Craig, 116
MOORHART, Jacob, 214
MOORHEAD, John, 191
MOOTZER, Daniel, 211; John,
211; Martin, 211
MORELAND, David, 183, 209;
James, 104
MORISON, John, 81; Phoebe, 54
MORRET, Gertrout, 253; Hartman,
36; Hortenan, 253; Jacob,
253; John, 253, 274; Michael,
253
MORRIS, ---, 232; Jane, 74;

Nancy, 74; Robert, 111
MORRISON, Agness, 136; Anna,
136; Anthony, 61; Catherine,
136; Daniel, 54; Esther, 154;
Grizzel, 136; Hance, 141;
James, 127, 136, 154; Jas.,
54; Jean, 127; Jeanet, 67;
John, 25, 31, 38, 39, 54, 67,
84, 157, 230; John Pollock,
141; Lucas, 141; Lydia, 157;
Margaret, 141; Mary, 127,
136, 157; Noble, 127; Phoebe,
54; Robert, 12, 67, 157;
William, 67, 81, 136, 255
MORRON, James, 273
MORROW, Alexander, 39; Eleanor,
279; James, 273; Jane, 61;
John, 263; John S., 227;
Nancy, 39; Robert, 112;
William, 12, 39, 118
MORTIMER, John, 67
MORTON, Edward, 22, 85, 123,
126; Japheth, 22; William,
123, 124
MOTZER, Martin, 57
MOUNTZ, Adam, 265
MOUTZ, Stophel, 5
MOWER, George, 134, 174
MOWERS, George, 144
MOYER, Barbara, 236; Christian,
236; Henry, 236; Isaac, 236;
Jacob, 236; John, 236;
Samuel, 236
MOZER, John, 83; Magdalena, 98
MULL, Rebecca, 261
MULLEN, Hugh M., 239
MULLERSHOCK, Peter, 78
MULLIGAN, Thomas, 184
MULLIN, John, 257
MUMMA, Frecerick, 125; John,
125, 163, 186, 211, 236, 237,
254, 260; Margaret, 254;
Mary, 254; Samuel, 254
MUMPER, Christina, 237; John,
237
MUNRO, Margaret, 235; Ruben,
235; William, 188, 235
MURDOCK, Agness, 19; Alexander,
21; John, 11; Sarah, 11
MURKLAND, Alexander, 194; Mary,
194
MURPHY, Anne, 115; Elizabeth,
220; James, 220; Jeney, 130;
John, 115, 220; Paul, 172;
Samuel, 131; William, 220
MURRAY, Agness, 48; Alexander,
29, 31, 35, 39, 48; Alexr.,
29, 44; Ann, 39, 191; David,
45; Elizabeth, 19, 199;
George, 212, 216, 226;
Halbert, 39; Isabella, 48;
James, 39; Jean, 29; John,

320

OLFINGHER, George, 165
OLIVER, Polly, 239
OLLINGER, George, 197; Justina,
197; Sarah, 197
O'NEIL, John, 17
ORMSBY, Oliver, 185
ORNER, Abraham, 125, 160; Ann,
125, 160; David, 125;
Elizabeth, 125, 160; John,
160; Margaret, 125, 160;
Martin, 160; Mary, 125, 160;
Sarah, 125, 160; Susan, 125,
160
ORR, Frances, 6; Jane, 242;
Jean, 55; John, 55, 113, 117,
120, 124, 139, 153, 191, 242;
Martha, 55, 242; Mary, 55,
242; Rachel, 55, 242;
Rebecca, 242; William, 55,
85, 117, 120, 124, 242
ORRIS, Adam, 135; Catty, 142;
George, 135; Henry, 135;
John, 135; Joseph, 135, 142;
Mary, 142; William, 135
ORWAN, John, 64
OSBORNE, Samuel, 32
OTTENBERGER, Catherine, 2;
Jacob, 2
OTTLEY, John, 117
OVERLY, Adam, 87
OWEN, John, 186, 197, 204, 220;
Mariah, 219
OWENS, Benjamin, 221; James,
219; John, 176, 221; Mary,
193; William, 219

-P-
PAGE, Mary, 230
PAGUE, Jacob, 222; James, 222;
John, 222; Molly, 222; Peter,
222; Philip, 222; Rebecca,
222; Samuel, 222; William,
222
PAINTER, Catherine, 149;
George, 43; Hannah, 43
PALEN, Jacob, 104
PALLEY, Thomas, 14
PALM, Jacob, 177; Margaret, 177
PALMER, Catherine, 276
PARKER, Alexander, 42; Andrew,
55, 76, 98, 122, 127, 142;
Elizabeth, 123; George, 171;
J. B., 231; James, 55; John,
42; Margaret, 42, 98; Mary,
42, 239; Rebeca, 55; Richard,
190; T. B., 221; William, 190
PARKINSON, Robert, 167
PARKISON, Ann, 97; Catherine,
97; Catreen, 102; David, 102;
Elizabeth, 97, 102; Jane, 90;
Jeams, 102; Jean, 97; John,
97, 102; Joseph, 102;

Margaret, 102; Margret, 102;
Rachel, 102; Richard, 97,
102; Thomas, 102; William,
102
PARSEL, John, 139; Rachel, 139
PARSONS, Catherine, 54; Samuel,
54
PATERSON, Hannah, 43; John, 43;
Martha, 43; Millard, 43;
Robert, 43, 100; Samuel, 43;
Timothy, 43; William, 43
PATON, William, 4
PATRICK, James, 134; Polly,
134; Sarah, 134; William, 134
PATTEN, David, 6; Margaret, 68;
Robert, 6; Thomas, 6, 68;
William, 6, 68
PATTERSON, Alexander, 230;
Andrew, 201; Ann, 81, 118,
131; Benjamin, 120; Catherine,
152, 207, 230; Charles, 162,
164; Christopher, 192;
Elizabeth, 162, 209; Esther,
22, 131; Ezra, 128; Francis,
208; George, 71, 134, 162,
209; Grisald, 131; Holmes,
162, 209; Isabella, 22, 230;
James, 22, 152, 195; Jane,
131, 162, 219, 230; Jesse,
215; John, 22, 80, 81, 113,
118, 128, 136, 147, 152, 192,
210; Josiah, 128; Margaret,
230; Mary, 25, 131, 190, 192,
201; Mary Ann, 192; Nancy,
162, 187; Obidiah, 113, 128;
Polly, 113; Robert, 9, 10,
37, 74, 83, 93, 113, 128,
134, 135, 152, 207; Ruth, 25,
152; Sarah, 74, 113, 131;
Thomas, 113, 131, 151, 174,
188, 255, 269; William, 22,
25, 26, 192, 230; Zacheus,
128
PATTISON, Chas., 158; George,
50, 55, 60, 106, 114, 158,
168, 198, 199, 232, 236, 240;
Holmes A., 221
PATTON, Elizabeth, 78, 122;
Hugh, 44; James, 93; Jannet,
68; John, 18, 54, 62, 68,
122; Mary, 122; Rebecca, 68;
Richard, 151; Robert, 54, 68;
Sarah, 151; Thomas, 122;
William, 54, 67
PAUL, Isaac, 189
PAULY, Sarah, 1
PAWLEY, John, 2; Sarah, 2
PAXTON, David, 246; James, 153;
John, 245, 246
PEA, Mary, 222, 224; Nancy,
225; Sarah, 222

PEACE, John, 196
PEBLES, Alexander, 5, 78, 141,
234; Robert, 78
PEDEN, Agness, 204; John, 24,
204; Margaret, 204; Mary,
204; Robert, 204; Ross, 204;
William, 204, 205
PEEBLES, Alexander, 10, 192,
272; Elizabeth, 272; John,
119, 121; Margaret, 119;
Robert, 144, 174, 229, 272
PEFER, Eve, 248
PEFFER, John, 235; Philip, 216;
Rachel, 216
PEIFER, George, 88
PEIRCE, Jane, 123; Jos., 90
PELSE, Catherine, 174;
Christian, 174; James, 174;
Mary, 174
PENCE, Elizabeth, 251; George,
251; Philip, 251
PENEWELL, Agness, 4
PENN, John, 151
PEPPER, Philip, 107
PERRY, Martha, 92; Samuel, 8
PESH, Elizabeth, 158; Joseph,
158
PETERS, George, 140; John, 198,
250; Margart, 104; William,
104
PETTIGREW, James, 140, 150,
154, 199
PFEFFER, Philip, 99
PFIESTER, Philip, 68
PFOUTS, Michael, 185
PFOUTZ, Anne, 117; David, 117;
Jacob, 26
PHILIP, Michael, 77
PHILIPS, George, 212; John, 80,
142, 213; Mary, 142; Michael,
142; Peter, 142
PHILLIPS, Mary, 6; Peter, 218;
William, 6
PHIT, Catherine, 165
PICKARD, Henry, 228
PICKLE, Rudy, 15
PIERCE, Andrew, 208, 274; Mary
Chambers, 274; Paul S., 123;
Rebecca, 274; Rebeckah, 208
PINCHSMITH, Charity, 143;
Henry, 143; Rebecca, 143
PINKERTON, John, 166, 221;
Margaret, 166, 221; Polly,
166; Thomas, 166
PIPER, Capt. James, 238;
Elizabeth, 82, 94; James,
279; Jane, 94; Mary, 94;
Robert, 207; Samuel, 249;
William, 82, 94
PLANK, Jacob, 263
PLITT, Catherine, 277
PLUNKET, Isaac, 145; Lydia, 145

POLLINGER, Abraham, 67, 197;
Elizabeth, 67
POLLOCK, Alexander, 162; Ann,
93, 175; Betsy, 227; Ellinor,
162; Galvez, 93; Grace, 141;
James, 70, 93; Jared, 110;
Jarrett, 93; Jean, 162; John,
16, 70, 71, 141, 162; Joseph,
227; Mary, 93, 110, 227;
Nancy, 81; Oliver, 93, 110;
Rosetta, 93
POOL, John, 228
POORMAN, Mary, 25
PORER, Agness, 245
PORTER, Agness, 5; Ann, 216;
Caroline, 216; David, 5;
Elenor, 142; George, 216;
Hugh, 3; James, 145, 169;
Joseph, 3, 139; Mary, 5, 61,
216; Moses, 61, 216; Robert,
3, 5, 90, 170, 192, 216, 222;
Saml., 5; Sarah, 5;
Washington, 5; William, 3,
208
PORTERFIELD, Agness, 18;
Hannah, 18; James, 18; Jean,
18; John, 18; Samuel, 18;
Sarah, 18; William, 18, 62
POSTLETHEWAIT, Saml., 97
POSTLETHWAIT, Saml., 50, 56, 75
POSTLETHWAITE, John, 23, 167;
Joseph, 167; Matilda, 167;
Samuel (Saml.), 11, 27, 101,
114, 124, 147, 152, 162, 164,
167, 171, 185, 223, 227
POTTS, Elizabeth, 114; Hugh H.,
114; Samuel, 263
POWER, Agness, 91; Alexander,
52, 74, 95, 181; Captain
William, 172; Edward, 181;
Fatima, 172; James, 172, 181;
John, 172; Joseph, 181; Mary,
181; Tamar, 181; William,
181, 184
POWERS, Grizzle, 52; James, 49
PRATZ, Abraham, 125; Chatarina,
125; Conrad, 125; Daniel,
125, 237; Elizabeth, 125;
Frederick, 125, 237; Henry,
237; Jacob, 125; John, 125,
237; Magdalena, 237; Philip,
125; Simon, 125; Thomas, 125
PREBLES, Robert, 260
PREEKER, Jacob, 143; Mary, 143
PRICE, Philip, 130
PRINDLE (Brindle), Magdalena,
260; Melchor, 260
PUE, Rebeka, 37
PURCELL, Edw., 1
PURDY, Elizabeth, 44; James,
95, 205, 250; John, 44, 72,
95, 122; Margaret, 95;

7; Margret, 7; Rebeka, 7; Robert, 7; William, 7
RYLEY, Anna Maria, 181; Thomas, 181

-S-
SADLER, Isaac, 74
SAILOR, Henry, 212; John, 28, 218; Mathias, 104; Samuel, 28
ST. CLARI, Gen., 52
SALSBURY, Christian, 35; Daniel, 35; Henry, 35; Peter, 35, 161; Philip, 35; Salome, 35; William, 35
SAMPLE, Agness, 266; Chambers, 55; David, 61, 102; Elizabeth, 55; James, 55, 266; John, 55, 127, 266; Joseph, 55; Kesiah, 55; Samuel, 55, 244, 266
SANDERS, Alexr., 228; George, 245; Jacob, 234
SANDERSON, Alexander, 70, 105, 112; Alexr., 105; Elizabeth, 105; George, 70, 83, 105, 111, 112; James, 105, 135; Jane, 70; John, 63, 70, 83, 112, 133, 253; Letice, 81; Letuce, 118; Lydia, 157; Mary, 105, 111, 112, 133, 277; Rebecca, 139; Rebeccah, 277; Robert, 70, 83, 111, 245; Samuel, 81; Sarah, 83; William, 105, 112, 121, 139
SANDS, George, 80, 178; John, 80; Mary, 178
SANNO, Michael, 273
SAUNDERS, Christy, 95
SAYERS, James, 69
SCADEN, Thomas, 64
SCANDRETT, James, 72, 78
SCHENK, George, 106; Mary, 106
SCHLOUNER (Schlonner), John, 80
SCHNEIDER, Eleanora, 109; John, 109; Michael, 109; Samuel, 109; Sera, 109
SCHNYDER, George, 195; Susannah, 195
SCHONS, John, 195
SCHOP, Barbara, 186
SCHRAM, Joseph, 180
SCHULER, Christopher, 271
SCHWEITZER, Frederick, 102
SCHWENDT, George, 280; John, 280; John Nicholas, 280; Magdalena, 280; Maria, 280; Nicholas, 280; Peter, 280; Philip, 280
SCOT, John, 161; Mary, 161; Robert, 25, 44
SCOTT, Andrew, 167; Elizabeth, 77; Isabel, 96; Jane, 167;

John, 31, 45, 57, 66, 77, 83, 93, 96, 141, 160, 167, 172, 176; Joseph (Jos.), 77, 164, 167; Margaret, 91; Mary, 163, 164; Matthew, 77; Mattw., 66; Rob., 12; Robert, 77, 167; Thomas, 37, 82; William, 9, 33, 36, 60, 75, 77, 156, 163, 167
SCOULER, John, 204
SCOULLER, John, 11, 23, 31, 40, 48, 142, 188, 195, 217, 219, 233, 237, 242, 246, 250
SCROGGS, Alexander, 63; Allen, 63; Aron, 63; Ebenezer, 63; Elijah, 63; Elizabeth, 63; James, 63; John, 63; John A., 170; Mary, 63; Moses, 63; Rachel, 63; Sarah, 63
SCROGS, James, 40
SEARER, Catherine, 243
SEARIGHT, Alexander, 184; Francis, 184, 185, 208; George, 184; Gilbert, 184; William, 185
SEELY, Eliza, 175
SEEVER, Michael, 152
SEFFER, John, 36
SEIBERT, Daniel, 202; Jacob, 202; Nancy, 202
SEIER, David, 251
SEIRAH, Adam, 117; Catherine Elizabeth, 117; Daniel, 117; Elizabeth, 117; George, 117; Jacob, 117; John, 117; Margaret, 117; Mary, 117
SELIARS, Martin, 124
SEMPLE, Elizabeth, 172; Jane, 172; Jos., 9; Joseph, 9, 172; Robert, 59
SENDER, Philip, 106
SENSBORG, John, 214
SEVERS, Abraham, 275; David, 275; Elizabeth, 275; George, 275; Jacob, 275; John, 275; Leah, 275; Mary, 275; Michael, 275; Rachel, 275; Sally, 275
SEVILER, Christopher, 276; John, 276
SHADE, John, 98; Maria, 98; Mary, 229
SHAFER, Barbarah, 212; Betsy, 212; Catherine, 212; David, 212; Deborah, 212; Elizabeth, 212; Henry, 212; John, 212; Mary, 212; Nicholas, 212; Petre, 212; Rozena, 212; Sarah, 212; Susy, 212
SHAFF, George, 102
SHAFFER, Elizabeth, 197; John, 197

328

SNIBUL, Jacob, 8
SNIDER, Frederick, 64; John,
159, 274; Michael, 64
SNIVELY, Elizabeth, 126, 265;
Fanny, 126; George, 126;
Henry, 126; John, 126, 265;
Nancy, 126; Polly, 126;
William, 260
SNIVLEY, John, 277
SNODY, Adam, 195; Benjamin,
195; John, 41, 195; Johnston,
195; Mathew, 195; Matthew,
195; Polly, 195; William,
195; William Johnston, 195
SNOWDON, Sally, 127
SNYDER, Christiana, 211;
Conrad, 245, 264; David, 47,
228, 250; Elizabeth, 228,
265; Henry, 225; John, 254,
265, 266; Merchor, 228;
Nicholas, 106; Philip, 229;
Susan, 266; Susanna, 264
SOLANDER, John, 256
SOLENBERGER, ----, 51
SOUDER, Catherine, 174; Caty,
174; David, 174; Jacob, 174;
Polly, 174
SOUR, Barbara, 118; Barnhart,
118
SOUTER, John H., 141
SOWERS, Adam, 244; Elizabeth,
254; Jacob, 254; Mary, 244;
Sarah, 254
SPADE, Rachel, 147
SPAHR, Eliza, 220; Frederick,
220; Isaac, 220; John, 220;
Joseph, 220; Nancy, 220;
Polly, 220; Samuel, 220;
Simon, 220; Susan, 220
SPANGLER, Peter, 113, 248;
Philip, 248
SPARK, Henry Ludolph, 104
SPEAK, Fredk., 196
SPEAR, Elizabeth, 259; William,
259
SPEEDY, Jean, 67
SPENCER, Joseph, 73
SPESS, John, 173
SPONG, Elizabeth, 147; Jacob,
147
SPONSIER, Alexander, 198;
Elizabeth, 198; George, 198
SPONSLER, Elizabeth, 180;
George, 180
SPRIGLE, Joseph, 217
SPROAT, Betsy, 169; Elizabeth,
168; Eves, 168; Isabella,
168; John, 7, 45, 103; Nancy,
169, 202; William, 7
SPROUT, Agness, 135; Alexander,
135; Catherine, 208;
Elizabeth, 135; Eve, 135;

Isabella, 135; Jean, 135;
John, 135; Mary, 135;
William, 135
SQUIER, Jacob, 213, 247
SRUOYER, Jo., 269
STAGGERS, Conrad, 144; Jacob,
144; John, 144; Mary, 144
STAGMAN, John, 107
STAHL, Abraham, 161; John, 161;
Margaret, 161; Peter, 161;
William, 161
STAIR, John, 15; Mary
Magdalane, 15
STAKEMILLER, William, 236
STALL, Daniel, 188
STANBRIDGE, Christopher, 181;
Elizabeth, 181; George
Livingston, 181; John, 181;
John Christr., 181; Mary Ann,
181; Sarah, 181; Susan Mary,
181; Thomas, 181; William,
181
STANDLEY, Samuel, 244
STANLY, Nathal., 20; Samuel,
202
STANSBERRY, Thomas, 238
STARR, Elizabeth, 2; Jane, 247;
John, 2, 85; Mary, 2; Moses,
2; Rachel, 2; Samuel, 266
STARRETT, James, 35; Robert,
168
STAUBB, Daniel, 121
STAYMAN, Abraham, 89, 241;
Elizabeth, 88; Jacob, 89;
John, 88; Joseph, 88; Katron,
88
STEAIR, Jacob, 213
STEEL, Catherine, 149; David,
1; Eliza, 216; Elizabeth, 53;
Eph., 127; Ephraim, 25, 98,
101, 275; Esther, 275; John,
6, 15, 157, 158, 221, 275;
Margaret, 216; Mary, 183,
207, 214; Morris, 169;
Nathaniel, 11; Rev. John,
167; William, 158
STEEL (Stahl), Ann, 59;
Anthony, 59; Elizabeth, 59;
Eve, 59; Mary, 59; Morris,
59; Paul, 59
STEELE, Ephraim, 89; John, 89,
248; William, 89
STEELMAN, James, 9; Mary, 275
STEEN, John, 159
STEIGLEMAN, Elizabeth, 277;
John, 277; Mary, 277; Rachel,
277; Sarah, 277; Wilkenson,
277
STEMAH, Christian, 160
STEMAK, Christion, 125
STEPHEN, Catherine, 17;
Elizabeth, 230

STEPHENS, Elizabeth Henning, 225; Hannah, 225; James, 27; Mary, 225; Thomas, 225
STEPHENSON, John, 258; Margaret, 258; Thomas, 258; William, 273
STEREATT, David, 140
STERET, David, 227
STERETTS, Mr., 76
STERRET, Brice I., 214; David, 255; Isabella, 157; John, 120; Rebecca, 3
STERRETT, Agness, 101, 168; Alexander Wilson, 278; Brice I., 140; Brice Innes, 35, 168, 278; Daniel, 140; David, 16, 18, 35, 99, 140, 154, 168, 172, 227, 278; Elizabeth, 35, 154, 172; Isabella, 278; James, 56, 154; Jane, 278; John, 35, 101, 168, 172; Margaret, 168; Martha, 172; Polly, 154; Rachel, 35, 168; Robert, 35; Samuel, 154; Sarah, 172; William, 35
STEVENS, Arthur, 182; George, 216, 217; Hannah, 182; James, 182; John, 182; John Jefferson, 182; Richard, 182; Thomas, 182
STEVENSON, Elizabeth, 278; George, 4; James, 46, 62, 227; Jane, 227, 279; John, 46, 227, 279; Margaret, 227, 279; Mary, 46, 129, 227, 279; Rachel, 30; Robert, 74; Thomas, 30; William, 18, 46, 140, 227, 279
STEWART, Alexander, 20, 175; Alexr., 172; Archd., 20; Archibald, 44, 113; Catherine, 20; Dr. Alexander, 233, 234; Elizabeth, 2, 225; Isabella, 44; James, 20, 44; Jane, 233; Jean, 20; Jeney, 44; John, 44, 90, 113, 222, 225; Joseph, 70; Kathrine, 70; Margaret, 79; Mary, 20, 44, 70; Robert, 2, 225; Samuel, 44; Thomas, 44; William, 44, 233
STIEVICK, Abraham, 176
STINE, George, 136
STITT, James, 169
STOCKDALE, Elizabeth, 275; John, 275
STOCKTON, Agness, 243; Robert, 243
STOFFER, Henry, 239
STOKES, Samuel, 175
STONAKER, Jacob, 267

STONE, Barbara, 251
STONEBRING, George, 279
STONER, Christian, 164; Elizabeth, 164; John, 130, 164
STONES, Andrew, 24, 49; Ann, 24; James, 24; John, 24, 105; Margaret, 24; Martha, 105; Peter, 24, 46, 49
STORY, Jane, 146; John, 25
STOUGH, Catherine, 178; Elizabeth, 178; Hanes, 178; Jacob, 178; Margaret, 178; Nicholas, 178; Samuel, 178; Susanna, 178; William, 178
STRATTON, Lot, 65
STRAUSE, Ephraim, 87
STREN, Mary, 186
STRICKLER, Henry, 277
STROCK, Jacob, 196, 251; Joseph, 36
STROEH, Jacob, 195; Joseph, 195
STROEK, Jacob, 265
STRONG, William, 219
STROOP, George, 100, 165, 197, 222
STROUP, Peter, 148; Rosina, 186
STRUCKLER, Conrad, 271
STRUNK, John, 99; Polly, 99
STRUUBE, Andrew, 5
STUART, Archibald, 76; Hugh, 122; Isabella, 205; John, 50, 205; Mary, 34; Robert, 205; Samuel, 23, 34; William, 205
STUBBS, George, 173, 274
STUCKEY, Martin, 220; Rosanna, 220
STUMBAUGH, Jacob, 25; Mary, 189; Peter, 175; Rebecca, 189
STURGEON, Fanny, 119; Peter, 13; Samuel, 119
STURGES, Mary, 219
STURM, David, 175, 281; Elizabeth, 175; George, 175; Sophia, 281
SUCH, Thomas, 50
SULENBERGER, Anna Elizabeth, 165; Henry, 165; Jacob, 165; Joseph, 165
SUMMERS, James D., 254
SUNBAY, Elizabeth, 44
SUNDAY, Henry, 234
SURMIS, Martin, 210
SWAIR, Margery, 180
SWAN, Joseph, 18
SWANEY, Ann, 83
SWANGER, Abraham, 26; Christty, 136; David, 136; Jacob, 136; Mary, 136; Michael, 136; Nicholas, 136; Paul, 136
SWARTZ, Annamare, 36; Caspar, 36, 73; Casper, 36;

132; John, 128, 269; Joseph,
269; Mary, 128; Rachel, 154;
Rebecca, 128; Thomas, 128,
132, 255, 269; William, 22
TRIMMER, Andrew, 216
TRINDLE, Agness, 7; Alexander,
245; Alexr., 4, 7; David,
246; James, 7; Jane, 246;
John, 4, 7, 245, 246;
Lucinda, 246; William, 7, 246
TRITT, Peter, 201
TRONVINGER, Eve, 211
TROTTER, Elizabeth, 271; Jane,
149; Matthew, 87; William
Hunter, 271
TROUDT, Adam, 125
TROUGH, John, 198; Rudolph, 198
TROW, John, 33
TUCKER, Susannah, 232
TULLY, James, 60
TURNER, Daniel, 103; James, 52,
103, 134; John, 103; Joseph,
103, 104; Rebeccah, 71;
Samuel, 81

-U-
UHLER, Frederick, 124; Tedrick,
99
ULCH, John, 276
ULLRICK, Catherine, 169
ULSH, Jacob, 195
ULTZ, John, 264
UNDERWOOD, Ann, 244; Elisha,
74; James (Jas.), 205, 276;
John, 139, 205; John Dickson,
244; Margaret, 244; Sarah,
244
URIE, Grizzle, 264; John, 3,
171, 184; Margaret, 164;
Thomas (Tho.), 76, 122, 142,
146, 164, 167, 168, 173, 231,
264
URWIN (Irwin), Daniel, 91;
Elizabeth, 92; Jane, 92;
John, 91; Maria, 92;
Susannah, 91
UTTER, Saml., 66, 124; Samuel,
121
UTTEY, Barbara, 216, 221;
Betsy, 216, 221; Moses, 216;
Peter, 216; Samuel, 216, 221;
Susannah, 216

-V-
VAN CAMP, Abigail, 129;
Alexander, 87; Andrew, 87,
130; Ann, 129; Catherine,
129; Deborah, 87, 129;
Elizabeth, 87, 129; James,
87, 130; John, 129; William,
87
VANBRUNT, Rutgart, 26

VANDERBELT, David, 256; Eliza,
256; Elizabeth, 256; John,
256
VANFOSSEN, Nathan, 95
VANHORN, Jane, 116, 239;
Joseph, 116; Mary, 116
VANMEATER, Elizabeth, 34
VICKMAN, Adam, 191
VINCENT, James, 61; John, 217;
Nancy, 135
VOGEL, Wilhelm, 110

-W-
WACK, John, 161
WADDEL, James, 128
WADLE, Francis, 239
WAGGONER, Abraham, 152;
Catherine, 152; David, 238;
Elizabeth, 171; George, 152,
186; Henry, 182; Jacob, 117,
152, 182, 262; John, 117;
Magdalena, 117; Magdalene,
117, 182; Michael, 117;
Nelly, 266; Philip, 152, 171,
266
WAGGONER (Smithly), Polly, 117
WAGONER, Peter, 74
WAKEFIELD, Matthew, 4
WALACH, John, 72
WALEIS (Wallace), Elizabeth,
161; Thomas, 161
WALKER, Ann, 213; Eleanor, 272;
Elizabeth, 11, 153; Isabel,
11; Isabella, 153; Jacob,
215; James, 71, 83, 153, 213,
272; Jane, 83, 153; Jean, 83;
John, 21, 43, 71, 83, 125,
159, 213; Jonathan, 56, 144;
Joseph, 263, 269; Lucy, 56;
Margaret, 180; Margret, 83;
Mary, 71, 83, 149, 153;
Peggy, 159; Rachel, 50;
Robert, 11, 22, 47, 50, 159,
180; Samuel, 11, 153; Thomas,
142; William, 50, 83, 153,
180, 213
WALKUB, Nesbit, 168
WALLACE, Agigail, 133; Agness,
117, 133, 142, 168; Ann, 258;
Chrsitiana, 168; Eliza, 176;
Elizabeth, 78, 108; Grace,
181; Hugh, 28, 44, 50, 76,
115; Isabella, 108; James,
109, 133, 168, 176, 195, 221,
256; James Hamilton, 116,
117; John, 77, 78, 142, 153,
195, 258; John Swishelm, 176;
Jonathan, 133; Joseph, 78,
133; Margaret, 115, 195, 201;
Martha, 78, 124, 181; Mary,
78, 176, 268; Moses, 78, 108;
Mr., 66; Nancy, 195; Nelly,

332

334

105, 170, 248; Matthew, 62,
78, 269; Mrs., 25; Nathaniel,
16, 102; Peggy, 251; Rebecca,
60; Samuel, 20, 79, 102, 234,
269; Sarah, 18, 24, 27, 79;
Susanna, 24; Thomas, 61, 72;
William, 15, 18, 52, 78, 79,
170, 172, 234, 269
WILT, John, 86
WINGERT, Henry, 186; John, 117
WINGLEY, Sally, 272
WINING, Cadarina, 186
WISE, Elizabeth, 158; Felix,
158; Frederick, 75; George,
75, 146, 158, 202, 203, 212;
George Crop, 202; Hendricks,
202; Henry, 75; Jacob, 9, 60,
75, 136, 195, 202; James,
202; John, 75, 202, 259, 278;
Martin, 75; Mary, 158, 202;
Michael, 158; Phillex, 36;
Polly, 212; Rachel, 202;
Rebeckah, 202, 203; Thomas,
115
WISEMAN, George, 126, 138;
Hester, 239
WISER, Christy, 106
WISHARD, John, 103
WISLER, Catherine, 212;
Christen, 219; Christian, 212
WISSLER, Christian, 280
WISTER, Daniel, 100
WITHROW, William, 18
WITMER, Jacob, 58
WITMORE, Abraham, 147; Anne,
147; Esther, 147; Henry, 58;
Jacob, 147; John, 147
WITZEL, George, 13; Jacob, 13,
45; John, 13; Martin, 13;
Mary, 13
WOIST, Christian, 232
WOLF, Adam, 97; Andreas, 9;
Andrew, 214; Anna Maria, 97;
Barbara, 214; Christian, 270;
Christiana, 136; Christina,
214; Christopher, 214; David,
269; Elizabeth, 163, 214,
269; Eve, 214; George, 163,
214; Jacob, 12, 152, 171,
192, 219, 269, 270; Jean,
210; John, 171, 180, 186,
203, 214, 236, 266, 269, 270;
Katrene, 214; Kitty, 150;
Leah, 163, 214; Margaret,
152, 214; Mary, 152, 163,
192, 266; Mathias, 192;
Peter, 192; Philip, 152, 171;
Samuel, 214; Valentine, 136
WOLFE, Catharine, 9;
Christianan, 9; Elizabeth, 9;
Henry, 9; Jacob, 9; Leonard,
9; Margaret, 9; Mary, 9

WOLFF, Ann Catherine, 161;
Conrad, 161; Daniel, 161;
Jacob, 161; John, 161; John
Conrad, 161; John Henry, 161;
Joseph, 161; Michael, 161;
Peter, 161
WONDERLICK, Daniel, 126
WOOD, George, 100; James, 60
WOODARD, Matty, 194
WOODBURN, Agness, 75, 263;
Eliza, 200; George, 75, 263;
James, 44, 75, 76, 200, 263;
Jane, 263; John, 80, 151,
153, 171, 263; Major James,
115; Margaret, 263; Mary, 22;
Peggy, 75; Saml., 248, 268;
William Henry, 263
WOODLAND, John, 263; Richard,
263
WOODNEY, Polly, 81; Samuel, 81
WOODORD, Benjamin, 194;
Cathrene, 194; John, 194;
Matty, 194; Polly, 194
WOODS, Alexander, 60, 216;
Alexr., 157, 213, 228;
Andrew, 100; Ann, 60; David,
41, 49, 96, 99; David H.,
174; Elizabeth, 41, 99, 215;
Esbel, 32; George, 32; Hugh,
32, 114; James, 32, 42, 48,
79, 114; Jane, 60, 65, 99,
100, 174, 204, 235; Janet,
41, 48; Jean, 34, 100, 215,
255; Jenny, 80; John, 32, 46,
68, 119, 143, 174, 201, 225,
227, 259; Lilly, 255;
Margaret, 227; Mary, 41, 48,
80, 215; Matthew, 204; Meary,
99; Nathan, 41, 48, 49, 99,
107, 174, 215, 255; Richard,
32, 48, 49, 79, 88, 109, 145,
183, 193, 194, 238, 253, 255,
269; Robert, 32; Samuel, 41,
49, 79, 80, 82, 99, 174, 193,
215, 255, 278; Thomas, 41,
79, 255; William, 32, 41, 42,
43, 48, 79, 99, 255
WOODWARD, Benjamin, 222; Elis,
102, 142, 222; Elizabeth, 155
WOOLF, Catherina, 10;
Elizabeth, 10; Henry, 122;
Jacob, 10; Jeremiah, 10;
John, 10; Mary, 10; Regina,
10
WORK, Alexander, 50; Jenet, 80;
John, 80; Martha, 80, 81;
Miriam, 63; William, 63, 80,
170
WORKMAN, Margery, 165, 273;
Rebecca, 165; Saml., 165
WORLEY, Abraham, 139
WORMLEY, Anna Maria, 75;

66711627R00188

Made in the USA
San Bernardino, CA
15 January 2018